Critical Concepts

An Introduction to Politics

THIRD EDITION

EDITED BY JANINE BRODIE AND SANDRA REIN
UNIVERSITY OF ALBERTA UNIVERSITY OF ALBERTA

PEARSON
Prentice Hall

Toronto

For our students

National Library of Canada Cataloguing in Publication

Critical concepts : an introduction to politics / edited by Janine Brodie and Sandra Rein. — 3rd ed.

Includes bibliographical references and index.

ISBN 0-13-123815-9

1. Political science. I. Brodie, M. Janine, 1952– II. Rein, Sandra, 1971–

JA66.C75 2005 320 C2004-901842-6

ISBN 0-13-123815-9

Vice President, Editorial Director: Michael J. Young
Executive Acquisitions Editor: Christine Cozens
Marketing Manager: Ryan St. Peters
Developmental Editor: John Polanszky
Production Editor: Söğüt Y. Güleç
Copy Editor: Rohini Herbert
Proofreader: Tara Tovell
Production Manager: Wendy Moran
Page Layout: Christine Velakis
Permissions Research: Amanda McCormick
Art Director: Mary Opper
Cover and Interior Design: Lisa Lapointe
Cover Image: Courtesy of CP Archive

Cartoons used with permission of Malcolm Mayes, the *Edmonton Journal.*

Statistics Canada information is used with the permission of the Minister of Industry, as Minister responsible for Statistics Canada. Information on the availability of the wide range of data from Statistics Canada can be obtained from Statistics Canada's Regional Offices, its World Wide Web site at http://www.statcan.ca, and its toll-free access number 1-800-263-1136.

2 3 4 5 09 08 07 06 05

Printed and bound in Canada.

PEARSON
Prentice Hall

Brief Table of Contents

PEARSON Education Canada The Pearson Education Canada **COMPANION WEBSITE**

A Great Way to Learn and Instruct Online

The Pearson Education Canada Companion Website is easy to navigate and is organized to correspond to the chapters in this textbook. Whether you are a student in the classroom or a distance learner you will discover helpful resources for in-depth study and research that empower you in your quest for greater knowledge and maximize your potential for success in the course.

Companion Website

[www.pearsoned.ca/brodie]

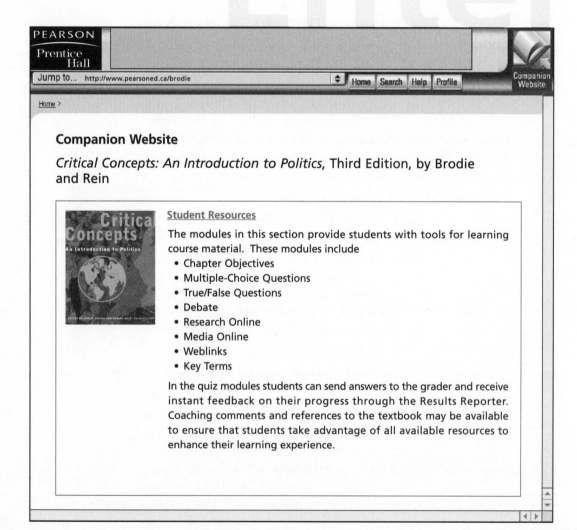

PEARSON Prentice Hall

Jump to... http://www.pearsoned.ca/brodie

Home Search Help Profile

Companion Website

Home >

Companion Website

Critical Concepts: An Introduction to Politics, Third Edition, by Brodie and Rein

Student Resources

The modules in this section provide students with tools for learning course material. These modules include

- Chapter Objectives
- Multiple-Choice Questions
- True/False Questions
- Debate
- Research Online
- Media Online
- Weblinks
- Key Terms

In the quiz modules students can send answers to the grader and receive instant feedback on their progress through the Results Reporter. Coaching comments and references to the textbook may be available to ensure that students take advantage of all available resources to enhance their learning experience.

Detailed Table of Contents

Preface

The world has changed since the second edition of this text was published in the spring of 2001. The destruction of the World Trade Centre and the attack on the Pentagon on September 11, 2001, have set in motion a series of events, including the "War on Terror" and the attack against Iraq, which have intensified global insecurities and generated countless personal tragedies. The political world is marked by uncertainty and insecurity. These traumatic international events have been accompanied by the worldwide rise of HIV/AIDS infection, growing environmental concerns, a yawning gap in income and well-being between the rich and the poor both within and among countries, and increasing evidence of corporate and governmental corruption. From Enron to the Sponsorship Scandal, people have a sense that if politics matters, it is a very "dirty business." The contributors to this third edition of *Critical Concepts* explore the many ways in which politics matters in our daily lives. We believe that students are better prepared to engage in contemporary political debates after they have been introduced to the critical concepts that political scientists use to make sense of the complexities of the political world.

This text explores key and contested political concepts, arising from the Western tradition of political thought, the evolution of political regimes and institutions, civil society, and the international and global systems. This third edition has a number of innovations. We have expanded both the introductory section on political thought and organized it around themes, such as justice, ethics, and democracy, which have animated political debates since the ancient era. We have also expanded the final section on global perspectives to include issues of poverty, development, and global order. In addition to reorganizing the major themes of the text and significantly revising chapter content, we have added new chapters on justice, civil society, political violence, poverty, and good governance. Our objective in this third edition, however, remains the same as in the first: to introduce students to the fundamentals of political science, to engage them with key and enduring debates, and to explore the conceptual shifts and uncertainties emerging in the current era of ever-intensifying globalization. Most importantly, the chapters in this text are designed to challenge students with the political issues and ethical dilemmas that they confront daily. Each chapter attempts to frame these issues as part of the disciplinary heritage of political science and to make them accessible to first-year students.

Introductory courses are often a challenge for political science instructors because of differing philosophies about how best to acquaint students with the complex world of politics. Some are convinced that an introductory course should concentrate on the foundations of political analysis, most notably the canons of Western political thought. These instructors place great emphasis on the study of great thinkers. Others prefer a course that serves as an intensive institutional primer, reasoning that students require a working knowledge of the mechanics of political life before they can explore more advanced subject matter. These instructors focus on key political institutions, such as regimes, bureaucracies, and constitutions. Still others suggest that foundations and mechanics will come with time and that the primary goal of an introductory course should be to offer students a sampling of the many intriguing perspectives on the political world that political science offers. Each of these perspectives has merit, considering the many dimensions of political life.

There is no equivalent in political science to the laws of supply and demand in economics or the laws of motion in physics. Neither is there a neutral doorway into the political world. Any entry to the study of politics is already saturated by, among other things, history, political ideas, institutional constraints, and power inequalities among political actors. Moreover, students come to their first course in political science already influenced by and engaged in the political world around them. Political science offers few road maps to move from the simple to the complex, in part because politics is always complex, especially for students who study politics in this era of increasing uncertainty.

A Chinese proverb goes something like this: "May you live in interesting times." In many respects, students of politics have always lived in interesting times. The most enduring work in political science has taken up the challenges of "its time," both in order to make sense of political life and to change and improve it. Political scientists have studied the ravages of war, of industrialization, of colonialism, and of genocide. They have also advanced the causes of human rights, good governance, individual well-being, and peaceful co-existence within and among states. Today's students of politics will go on to face many similar challenges, but they will also confront new ones in this emerging era of globalization. More than ever before, citizens are asked to consider the implications of the political decisions not only for the future of their neighbourhood and country but also for the planet.

Globalization consists of complex and multiple processes that reach from the transnational to the daily lives of the average citizen. While we may quibble about exact definitions, there is no doubt that we now find ourselves immersed in a process of complex social change. In fact, some argue that today's social changes are similar in magnitude and scope to those of the Industrial Revolution. Today, a space station prepares to explore the vastness of the universe, geneticists create new forms of life, and new technologies allow information and digital cash to travel around the globe at the speed of light. The world, it seems, is getting smaller. But, it also seems more fragmented and difficult to comprehend. Globalization, as this text emphasizes, is a contested concept in political science that has many subtle and contradictory influences on political life. Some celebrate the globalization of national economies and cultures because it promises to transcend barriers to finding global political solutions to serious political problems such as famine, mass migration, global warming, and the HIV/AIDS epidemic. At the same time, citizens and students of politics are becoming increasingly aware that globalization is challenging the continuing viability of sovereign and national democratic governance as we have come to understand these terms. These challenges are particularly unsettling for the discipline of political science. Modern political institutions, political processes, and theories of politics have been built up around the assumption of state sovereignty. Globalization, in other words, complicates the question of where to begin the study of politics as well as politics itself.

This introductory text is designed to address both the fundamentals of political science and many of the current challenges to governance in the twenty-first century. It examines the critical concepts that we believe students should master during their first encounter with political science. Each chapter introduces a critical political concept, describes its importance in the study of politics, and outlines the debates that the concept has engendered in political life and for the discipline of political science. Each chapter also explores how the contemporary political environment challenges the meaning and relevance of these concepts. The text acquaints students with traditional debates in political science as well as those recently introduced to the discipline by, for example, feminists, ecologists, and postmodernists.

The text is divided into four sections examining: (1) the politics of ideas (2) foundations of governance, (3) arenas of politics, and (4) global perspectives. The contents of each section are as follows:

Part I, *The Politics of Ideas,* explores a broad range of political, philosophical, and ethical issues that lie at the core of the study of politics. Chapter 1 ("Power and Politics") introduces many of the critical concepts, such as power, authority, and sovereignty, which are developed in later chapters. Chapters 2 to 6 ("Justice," "Ethics," "Democracy," "Liberalism," and "Radical Politics") explore the foundations of Western political traditions and institutions and the critiques of liberal democratic governance. These chapters also describe how political ideas and ethical decisions influence both the study and the practice of politics.

Part II, *Foundations of Governance,* begins by explaining the elementary relationships among the historical development of the state, the market, regime types, and international political economy. This exploration of political regimes is followed by a detailed account of the evolution of the liberal democratic state and its three principal forms—the *laissez-faire,* welfare, and neo-liberal state. The remaining chapters provide detailed accounts of the development of and challenges facing the central institutions of modern governance, especially in liberal democracies, such as Canada. These include constitutions and the rule of law (Chapter 9), citizens and citizenship (Chapter 10), community (Chapter 11), public bureaucracy (Chapter 12), and elections and electoral systems (Chapter 13).

Part III, *Arenas of Politics,* explores less formal influences on political outcomes, including the most basic units of liberal democratic politics at the level of nation, community, group, and individual. The section begins with a look at issues surrounding political representation (Chapter 14). Subsequent chapters examine the important contemporary issues of diversity, culture (Chapter 15), the role of civil society (Chapter 16), local politics (Chapter 17), gender (Chapter 18), and the political role of violence (Chapter 19).

Part IV, *Global Perspectives,* shifts our focus to the international and transnational domains. This section includes more familiar foci and debates in the study of the world order (Chapter 20), post-Cold War politics (Chapter 21), international relations (Chapter 22), the role of international organizations (Chapter 23), emerging international financial infrastructure (Chapter 24), the growth and definition of global poverty (Chapter 25), and the role of global good governance (Chapter 26).

This text has been designed for a first-year political science course. It has a number of innovations that will contribute to a successful first encounter with political science. Each chapter provides study questions, suggested further readings, and websites for further research on the topic. Key terms are identified within the text and defined in a glossary at the end of the book.

Supplements

No matter how comprehensive a textbook is, today's instructors and students require a complete teaching package. *Critical Concepts: An Introduction to Politics*, Third Edition, is accompanied by the following supplements:

Supplements for Instructors

Instructor's Resource Manual. *The Instructor's Resource Manual* features a variety of teaching resources including chapter objectives, chapter summaries, and lecture suggestions.

PowerPoint Presentation. A set of PowerPoint slides offers additional lecture aids for each chapter in the text.

Test Item File. This test bank contains multiple-choice, true/false, and short answer/essay questions for every chapter. The *Test Item File* is available in both Word and TestGenerator formats. TestGenerator is compatible with both Windows and Macintosh software.

Instructor's Resource CD-ROM. The instructor supplements listed above are conveniently available on one Instructor's Resource CD-ROM.

Media Supplements

Companion Website (www.pearsoned.ca/brodie). An interactive website is available for instructors and students who use *Critical Concepts: An Introduction to Politics*, Third Edition. Visitors will find a range of interactive resources, including self-assessment quizzes, available in every chapter that can be emailed to instructors or teaching assistants.

Acknowledgments

Many people deserve our thanks and appreciation for their contributions to this ongoing project. First, the authors wish to thank Christine Cozens, John Polanszky, and Söğüt Y. Güleç of Pearson Education Canada, as well as Rohini Herbert and Tara Tovell for their editorial magic. Undoubtedly, this third edition could not have been completed without the very capable support of the staff of the Department of Political Science at the University of Alberta—Cindy Anderson, Marilyn Calvert, Tara Mish, and Sharon Moroschan. Although Sharon retired this year, her many contributions to all three editions of this text are embedded in each and every page.

During the preparation of this new edition, valuable and much appreciated reviews were provided by a number of colleagues from across the country, including Toivo Milan at Wilfrid Laurier University, Michael K. McDevitt at Champlain Regional College, and Nick Baxter-Moore at Brock University.

We also want to extend our thanks to Malcolm Mayes, editorial cartoonist at the *Edmonton Journal*, who has once again generously volunteered to lend his obvious talents, political insights, and, above all, his sense of humour to this project. Selecting the cartoons for each chapter was one of the greatest pleasures of editing this book. A library of his work can be found at www.artisans.com.

Janine Brodie and Sandra Rein
Edmonton, Spring 2004

About the Editors

Janine Brodie

Janine Brodie is a professor of political science and Canada Research Chair in the Department of Political Science at the University of Alberta. Dr. Brodie served as Department Chair from 1997 to 2003. She was elected as a Fellow of the Royal Society of Canada in 2002. Before joining the University of Alberta in 1996, she was also the first Director of the York Centre for Feminist Research, the John Robarts Chair in Canadian Studies at York University, and the University of Western Ontario Visiting Chair in Public Policy. She has published widely in the areas of Canadian politics, gender and politics, and globalization and governance.

Sandra Rein

Sandra Rein is a doctoral candidate in the Department of Political Science at the University of Alberta. Ms. Rein has held a Social Science and Humanities Research Council (SSHRC) doctoral fellowship, a University of Alberta dissertation fellowship, and a doctoral fellowship from the Department of Foreign Affairs and International Trade (DFAIT) as part of the Mine Action Research Program with York University. Ms. Rein's primary fields of interest include international political economy, international relations, and social theory. Ms. Rein is currently completing a dissertation on the Marxist–humanist theory of Raya Dunayevskaya and its application to globalization.

About the Cartoonist

Malcolm Mayes

Malcolm Mayes was born in Edmonton, Alberta, in 1962. He drew extensively throughout his childhood and by his late teens was selling his artwork on a regular basis. A love of cartooning and interest in newspapers steered him naturally toward political comment. He studied design art for two years at Grant MacEwan College in Edmonton and freelanced for a dozen Alberta weeklies before landing a full-time position at the *Edmonton Journal* in June 1986.

Mayes is one of Canada's most widely read political cartoonists; his work has been published in over 150 Canadian publications, including *Maclean's*, the *Toronto Star*, *Montreal Gazette*, and *Ottawa Citizen*. He's won numerous internal Southam awards and was nominated twice for a National Newspaper Award. In 1996 he published a cartoon collection entitled *Political Asylum*.

Mayes was an early entry in cyberspace, becoming one of the first cartoonists on the continent to go digital. He created animated political cartoons that were featured on Microsoft's News Website. He is also the founder of Artizans.com—a comprehensive online service that delivers digital artwork to publications around the world.

Malcolm's twin daughters, Michelle and Kelsey were born in 1991. He currently lives in an old house on a quiet treed boulevard in central Edmonton.

PART

I

The Politics of Ideas

There is rarely a simple answer for why political events unfold as they do. Political outcomes are the combined product of many forces that often clash and pull in opposite directions. Some of these factors are immediate and observable, while others are more distant and concealed, lodged in historical legacies and political traditions. There is, however, one inescapable constant in political analyses. Everything political is embedded in ideas—in the way we understand the political world around us. All political and social interactions, both harmonious and conflict-ridden, are informed and directed by ideas. The six chapters in this section of the text provide an introduction to the key concepts and different streams of political thinking that have structured politics in the West for millennia. Many introductions to political thought follow its historical development from ancient to contemporary thinkers—from Plato to NATO. The chapters in this section link particular ideas about politics to historical contexts; however, they are organized around the critical and enduring concepts of power, sovereignty, and authority, justice, ethics, democracy, liberalism, and radicalism. We will discover that the questions of how we ought to live together and govern ourselves have always animated political thought and debate. We will also find that the issues of morals, fairness, inclusion, freedom, and change rest at the very heart of political choice and action. Political life, however constrained by historical and structural factors, is fundamentally about the choices that we make and about the consequences of those choices.

CHAPTER 1

POWER AND POLITICS

Objectives

We often encounter the flat assertion that "power and politics are everywhere." And so they are, but this truism does not give us any guideposts indicating where or how to begin to study political power. The world of politics is complex, fascinating, and multi-dimensional. The study of politics can lead us to the most diverse of places, among them, the home, the workplace, political party organizations, and the bureaucracy. Political science is increasingly inclusive about the terrain of politics and political study. But, in order to enter the complex world of politics, we have to carry with us some basic conceptual tools, not the least of which is an understanding of the concepts of power and politics.

JANINE BRODIE

This chapter introduces many of the critical political concepts that will be revisited and explained in greater detail throughout this text. In particular, we discuss the relationship between politics and power. We then explore a few of the many faces of political power, among them, "power to," "power over," knowledge and power, sovereignty, and authority, especially Weber's distinctions among traditional, charismatic, and legal-rational authority. The chapter next introduces some of the dominant approaches to the study of politics—institutional, pluralist, elitist, and class approaches. Finally, we touch on some of the ways that the current era of globalization is challenging the meaning and continuing relevance of key components of modern governance.

Introduction

Aristotle, contemplating political life over two thousand years ago, made an enduring observation about the human condition. "Man," he said, "is by nature a political animal." Aristotle quite literally meant *man,* indeed only the men of Ancient Greece's ruling class. Contemporary political theorists now understand Aristotle's man as a representation of all people and politics as an ever-present force in all societies. Whenever two or more people come together, there is politics. Politics, whether we recognize it or not, informs how we think about others and ourselves and flows through all social relationships. It is the glue that holds these relationships together. It also is the friction that erupts in disagreement and conflict, sometimes tearing friendships, communities, and nations apart. Politics is all around us, not unlike the air we breathe. And, like air, it is often difficult to see, to capture, and to study. Politics, whether experienced at the level of the individual, the community, the country, or the globe, is constantly shifting. The push and pull of conflict and consensus mean that political life is always moving in directions that we can never fully predict.

The instabilities of contemporary politics provide an obvious example. No one could have predicted the terrorist attacks of September 11, 2001, although many explanations have been offered about why they occurred. Neither could we have predicted the ongoing ramifications of that fateful day in global politics or in our daily lives. Beyond the personal tragedies of the victims, September 11 was followed by concerted military reprisals, costing thousands of innocent lives, accelerated terrorist activity across the globe, and the dubious occupation of Iraq by a "coalition of the willing," even though there was no credible evidence to suggest that its brutal dictator, Saddam Hussein, was at all implicated in the terrorist attacks. In a few short years, the optimism that rang in the new millennium has quickly and dramatically given way to the destructive unilateralism of an angry superpower, strained international alliances, intensifed surveillance, increased racial profiling, assaulted individual liberties, and, of course, created endless queues at airports.

Uncertainty and unpredictability were for Karl Mannheim, writing over 70 years ago, at the very heart of the definition of politics. He drew a fundamental distinction between administration and politics. The administration of our daily lives was routinized, ruled based, and predictable—what he called the "routine affairs of the state." Politics, in contrast, was the play of irrational forces, social competition, and struggle. Mannheim identified two main sources of irrationalism—uncontrolled competition and domination by force. Both conditions, he argued, "constitute the realm of social life which is still unorganized and where politics becomes necessary" (1936, 115–116).

How then are we to understand, let alone study, something that is so fundamental to our daily lives and yet so fluid and so unpredictable? Some argue that an all-embracing approach to the study of politics, one that sees its operations and consequences everywhere, is not very useful. How are we to distinguish a political relationship from other kinds of relationships? If politics is everywhere, they point out, then it is nowhere. The discipline of political science, however, rests on the basic premise that politics does have a number of defining characteristics that make it more tangible. While there is considerable debate about what these characteristics are, political scientists agree on at least one point of departure. Politics is about power, and political science is devoted to the study of its various uses, organization, and outcomes. Who has political power, and why? How does it flow through institutions and societies, and to what end? Where does political power come from? Can it be used to build a better society?

Politics and Power

THE PRIMARY LINK BETWEEN POLITICS AND POWER HAS BEEN A PERENNIAL issue for students of politics. Niccolò Machiavelli (1469–1527) is sometimes called the first political scientist because he distinguished between the "is" and the "ought" of politics. While religious and moral codes tell us what action we ought to take, the grim realities of politics are more often concerned with what is. Almost 500 years ago, Machiavelli, in his famous book, *The Prince*, advised the ruling elite of Italy to give up any notion of governing according to moral ideals and, instead, to use the power of both force and persuasion to disarm opponents. He believed that political survival and moral codes were often incompatible and that princes sometimes had to violate moral norms to hold onto political office. The end—staying in power—could justify amoral and brutal means. For Machiavelli, politics was mostly about the effective exercise and consolidation of political power and position. Early in the twentieth century, the great Russian revolutionary, Vladimir Lenin, defined politics in a similar way as "who does what to whom" (quoted in Guy, 1995, 5). Perhaps the most often quoted definition of politics comes from Harold Lasswell, a distinguished American political scientist writing in the 1930s. For him, the study of politics was about "who gets what, when, and how" (1936).

Yet, to say that politics is about the exercise of power only begs the obvious question—what is **power**? Most political scientists agree about the ubiquity of power. As Amos Hawley explains, "every act is an exercise of power, every social relationship is a power equation, and every social group or system is an organization of power" (1963, 433). Think about how often in our daily conversations or in the media we hear the word "power." This person has power, that person is seduced by power, another person is on a power-trip, while Ford trucks have more power, and Joe Sakic has perfected the power play. Do these various usages convey the same or different meanings? In fact, we find little consensus in political science about the meaning of power. Like politics, it has many faces. There are literally dozens of definitions of power. At the most basic level, power is understood as "bringing about consequences." Power, in other words, makes something happen that probably would not happen in its absence. But, beyond that, there is widespread disagreement about the fundamentals of power. For example, how is power acquired? Is it through wealth, knowledge, cunning, good looks, force, race, or something else? How do we experience power? Is it through influence, coercion, control, or some other mechanism? Are we even aware when power is weighing down on us? Who benefits—individuals, select groups, or the community? Who decides how power will be used? (Philp, 1985, 635)

Power to and Power over

Political scientists have generally treated power in one of two ways, either as power to do something or as power over something. **Power to** connotes the realization of personal or collective goals or, in today's parlance, "being empowered." (Kourvetaris, 1997, 41). The popular notion that, in democratic systems, power ultimately rests in the hands of citizens conveys the idea of "power to" realize social consensus and collective goals through democratic institutions, such as elected legislative assemblies. Through democratic practices, citizens are supposed to be able to hold their political leaders accountable for their actions and, if need be, throw them out of office.

For political cynics, this idea of "power to" is, at best, naive and, at worst, an outright sham. They argue that people are encouraged to believe that they can change political outcomes or govern themselves democratically when, in fact, the present and the future are already determined by the capitalist class, political elites, faceless bureaucrats . . . the list is of potential conspirators is endless. Such fatalism, however, does not square with history. One need only think of the lone student staring down a tank in Tiananmen Square, the droves of Yugoslavians who stayed away from work and packed the streets until Milosevic left office, or Rosa Parks, who refused to go to the back of the bus in a racist American south, to realize that people, individually and collectively, have the power to bring about political change. But, the fight for political change always exacts costs, whether it is the small investment of time to attend a political rally or write a letter to a public official or the ultimate cost of one's life. If the graveyard of history is filled with political elites, even larger graveyards are filled with those who opposed them.

The notion of **power over**, in contrast, conveys the idea of disempowerment. It tells us that there are forces outside us that constrain and direct our actions, making us do things that we would not otherwise do and that might be contrary to our interests and well being. Robert Dahl's definition of power is a good example of the idea of "power over." For Dahl, "A has power to the extent that A makes B do something that B would not otherwise do" (1961, 203). Dahl's thinking about power was very much influenced by the behavioural approach to politics that dominated Canadian and American political science thinking in the 1960s and 1970s. **Behaviouralism** highlighted individual political actors and their interactions, rather than political institutions or systems of inequality embedded in society. Behaviouralists made great use of public opinion polling—large surveys of the attitudes and actions of both ordinary people and political leaders—because they believed that the individual, whether citizen and leader, was the basic unit in the study of politics.

Behaviouralists also assumed that by studying individuals scientifically—that is with surveys and statistical calculations—they could discover fundamental laws about political behaviour. In much the same way that natural scientists were able to discover the laws or building blocks of nature, behaviouralists aspired to discover the laws of politics—laws that operated everywhere and at all times that could explain such things as, for example, how revolutions occur. Political scientists, unfortunately, have proved time and again that politics defies regularity and prediction. We were not able to predict September 11 or the collapse of Soviet-style communism, although, arguably, these are the two most significant political events of recent decades. To be fair, economists wedded to the science of the market have not done much better, being unable to predict with precision the onset of the nine deep recessions that have hit capitalist economies since the Great Depression of the 1930s. The problem, it would seem, is not the discipline of study but, instead, the questionable assumption that the complexity of human relations can be reduced to timeless scientific generalities.

Ahistorical and individualized approaches to power contrast greatly with societal approaches, such as class analysis, that locate power and political conflict in the economy and the historical organization of societies. Consider, for example, the depiction of "power over" provided by Karl Marx and Friedrich Engels in the *Communist Manifesto.* "The history of all hitherto existing society," they write, "is the history of class struggles. Freeman and slave, patrician and plebeian, lord and serf, guildmaster and journeyman, in a word, oppressor and oppressed, stood in opposition to one another." Marx and Engels, and many after them, were trying to convey an important point: people are political animals; they are also born into specific historical contexts and patterns of politics before they take their first breath of air. At different times and in different places, to be born black, Aboriginal, female, or working-class was already to be in a position of being subjected to "power over" within the broader historical contexts of racism, colonialism, sexism, and capitalism. To paraphrase Marx, people engage with a political world marked by profound imbalances in political resources—in other words, under conditions not of their own choosing.

Power and Knowledge

More recently, some political theorists, particularly those associated with postmodern analyses, such as Michel Foucault, have rejected the idea that power is simply a thing to possess or to hold over other people. Foucault argued that thinking about power as something outside us, to be gained, lost, or used to empower or to disempower is not the only or perhaps the most appropriate way to think about power. Instead, he suggested that the "real power" of power is productive. For Foucault, we never stand outside power but, instead, are created (produced) by it. Power runs through all social relations, indeed, through our bodies like capillaries. These capillaries of power can be so innocuous, even commonsensical, as to be undetectable. They, nonetheless, have a defining influence on the way we think and behave.

Foucault advanced the idea that power is embedded in the way we think about things, in knowledge systems that tell us what exists, who we are, what is true. He used the term *discourse* to convey the idea of the inseparability of power and knowledge. Foucault expanded modern thinking about power to include the ideas of **disciplinary power** and **dividing practices**. Disciplinary power exacts appropriate behaviours, not through force, but by defining what is normal. Dividing practices stigmatize those who do not fit the mould by naming them scientifically as being different or abnormal. People exercise productive power over themselves and others quite unconsciously. For example, when a scientific discourse defines what is normal, we both discipline ourselves to fit this definition in order to avoid social rejection and, in turn, reject those who, through dividing practices, do not conform. Long before we act, we have power inscribed on us through these disciplinary and dividing practices. As Foucault explains, power and knowledge directly imply one another. This means that there can be no knowledge "out there" that is free of power relations to be used for good or evil. Claims to knowledge are also claims to power. Fields of knowledge categorize, discipline, and divide people for the purposes of social control. Modern governments, Foucault argued, use these various categories to manage populations.

Foucault's work focused on the dividing and disciplinary practices that came out of the scientific naming of homosexuals, the mentally ill, and criminals. More generally, Foucault argued that the accepted truths of knowledge and their resulting disciplinary practices are like a panopticon. The panopticon was a model prison designed such that the prisoners could always be watched but could never see the guard. The beauty of the design was that prisoners would eventually come to behave as if they were being watched even if they were not (Fink-Eitel, 1992, 50). Foucault used the analogy of the panopticon to convey the idea that knowledge systems work in the same way, producing appropriate behaviours without coercing them.

Foucault's approach to power has been criticized for being too all encompassing and for effectively foreclosing the possibility of individual action, political contestation, and political change. Foucault, however, resisted this interpretation of his work. He recognized that there were situations where opportunities for political opposition were limited, but he called these examples of domination, rather than power. Foucault argued that some states of domination can be so complete that there is no room for resistance. "Slavery," for example, "is not a power relationship when man is in chains" (quoted in Simons, 1995, 82). Foucault's point, in other words, was that the exercise of power always presupposes resistance.

Foucault never had the opportunity to fully respond to his critics. He died of AIDS in the mid-1980s. His work remains important because it underlines the critical notion that knowledge contains power and the reverse. His conception of power challenges us to take responsibility for the power relations embedded in the way we think about the world and ourselves. Consider, for example, the power relations embedded in recent changes in thinking about social welfare recipients. For most of the post-war period, those receiving assistance did so as a right of citizenship that could be claimed by those in need. These citizens were seen to need state support because of a broad range of factors, many of them beyond the control of the individual, such as recessions, disability, and illness. Moreover, it was assumed that any one of us could fall victim to these unhappy fates. Now, it is common to refer to these same citizens as welfare dependents. The term *dependence* conveys the idea that welfare recipients, like drug addicts, are lesser individuals and somehow responsible for their own plight (Fraser and Gordon, 1994). Those in economic need are thus divided from the rest of us as "abnormal." And, in order to avoid a similar fate, others accept the discipline of the workplace, even if the jobs available are insecure, undervalued, or dangerous. Nowhere in this discourse are we invited to entertain the idea that most of us are dependent on the job market as a mark of our normality. We are all dependent in one way or another, but the discourse on welfare dependency stigmatizes those who depend on the state, however temporarily, to meet their basic needs for survival.

Authority

Other writers have located power in institutions and value systems. This approach also tends to emphasize the idea of power as **authority**, rather than as force, although the two are usually mutually reinforcing. In cases of authority, individuals adjust their behaviour because they concede to the authority associated with an institution. Consider the following two scenarios. In the first scenario, you are driving down the street, and a police officer demands that you stop your car. You are likely to comply. In the second scenario, an ordinary person demands that you stop your car. In this case, you may stop or, instead, lock your doors and speed down the street. What is the difference? It is the authority vested in a policeman's uniform. Authority is "socially approved power" that entails both legitimacy and impartiality (Kourvetaris, 1997, 51). Someone is accorded power and legitimacy, less for who they are personally than for the institution that they represent, whether that be the police, the judiciary, or elected office. This legitimacy is often backed by the threat of sanction or punishment. Most us of obey the law both because we believe in the rule of law and because we realize that failure to comply with the law might very well result in a fine or jail sentence. Similarly, those in positions of power lose their legitimacy if they fail to adhere to institutional norms and expectations. A policeman on "the take" or a political leader caught lying to the public are examples.

Max Weber (1864–1920), one of the fathers of modern social science, argued that societies have been governed by three different kinds of authority: traditional, charismatic, and legal-rational. **Traditional authority** was the social glue that held together pre-industrial societies. Power was vested in certain individuals because of custom or heredity. The chief or the king was obeyed because that was how it was intended or how it had always been. While traditional authorities might take advice from others, including a god, their authority was individual and incontestable. **Charismatic**

authority was similarly vested in individuals. It, however, was grounded in the personal qualities of the charismatic leader, rather than in tradition or in birth. Weber argued that charismatic leaders tend to gain authority during periods of profound crisis and social upheaval. Their authority, he argued, grows out of "a certain quality of an individual personality by virtue of which he is set apart from ordinary men and treated as endowed with supernatural, superhuman, or at least specifically exceptional powers and qualities" (quoted in Bendix, 1960, 88). The social upheaval of the Great Depression in the 1930s, which saw the rise of fascist dictators, such as Hitler in Germany and Mussolini in Italy, provides obvious examples of what Weber meant by charismatic authority.

Weber saw both traditional and charismatic authority as fleeting in modern societies, which were increasingly governed by **legal-rationalism**. This kind of authority is based in the rule of law and in the bureaucratic and impersonal procedures of modern institutions, such as the courts, constitutions, bureaucracy, and legislatures. Legal-rational authority is accorded to leaders who hold positions in and abide by the rules of these institutions. They, in turn, are considered legitimate by the public. In a legal-rational system, claims to authority, even by charismatic leaders, are unlikely to be considered legitimate unless they are framed within a system of legal-rationality. To put the point more clearly, no matter how charismatic an individual or how royal a bloodline, a person could not make claims to political leadership and authority in a legal-rational culture unless accorded legitimacy by, for example, a democratic election.

Although these different kinds of authority tend to characterize different kinds of society, from the simple to the complex, all can be found in contemporary culture. A religious leader or one's parents or teachers make claims to traditional authority, although many traditionalists lament that these claims do not hold the force that they once did. Any day of the week, you can find someone on television linking the problems of the world to the decline of religious deference or the authority of the family. Charisma also remains a formidable force in political life. The international political stage still affords a role to charismatic leaders, such as Robert Mugabe of Zimbabwe, who grounds his political power both in force and in the force of personality. Yet, in a world dominated by legal-rational authority, these leaders are condemned as illegitimate.

State and Sovereignty

The rise of legal-rationalism is intimately tied to the ideas of sovereignty and the birth of the modern state. Traditional leaders, especially the rulers of feudal Europe, claimed sovereignty in their person. **Sovereignty** means supreme power. There is no question or debate about the right to exercise power where sovereignty has been established. In feudal societies, power and authority were dispersed and divisible, often shared and struggled for among the nobility, the monarch, and the Church. Gradually, from the fifteenth to the seventeenth centuries, coinciding with the demise of feudalism and the ascendancy of capitalism, political power began to consolidate both territorially and practically within the early predecessors of the modern state. These predecessors took on two dominant personalities—the "absolute" monarchies of France, Prussia, Austria, Spain, and Russia and the "constitutional" monarchies and republics, based on representative government, which were beginning to take form in England and Holland (Held, 1996, 66). In absolute monarchies, the sovereignty of traditional hereditary monarchs, such as King Louis XV of France, who ruled from 1715 to 1774, was effectively imposed on the state through the person of the King. Louis XV, for example, pronounced that "*l'état, c'est moi.*" Absolute monarchs maintained that their power was God-given and, thus, to disobey the monarch was to disobey God, which was the greatest offence in premodern times. Absolute monarchies eventually crumbled in the face of democratization, class conflict, and the idea of popular sovereignty—that is, the idea that political power ultimately rested in the hands of all citizens instead of leaders alone. Absolute monarchies, nonetheless, provided the institutional underpinnings of the modern state, especially the centralization of political, military, and administrative powers within defined territorial boundaries (Held, 1996, 68).

During the past four centuries, the modern state has taken on a number of different forms, ranging from representative democracies to fascist dictatorships to communist regimes. Regardless of form, states share one defining characteristic—the non-negotiable claim to sovereignty. All modern states claim the supreme and indivisible power to rule over a national territory. This non-negotiable monopoly of state sovereignty was recognized formally in the Peace of Westphalia in 1648, which cast the world community as consisting of "sovereign states." These states controlled their own territories and could legitimately use force to repel threats to national security and sovereignty arising either from domestic politics or external threats (Held, 1996, 69). This idea of the fusion of power, sovereignty, authority, and legitimacy, which structures current thinking about politics, is clearly conveyed by Weber's often-cited definition of the **state**. He called it "a human community that successfully claims monopoly of the legitimate use of physical force within a given territory" (quoted in Gerth and Mills, 1958, 78).

To sum up, the study of politics revolves around a number of critical concepts, among them, power, authority, legitimacy, sovereignty, and the state. But political scientists have adopted quite distinct perspectives on how politics works within and among national territories. Next, we will briefly review four broad approaches, each of which serves as a guidepost to explore the complex world of politics. Institutionalism, pluralism, elite analysis, and class analysis are only four among the many perspectives that political scientists have adopted in order to compare and explain the political world around us. Approaches are simply perspectives. They highlight one part of the complex matrix of political life, often to the exclusion of others. Approaches to politics are neither true nor false, only more or less useful in helping us understand political events. But, as we will see, using one approach rather than another forces us to accept a number of other assumptions about the nature of political actors, the basic structures of social organization, and the appropriate ways to achieve political change. Theories of politics are also theories of society, providing answers to such questions as what the basic units of political society are and how power is distributed.

Approaches to the Study of Politics

Institutionalism

Early political scientists defined their task as explaining those things obviously contained within the political sphere, especially laws and institutions and formal political processes, such as elections. Institutionalism provided a descriptive and comparative analysis of the institutional infrastructure of the liberal state. Texts focused on such questions as the differences between parliamentary and congressional systems, federal and unitary systems, a separation of power versus a fusion of power, and written versus unwritten constitutions. A.V. Dicey's book *An Introduction to the Study of the Law of the Constitution*, first published in 1908 and reprinted many times and in many languages since then, is a classic example of the legal-institutional approach.

The events leading up to World War II created doubts that institutionalism could explain how politics really worked. For example, the horrors of Nazi Germany could not be predicted or explained by studying its constitution. How could the politics of a country with a history of constitutionalism take such a turn? Could something similar be prevented in the future? The institutional approach could not provide answers to these questions.

Advances in scientific polling, after World War II, also created doubts about whether liberal democracies actually worked in the way that institutionalists assumed. Institutionalists assumed that citizens behaved in the way that democratic theory prescribed. In theory, at least, citizens were active and informed, could identify and prioritize the political choices offered to them at election time, and voted accordingly. Early public opinion polls, however, showed that most citizens did not pay attention to politics, even fewer were active in political parties and other political organizations, most had trouble distinguishing between the political right and the political left, and most did not understand the implications of particular policy choices. This mismatch between political theory and political behaviour encouraged political scientists, overwhelmingly located in the United States, to rethink the relationship between society and the state.

The questions posed by institutional analysis, however, remain important to political scientists today. In fact, introductory textbooks such as this one devote a great deal of effort to clarifying the distinctions between different kinds of legal and political institutions. In past decades, there also has been a renewed interest in the impact of institutional design on public policies. Neo-institutional studies demonstrate that political institutions can have impacts on policy outcomes that are quite independent from other political factors, such as national histories, political ideologies, and political actors. For example, recent cuts to social programs have been less pronounced in countries with proportional representation electoral systems than in those with plurality systems.

Pluralism

Post-war political science took on the task of developing an approach to politics that would explain the realities of modern politics and, at the same time, preserve the idea of the superiority of a democratic system. Strongly influenced by liberal political thinking, the **pluralist** school argued that although the individual remained the basic unit of democratic politics, the sheer size and complexity of modern society had long ago ruled out a democratic politics revolving around the informed and active democratic citizen. Instead, pluralists saw politics as the play for preferred policy outcomes among an endless variety of competing groups in civil society.

From this perspective, the governance of modern society is far too complex and the society too large to nurture the direct political participation of everyone in the political process. Instead, individuals join groups that promote their interests. Since modern citizens have many interests, they may hold memberships in many different kinds of groups, ranging from a parent–teacher organization to an association to abolish capital punishment, a gun collectors club, or a lesbian and gay choir. Many of the groups to which citizens belong have a direct interface with the public sphere, but most do not. According to the pluralists, groups become politically active around political issues that concern or affect their members. They make coalitions and compete with other groups for preferred policy outcomes. No one group is a permanent player in pluralist politics. Neither does one group always win. Different groups with different resources move in and out of the political sphere when their interests are affected. Politics is a constant play of groups that both advance the interests of their respective memberships and check the power of other groups. Everyone gets to play, and there are no winners assumed at the onset of a political debate. As prominent pluralist theorist Robert Dahl contended, "all active and legitimate groups in the population can make themselves heard at some critical stage in the process of decision making" (1956, 137).

The pluralist approach was very much committed to promoting the idea that both the democratic citizen and the democratic system, although somewhat modified, were alive and well in post-war America. Their message was that democratic pluralism was a system of governance that could and should be emulated in countries emerging from the rubble of fascism and World War II as well as in new countries recently released from the bonds of European colonialism. Citizens were free to join groups, to advance their interests, and to choose group leaders, and, indeed, to become leaders themselves to represent their interests in the policy process. As importantly, the state was not predisposed to favour one group over another. The game of politics, in other words, was not stacked for or against anyone. Pluralists viewed the state as neutral, serving to mediate among competing groups and to strike compromise and consensus in public policy. From a pluralist perspective, the state processed group demands or inputs and converted them to public policies or outputs. Officials inside the state did not adopt policies that were self-serving and the institutions of government did not manipulate democratic processes to favour some groups over others. The strength of democracy on the ground, as it were, in clubs, groups, and communities, in turn, was a powerful preventive to the rise of authoritarian or corrupt regimes.

Elitism

At the same time that the pluralist school was advancing its celebration of democratic pluralism, the approach found powerful critics both inside and outside the United States. E.E. Schattschneider, an American political scientist and liberal thinker, criticized the pluralist school for misrepresenting the extent and nature of group membership in the United States. Most group members were decidedly middle class, and most groups rarely engaged directly with politics. Schattschneider mused that if there were a pluralist heaven, then "the heavenly chorus sings with a strong upper-class accent." Schattschneider also argued that political institutions were not neutral but, instead, set in motion what he termed a "mobilization of bias" (1960, 29). Others argued that the singular focus of the pluralist approach on the decision-making process obscured the fact that power is also exercised, perhaps even more strongly, when issues never make it to the public agenda and when no decision is made. In these cases, inaction would obscure and preserve an unequal and power-saturated status quo (Bachrach and Baratz, 1970).

The most sustained criticism of the pluralist approach in the United States, however, came from the new elite theorists. They revived a long tradition of elite theorizing about the possibility of sustaining a meaningful democracy in modern societies. Elite theorists, for different reasons, argued that a select few, in all societies, manipulate the levers of government for their own advantage. President Dwight Eisenhower, just before departing from office in 1960, warned the American public of the growing power of what he termed the "military-industrial complex." Himself a former general and war hero, Eisenhower argued that a triad of military leaders, arms manufacturers, and sympathetic public officials posed a threat to American democracy. Elite theorist C. Wright Mills fleshed out the "military-industrial complex" in his famous book *The Power Elite*, which appeared on bookshelves beside Robert Dahl's pluralist primer, *Preface to Democracy*, in 1956. Elite theory has a long tradition in political theory and in the evolution of political science. It is based on a very different view of society from the one advanced in the pluralist model. While pluralism focused on individuals in groups, elitism proposed a stark divide between the few and the many. The few, the elite, occupy the most powerful positions in the central institutions of society—the military, religion, economy, politics, and culture. The few hold the power, while the many do not.

There is little debate about the fact that there are leaders and followers in all societies—the questions posed by elite theory are, first, is this a good or bad thing, and second, do elites threaten democracy? Plato advanced the idea that good governance was best achieved when an elite of "philosopher kings," endowed with wisdom, virtue, and prudence were given the exclusive power to rule. At the turn of the twentieth century, Italian sociologists Vilfredo Pareto (1848–1923) and Gaetano Mosca (1858–1941) claimed that elite rule was an inevitable fact of human existence. For these elite theorists, all societies were characterized by a fundamental truth: the few (elites) rule the many (masses). Pareto advanced this dichotomous model of society quite starkly. "Whatever certain theorists may like to think," he wrote, "human society in fact is not a homogeneous thing, and different individuals are physically, morally, and intellectually different" (1978, 247). A few excel, and the great majority are average.

Mosca presents a similar depiction of social organization. "In all societies," he contends, "two classes of people appear—a class that rules and a class that is ruled." The first class performs "all political functions, monopolizes power, and enjoys the advantages that power brings" and controls the second class (quoted in Knuttila, 1987, 50). Pareto and Mosca advanced the case that elite rule is a basic fact of human existence and inevitable. A meaningful democratic politics, therefore, was neither possible nor desirable. It is perhaps for this reason that European fascists of the 1930s embraced these theorists, especially Mosca, and their anti-democratic thought. It is a short leap from the repugnant claim that some people are naturally superior to all kinds of pathological political practices and regimes.

Perhaps the most often cited elite theorist, Roberto Michels (1876–1936) also argued that elite rule was inevitable, although not necessarily desirable. Michels was active in social democratic politics and observed how elites captured the party organization, even though party ideology was committed to democracy. According to Michels, modern society was governed by what he called "the iron law of the oligarchy" (rule by a few). Modern societies require large and complex organizations that are characterized by specialization and division of labour. The latter creates a hierarchy in which a few, because of their organizational position and skills, gain experience, expertise, power, and control. As the elite's skill set grows, it becomes increasingly distant from the rank-and-file of the organization who, in turn, grow apathetic and disempowered. It is through this process, according to Michels, that democracy inevitably leads to oligarchy, or elite rule (Knuttila, 1987, 52–3). Michels' point was that elites gain their power because of their strategic position within modern organizations and not because of human nature.

Most elite studies now identify powerful institutions and key figures within them as the starting point of their analyses. These studies often find that the elite of a variety of sectors, including politics, the military, the media, and business, are overwhelmingly white, wealthy, and male. They share similar backgrounds, attend the same elite schools, frequently interact socially and through marriage, and share similar values and opinions. But, these similarities do not necessarily demonstrate that we are governed by oligarchy or that the study of elites tells us all that we need to know about power and politics. Pareto once mused that "history is the graveyard of elites" (1976, 249), and in some ways it is. There are few examples in politics where there are no leaders and followers. The starting point of elite theory, that society is composed of two groups—the elite and the masses—seems obvious and, thus, for many, is an appealing approach to the study of politics. Few would argue that the study of political and other institutional leadership is not important, but this does not mean we can explain politics through the narrow lens of elite analysis and its intellectual cousin—conspiracy theory.

Critics of elite theory argue that it overemphasizes the cohesion of elites. As we know, there is considerable conflict and competition among the powerful. What factors determine the winners and losers in struggles among the elite? Others suggest that elite theory ignores the institutional constraints that make it impossible for elites to ignore the masses. Elected officials, for example, still have to get elected by the people. Finally, others, especially Marxist critics, suggest that elite analysis is simply a poorly theorized class analysis, which fails to locate elites in the broader historical–economic context and ignores the ever-present tensions arising from class conflict.

Class Analysis

There are many variations of class analysis, but each envisions society as being divided into hierarchical strata or ranks that have unequal access to power, authority, and influence. Sociologists call this the study of social stratification. In these social divisions, political scientists, following from the work of Karl Marx, see social classes, antagonistically grounded in the organization of the economy, while followers of Max Weber see status groups that can be ranked on the basis of wealth and prestige. Karl Marx's theory of the capitalist organization of politics and society is explained in more detail later in this volume. Here, we will concentrate on the concept of social class and its implications for the study of politics.

Although social stratification has always been recognized in political theory, Marx was the first to develop a comprehensive theory of social class. Marx, as we saw earlier in this chapter, believed that all societies were divided along class lines and that, moreover, classes were necessarily and always in conflict over the distribution of material resources in society. Marx provided an overarching explanation of politics grounded in the historical organization of the economy. He argued that the "economic structure of society" was "the real foundation" from which arises a society's legal structure and politics (1970, 21). Although Marx argued that a focus on the way economies are organized and the class divisions that result explained the politics of all societies, the bulk of his writings on social class pertain to the emergence of capitalism and industrialization in Europe. He contended that democratic government was the result of a political revolution of a new class—commercial and industrial capitalists or, as Marx called them, the **bourgeoisie**.

At the same time, the emergence of capitalism created another new class—the working class or the **proletariat**—who sold their labour to capitalists and were exploited by them. Marx's careful analysis of the logic of capitalism led him to conclude that in time, the middle class would be absorbed into the working class and the living conditions of the working class would become more and more desperate. The politics of capitalist societies would then revolve around a struggle between capitalists and workers. The working classes of the world, through revolution, would ultimately win and establish a communist society. Capitalism, unlike previous systems, Marx concluded, had a distinctive identifying feature. As he and Engels put it in the *Communist Manifesto,* capitalism "has simplified the class antagonisms. Society as a whole is more and more splitting up into two great hostile camps, into two great classes directly facing each other, bourgeoisie and proletariat" (1952, 8).

Marx's work on social class and the inevitability of class conflict significantly influenced political science as well as the politics of the twentieth century. Nonetheless, many of the political developments of the twentieth century also suggested to many that Marx's analysis was too extreme and failed to account for many of the subsequent changes in the stratification of society. His work has been criticized for its *economic determinism*—that is, for reducing the explanation of all social phenomena to a single factor, the organization of the economy. Others argue that, contrary to Marx's prediction, the middle class did not disappear as capitalism matured but, instead, grew to be an important political force. White-collar workers and professionals do not fit easily into Marx's scheme of class conflict because they are neither capitalists nor working class in a traditional Marxist definition of these terms. Finally, others, following from the work of Max Weber, argue that social stratification occurs along many dimensions due to a variety of factors, not solely due to one's position in the organization of economic relations.

When Weber contemplated the ways that societies were stratified, he saw quite a different world from the one Marx did. The starkly oppressive conditions of emerging industrialization had been somewhat improved, the working class had organized into unions and socialist political parties, democracy had expanded, and, as Weber saw it, society was increasingly governed by legal-rational authority and large bureaucracies. He argued that social stratification could no longer be studied as a product of social class alone. For Weber, social class remained an important determinant of power, but it was not the only factor. Modern society was divided into many status groups whose positions on the social hierarchy were also determined by prestige and by political power. Prestige could involve things as intangible as tastes and patterns of consumption that are socially valued, such as driving a Mercedes or being a celebrated author. This kind of social power, while not entirely unrelated to social class, is not reducible to economic relations alone. Weber's work on status groups encouraged political scientists and sociologists to explain social divisions in influence and power on the basis of a variety of factors, including patterns of consumption, the social prestige assigned to some professions, such as medicine or law, and such factors as ethnicity, gender, race, and religion. Weber's work also encouraged political scientists in the United States, where the Marxist tradition was not strong, to talk about class divisions in non-antagonistic ways. Social class was analyzed along a continuum—upper class, middle class, and lower class—without any notion of exploitation or conflict among these groups. Weber's work, nonetheless, underlined the many ways that power and influence are unequally distributed in society, quite often on the basis of characteristics we are assigned at birth, such as gender and race.

To sum up, the institutional, pluralist, elite, and class approaches to the study of politics are only four among many ways to view the political world. They do, nonetheless, highlight many of the critical concepts in political science. Institutionalism emphasizes the importance of formal political institutions and how constitutions structure the rules of the political game and, thus, often, the outcome. Pluralists, in contrast, emphasize the informal ingredients of power, individual political actors, and the competition among groups for their preferred policy outcomes. They emphasize the play of politics from the bottom up, from the citizen to the state, while elitism focuses on the opposite flow, from leadership down. Although the elite approach probably exaggerates the isolation and independence of elites from the vast majority, it does point to the ways that ordinary citizens are often distanced from the political world and lack the expertise and information to engage in effective political participation. Finally, the class approach points to the ways in which power and influence are unevenly distributed in societies on the basis of social structure, position, and identity. Whether we agree with Marx or with Weber about the singular or multiple causes of social stratification, the class/status approach tells us that we can never study the individual political actor outside the context of history or the broader social divisions of power and influence. Having traced many of the key perspectives of the political world, this chapter concludes with a discussion of some of the new challenges facing political science in the twenty-first century.

Politics in the Twenty-First Century

IN RECENT YEARS, THE TRADITIONAL APPROACHES AND CONCERNS OF THE discipline of political science has been challenged by, among others, feminist, postcolonial, and postmodern perspectives. The current era of intensifying globalization, however, poses perhaps the most far-reaching challenges to both the study and the practice of politics in the twenty-first century. As the chapters in this book explain, globalization has eroded familiar political institutions and patterns of politics without signalling what will or should take their place. Contemporary politics are marked by uncertainty and transition.

Although increasingly present in our daily vocabularies, globalization is very much a contested concept. At the very least, globalization can be understood as an unfolding political drama involving a number of transformative processes, some reinforcing and others contradictory. These processes stretch social, political, and economic activities across political frontiers and the formal boundaries of the national state. In so doing, they intensify interdependencies, accelerate social exchanges, and blur the boundaries among the local, the national, and the global (Held and McGrew, 1999, 484). As these epochal shifts become inescapable facts in our daily calculations, it is important to unpack globalization into its component parts, especially to distinguish between transformations in our social world and the governance of these changes. Beck calls the first **globality** and the second **globalism** (2000).

Globality refers to epochal shifts in social and political and organization that have irreversibly altered the political world and our daily lives. Globality focuses our attention on new technologies, social and political issues that transcend territorial boundaries, and the possible emergence of the planet as the relevant space for political action. Beck argues that globality is an unavoidable and irreversible fact of twenty-first century politics with "all interventions, victories, and catastrophes" occurring on a local–global axis (2000, 11, 15). September 11 and its ongoing reverberations everywhere illustrate this point forcefully.

Globalism, in contrast, refers to the transnational embrace of a common world view and institutions of governance. As many of the chapters that follow explain, the embrace, in varying degrees, of neo-liberalism by most national governments and by international organizations approaches this idea of a common world view. Many commentators on globalization, both for and against, fail to distinguish between globality and globalism. Recognizing the difference between these two concepts, however, is an important key to understanding contemporary politics. The distinction allows us to recognize the profound changes that define this globalizing era while leaving open to analysis and activism the essential questions of how these changes will translate into public policies and political institutions. The progressive shaping of the planet into an interdependent whole may be inevitable, but contrary to the pronouncements of the promoters of neo-liberal globalism, there is nothing inevitable about the way this process should be governed.

Summary

This book focuses on critical concepts in political science. A concept is generally understood as an idea—a representation of a class of things or practices. The adjective *critical* is meant to convey three meanings that are elaborated in the chapters that follow. The first is that the concepts we identify are critical to our understanding of power and politics. Such concepts as justice, democracy, the state, and international relations, to name a few, have been the bread and butter of political science since its conception. Second, the adjective "critical" is meant to convey the idea that these concepts are contested—subject to ongoing debate and struggle about their very meaning and practice. Finally, these concepts are critical because the stakes of politics—of who wins, loses, or is simply ignored—generally hinge on how foundational political concepts are commonly understood and embedded in our political institutions.

There is an old cliché that says, "We cannot understand where we are going unless we understand where we have been." This cliché resonates in contemporary political affairs. As we debate today's political issues, it is important to realize that similar questions vexed other societies and that, through politics, they arrived at either reasonable or horrible solutions. The kind of politics we will have in an era of globalization, as well as the solutions we find to global coexistence, is still ours to create, although, as Marx would remind us, not necessarily under conditions of our own choosing. Globalization challenges old assumptions and creates new political problems. It does not, however, release us from the responsibility of constantly revisiting the fundamental political questions of what is and, more importantly, what ought to be.

Discussion Questions

1. Think about your day. How often did you encounter politics? What kind of politics did you encounter? Were there some encounters that entailed more power than others? Why? In what ways could you have resisted that power?
2. Compare and contrast the approaches to politics discussed in this chapter.
3. What ought our politics look like in the twenty-first century? Why?

References

Bachrach, Peter and Morton Baratz. 1970. *Power and Poverty: Theory and Practice.* New York: Oxford University Press.

Beck, Ulrich. 2000. *What is Globalization?* Translated by Patrick Camiller. London: Polity Press.

Bendix, Reinhard. 1960. *Max Weber: An Intellectual Portrait.* Garden City, N.Y.: Doubleday.

Bentley, Arthur. 1935. *The Process of Government.* Evanstown, IL: Principia Press.

Bottomore, Tom. 1979. *Political Sociology.* London: Harper and Row Publishers.

Brodie, Janine. 1995. *Politics on the Margins: Restructuring and the Canadian Women's Movement.* Halifax, NS: Fernwood Publishing.

Dahl, Robert. 1956. *Preface to Democratic Theory.* Chicago: University of Chicago Press.

———. 1961. *Who Governs.* New Haven, CT: Yale University Press.

Dicey, A.V. 1908. *An Introduction to the Study of the Law of the Constitution.* 7th edition. London: Macmillan.

Fink-Eitel, Hinrich. 1992. *Foucault: An Introduction.* Philadelphia: Pennbridge Books.

Foucault, Michel. 1977. *Power/Knowledge.* New York: Pantheon.

Fraser, Nancy and Linda Gordon. 1994. "A Geneology of Dependency: Tracing a Keyword of the US Welfare State." *Signs,* 19, no. 2 (Winter).

Gerth, H.H. and C.W. Mills, eds. 1958. *From Max Weber: Essays in Sociology.* New York: Oxford University Press.

Guy, James John. 1995. *People, Politics, Government: Political Science: A Canadian Perspective.* Scarborough, ON: Prentice Hall.

Hall, Stuart. 1996. "The Question of Cultural Identity." in Stuart Hall, David Held, Don Hubert and Kenneth Thompson, eds. *Modernity: An Introduction to the Modern Social Sciences.* London: Blackwell.

Hawley, Amos. 1963. "Community Power and Urban Renewal Success." *American Journal of Sociology.* Vol. 68 (January).

Held, David. 1996. "The Development of the Modern State." in Stuart Hall, David Held, Don Hubert and Kenneth Thompson, eds. *Modernity: An Introduction to the Modern Social Sciences.* London: Blackwell.

Held, David and McGrew, Anthony. 1999. "Globalization." *Global Governance.* 5, no. 4.

Knuttila, Murray. 1987. *State Theories.* Toronto: Garamond.

Kourvetaris, George. 1997. *Political Sociology: Structure and Process.* Boston: Allyn and Bacon.

Lasswell, Harold. 1936. *Politics: Who Gets, What, When and How.* New York: McGraw-Hill.

Mannheim, Karl. 1936. *Ideology and Utopia.* New York: Harvest Books.

Michels, Roberto. 1962. *Political Parties.* New York: The Free Press.

Mouffe, Chantal. 1992. *Dimensions of Radical Democracy: Pluralism, Citizenship, Community.* London: Verso.

Pareto, Vilfredo. 1978. *Sociological Writings.* Oxford: Basil Blackwell.

Persky, Stan. 1992. "City without Citizens." in Max Wyman, ed. *Vancouver Forum: Old Powers, New Forces.* Vancouver: Douglas McIntyre.

Philp, Mark. 1985. "Power." in Adam Kuper and Jessica Kuper, eds. *The Social Science Encyclopedia.* New York: Routledge.

Schattschneider, E.E. 1960. *The Semi-Sovereign People: A Realist's View of Democracy.* New York: Holt, Reinhart and Winston.

Simons, Jon. 1995. *Foucault and the Political.* New York: Routledge.

Walzer, Michael. 1984. "Liberalism and the Art of Separation." *Political Theory,* 12 (August).

Further Readings

Bottomore, Tom. 1979. *Political Sociology.* London: Harper and Row Publishers.

Hall, Stuart, David Held, Don Hubert and Kenneth Thompson, eds. 1996. *Modernity: An Introduction to the Social Sciences.* London: Blackwell.

Knuttila, Murray. 1987. *State Theories.* Toronto: Garamond.

Weblinks

American Political Science Association
www.apsanet.org

Canadian Political Science Association
www.sfu.ca/igs/CPSA.html

Department of Political Science, University of Alberta
www.ualberta.ca/~polisci/index.html

International Studies Association
www.isanet.org

CHAPTER 2

JUSTICE

Objectives

This chapter examines the concept of justice as a central thread in the legacy of Western political thought. While the study of politics most often poses the question of how it is that human beings organize themselves, political theory poses the question of how we *ought* to organize ourselves. Although fundamental concepts in Western political theory may seem distant from our daily lives, they are central to the vocabulary of contemporary political discourse. Of these concepts, justice is the most foundational and the most vexed. In many ways, a history of Western political theory can be viewed as a prolonged debate about the very meaning of the concept of justice. Understanding how different formulations of justice are and have been defended and articulated offers students of politics a rich resource for making sense of contemporary political debates. For instance, all political debates involve some evaluation of how we think we might best live together, what we decide are our central values, what we hold to be common among us, and what dimensions of life we call "political." The objective of the chapter is to give students a deeper sense of the ways that the idea of justice has been understood and philosophically defended in order that they might be more prepared to decide for themselves which of these legacies they find most helpful in thinking through the kinds of political arrangements they want to endorse. Three definitions of justice are explored: justice as the outcome of a way of life, justice as the rational ordering of our common life, and justice as the ability to deliver on promises.

CATHERINE KELLOGG

Introduction

The history of Western political thought is a long and interesting struggle over the meaning and definition of **justice**. On the one hand, justice can be understood as a way of living—what the ancient Greeks called a disposition of the soul. The Greeks linked their definition of justice to the question "How should I live in order to be a good person?" For the Greeks, the question "How ought *I* to live?" was inseparable from the question "What might be a just form of political life?" or "How ought *we* to live?"

On the other hand, we think of justice much more regularly as a state of common or public affairs. For instance, the late Canadian Prime Minister Pierre Trudeau campaigned in the 1968 election on the platform of a "just society." Insofar as he was calling for a robust set of "universally" accessible social services and a politics of inclusion, he was talking about what we *ought* to share in common. He also was alluding to our common capacity for reason and, thus, our ability to build a rationally organized and equitable political community. As we will see in the second section of this chapter, modern political theory is preoccupied with the idea that in order to create a just world, we must first investigate what is common to us as human beings. Most modern political thinkers insist that we share reason in common. **Reason**, in other words, separates human beings from other sentient creatures. This approach to justice de-emphasizes the question of what kind of life we should live and emphasizes instead the question of how we should rationally proceed or what we should *do*.

When justice is understood in terms of our common capacity for reason, it suggests that no matter how tall or old or law abiding, we are all equally worthy of participating in deciding what our common future might be. This conception of justice is, thus, already linked in the great social experiment of the modern era: democracy. This is because **democracy** refers to the rule of the people, or the will of what is common or general to us, which for all democratic thinkers was our ability to reason.

These two prevailing ways of thinking about justice implicate a tension between the way of life or set of values of a people and the individual who is the bearer of reason. It is most clearly seen in the most enduring legacy of modern political thought: **liberalism**. Liberalism has charted an interesting path between the idea that, on the one hand, "individuals" rationally produce themselves and their communities and, on the other, the idea that individuals are the product of their communities' values. Current debates about the limits of liberalism lead into the final section of this chapter. No matter how you slice it, liberalism holds fast to the idea that for the purposes of politics, we must understand that all individuals are identical: equal, free, and rational. While liberals are committed to the sanctity of the individual, each individual is understood to be *politically identical* to every other individual. As we will see in the final section of this chapter, many contemporary approaches to justice concern the limits and possibilities of liberalism's promise to deliver a just and equitable society.

Defining Justice I

THE WORD *JUSTICE* DEFIES CLEAR DEFINITION. IN ITS CONTEMPORARY USAGE, justice usually refers to something like an "ideal" of perfection or goodness toward which we collectively strive. It is the "ought" to which we can compare the "is." Politically, it is most often linked to an idea of law. It is the ideal that we hope our laws might achieve. In this sense, justice is often the thing or idea that prompts people to act and change laws. "No justice, no peace" is a familiar refrain at all kinds of protest events.

In our contemporary usage, we also tend to think that identifying what might be a "just" solution to a problem is something that ought to be assigned to those who are mature and experienced. We believe that those to whom we entrust decisions about how to come up with just solutions require something like wisdom or prudence. We call, for instance, judges at the highest level of office, *justices*—they are understood to be "justice" incarnate. While there is an important contemporary debate in Canada about whether or not the courts have a place in making decisions about politics, there is a widespread agreement that judges should be people who have lived, reflected, and studied so that they might be able to come to wise or prudent decisions. This is because we understand that delivering justice—making ideals deliver on their promises—is understood to be work best left to people with a certain kind of expertise.

And finally, many people understand justice in **quasi-divine** terms. Justice is often understood to be the decision that God, were s/he to exist, might make. Justice here, is thought of as something more like art than science; we might not know much about it, but we know it (aha, justice) when we see it. These three ideas—justice as an ideal, justice as a dividend of wisdom, and justice as a quasi-divine force—come to us from the ancient Greek philosophers Plato and Aristotle.

Justice and a "Way of Life"

Importantly, both Plato and Aristotle approached the question of justice not so much in terms of a state of public affairs but, rather, as a state of the soul. The Greeks asked the question, "What might be a just way of living?" There is much to be learned from the idea that justice pertains to a way of life for both singular souls and for a particular people. For instance, in his most famous dialogue, *The Republic*, Plato understands justice to be a kind of natural ordering force in the universe, ordering both our souls and the world around us. In his view, justice is a quasi-divine eternal "light" of the world, and he thinks that our way of life should be dedicated to discovering it. Indeed, Plato suggested that to live in pursuit of riches or power or glory in this temporary physical world, rather than in pursuit of the eternal ordering perfection of justice, is a life not worth living. To get at this idea, Plato employs a long analogy between the just soul and a just city. For Plato, we are just when we realize that the soul, which is the seat of moral, intellectual, and spiritual life, should "rule" over the body or the senses. And by analogy, the city is just—it is in the right order—when the "class" of people who are most suited to this ability rule over those who are not.

Plato's extraordinary aim in this text is to prove the *existence* of justice. In other words, he sets out to prove that there is something "good" that is a real force in the universe, that it has a real presence. For Plato, justice is not simply something that we human beings "make up" or believe in. Plato argued that justice is the most "real" thing, and that all other "things" are mere illusions. Indeed, he argued that those things we can experience through our senses—from rocks to art—are as false as shadows on the walls of a cave. Plato claims that not only does justice, or "the good," exist, but it is only by its existence that we can know anything at all. Justice is to knowledge as light is to our sense of sight. Without justice we cannot know anything, in the same way that without light, we cannot see anything. And while we cannot really "see" light, we know that it is the foundation for our ability to see. On the same grounds, Plato says that while we cannot "see" justice, we know that it is the foundation for our ability to know anything at all.

On his saying so, we must work hard to "know" things as they really are, in their "ideal" or perfect form and not as they appear to us through our senses. Knowing this ideal, moreover, can only be apprehended through our souls. For Plato, this attempt to know things—including our cities and us—as they really are is the only possible important way of life. This is what he calls the examined life or the life of contemplation. Indeed, he presents a long argument about how we should be educated to examine the world and ourselves in its wholeness and perfect, harmonious integration. And as we learn to know things in their "ideal" form, we are on our way to knowing justice. When we know justice, we have, in fact, become just.

The question of the just city follows directly from the discussion about the just soul. On Plato's account, the city is made up of three classes of people, two of whom simply cannot *fully* know what this extraordinarily good thing is because they do not have the right kind of souls. These two classes, however, *can* know that they do not fully know it and can agree to be ruled by those who do. The third class of people fully knows the whole and justice. They can decide most appropriately what is good for the whole community. They alone will rule "justly"—that is, in the interests of all, because they know fully and deeply all of those interests.

For our purposes, what is interesting about the way that Plato describes justice is that we do not know it in the same way that we can know that two plus two equals four. Rather, knowing justice operates more as a kind of revelation. *Aha,* we say, *that* is what justice is. Justice is a force that some of us can know completely, but this form of knowing is not entirely rational. It cannot be worked out entirely through the processes of deduction and induction.

Plato's most famous student, Aristotle, agreed that justice emerged from a particular way of life. For Aristotle, as for Plato, the only possible "good" way of life was one of contemplation, deliberation, and thought. Aristotle, however, disagreed with Plato's claim that justice was an eternal, natural force. In his view, it made no sense to talk about one supreme force ordering all things. Instead, it made more sense to talk about each thing—including, importantly, human beings—having its own "good" or end. What was interesting about most things in the world, including human beings, as far as Aristotle was concerned, is that they grow and change. The seeds of plants look very much alike, but when planted, one will grow into a corn plant and another into an oak tree. This suggested to Aristotle that each thing might be said to have latent possibilities that proper care would develop. We know what an acorn is because we have seen the mature oak tree. The "good" of the acorn, the end at which the acorn aims, is the mature oak tree, and the "good" or end of honeysuckle pollen is the mature honeysuckle plant. On the basis of this insight, he suggested that we cannot proceed from the premise that all things and activities—from darts to statecraft—must end *somewhere* to the conclusion that they must all end *in the same place.* Just because all things and activities have their *own* good, it does not necessarily require that there must be one chief good. All activities do have a final destination toward which they strain—their good. But they all end in different places. Just as oak trees must become mighty, so too must human beings *become* good.

On the basis of the insight that things become "good" when they become fully developed, Aristotle argued that human beings could only become good when they learn to be ethical in a community of other human beings. This is because it is only through the *practice* of living together that we can learn how to become fully developed as human beings. Aristotle names *ethics* the process of practising how to be good at being human, and he names *politics* as the practice of living together. These are uniquely linked in his theory. One can only become ethical through practising politics. Significantly, Aristotle argues that we must approach specific political and ethical situations again and again in our lives before we can develop the qualities or habits required to do them justice. We study ethics "not to know what goodness is, but how to become good men, since otherwise it would be useless" (*Nichomachean Ethics*, 1103b, 27–9).

For Aristotle, then, unlike Plato, justice is not an eternal or natural force in the universe but, rather, an outcome that emerges from certain practices or habits. What he calls general justice is simply the disposition to obey the laws of *any* city. But what interests Aristotle is justice in its *particular* sense, which he says is the disposition to give or take only a fair, or equal, share of a limited number of particular good things in a *given* city. And the two kinds of particular justice Aristotle introduces us to—distributive justice and rectificatory justice—do those two things in turn. The first, **distributive justice**, is the *fair* way of dividing up good things, and the second, **rectificatory justice**, is the *equal* way. Distributive justice is a principle for dividing up the goods of a society that gives equal shares to equal persons, and unequal shares to unequal persons. It is a principle of proportion that says the "better" people get more, and the "worse" people get less. This is what Aristotle means by fair. Distributive justice is a relative term for Aristotle because different regimes, different political constitutions, have different understandings of who gets to count as "better" and, thus, deserve the greater share.

Aristotle's second kind of justice, "rectificatory" or "corrective" involves transactions and is the application of a simple arithmetic equality to the persons and goods involved: equal shares for everyone. Thus, the judge (who is what Aristotle calls a personified Justice) divides "goods" in half, taking from those who have taken too much and restoring it to those who have too little.

Defining Justice II

MANY OF YOU MAY HAVE RECOGNIZED THE DEFINITIONS PRESENTED IN OUR FIRST attempt to define justice but also may have wondered what happened to the idea most regularly associated with justice—**fairness**. While *fairness* may seem a simple term, as Aristotle's analysis of justice indicates, it is, in fact, a relative concept. What comes to count as "fair" or "just" depends on the form of political life we inhabit, what values we hold, and what forms of knowledge predominate. In the modern period, we can see that the idea of justice (or fairness) takes on specific contents that were uniquely tied to the kinds of political forms, ways of life, and forms of knowledge that emerged then. Specifically, justice in the modern era is associated with the political form of popular sovereignty, a capitalist mode of producing wealth, and the form of knowledge called science.

The *form* of political life that dominates the modern period is the modern representative state, and this had a dramatic impact on the ways that modern political philosophers thought about the just or equitable distribution of political power. The modern state placed political power, for the first time, not in the hands of a single ruler but in the hands of the people in general. Our common sense understanding of "fairness," which implies a notion of equal distribution, then, emerges from and works with this very kind of political power. **Popular sovereignty**, or popular rule, is about distributing the ability to rule or govern equally among the people generally.

The *way* of life that emerged during the modern era was, of course, capitalism, and this had a dramatic impact on the ways that modern political philosophers thought about "wealth" and its distribution. Forging a link between the question of "fair distribution" of the common wealth and the inherent dignity of the individual, including his or her rational power to accumulate that wealth, turns out to be a central question posed by modern political philosophy.

The form of *knowledge* that emerged in the modern period was science. It also had a dramatic impact on the ways that political philosophers thought about justice. According to the modern political philosophers, in order to determine what justice might consist of, we must examine human beings generally to discover what is common to us all, in the same way that a scientist might examine many different blades of grass to discover the properties of grass. The shift in emphasis here is important. The way that science proceeds is not by asking how *a* person might *live* but, rather, by asking what *the* person—any person—might *be*.

Nature, Reason, and Sovereignty

The questions of justice in the modern era no longer centred, as they did in ancient Greece, on how we ought to live. According to modern political theorists, we no longer need to investigate the contents, ordering, and habituation of our souls in order to understand justice. Rather, we need to know what it is that human beings *are* and what we all share in common. Most modern political theorists worked with the idea that while human beings are continuous with the natural world—we are natural beings—what separates us from other sentient creatures is our ability to reason. Each of the modern political theorists suggests that we can use our reason to "overcome" our "first" nature so that we might more fully have control over ourselves and the world we live in and no longer be directed by the blind forces of nature. Each of the philosophers we will overview here claim that we will do this by way of learning a kind of second nature. This second nature takes the form of a rational agreement or contract with each other, an agreement to form a civil society that will help us become sovereign over us. The *is*, to which modern political theorists apply themselves, is our nature itself, and the *ought* is a world in which we might become sovereign over ourselves so that we might rationally and collectively determine our common future. In this modern view, the study of politics begins from the study of who human beings "naturally" are.

The convention that is most often associated with this modern tradition is the idea that at some mythical point in time, human beings exited a "state of nature" in which they were little more than beasts. Because of their reason, however, these beasts entered into a "contract" with each other to develop themselves as beings capable of living in peace, in civil harmony, and rationally harvesting the bounty of the earth. Now each of the social contract theorists—Hobbes, Locke, and Rousseau—understands what our "nature" as beasts might have been quite differently, and each imagines this reason we had differently, and, consequently, each imagines different kinds of contracts we might have entered into in order to attain civil peace and rational control. Thomas Hobbes, for instance, in his great text *Leviathan*, argued famously that without a higher power to keep us in awe, our lives as natural beings would have been one of constant war. He suggested that our lives in the "state of nature" would have been one of unceasing struggle for power over each other. Because we are, naturally, little more than wild beasts, our lives in the state of nature would have been "brutish, nasty, and short."

Fortunately, Hobbes tells us, what we share in common, what makes us different from other kinds of wild beasts, is a rudimentary kind of reason that is little more than a self-preservative force. It is the awareness of our impending mortality. However, because we have this capacity in common, he suggests that we found a way out of the war of all against all. In order to protect ourselves from our instinctual or natural ways that constantly threaten to erupt, he suggested that we should agree to give over all of our powers to a new entity, a state, which would have ultimate authority over our lives. Only with a power this immense could we be sure to continue as a species. Importantly, this new political state is a representation of who we are—a portrait of "us" as we are, in common. We are equal under this sovereign, to the extent that we have all agreed to it, and we are equally subjected to its power. The only idea of justice Hobbes suggests we can pursue is one in which we agree to keep our contracts with each other to continue to agree to this overarching power. This idea of justice is meant to preserve the only kind of freedom Hobbes thinks is truly important. This is the freedom to stay alive and not to wreak destruction on the world and us.

By way of contrast, John Locke, writing less than a hundred years after Hobbes, suggested that in our natural state, we were already equal, free, rational, peaceful coexistents. Consequently, the kind of contract we would/should enter into is one that gives the government or the state only limited powers over our lives. In his *Second Treatise of Government*, Locke added a fascinating addition to the social contract tradition: the idea that we naturally "own" our bodies, our labour, and ourselves. We contract with each other to give up executive power to the state in order that it might protect our "lives, liberty, and estates." In his view, the state's role is not much more than an arbiter for deciding that we should honour our contracts with each other regarding the ways that we divide up the bounty of the earth. Justice, here, is meant to preserve a kind of natural liberty to which we are born and to distribute the goods of the earth in such a way that those who are good at accumulating them will be able to keep them.

Writing in the years leading up to the French Revolution, Jean-Jacques Rousseau suggested that in our natural state, we were dumb beasts but benign, equal, free, and loving ones. In his view, the scheme to enter into a contract with each other was, in fact, an evil plot hatched by those with the end of grabbing property from their fellows. The form of civil society that Rousseau saw around him was one in which we had, in fact, lost our natural liberty, our natural equality, and our natural goodness. We had become enslaved to each other and to the needs we had developed. Consequently, Rousseau suggested that we needed a *new* kind of social contract.

Rousseau thought that through developing proper laws, laws that emerged from our ability to reason, a semblance of man's original condition of both freedom and equality could be recaptured. Now, Rousseau is clear that we should *not* do this in such a way that we give up power to some absolute or arbitrary power (*à la* Hobbes), as this does not safeguard liberty. Neither should we simply give our power over to legislators who we will keep us in check with an executive that stands over them (*à la* Locke), as this does not safeguard equality. Rather, Rousseau claimed that in order to re-find our lost equality and liberty, we should become *ourselves* legislators, with each involved in making laws. In this way, not only would we regain some of the freedom we lost in the circuit out of the state of nature and into civil society, we would reinstitute a political equality that reflects the natural equality we had in our original state.

Defining Justice III

WE REGULARLY USE THE PHRASE *TO DO JUSTICE* TO SOMETHING. JUSTICE, IN this view, refers to the ability to deliver on promises. In the contemporary period, we have seen many political theorists attempt to think through whether the ways that the modern emphasis on what is common, general, or universal to us has led to substantive forms of equality and freedom. For instance, if justice is the ability to deliver on promises, then such universal political categories as *citizen* should display sensitivity to what they claim to include. What makes general or universal categories truly universal, in other words, is that they can be applied to every particular case without violation. But notwithstanding the attempt to make *citizenship* a truly universal category, women, immigrants, visible minorities, Aboriginal people, lesbians and gays, the disabled, the poor, the disenfranchised, or the overlooked continue to insist that they have not been adequately represented by our public institutions or public discourses. These struggles are understood to be "social justice" struggles because they attempt to hold universal categories to their word.

In fact, if modern political thought was characterized by the claim that human reason was an adequate resource for the development of universality, contemporary political thought can be characterized by *challenges* to universalism, challenges that claim that the pre-eminent form of modern political life—the liberal democratic state—is not the only site of politics or power. Work, the family, and processes of producing and distributing wealth are sites where substantive freedom and equality are demonstrably missing. What this has meant is that arenas of social life previously considered apolitical have become politicized and subjected to public contestation.

Contemporary Challenges

Contemporary phenomena such as Marxist, feminist, and anti-racist thought all work through challenges to claims about the justice delivered by universality. Each of these approaches to the question of "justice" claims that our concrete differences from each other, differences upon which real discrimination and oppression rest, are, in fact, covered over by the liberal ideal that for the purposes of politics, we must be understood to be identical to each other.

For instance, Marx claimed that while the liberal democratic state insists that we are all free and equal in our "ideal" or identical form as "citizens," we continue to be vulnerable to exploitation and inequality as workers. The increasing gap between the rich and the poor in Canada, as well as the increasing gap between the North and the South, has indicated that this is the case. Indeed, while there has been a recurring debate about whether Marx thought that capitalism should be overcome and replaced because it is *unjust,* what most critics seem to overlook is that Marx's most devastating normative critique is directed toward modern notions of justice themselves. This is why Marx suggests that communism will be, in a certain sense, beyond justice. The reason Marx tells us that communism will be *beyond justice* is because it will be beyond modern universal categories that necessarily generalize. The Marxist critique of justice is that unlike capitalist society, communist society will be one in which *each* will give according to her ability and each will receive according to her need. For justice to be rendered justly, Marx suggested that it would have to be rendered on a case-by-case basis in concrete circumstances.

Many feminists and anti-racists similarly argue that abstract notions of freedom and equality often disguise the ways in which concrete and embodied subjects are rendered unequal by sexism and racism.

For instance, the family is still an arena of social life in which women are expected to care for the young, the old, and the sick, and, at the same time, are increasingly expected to participate in the labour market. In a similar vein, the labour market, with its famed "glass ceiling" has remained stubbornly attached to racist and sexist ideas about who should be promoted, who might be considered worthy of advanced education, and so on. The ideal, identical subject of liberal individualism is not emancipated from all processes of subordination. Like Marxists, feminists and anti-racists argue that if the modern political categories of universality were to actually deliver on their promises, then all areas of social life would be subject to rational control, including work, education, leisure, and family. In this sense, contemporary political thought has challenged the claim that for the purposes of political life, we are or should be considered to be identical. This comes with the observation that political life extends beyond formal processes of representation and into arenas of life previously considered un- or apolitical. Feminist and anti-racist claims about the racist and sexist dimensions of the seemingly "apolitical" or private realms of the family or the market, have, in fact, worked to politicize them.

Summary

This chapter has reviewed a series of approaches to the question of "justice" that have been posed throughout the history of Western political theory. We have reviewed the shift from the Ancient Greek preoccupation with justice as a way of life to the modern idea that justice is bound up with our common capacity for reason. In the classical view, justice was fundamentally bound up with a life of contemplation and introspection; in the modern view, insofar as we have a common capacity for reason, we are capable of directing our common futures in a rational and equitable fashion. The shift of focus from antiquity to modernity is the shift from thinking to acting, or from *discovering* justice to *making justice happen.* And in the contemporary period, we have seen that many political thinkers are questioning and reassessing the quality of "justice" promised by the dream of modern political thought. These thinkers have asked whether the attempt to find what is common or universal to us for the purposes of our shared political life actually delivered a life of true equality and freedom. They ask whether justice has been done to the modern understanding of "justice." What we have discovered is that the critical concept *justice* carries a wide variety of meanings in Ancient Greek philosophy, modern political thought, and contemporary political thought.

Discussion Questions

1. Which of the ideas of justice discussed in this chapter seem the most appealing to you, and why?
2. We suggest here that justice can be thought of as a "way of life" that trains the soul. Is there a more contemporary way of saying this, or do you think that this is a thought that disappeared with the disappearance of the Ancient Greek world?

3. Modern political thinkers thought that "reason" could free us from nature. Do you think that this is a useful way to think about politics?
4. We have suggested here that contemporary challenges to ideals of universality have worked to politicize arenas of life previously not considered political. Can you think of more examples of this process of politicization?

References

Aristotle. 1948. *Politics.* Translated by Ernest Barker. Oxford: Oxford University Press.

———. 1985. *Nicomachean Ethics.* Translated by Terence Irwin. Indianapolis, IN : Hackett.

Hobbes, Thomas. 1977. *Leviathan.* Hammondsworth: Penguin.

Locke, John. 1965. *Second Treatise on Government.* New York: Mentor Press.

Marx, Karl and Friedrich Engels. 1968. "The Communist Manifesto" and "Critique of the Gotha Programme," in *Selected Works.* London: Lawrence and Wishart.

Plato. 1987. *Republic.* Translated by Desmond Lee London: Penguin Books.

Rousseau, Jean-Jacques. 1964. *A Discourse on the Origins of Inequality* and *The Social Contract* New York: St. Martin's Press.

Further Readings

Chomsky, Noam. 1997. *Perspectives on Power: Reflections on Human Nature and the Social Order.* Montreal: Black Rose Books

Cohen, G.A. 2000. *If You're an Egalitarian, How Come You're So Rich?* Cambridge, MA: Harvard University Press.

Fisher, William F. 2003. *Another World Is Possible: Popular Alternatives to Globalization at the World Social Forum.* New York: Zed Books.

Harvey, David. 1996. *Justice, Nature and the Geography of Difference.* Cambridge, MA: Blackwell Publishers.

Young, Iris Marion. 1990. *Justice and the Politics of Difference.* Princeton, NJ: Princeton University Press.

Weblinks

Network for Social Justice
www.socialjustice.org

The Internet Encyclopedia of Philosophy: Hobbes
www.iep.utm.edu/h/hobmoral.htm

The Internet Encyclopedia of Philosophy: Locke
www.iep.utm.edu/l/locke.htm

CHAPTER 3

ETHICS

STELLA GAON

Objectives

The objective of this chapter is to demonstrate how political life, from the decisions of high courts to informal individual choices, is permeated with ethical assumptions and beliefs. Ethics guide both our assessments and criticisms of political claims. In a recent federal election, for example, Canadians were asked to choose between two competing sets of ethical values. One stressed the role of the market in providing for the well-being of Canadians, while the other stressed a more active role for the state. The election, therefore, raised an ethical conflict between those who believe that the market provides such goods as health care more efficiently and those who believe that such basic goods should never be produced for profit. Both before and after the events of September 11, 2001, we also witnessed on an international level the kinds of profound political antagonisms that can erupt when ethical beliefs about the best way to live come into conflict.

We begin by discussing the relationship between ethics and politics. We then provide a working definition of the concept of *ethics*, and describe three prominent views that have developed over the ages. In each case, we provide examples of how these different ethical theories inform particular political positions. We pay special attention to how the critical concepts of *reason*, *legitimacy*, and *autonomy* have influenced political thought and practice during the modern era. Throughout the chapter, we emphasize the importance of making visible the ethics of politics. But we also stress that political interests are often supported and served by particular ethical beliefs. The question of whether political interests influence moral perspectives is raised in the context of contemporary challenges to modern moral and political thought. Our conclusion is that it is necessary both to criticize political claims on moral grounds and to question ethical perspectives and approaches on political grounds. The conversation between ethics and politics, in other words, flows in both directions.

Introduction

It is common to think of ethics and politics as two entirely separate spheres. For example, politics is often understood in terms of the mechanics, strategies, and structures of power. The question of ethics, if it arises at all, is often limited to reflection on a politician's or ruler's personal integrity. Ethics is generally understood as strictly a personal matter, one that does not have much bearing on the political realm. Yet, political arguments and decisions are thoroughly saturated with ethical claims, assumptions, and beliefs, whether or not these are explicit. For instance, should governments support medical developments in the fields of biotechnology and genetic manipulation (such as genetically modified foods and cloning)? Are property rights for music and books desirable in a digital universe? Should there be legal limitations on fundamental freedoms, such as free speech, in a democratic society—for example, in the case of racist or hate speech or, more recently, in the case of suspected threats against the state? Is it legitimate for one country to aggress another by means of military interventions or economic sanctions in order to address human rights violations or to replace non-democratic political regimes with democratic ones, as in Kosovo or Iraq? Each of these political questions requires one to take a particular ethical stance, and each has profound moral implications. The ethical questions may not be answered to everybody's satisfaction, if at all. Nonetheless, it is important to bring ethical issues forward in political debates because a conflict over ethical beliefs often drives political conflicts. For this reason, it is necessary to learn how moral assumptions play out in the political sphere and to develop arguments that can be used either to contest or support them.

Defining Ethics

IN ENGLISH USAGE, BOTH *ETHICS* AND *MORALITY* REFER TO A BELIEF OR SET of beliefs about what one ought to do, how one ought to live, and what ought to be the case. The word **ethics** comes from the Greek *ethos*, which means the general way of life and customs of a people; an *ethos* encompasses a society's cultural, traditional, religious, social, and political norms. The word **morality** is related to the Latin *mores*, which is a synonym for the Greek word *ethos*. *Mores* are customs of a people that are considered socially beneficial. *Mores* sometimes develop into formal laws. The words *ethics* and *morality* may be used interchangeably, although some philosophers distinguish between them for the purposes of a specific theoretical argument.[1]

Ethics is generally broken down into two components: theoretical study and practical application. In its theoretical sense, ethics is a branch of philosophy that studies what is *good* and what *ought* to be the case. Theoretical ethics investigates such questions as: How do we know what is the right decision or action? What kinds of arguments should count when one is trying to justify a moral belief? What role should community values or traditions play in ethical deliberation? What is "happiness," and does it contribute to a "good" life? What is the best way to achieve these often elusive goals? These are all "theoretical" questions in the sense that they are *general* in nature: they do not refer to any *particular* ethical question or case.

Practical ethics, in contrast, does refer to the study of particular problems and cases, and attempts to devise specific solutions to them (Birsch, 1999, 2). Contemporary examples of issues in practical ethics include the moral and political questions of abortion, euthanasia, cloning and reproductive technologies, legal punishment and the death penalty, world hunger, environmental issues, and the moral treatment of animals. Theoretical and practical ethics can be understood as two sides of the same coin, since people often apply their theoretical insights to specific practical problems. Similarly, the ongoing quandaries of politics and law often provoke further theoretical reflection. What is at issue in both cases, moreover, is what a person, community, or society believes is the *good* or *right* thing to do.

Ethics and Politics through the Ages

AT ITS CORE, THE HISTORY OF WESTERN POLITICAL THOUGHT IS ONE OF ongoing reflection about how to change what *is* to the way we think it *ought* to be. This moral reflection about the just society includes considerations of how we should organize ourselves for the maximum good of each person, what role the state should play in citizens' personal lives, whether individual or the collective good should take precedence in political deliberation, and how to judge whether political power is being used for good ends (legitimately) and when it is being used unjustly (illegitimately). As soon as we direct these kinds of **normative** questions to the realm of politics, we are drawing on ethics because we are trying to decide what *ought* to be the case within a particular political context or practice.

Of course, over the ages, there has been a series of changes in the general understanding of the relationship between ethics and politics. Moreover, at no point has there ever been uniform agreement about what constitutes the truly ethical decision or act. For example, ancient philosophers, such as Plato and Aristotle, both stressed the important role of the state in producing virtuous citizens. They disagreed, however, about whether it is the theory or the practice of political justice that ought to be emphasized and about exactly what justice entails. Similarly, medieval thinkers

St. Augustine and St. Thomas Aquinas both ranked divine wisdom over the political authority practised by human beings. Nonetheless, they took different positions on the question of what moral role the state might still be expected to play.

Modern Ethics and Politics

IN MODERN POLITICAL THOUGHT—A TRADITION THAT CAN BE SAID TO BEGIN in the sixteenth century with Niccolò Machiavelli and Thomas Hobbes and to continue into the eighteenth and nineteenth centuries with John Locke, David Hume, Immanuel Kant, and Georg Wilhelm Friedrich Hegel—the virtues of rational self-determination and freedom became the guiding moral and political principles. These values replaced both the ancient virtues of citizenship, manliness, and courage that were held by classical Greek philosophers as well as the medieval Christian virtues of charity, humbleness, and faith.

The value of self-determination—that is, the capacity to determine one's own goals for oneself rationally—is called **autonomy**. In the Western world, this quality is generally taken as a fundamental moral good. It applies both to individuals as well as to states in their sovereignty. The moral value of autonomy stems from one basic assumption. It is that the capacity to **reason** is what distinguishes human beings from animals and is, therefore, our most precious quality. Moreover, since everyone is at least potentially rational, everyone is likely to consent to ideas about justice if they are justified by good reasons. Contemporary moral and political thinkers who follow in the tradition of those such as Hobbes, Locke, and Kant, in other words, agree that reason is the most reliable authority on all matters moral and political. They argue that when each of us determines for *ourselves* what is morally good on the basis of good reasons, we are acting in the most ethically responsible way because we are acting autonomously. In this sense, rationality confers **legitimacy**, or "rightness," on our moral and political acts. In this approach, private beliefs and cultural differences are considered irrelevant. Thus, in the modern era, we often distinguish sharply between public and private concerns. Yet, notwithstanding their general agreement about the critical concept of autonomy, contemporary thinkers disagree about its specific ethical and political implications. It is possible, therefore, to identify a number of distinct ways of arguing for moral and political legitimacy within this broad frame.

Utilitarian Ethics

One form of rational justification for moral claims is called **consequentialism**. This theory suggests that in order to judge the legitimacy of political and moral beliefs, one needs to consider only the consequences of the action or the decision. **Act utilitarianism** is a common variant of consequentialism. This approach stresses the utility (or use-value) likely to result from one's act. In moral theory, *utility* is defined in terms of an increase of pleasure and/or a decrease of pain. Act utilitarianism rests on the premise that "an action is morally bad if it harms someone, whereas it is morally good if it helps or benefits someone" (Birsch, 1999, 31).

The utilitarian argument was formulated in the eighteenth and nineteenth centuries by Jeremy Bentham, John Stuart Mill, and William James. Bentham believed, for example, that the only meaning of the term *good* is "pleasure," and that the only meaning of the term *evil* is "pain." He further argued that the moral principle of utility (so defined) could be applied to the sphere of criminal law in two ways. First, he argued that if an act does not cause a calculable injury or harm, it should not be punished. Second, he contended that if an act does cause harm, the punishment should be determined with a view to providing harm to the offender that is greater than the pleasure or benefit gained from the criminal act. In this way, the punishment will serve as a deterrent.

Another act utilitarian is the British political philosopher John Stuart Mill, who is best known as a social reformer, particularly with regard to the issue of minority rights. He argued that in order to know what one ought to do, one must calculate the greatest good or happiness for the greatest number. Thus, for Mill—as for Bentham—the basic moral norm is that one ought to act and one ought to be motivated to act so as to maximize utility or pleasure as much as possible. Like all consequentialists, Mill believed that one should rationally calculate the likely consequences of one's actions and weigh the potential harms in comparison with the potential benefits in order to determine whether an act or decision is ethically good.

The ideas that the consequences of actions are of key moral significance and that consequences can be rationally calculated have been brought to bear directly on the field of politics in a number of ways. Indeed, one way of deciding whether a particular piece of legislation is legitimate is to consider whether it ultimately causes more harm or more good. A ground-breaking case in legal jurisprudence provides one salient example: the Canadian Supreme Court case *R. v. Oakes* (1986).

David Oakes was arrested and subsequently found guilty of possession of illegal narcotics. According to a section of the *Narcotic Control Act* then in effect, anyone found guilty of possession also was guilty of trafficking in a narcotic *unless* he or she could prove otherwise. The trial judge, therefore, found Oakes guilty of trafficking as well. Oakes appealed the decision to the Supreme Court of Canada on the grounds that the *Narcotic Control Act* violated his constitutional right to be presumed innocent until proven guilty (s. 11d of the *Canadian Charter of Rights and Freedoms*). His argument was that while he was guilty of possession, he had not been *proven* guilty of trafficking. He had simply been *presumed* guilty. Oakes argued that in putting the burden on him to prove his innocence, the *Narcotic Control Act* was making an unconstitutional demand.

The Supreme Court found in Oakes's favour. What was most interesting about this case, however, was that the unanimous ruling set the ground rules for all future cases about when a government is entitled to limit someone's fundamental rights (as laid out in the *Charter*) and when it is not. Specifically, the ruling in Oakes sets out two tests that the state must satisfy. These tests concern the *social good or end* the legislation is supposed to achieve and the *means* the government uses to achieve it. The fundamental question here is whether the means are appropriate to the end—particularly when the means limit one of our fundamental *Charter* rights.

In this case, the point of limiting the right to be presumed innocent until proven guilty is to protect society from the dangers of drug trafficking. The judges agreed that this is, indeed, an important objective. However, the means used to achieve it have to be legitimate as well. In order to satisfy this second test, the Crown had to answer three questions. First, are the means rational, or are they arbitrary or unfair? Second, is there a better way of achieving the same social good—one that does not limit a person's or a group's rights to as great an extent? Third, are the means proportional to the ends? The more severe or harmful the effects of a legal measure, the more important the social objective must be.

The Supreme Court ruled that the Crown failed to satisfy the second test. They argued that it is not rational to believe that someone holding only a small quantity of narcotics intends to sell them. In other words, the means used to protect society from the dangers of drug trafficking were irrational and were, therefore, deemed illegitimate. The section of the *Narcotic Control Act* was ruled unconstitutional and was subsequently changed. Since these various tests were set out in *R. v. Oakes,* the Crown can only uphold legislation that limits our fundamental rights if it provides good arguments based on these fundamental utilitarian principles.

Virtue Ethics

Virtue ethics shares with all modern moral philosophy the understanding that ethical values must be supported with rational arguments. In this case, however, the values that are upheld are derived from particular conceptions of the good person, rather than from conceptions of the good act. This theory begins from the basic insight that "virtues help persons to achieve well-being or live good lives" (Birsch, 1999, 81). This approach can be traced back to Aristotle, who held that human beings, like all other beings and things, have a distinctive purpose that makes us what we are. Specifically, the capacity to reason is what distinguishes human beings from all other animals. Therefore, the distinctive form of flourishing that humans can achieve will put this capacity into practice. This means that the intellectual virtues are of primary moral significance with respect to the end or purpose of human life. As Birsch explains, "in virtue ethics, the ethical standard will not be a rule or a principle that designates ethical actions but rather *a moral model or ethical ideal of the virtuous person* (1999, 83; original emphasis). Thus, whereas the utilitarian is likely to ask him- or herself how much good (or harm) will result from a specific act, the virtue ethicist is much more likely to ask what kind of person would undertake such an act, whether he or she wants to be such a person, and whether there is a place for such a person in his or her cultural context. The virtue ethicist, thus, contemplates the *ethos* of the community.

A derivative of virtue ethics is **communitarianism**. Communitarians believe that ideals of the good life and the virtuous person are culturally specific. Each community has a different conception of what is good, and each community will produce individuals in different ways. This version of virtue ethics can be traced to the German philosopher G.W.F. Hegel, who argued that individual morality is a product of the society in which one lives. Contemporary moral and political theorists Alasdair MacIntyre and Charles Taylor follow in this tradition. They emphasize that any rational principle of justice that distinguishes between what is morally right and what is morally wrong also will embody particular, tradition-based ideas concerning the purpose and meaning of human life.

Taylor, for instance, argues that moral judgments are never strictly rational. Instead, principles, values, and beliefs are formed, in part, by a society's cultural traditions. He therefore suggests that in order for *different* cultural groups—such as francophone and anglophone Canadians, or Aboriginal peoples and Canadians of European descent—to come to an agreement about principles of justice, there must be a "fusion of horizons" (1994, 67). By this he means that a meeting of cultures necessarily requires the development of a *common* moral horizon. The production of common ground among different moral views, in turn, requires all parties to open their own moral standards and norms to criticism and change. Whereas a utilitarian might only weigh the outcome of a law or policy with respect to its implications for the individual, a communitarian begins from the understanding that individuals are products of their social and cultural environments.

Elements of communitarianism applied to the public realm are found in Canada's *Multiculturalism Act*. This *Act* provides for the rights of specific groups to exercise and maintain their religious, cultural, ethnic, racial, and national beliefs and identities in Canadian society and politics. It is aimed, moreover, at enhancing Canadian identity and national unity in general—a goal that has no place in an individualist approach to ethics and politics. Although people from different cultures may never agree completely about the right way to live, they can negotiate overlaps between their positions that allow for agreements to be reached. In this way, conflicting conceptions of justice might ultimately be harmonized. Communitarianism, Taylor suggests, is a particularly useful ethical approach to political questions arising from cultural differences in pluralistic societies like Canada's.

Rule-Based Ethics

One of the most influential moral theories with regard to contemporary politics is called **deontology**. This liberal, individualist approach to ethics and politics emphasizes the principles or rules upon which one judges or acts. It is strictly a formal, rule-based moral theory. It ignores all questions concerning the consequences of actions, one's relationship to others in a community, or one's commitment to particular traditions or beliefs. Deontologists maintain that the only *morally* relevant question is whether or not one has acted on the basis of a principle that can be rationally defended. Rather than reflecting on the kind of person one is (communitarianism) or estimating the good that will result (utilitarianism), the deontologist investigates the *reasons for* one's act.

This theory was most fully developed by the German philosopher Immanuel Kant, who is best known for what he called the *categorical imperative.* According to this formula, the only morally right act is one that satisfies the requirement that it would be rational for one to will (agree to, or choose) that one's act becomes a universal law (Kant, 1993, 42). If one can universalize one's act without contradicting oneself, Kant argued, then one's decision is ethically right because it is rational. It is, therefore, one's moral *duty* to undertake it. If you are planning to vote in an election by mail, for example, and if by mistake you receive two ballots instead of one, what should you do? A deontologist would argue that it is contradictory and, thus, morally wrong to take advantage of this situation. For, if everyone did so, the electoral process would no longer work. In other words, since your goal is to have the opportunity to elect the candidate of your choice, it would be counterproductive to act in such a way that, if your action was followed universally, it would no longer be possible to vote at all. Thus, it is your moral duty to destroy the second ballot.

This rule-based approach to moral theory has enormous political currency. Consider the ethical values of equality or basic human rights as expressed in the *Canadian Charter of Rights and Freedoms.* The rights not to be tortured or imprisoned arbitrarily, for example, are upheld in Western democratic countries on principle, or *categorically.* These rights are upheld regardless of what consequences they may have and regardless of the particular religious beliefs, gender, sexual orientation, cultural traditions, or personal characteristics that distinguish people from one another. For instance, every individual has a right to a fair trial, even when there are completely reliable witnesses to a crime; no matter how compelling the evidence, individuals are never held in jail automatically. These principles can be supported on rational grounds. Specifically, it is argued that it is irrational (contradictory) to treat one person in one way, while treating someone else in the same situation in a different way.

Deontological moral theories are *universalist* in orientation because they make no exceptions among rational beings. They are also *individualist* because they suggest that moral action is something that *each* person can and should decide on his or her own. In fact, Kant believed that one is not morally virtuous if one is influenced by others. If one relies on culture or tradition for moral norms, for example, one is not acting morally. Kant can be credited with laying the theoretical ground for the powerful political belief in the universal good of autonomy, or rational *self*-determination. For example, his theory explains the discomfort people may feel when asked to choose on someone else's behalf or, similarly, when one country usurps the sovereignty of another.

A common derivative of deontology is **social contract** theory. The ancient Greek philosopher Socrates was the first political thinker to articulate a version of social contract theory. He claimed that it was right that he be put to death after he was tried and found guilty of impiety because by living in Athens and benefiting from its laws, he had entered into an implicit contract with the state to abide by its rules. But social contract theory was not fully developed until the modern era. Both Hobbes and Locke emphasized that it is rational for individuals in societies to agree to certain restrictions of their freedom—for example, by following laws, paying taxes, or respecting the property of others. Hobbes argued that it is rational to agree to such restrictions because of the physical and psychological security that they provide, whereas Locke reasoned that such restrictions are both desirable and legitimate when they are the will of the majority.

Jürgen Habermas and John Rawls are two contemporary philosophers who follow in the tradition of deontology and social contract theory. Habermas modified Kant's moral theory to accommodate the fact that even though everyone may be capable of acting rationally, not everyone will share the same political beliefs or interests. In Habermas's view, when it comes to moral claims that affect other people, we cannot decide by ourselves. Habermas (1990) therefore argues that moral and political claims can be considered legitimate when everyone who is affected by them has engaged in a procedure of fair discussion aimed at a rational consensus.

Social contract theorist, John Rawls, devised a different method for establishing the basic principles of justice. Rawls suggests we imagine we have an opportunity to choose fundamental principles of justice from behind a "veil of ignorance" (Rawls, 1971). What he means by this is that in order to determine what is just, we should try to imagine what we would agree on if we did not know whether we were poor or rich, able-bodied or disabled, female or male, and so on. A veil of ignorance is the ignorance of one's identity and one's place in the social hierarchy. Rawls speculates that if we were to proceed this way, we would choose just principles—principles that do not harm or advantage anyone in particular—because we would not know if we would be personally advantaged by them or not. For example, he thinks it is most likely that a group of people who did not know anything at all about their individual social and economic standing would agree that equality should be enshrined in the constitution as a fundamental principle of justice. If principles of justice enshrined in our constitutions and charters are chosen rationally and fairly in a procedure like the one he describes, Rawls concludes, then not only will the principles themselves be legitimate, the laws based upon them will be legitimate, too.

Habermas and Rawls develop different procedures for determining the moral good, but both are rule-based moral theorists, and both focus on the procedure, rather than the outcome (as in utilitarianism and communitarianism), of moral reasoning. For both, the most important moral question is whether the principles that a person or a state acts upon are rationally defensible and universally acceptable.

Contemporary Ethical and Political Challenges

MORAL REFLECTION ABOUT HOW WE OUGHT TO LIVE COLLECTIVELY HAS always changed as a result of political and historical transformations in society, and it continues to change. Indeed, many theorists understand the present moment as one of crisis for the modernist belief in human reason and the promise of freedom and moral legitimacy that it once held. The crisis is due, in part, to rapid technological advancements made during the twentieth century and to the proliferation of social differences in multicultural societies. But it is also due to increasing pressure from marginalized groups who were previously silenced in public discourse—among them, women, disabled people, racial minorities, gays and lesbians, and citizens of countries that have gained independence from colonial empires and states.

This moment has been characterized variously as "late modernity" and as the "postmodern condition" (Lyotard, 1984). However, it is too early to tell whether it will give rise to a new, distinct tendency in the history of political thought. What *is* clear is that ethical questions of social organization, of state involvement in citizens' lives, of how to balance individual and collective needs, and of the legitimacy of political power are being asked forcefully and anew. The moral beliefs associated with **modernity** are being challenged from the explicitly political perspectives of Marxism, feminism, anti-racism, post-colonialism, and queer theory. These analyses have raised significant questions about whether the emphasis on universal reason trivializes politically significant differences among people and whether it thereby serves the interests of privileged social groups. Consequently, the rationalist foundations of ethical and political thought have begun to crumble. In their place, new ethical questions have recently begun to emerge. Primary among these is the question: are we sufficiently responsible to other persons, in all their differences and otherness? The politics of the twenty-first century undoubtedly will give rise to ethical and political perspectives yet to be articulated.

Summary

This chapter has examined the relationship between ethics and politics and has shown that the conversation between them flows both ways. We have outlined how answers to basic ethical questions at the root of political thought have changed over time and how they continue to do so. In particular, the modern moral emphasis on reason and individualism developed only after the medieval period. Modern moral theories differ from one another. But they all arise from the understanding that human reason is a fundamental resource for answering moral and political questions. In this chapter, we have seen that utilitarianism, virtue ethics, and rule-based moral theories share the belief that if moral claims are to be applied to the public realm, they must be grounded on reasons. However, recent scholars have questioned whether the critical concept of reason and the traditional notion of legitimacy are adequate to political issues that face us today. Certainly, each moral theory does illuminate certain political views. As discussed in this chapter, utilitarianism can apply to legal interpretation, communitarianism can support multicultural policies, and rule-based theories can justify universal human rights. But the modernist approach is also limited. It may not be suitable to address politically significant differences among people that now are so central to the formation of contemporary political identities and conflicts. We have shown in this chapter that just as ethical assumptions can inform political claims, so, too, do political issues inform and challenge moral beliefs. Ethics and politics are always deeply entwined.

Endnote

[1]For example, political philosopher Jürgen Habermas uses the term "ethics" to refer specifically to values that are held by individuals privately, based on their personal histories, culture, traditions, and religious beliefs. He uses the term "morality," in contrast, to refer to values that can be supported with rational arguments and that can be agreed to publicly by all people, regardless of what their culture, their religion, or their personal histories happen to be.

Discussion Questions

1. Do you think it is possible for people of different cultural backgrounds and religious traditions to agree on what is morally right or wrong, and if so, on what grounds might they do so?
2. Is it legitimate for the government to implement health-care and schooling policies for the public good, or are decisions about health and education best left to the discretion of private citizens, and why?
3. To what extent does reason play a part in your moral deliberations and decisions, and to what extent do you think it should play a greater part?

References

Beatty, David. 1991. "The End of Law: At Least as We Have Known It." Richard Devlin (ed.), *Canadian Perspectives on Legal Theory.* Toronto: Emond Montgomery Publications Ltd.

Birsch, Douglas. 1999. *Ethical Insights: A Brief Introduction.* Mountain View, CA: Mayfield Publishing.

Eldridge v. B.C., [1997] 3 S.C.R. 624.

Habermas, Jürgen. 1990. *Moral Consciousness and Communicative Action.* Translated by Christian Lenhardt and Shierry Weber Nicholsen. Cambridge, MA: The MIT Press.

Jackman, Martha. 1998. "'Giving Real Effect to Equality:' *Eldridge v. British Columbia (Attorney General)* and *Vriend v. Alberta.*" *Review of Constitutional Studies* IV, 2: 352–371.

Kant, Immanuel. 1993. *Grounding for the Metaphysics of Morals: On a Supposed Right to Lie because of Philanthropic Concerns.* Third Edition. Translated by James Ellington. Indianapolis: Hackett Publishing.

Lyotard, Jean-François. 1984. *The Postmodern Condition: A Report on Knowledge.* Translated by Geoff Bennington and Brian Massumi, forward by Fredric Jameson. Minneapolis: University of Minnesota Press.

Rawls, John. 1971. *A Theory of Justice.* Cambridge, MA: Harvard University Press.

R. v. Oakes, [1986] 1 S.C.R. 103.

Taylor, Charles. 1994. "The Politics of Recognition." Amy Gutmann (ed.), *Multiculturalism: Examining the Politics of Recognition.* Princeton, NJ: Princeton University Press.

Further Readings

Jacobs, Leslie A. 1997. *An Introduction to Modern Political Philosophy: The Democratic Vision of Politics.* Upper Saddle River, NJ: Prentice-Hall.

Liszka, James Jakób. 1999. *Moral Competence: An Integrated Approach to the Study of Ethics.* Upper Saddle River, NJ: Prentice-Hall.

Lukes. Steven. 1991. *Moral Conflict and Politics.* Oxford: Oxford University Press.

Weblinks

Dalhousie University's Applied Ethics Site
www.ethicsweb.ca/resources

Ethical Updates
http://ethics.acusd.edu/index.html

Philosophy in Cyberspace
www-personal.monash.edu.au/~dey/phil/ethics.htm

CHAPTER 4

DEMOCRACY

Objectives

This chapter examines one of the most critical concepts of the current era—democracy. **Democracy** is a critical concept because it highlights the question of the "public." The distinction between what is public and what is private has been extremely important to the study of politics. This chapter begins by showing how the concept of democracy involves the question of the public. The chapter then provides a brief history of democratic thought, from the philosophers of the *polis* of Ancient Greece to today's theorists of radical democracy. We find that dramatic shifts in thinking about democracy often occur in periods of social change, when societies are forced to reflect on themselves and on their assumptions about the fundamentals of social organization and governance. The current era of globalization is just such a period of reflection. Key assumptions about governing, such as the nature of the capitalist market and its relationship with the state, are now being revisited and reformulated. More specifically, contemporary thinkers are suggesting that many dimensions of human experience, such as sexuality, the family, and "private" property, are, in fact, political in nature and are therefore public concerns. Some contemporary theorists of democracy question the distinction between "public" and "private" set down by the tradition of liberal democratic theory. In this sense, contemporary democracy is said to be "in crisis." As a way of trying to understand this current crisis, the chapter concludes by introducing ongoing debates in contemporary democratic thought.

CATHERINE KELLOGG

Introduction

The word *democracy* comes from the Greek *demos* (people) and *kratos* (rule). In the classical literature we refer to, democracy means the "rule of the many." It is generally contrasted with the "rule of the few" (aristocracy) or the "rule of one" (monarchy). More recently, however, *democracy* is used to refer to its literal translation as "the rule of the people." Simply put, democracy is any form of government in which the rules of society are decided by the people who will be bound by them. This is how the concept of democracy implicates the public: it suggests that public affairs—the rules of society—should be decided by the public itself.

What is distinctive about theories of democracy is their common insistence that the authority of the state begins and ends with the public. At the root of the practice of democracy lies a faith in the capacity of people to decide key issues of governance for themselves. While this belief is the central tenet of democratic theory, it is not limited to classical democratic theorists, such as Jean-Jacques Rousseau or John Stuart Mill. It is also found in the editorial pages of our newspapers. Indeed, the view that governments should operate only through the "will" of the people is so widespread that the only regimes in the modern world considered legitimate are those based on popular consent. Despite the widespread appeal of democracy, anyone who looks closely at this concept is bound to notice that it means many different things to different people. Indeed, Robert Dahl explains that a "term that means anything means nothing. And so it has become with 'democracy' which nowadays is not so much a term of restricted and specific meaning, as a vague endorsement of a popular idea" (Dahl, 1989, 2). Not only does the word itself imply the "populus" or the public, but also democracy as an ideal receives seemingly unanimous support the world over. For instance, the vast majority of national constitutions in the world today claim to be democratic. It is precisely the popularity of this concept that leads our political leaders to use the word *democracy* when they are stuck for something to say. Like the British politician of the late nineteenth century who, when asked a difficult question, always mentioned the name of the popular Liberal party leader Gladstone because the five minutes of cheering that ensued gave him time to formulate an answer, the word *democracy* has been used to navigate politicians out of many tight spots. The word is often used simply as a synonym for *good*. In short, democracy is hailed as the master principle of our age.

Theory and Crisis

DEMOCRATIC THEORY IS THE DOMINANT FRAME OR THEORY THROUGH which we organize and make meaningful the world of politics. In fact, constructing theories is nothing more than the process through which we organize and make our lives meaningful. Even when we are performing a mundane task, we are doing so within a set of assumptions that have rendered that activity meaningful in some way. In this sense, all social life is founded on theory—a compilation of ideas that tell a coherent story about a given human practice. Theory is an activity that goes on all the time, even when we are unaware of it. But at certain moments the theories making our lives meaningful no longer seem to fit our experience or make sense of the world. These are times of *crisis*.

Theory becomes visible when we are forced to become aware of a human practice that has, in the past, seemed most ordinary and most untheoretical. Theory becomes visible when the ideas ordering ordinary human practices stop making sense.

Like every other kind of human activity, politics has its own set of theories. Political theories are interpretations—coherent stories that order and make sense of the world—about politics. In fact, the history of political thought can be understood as the history of waves of *crisis* that have forced human beings to reflect upon practices of human governance—democratic and otherwise. One of the most interesting things about the current state of democratic theory is that it is now at a point of crisis. This crisis in democratic theory stems from a variety of factors including a crisis in contemporary practices of democracy. Many issues that until now were not understood to belong to the tradition of democratic thought have come into view. For instance, democracy has generally been taken to mean something as simple as the representation of citizens in legislatures where we are recognized as "formally" equal. But certain thinkers have begun to question whether formal equality can mean anything very profound when we are so demonstrably unequal to each other with respect to our access to other kinds of power. The power at work in the areas of our lives previously considered "private," for instance, our workplaces, our families, or the "private sector"—the capitalist market—is perhaps as important politically as are the formal processes of political decision making. Can we consider truly democratic a set of political and social arrangements that render us formally equal to each other when the way that we actually live our lives is increasingly unequal? What are the real requirements of democratic citizenship? In order to begin making sense of these questions, we will look at three historical "models" of democratic thought.

A History of Democratic Theory

DEMOCRACY MEANS, AND HAS MEANT, A GREAT NUMBER OF DIFFERENT things to different people. However, Canadian political theorist C.B. MacPherson tells us that "in looking at models of democracy . . . we should keep a sharp lookout for two things: [the theory's] assumptions about the whole society in which the democratic political system is to operate, and its assumptions about the essential nature of the people who are to make the system work (which for a democratic system means the people in general, not just a ruling or leading class)" (MacPherson, 1977, 5). The following section offers a brief history of democratic theories. It pays particular attention to the assumptions those theories make about the essential nature of both society and the people who inhabit it.

Ancient Greek Democracy

The development of democracy in Athens during its "golden age"—which lasted for about 50 years in the fifth century BCE—has been the source of inspiration for much modern democratic political thought. For instance, the modern ideals of equality before the law, liberty, and respect are often traced to the ancient Greek *polis*. This small, self-contained institutional form nurtured intense communal life. The *polis* formed the ethical model for subsequent thinkers as diverse as Thomas Hobbes, John Locke, Alexis de Tocqueville, Jean-Jacques Rousseau, and G.W.F. Hegel.

The Greek word *polis* is the root for a range of English words, including *politics, politician, political,* and *police*. While there is no exact English equivalent, *polis* is commonly translated as both *state* and *city* because it possesses the attributes of both. Central to the life of the Athenian *polis* was smallness of scale. Although scholars do not agree on precise figures, it is estimated that some 300 000 people lived in Athens at its height. Only 40 000 however, were citizens. The rest of the population—women, children, foreign residents, and slaves—were excluded from the ranks of the citizens and from formal participation in political life. The "public" realm, then, was actually made up of a very small percentage of the inhabitants of the Greek city state. The small size of the *polis* allowed citizens to partake of a distinctive communal way of life. Spheres of life we now consider non-political—religion, art, sport, and commerce—were all considered within the purview of politics. They were, therefore, subject to democratic deliberation. The small size of the *polis* also provided its citizens with a sense of active involvement in public affairs that has not been widely duplicated at any other time. Greek direct democracy was probably the most *participatory* form of politics that Western civilization has ever seen. Following approximately 50 years of flourishing, ancient Athens and its allies entered into a conflict with oligarchies that sided with Sparta. This conflict—known as the Peloponnesian Wars—ended with the complete defeat and occupation of democratic Athens. Precisely because the Greek city-state or *polis* was in crisis, Plato and Aristotle were impelled to think about politics in a new way and to write their important works. For instance, the trial and execution of Socrates—the political philosopher so admired by Plato—inspired Plato to question the validity of rule by those who were ignorant of the most pressing questions of the purpose of life. Perhaps, he suggested, Greek citizens were not truly able to rule themselves but required the leadership of those specifically trained in the art of state and soul-craft. Despite the democratic nature of the ancient Greek state, then, the political thinkers we most associate with ancient Greece—Plato, Aristotle, and Thucydides—were uniformly hostile to the direct democracy represented by the Greek *polis*.

Notwithstanding this hostility to democracy, both Plato and Aristotle were profoundly influenced by the participatory nature of the Greek city state. Significantly, Aristotle argued, "Man is a political animal." By this he meant that human beings could attain their full potential only by living in political association with each other. It is only through active involvement in the life of one's political community that citizens can know what is truly important. Thus, we can see that for the ancient Greeks, a good citizen was someone actively involved in the day-to-day running of their government.

The Middle Ages and Italian Republicanism

There is a strange silence in the history of democratic thought that begins shortly after the demise of Athenian democracy and ends with the early Renaissance. This period overlaps significantly with what we call the medieval period, or the Middle Ages, which are meant to mark the "middle" period between the collapse of the Roman Empire in the fifth century and the beginning of the Renaissance in the fourteenth. This silence in the history of political thought is a complex matter to explain, but in its simplest terms, the ascendancy of the Christian faith in the Western world, as well as the rise of feudal forms of social organization, meant that the "good" citizen of the Ancient Greek *polis,* was replaced by the "true believer." The Greek world view suggested that political good could be found in active participation in public affairs. This view was replaced by one that insisted that the "highest good" was to be found only in the next world. The idea that humans could organize their common futures democratically was replaced by the idea that everyone's fate was predetermined by God.

By the middle part of the medieval period, Europe was also dominated by **feudalism**. This form of social and economic organization was characterized by a strict hierarchy between the property-owning aristocracy and the landless peasants. This way of life emphasized the deeply held belief that people were fundamentally unequal; those who held power did so because they were essentially "better" than those whom they ruled. Feudalism was set against the backdrop of the Holy Roman Empire—a complex web of kings and rulers who were understood to rule by "divine right." The authority of these rulers was said to come directly from God. In short, throughout the Middle Ages, European politics was heavily influenced by three great supranational institutions: the Church, the Holy Roman Empire, and feudalism.

By the beginning of the sixteenth century, a number of political communities had established some form of popular control, especially in northern Italy. What eventually became the new "city states" or city republics were run by elected councillors. Councillors were ultimately accountable to male householders with taxable property. This notion of accountability represented an important challenge to the prevailing understanding that rule was God given. An outcome of this new social order was a return to the ideas of **civic republicanism** first articulated by Aristotle: the idea of active involvement in the state as a "good." For we recall that for Aristotle, human beings are essentially political and they only flourish when they are involved in making the important decisions of public life. Central to this idea is the notion of a political community with a shared history and a shared destiny. Thus, the Renaissance (literally, *rebirth*) was so named because it recalled many of the ideas of ancient Greek democracy.

Capitalism and the Liberal Revolution

The slow movement out of the Middle Ages typified by these revived ideas led from the Renaissance to the Enlightenment. If the Reformation was a revolution against the traditional church and the Renaissance was the revalorization of some of the ideas from Greek democracy, the Enlightenment was a revolution against traditional philosophy and science. It was a "movement" that sought to understand the world and humanity on a new basis. This period was accompanied by the growing belief that all people were equal because, no matter what their social position, each possessed the capacity for reason. The presumption of equality was revolutionary because it led people to challenge the validity of political institutions that distributed power and wealth unequally among citizens. Legitimate political power was seen to emanate from the people themselves; the people were seen to be the source of ultimate political and legal authority.

The Reformation and the Enlightenment were accompanied (and in some senses precipitated) by the end of feudal forms of life and by the rise of *capitalism* and market economies. While feudal society did have market activity—there were individual transactions of labour goods and services—it was not a market economy. In feudalism, most economic activity was for the purposes of immediate consumption, rather than for exchange. What was distinctive about capitalism was the newly emerging notion of "private property" and the accompanying right of an individual (or corporate entity) to exclude others from the use or benefit of it. Significantly, human labour itself also became a commodity that could be bought and traded on the market. The transformation from feudal forms of life (characterized by the predominance of the Church, absolutist sovereigns, and a landless peasantry) to a market of "free" producers and buyers was a complex one which had profound social, political, and cultural consequences. In short, the Reformation, the Enlightenment, and the emergence of capitalism were not separate events but, rather, events that mutually reinforced each other.

These mutually reinforcing events are together known as the *liberal revolution*, a crisis in governing which marks the passing from feudal society to what we now recognize as capitalist modernity. An organic, hierarchical, traditional society was rapidly being replaced by an individualistic, fluid, and pluralist society in which reason replaced custom as a standard by which to judge policy and institutions. Perhaps the most graphic representations of this liberal revolution were the American Revolution of 1776 and the French Revolution of 1789. Both revolutions were dramatic uprisings against traditional, hierarchical forms of rule, and both were infused with the energy and enthusiasm of the liberal slogan: *liberty, equality, and solidarity.*

Early Liberal Democratic Theory

The dramatic changes in political rule in Europe and North America brought with them the most important variant of democratic thought: *liberal democratic theory.*

This view was first articulated by such theorists as Thomas Hobbes, John Locke, and John Stuart Mill. The most important aspect of liberal democratic theory, and what distinguishes it from the models of democratic thought reviewed so far, was the belief in the importance of political, moral, and economic *liberty.* This variant of democratic theory clearly distinguished the public—understood as the institutions of the state—from the private. This was significantly different from the civic republicanism and the Greek *ethos* of the *polis* that preceded it. For both the previous models, the *public* included some dimensions of human life that were consigned to the private sphere in the modern model.

The notion of freedom was very important to these liberal thinkers, but it was a very specific kind of freedom. As C.B. MacPherson explains, liberal democrats believed passionately in the freedom to pursue private property. Moreover, liberal democrats, no less than the democratic theorists who preceded them, had a distinct view of what constitutes human nature and a distinct view of the whole society in which the democratic political system operates.

According to liberal democrats, individuals are rational maximizers of self-interest. That is to say, for most liberal democrats, individuals will rationally choose what is in their own best interests, even when those interests are not necessarily those that grant them the most immediate satisfaction. For example, individuals will choose to live under a government that restricts some of their destructive activities because it will also restrict the destructive activities of others. Thus, they will rationally choose to outlaw theft and to be policed because they will weigh their own desires to rob against the possibility of being robbed by others.

One of the most passionate defenders of this perspective was Thomas Hobbes. While he was no advocate of democracy in principle, his justification of government was that state authority, rather than monarchs or God, was created by individuals acting out of self-interest. People created the authority of the state to protect themselves from each other. Hobbes believed that individuals ought willingly to surrender their rights of self-government to a powerful single authority. Democracy, in this view, was the mechanism by which citizens could check the powers of the state against arbitrarily punishing its citizens.

John Locke revised Hobbes's argument with the view that "government" should be conceived as an instrument for the defence of "life, liberty and estate" (Locke, 1965). One important difference between Hobbes and Locke is that whereas Hobbes emphasized democracy as a mechanism for protecting *individuals* from the state, Locke understood democracy as a mechanism for protecting the *market* from the state. And here is the second important assumption shared by classical liberal democrats: the society in which the democratic political system operates is understood to be a capitalist one. This is why, in Locke's view, the state should leave the "private" economic transactions of individuals entirely unregulated.

In the nineteenth century, John Stuart Mill developed his important objection to the purely formal dimensions of the position laid down by earlier liberal democrats. Mill went far beyond previous liberal democrats with respect to *moral* freedom. Mill formulated his theory with a view to protecting iconoclasts or "free thinkers" from the imposition of conventional or traditional morality. In this sense, Mill was passionately dedicated to the protection of minorities within a majoritarian system.

Classical liberal democrats, then, constructed a relatively coherent theory of democracy. In it, the major institutions of modern governance—in particular, the various institutions of the state—were understood to be public and, therefore, subject to collective control. The modern distinction between the public realm of the state and the private, unregulated, and apolitical realms of the family and the economy was vital to this theoretical framework.

Contemporary Challenges

THE CONTEMPORARY PERIOD IS DOMINATED BY THE SO-CALLED "TRIUMPH" of democracy worldwide. One does not have to look very far to discover, however, that we are not living in the best of all possible worlds. As Amnesty International points out, grotesque violations of human rights, such as torture, are used on citizens in almost half the countries in the world, many of which describe themselves as democratic.

The conversation about what constitutes democracy is, thus, far from over. While the majority of contemporary democratic theorists continue to be preoccupied with the major questions of liberalism, they have shifted their focus from freedom to equality. As well, there are some radical democratic critiques of the public–private distinction laid down by liberalism that require important scrutiny. In the current era of globalization (and the subsequent waves of democratic protest against globalization), the fundamentals of democratic thought are being challenged. In the following section, we look at the debates among contemporary liberal democrats, who are divided over the question of what vision of "the good" should drive contemporary liberal democracies. One variant of contemporary liberal democracy suggests that democracy is a "good" because it provides a mechanism by which each individual is equally represented in processes of governing. These thinkers are opposed by those who suggest that this purely formal mechanism is inadequate because it covers over and, in fact, entrenches important *differences* between people. Finally, Marxist and radical democratic critiques of liberal democracy propose that without economic and social equality, political equality is next to meaningless.

Contemporary Liberal Democratic Theory

The transition from premodern absolutist states and traditional societies to modern liberal democratic representative democracies has been largely achieved in the Western world. Not surprisingly, therefore, liberal democrats are currently less concerned with the freedom of individuals from the arbitrary powers of the state than they are with the nature of the equality that democracies can deliver to their citizens. The most important debate among contemporary liberal democrats—known as the *liberal–communitarian debate*— takes the liberal notion of equality as its central focus.

John Rawls, for example, suggests that the only "good" of democracies lies in their ability to formally recognize the equality of each citizen. More precisely, Rawls argues that the only idea of "the good" that we can agree upon is a thinly conceived notion of political *tolerance.* Any other concept would be in some way threatening to the multicultural, diverse political culture in which we live. In other words, we can never agree that we *should* worship one particular kind of God, or even that we should worship at all; that we *should* hold certain kinds of values when raising our children, or that we *should* mate in these and not other ways. The only *should* we can agree upon is to be tolerant of a variety of ways in which to worship, instill values, make families and structures of kinship, and so on.

Noted communitarians, such as Charles Taylor and Alisdair MacIntyre, take issue with Rawls's vision of the "good." They say that this conception of democracy has no "end." It is not directed toward making us better patriots or even better people. The idea of tolerance, they argue, is nothing more than a *procedure* that suggests that we deal fairly and equally with each other. Recalling the civic republicanism first articulated by Aristotle, Taylor and MacIntyre maintain that political life involves much more than representation in democratic institutions; liberal democracies are forms of civic association in which we discover who we really are. In fact, they say that we do not discover our "identities" (as Canadians, as Muslims, or as lesbians) in isolation. We discover them in dialogue with each other—in the give and take of a "public" conversation. Communitarians take their point of departure from people's real sense of alienation from the formal public institutions that represent them. For example, Quebec nationalism or Western Canadian alienation suggests that not everyone feels recognized by Canadian democratic institutions.

Rawls and other liberals respond that this is precisely the price that citizens must pay for living in a society that treats us all as equals, regardless of our particular ethnic, racial, religious, sexual, or other identities. It is the very neutrality of the public sphere that protects our freedom as citizens. In this "liberal" view, our "freedom" and "equality" refer only to our common characteristics. These include our universal needs for such things as income, health care, education, religious freedom, and freedom of speech. Therefore, our public institutions need not strive to recognize our particular cultural identities in treating us as free and equal citizens.

Rawls proposes that the principle of equality is complete in itself and that the differences between us are, in the final analysis, politically irrelevant. In contrast, Charles Taylor understands, in his unique situation as an Anglophone living in Quebec, that the demand for public recognition (by such institutions as the state or schools) by a people is more than simply a psychological quirk. It is a constitutive feature of liberal democracies. Taylor and other communitarians recall the civic republican tradition first articulated by Aristotle when they suggest that something more than empty "equality" ought to govern the public sphere and that we might be better served to return to traditional religious or cultural values.

However, both these contemporary liberal democratic positions share the division between public and private laid down by the earlier liberal democrats. While communitarians like Taylor want to infuse public institutions, such as the judiciary or parliament, with a sensitivity to cultural differences between us, the question of the market, the family, or the very real political and economic differences between people are conceived only as "cultural." The question of economic equality—rather than political equality—does not appear as a variable in this dispute.

Marxist and Radical Democratic Critiques

The focus on economic equality is another way of talking about the compatibility of liberal democracy with capitalism. This compatibility has been questioned with most insistence by Marxist and radical democratic critics. Marx argued that historically and logically, capitalism is tied to the private ownership of the means of production—the right of individuals or corporate entities to the exclusive use of land, money, and labour power. This private ownership encourages wealth to accumulate predominantly in one class. It is, thus, surely not accidental, Marx argued, that the "rights of private property" are at the foundation of the whole constitutional and juridical superstructure we have come to know as *liberal democracy*. Marx felt that capitalism could tolerate "democracy" because in the final analysis, real power is not to be found in democratic institutions but instead rests with those who control the means of production.

Specifically, capitalists control the working class, not by means of exclusive political rights but by means of exclusive property. This means that even in its best and most democratic forms, capitalism can, and must, confine equality to a separate "political" sphere that does not, and must not, intrude into the economic sphere or subvert economic *in*equality. People in capitalist societies spend most of their waking hours in activities and relationships where there is no democratic accountability at all. This is true not only in the workplace, where they are likely to be under the direct control of others but also in all spheres of life that are subject to "market" imperatives. Liberal democracies, such as Canada, may indeed have a political sphere governed by "democracy," but at the same time, large areas of human life lie entirely outside the reach of democratic processes.

This critique of classical and modern liberal democratic theory has been most recently re-elaborated by a new form of democratic theory known as *radical democracy*. Like Marxists, radical democrats argue that traditional democracy has failed to deliver on its promise of real equality and civic participation. And like Marxists, radical democrats claim that a thorough-going understanding of democracy will entail extending the principles of democracy—freedom, equality, and solidarity—into every area of daily life: work, education, leisure, and home.

But radical democrats differ from traditional Marxists by insisting that class is not the only source of inequality in contemporary society. They argue that we are unequal in ways that go beyond the economic. For instance, the great disparity in real economic and political power between men and women, between white and non-white people, and between those who live in the "North" and those who live in the "South" reflects the inability of our "democratic" institutions to deliver any kind of substantive equality. Understanding democracy as nothing more than free-market capitalism accompanied by multi-party elections does a real disservice to the radical vision of emancipation offered by early liberal democratic theory. Radical democrats insist that if the principles of liberal democracy are to be taken seriously, the limited scope of freedom and equality offered by contemporary liberal democracies must be challenged.

This new strain of political critique also responds to the challenge of *globalization.* While the nation-state is still a key unit in the political order of the twenty-first century, it also is under attack. This attack comes both from within by those who look to subnational forms of authority as the focus of their activity and from without by supranational forces, such as transnational corporations, continental or hemispheric trade agreements, and so on.

In the present era the nation-state is less and less endowed with the power to curb the stark inequalities in social, political, and economic power, both nationally and internationally. In this sense, the current era is witnessing a "contraction" in the realm of what we can meaningfully talk about as "public." Increasingly, the values of the private sphere—the capitalist market on the one hand, and the family on the other—dominate questions of public policy. Nations are required to be increasingly efficient and competitive (the dominant values of the market), and public discourses of morality (family values) dominate the public realm, at the same time, as the accountability of the state to its citizens is increasingly restricted. This new era of so-called "global competitiveness" or globalization represents the crisis forcing democratic theorists to rethink the distinction between public and private at the heart of liberal conceptions of democracy. If the nation-state becomes less and less able to act as an arbiter of social life, this rethinking may involve the creation of a global democracy beyond the level of the nation-state.

Summary

This chapter has surveyed the way that democratic practices and theories have consistently raised the question of the relationship between what is "public" and what is "private." Beginning with a brief history of democratic thought, we found that dramatic shifts in thinking about democracy often occurred during periods of fundamental social change. We then investigated the direct and participatory nature of Greek democracy, the revitalization of that tradition in civic republicanism, and the rearticulation of democratic ideals of freedom and equality in early and contemporary liberal democratic thought. The fundamental premise of liberal democratic theory is the importance of individual, political, moral, and economic *freedom*. This democratic theory draws lines between the public and the private in terms that we might currently recognize. Specifically, the family and the market are carved off from what was understood as "public" and placed in the category "private." They are, thus, outside the purview of those issues that traditionally concerned democratic politics.

More recently, liberal, Marxist, and radical democratic theorists, especially in Western democracies, have shifted the emphasis from freedom to equality in questioning how all citizens of a democratic society can participate equally. They have asked whether the formal political equality of the contemporary liberal democratic state is truly adequate to satisfy the important differences between us. Does democracy require *economic* or simply *political* equality? Does democracy imply the end of social discrimination? In the shift in emphasis from freedom to equality, many contemporary democratic theorists are challenging the validity of the claim that the market or the family are private and, therefore, outside the bounds of democratic deliberation. Despite the apparent success of democracy as the dominant ideal and practice of governing worldwide, then, some thinkers in liberal democracies have grown increasingly critical of the equality democratic states are able to deliver to their citizens.

Discussion Questions

1. Do you agree with the modern liberal perspective that it is only the neutrality of the public sphere that protects our freedom as citizens?
2. Do you think that democracy should imply economic as well as political equality in the way that Marxist and radical democrats suggest?
3. According to this chapter, theory is something that becomes evident when the human practices it orders and makes meaningful come into crisis. Can you think of a set of human practices less complex than the democratic processes of governing to which this idea might apply?
4. According to this chapter, democracy is the dominant value of our age. What values are embedded within this term?

References

Aristotle. 1948. *Politics.* Translated by Ernest Barker. Oxford: Oxford University Press.

Bernal, Martin. 1987. *Black Athena: The Afroasiatic Roots of Classical Civilization.* New Brunswick: Rutgers University Press.

Connolly, William. 1991. *Identity/Difference: Democratic Negotiation of Political Paradox.* Ithaca: Cornell University Press.

Dahl, Robert. 1989. *Democracy and Its Critic.* New Haven: Yale University Press.

Dworkin, Ronald. 1977. *Taking Rights Seriously.* Cambridge, Mass: Harvard University Press.

Held, David. 1987. *Models of Democracy.* Cambridge: Polity Press.

Hobbes, Thomas. 1977. *Leviathan.* Hammondsworth: Penguin.

Kymlicha, Will. 1995. *Multicultural Citizenship.* Oxford: Oxford University Press.

Locke, John. 1965. *Second Treatise on Government.* New York: Mentor Press.

MacPherson, C.B. 1965. *The Real World of Democracy.* Toronto: CBC Publications.

———. 1977. *The Life and Times of Liberal Democracy.* Oxford: Oxford University Press.

Marx, Karl and Friedrich Engels. 1968. "The Communist Manifesto" in *Selected Works.* London: Lawrence and Wishart.

McIntryre, Alisdaire. 1981. *After Virtue.* Notre Dame: University of Notre Dame Press.

Mouffe, Chantal. 1994. *The Return to the Political.* London: Verso.

Philips, Anne. 1991. *Engendering Democracy.* Cambridge: Polity Press.

Rawls, John. 1971. *A Theory of Justice.* Cambridge: Harvard University Press.

Rousseau, Jean-Jacques. 1964. *A Discourse on the Origins of Inequality* New York: St. Martin's Press.

Sandel, Michael. 1984. *Liberalism and Its Critics.* Oxford: Clarendon Press.

Taylor, Charles. 1992. *Multiculturalism and the Politics of Recognition.* Princeton: Princeton University Press.

Trend, David, ed. 1996. *Radical Democracy: Identity, Citizenship and the State.* London: Routledge.

Further Readings

Aristotle. 1948. *Politics.* Translated by Ernest Barker. Oxford: Oxford University Press.

Held, David. 1987. *Models of Democracy.* Cambridge: Polity Press.

———. 1995. *Democracy and the Global Order.* Oxford: Polity Press.

MacPherson, C.B. 1973. *Democratic Theory: Essays in Retrieval.* Oxford: Oxford University Press.

Tocqueville, Alexis de. 1946. *Democracy in America.* New York: Knopf.

Wood, Ellen Meiksins. 1995. *Democracy against Capitalism.* Cambridge: Cambridge University Press.

Weblinks

Amnesty International
www.amnesty.org/ailib/intcam/femgen/fgm1.htm

Canadians for Direct Democracy
www.npsnet.com/cdd

Canadian Centre for Policy Alternatives
www.policyalternatives.ca

Democracy Watch
www.dwatch.ca

CHAPTER 5

LIBERALISM

Objectives

This chapter explores liberalism today, with attention to its basic commitments and to some shifts in the ways these commitments have come to be understood. As a critical concept, liberalism rests on two central values—freedom and equality of individuals—which it protects and supports in the form of rights. There has, however, been a shift toward a broader and more social understanding of these commitments. We begin by considering the central values—freedom and equality—with attention to the shifts in their meanings, and then we show what is involved in the idea of protecting them as rights.

DON
CARMICHAEL

Introduction

Liberalism is centrally committed to the **freedom** and **equality** of individuals. But there has been a considerable shift in the way this commitment is understood. In traditional liberalism, freedom and equality were valued in rather narrow and legal terms. Freedom was understood primarily as liberty, or the absence of legal interferences, while equality was seen mainly as equality before the law. These commitments are important in liberalism today, but they have come to be understood in broader and more social terms as the equal freedom of individuals to live on terms of their own choosing.

In these commitments, liberalism focuses on the individual. That is, liberalism understands the political community as an association of separate individuals, each with different and sometimes conflicting interests. No one individual is more important than any other; thus, all individuals (and their interests) must be respected equally. This is strongly tied to an insistence on the freedom of individuals to live as they choose. But this freedom is problematic. It is a wonderful thing in the abstract, but what happens when some individuals want to live in ways that others dislike? And what happens when these others are powerful enough to compel conformity? Consider the case of gay men and lesbian women living in a homophobic community. Their attempts to live freely will almost certainly be obstructed by others. For example, they may find it difficult to secure employment, housing, respect from their neighbours, or a welcoming church. On this account, their freedom and equality require some form of special protection.

Politically, therefore, liberalism is committed to political measures that protect and support the freedom and equality of individuals. For the most part, these measures protect activities or areas of life by establishing protective walls around them, typically in the form of **rights**. Within these walls, each individual is free to do as she or he chooses. These "walls" can be of different kinds. In some cases, whole aspects of society are walled off from regulation by the state. Traditional liberals typically regarded the economy in these terms, and religious practice is still seen this way today. Sometimes these "walls" are described as private versus public areas of life, where "private" indicates areas where individuals should be free from legal controls as opposed to the "public" areas that are legitimately subject to regulation. Perhaps the most familiar example of this approach today is the *Canadian Charter of Rights and Freedoms.* The Charter stipulates that a law may be declared invalid if it violates certain basic rights and freedoms, even if the law is enacted democratically and supported by the majority.

But a word of caution is important here. We noted at the start of this chapter that there has been a shift in the understanding of freedom and equality in liberalism, moving from a narrow and somewhat legal conception to a broader and more social conception of the equal freedom of individuals to live on terms of their own choosing. With this shift in the understanding of the values of freedom and equality, there has been a corresponding shift in the measures needed to protect and support them. In addition to protecting individuals from interference, liberalism now aims to support individuals in important areas of life in more positive ways by providing them with the resources they need to live as they choose. This shift in liberalism is tentative and ongoing, and as such, it occasions controversy and uncertainty. In this chapter, accordingly, we will explore liberalism today with attention to these changing understandings of its central commitments. Three critical concepts will be examined: *freedom* and *equality*, as the two value commitments of liberalism, and the idea of protecting these values as *rights*.

Liberty/Freedom

ONE OF THE GREATEST WORKS IN THE LIBERAL TRADITION IS JOHN STUART MILL'S appeal for individual liberty in *On Liberty*. Originally published in 1859, it is still compelling reading today. In this work, Mill argued that the best society is one that allows maximum individual liberty because, in the long run, this would facilitate the fullest possible development of individuals. But in which aspects of life should people be free? Mill answered this question by what has come to be known as **the harm principle**. If a person's conduct directly harms others, society has the right to control it. But where a person's conduct does not directly harm others, society has no right to control it. In such cases, individuals should be completely free. This means that individuals should be free even where their conduct is considered morally wrong or offensive. For example, sexual practices among consenting adults cannot effectively be prohibited. It also means that individuals should be free to act in ways that may harm themselves. If no one else is directly harmed, society has no right to interfere. Thus, individuals cannot legitimately be forced to use safety equipment, such as safety belts in cars and motorcycle helmets.

Freedom of thought was Mill's greatest concern. He noted that ideas can be expressed in ways that are harmful. For example, shouting "fire!" as a prank in a crowded theatre could cause a stampede and lead to death. Where ideas are expressed in a way that causes harm, the particular manner of expression may be restricted. But Mill believed that ideas themselves never cause harm, at least in the long run, and so he argued that there should be absolute freedom of thought and belief. Mill thought that censorship can never be justified because it always hinders truth. Even if an opinion seems completely mistaken, Mill argued, it might still turn out to be true or to contain a part of the truth. This partial truth would be lost if it were censored. Further, if we protect the truth of one opinion by censoring its rivals, the protected opinion will come to be held as a dogma and people will then lose the ability to determine for themselves what is true and what is not.

Liberty and Freedom Today

Mill understood **liberty** primarily in negative terms, as the absence of interference in an individual's life. This liberty was somewhat legal and institutional, and it suggested a minimal role for the state. The state has an important role in protecting individuals from interference by others, but the state must minimize its own interference in doing so. Today, **freedom** is understood in more positive terms, as the ability of people to live on their own terms. This freedom is broader and more social than the legal-institutional "liberty" of traditional liberalism. Contemporary notions of freedom involve more than the issue of non-interference. Freedom can be limited, and people can be "unfree" in a broader range of ways—for example, through ignorance, dependence, or incapacity or through not having access to the resources they need to fulfill the lives they have chosen. This opens the door to a wider and more positive role for the state in protecting freedom. It is not just a question of protecting people from interference, but of more actively making available to them the resources and supports they need to lead the lives they have chosen.

This has led to a different understanding of the relationship between freedom and equality. For many traditional liberals, these values were opposed. Efforts by the state to reduce inequality (or to make valued goods, such as education or health care, available on a more equal basis) invariably involve measures of regulation, which interfere, to some degree, with people's choices. Where liberty is understood as the absence of interference, these equalizing measures will be seen as restrictions of liberty. However this opposition between liberty and equality disappears when liberty is understood more broadly as freedom. Today, when the community provides public education or health care through the state, these provisions may be justified on grounds either of equality or of freedom. The equality justification, as we shall see in the next section, is to make such goods available more equally, especially to persons who otherwise would lack them. The freedom justification is that such goods are essential for people to be able to live on their own terms. These justifications are different, but compatible.

The upshot is that discussions of freedom today can be quite complex. Freedom is no longer just a matter of minimizing interferences in people's lives but of supporting their ability to live on their own terms. Making this support available frequently involves some restriction of choice, but this restriction may be justified where the restriction is trivial compared with the larger freedom it facilitates. Even safety legislation can be justified this way. The requirement to use a safety belt in a car or a helmet on a motorcycle is an interference in people's lives, but the interference may be considered negligible in relation to the freedoms it protects.

In liberalism today, then, discussions of freedom are sometimes quite complex and divisive. But these discussions generally operate within the following parameters. First, freedom of thought and belief is treated as an absolute value. While it is recognized that ideas can sometimes be expressed in ways that harm others and that such manners of expression may, therefore, be regulated, liberals insist that ideas, and access to ideas, should never be restricted. Second, there is firm support in liberalism for the freedom of people to live as they choose, whatever this might be, so long as their choices do not harm others. Third, it is recognized that the community (through the state) has an important role in supporting this freedom and that, as a result, it is sometimes necessary to restrict some freedoms in order to promote others that are more important.

Equality

As with liberty/freedom, equality has been understood in different ways. Three different kinds of equality may be distinguished. The first, equality of citizenship, means that the rights of basic citizenship must be equal among all citizens. This requires that all citizens be treated equally by the law and state agencies and that all citizens have equal opportunities to participate in the political affairs of the community.

This kind of equality is limited in an important way. It holds that people must be equal in their basic rights, but this does not mean that people must be equal in their ability to exercise these rights. For example, we all have an equal right to be represented by a lawyer when charged under the law. But there is no right to equality in paying the legal costs. We each pay what we can afford, and the result is that those who are better off may have a better chance of being acquitted.

Is this a problem? Opinions differ here. For some persons in the liberal tradition, equality requires only that we all have the same citizenship rights. Others, however, take the view that equality also requires equality in the ability to exercise these rights. This is sometimes called equality in the "worth" of rights. The concern for equality in this respect does not usually involve trying to make people equal but, instead, trying to remove any inequalities that might prevent them from exercising their rights adequately. In our legal example, this would take the form of legal aid—of ensuring that all citizens, whatever their means, are adequately represented by counsel, though perhaps not the most expensive counsel.

A third and even more controversial sense of equality is equality in the resources needed to live a good life. In this view, equality is taken to mean that all the resources of the community should be used to create the conditions and opportunities of a good life for all persons, considered equally as members of the community, and that this equality of citizenship trumps any individual inequalities of ownership or merit. This kind of equality can take different forms, ranging from the ideal of complete equality through to the more modest goal of correcting specific and problematic inequalities. Complete equality would mean distributing all community resources equally (perhaps qualified with reference to the varying needs of a good life as between different persons). The more modest strategy—sometimes called *social democracy*—seeks to diminish inequality, particularly by removing the inequalities that most severely limit the ability to live a good life.

These three types of equality differ significantly in the degrees to which they require actual equality of income and power among people. But behind these differences, they differ even more profoundly in their understanding of citizenship. On the first conception, citizenship is just a matter of equal rights and does not require any equalization of income or power. Individuals will be equal as citizens when they possess the same formal citizenship rights. In this sense, the poorest street person and Bill Gates are equal as citizens because they both possess the same rights. In the second conception, the street person and Bill Gates are not equal as citizens because they are dramatically unequal in their ability to exercise their rights. Indeed, there is a sense in which street persons are excluded from citizenship because they cannot exercise their citizenship rights effectively. Here, then, citizenship is not a matter of rights but of effective participation in the community. In the third conception, equal citizenship is again seen in different terms. In this case, citizenship consists in community membership, where the community (with all its resources) is understood as a common undertaking to bring about the conditions of a good life for all. Thus, equality of citizenship here means that all citizens must be in a roughly equal position to enjoy a good life.

Rights

A RIGHT IS THE ABILITY TO REQUIRE THE PERFORMANCE OF A SPECIFIC DUTY. MORE exactly, the claim that a person has a **right** means, first, that other persons or agencies have some definite duty and, second, that the person with the right can require the performance of this duty. For example, your right to free speech means (1) that other persons have duties not to interfere with you when you are giving a speech, and (2) that if they do interfere, you can require that they stop.

It is important to note that the right to free speech is different from the freedom itself. With the freedom, the focus is on you: what you are free to do. With the right, the focus is on other people: what they must do to respect your right. The right *protects* you in the freedom (1) by imposing duties on the part of others not to interfere with you in exercising the freedom, and (2) by giving you the power to require people to respect these duties. This means that the nature of any right depends on the duties it imposes on others. Earlier, in the discussion of equality, we saw that the right to a lawyer could take two different forms. It could be just the right to hire a lawyer if you can afford one. Here, the right imposes on the state the duty not to stop you from doing so. But the right could take a stronger form, as in the right to hire a lawyer if you can afford one and the right to have a lawyer paid by the state if you cannot afford one. Here, the right imposes a different set of duties on the state. Thus, the same expression—"the right to a lawyer"—can designate different kinds of rights, and the difference lies in the duties that the right requires.

One way to classify rights, accordingly, is in terms of what they protect. Some rights protect liberties (or choices), and they do so by imposing duties of non-interference on the part of others. Other rights protect claims to particular benefits (such as education); and they do so by imposing the duty to provide the benefit on specific persons or agencies.

Legal rights are rights that are protected at law. Here, the law protects rights by providing a mechanism (through the courts) for their authoritative adjudication and enforcement. For some theorists, this enforceability is essential to the idea of a right. But there is a broader sense in which we may talk of **moral rights**. If Mary agrees to meet John for coffee, it can reasonably be said that she has a duty to turn up and that John has a right to expect this, even though he has no legal power to require it. There is a rich variety of these moral rights and duties in our social practices today, and these rights can be very important. There was a time, just one generation ago, when the law made it very difficult for women to obtain abortions. Those who opposed the law typically asserted, "Women have a right to abortion." Sometimes, this meant that women *should* have a right to abortion and that the law should be changed to allow it. But sometimes, the claim meant, more strongly, that women do have a right to abortion because they have the right to control their own bodies and that the law violates these rights by making it difficult for them to obtain abortions.

Historically, these moral rights have sometimes been presented as **natural rights**. These are rights which, it is said, people possess "by nature," as human beings, and not just as members of particular societies. Thus, all societies must recognize and respect these rights because they are owed to people as human beings. For example, John Locke (1632–1704) held that people have natural rights to life, liberty, and property and that any laws that violated these rights would be illegitimate. Today, rights of this kind are commonly called **human rights**. These are asserted as standards which must be respected by all societies because, it is held, they are the rights of people as human beings. In most cases, they are "moral," rather than legal, rights because there are few legal mechanisms for their adjudication and enforcement. But they are still "rights" because they assert duties whose performance can reasonably be demanded even if they cannot legally be enforced.

Issues about Rights

Can There Be Human Rights?

It is troubling that human rights cannot ordinarily be enforced and that, as a result, there are so many cases where basic human rights are violated with impunity. It may seem on this account that human rights are not "really" rights at all, but this is mistaken. It is true that if a legal right is non-enforceable, then it cannot be a (legal) right. But this is because legal rights, by definition, are enforced by the courts. If the courts do not recognize a right, it cannot be a legal right. But it may still be asserted as a moral right. It may still be true that certain persons or agencies have specifiable duties in relation to the right and that the right-bearer is justified in demanding that these duties be performed. Where these conditions apply, the right exists. If it is not enforceable, it is still a right, just one that is not, or not yet, legally enforceable.

Justifying Rights

Suppose you believe that people have certain rights. How can you show this? Just two steps are necessary. First, you must make a good case for holding that some person or agency has certain duties in relation to the right. Second, you must make a good case for holding that specific people should have the power to require that the duties be performed. Both steps—the duties and the power to require their performance—must be justified in establishing the right.

It is important to remember this because rights are sometimes treated as if they involved only duties. For example, you have a duty to be pleasant to the people you deal with. It does not follow that people have a right to *require* this from you. Imagine: "Hey, you aren't being nice enough to me: smile better!" The two situations—where you just have the duty, and where others have a right against you—are quite different. With the duty, you are still free to decide for yourself whether (and how) to do it. You lose this freedom when others have a right against you. With the right, they acquire control over part of your life. On this account, rights are not necessarily good things, even where the duties they require are important. When we establish a right to the performance of a duty, we take a certain freedom away from people and this must be considered in justifying the right. Contrary to popular belief, then, rights do not necessarily increase freedom. Instead, a right extends one person's freedom and control by reducing another's and, specifically, by giving the first person a power over part of the other's life.

Is the Regard for Rights Individualistic?

It is sometimes said that rights are undesirably "individualistic," as if they denied the value of community. But this is not necessarily so. In giving people the power through rights to require performance of duties, we give them a kind of freedom over their own lives and we correspondingly diminish the freedom of others—but there is no reason to suppose that this sets individuals against one another or the community. What it does is protect individuals in important ways and free them from dependence on others.

It is unfortunately true that people sometimes think only of their *own* rights and that they use these rights as weapons against the community. But it is wrong to blame the idea of rights for this. A right can only be established where the community values the activity in question as worth protecting in the manner of a right. So, the establishment of rights does not imply any anti-community spirit. Instead, it reflects a certain kind of community—one where individuals are given extensive control over their own lives. Liberalism values this kind of community.

Summary

This chapter has outlined three key concepts of current liberalism: liberty/freedom, equality, and rights. In the case of liberty/freedom, we noted that there has been a shift away from the traditional and narrow understanding of liberty as the absence of interference toward a broader and more social understanding of freedom as the ability to live on one's own terms. This newer understanding is more easily consistent with the value of equality, although we also found that the idea of equality can be understood in three different ways, each reflecting quite different conceptions of citizenship. These two concepts—freedom and equality—are the central value commitments of liberalism today. The chapter concluded by showing how these values may be protected by establishing them as rights.

Discussion Questions

1. Where there is a conflict between the freedom of individuals and the desires of the community, which do you think should prevail? Suppose a few people want to do something that does not directly harm anyone but greatly offends the majority. Should the majority be able to forbid them? Can you think of issues that would put you on one side of this question and other issues that would put you on the other side?
2. Would you allow clearly racist books to be freely published and distributed? Should they be available through publicly funded libraries?
3. In your opinion, is citizenship better understood as a set of rights that people have as individuals (such as the right to vote) or, instead, as a range of responsibilities and freedoms that people have as members of their community?

References

Mill, John Stuart. 1859. *On Liberty*. In A.D. Lindsay (ed.), *Utilitarianism, Liberty, Representative Government* (pp. 61–170). London: Everyman's Library.

Further Readings

Macpherson, C.B. 1978. *The Life and Times of Liberal Democracy*. Oxford: Oxford University Press.

Mill, John Stuart. 1859. *On Liberty*. In A.D. Lindsay (ed.), *Utilitarianism, Liberty, Representative Government* (pp. 61–170). London: Everyman's Library.

Rawls, John. 2001. *Justice as Fairness: A Restatement*. Cambridge, MA: Harvard University Press.

Taylor, Charles. 1992. *The Ethics of Authenticity*. Cambridge, MA: Harvard University Press.

Weblinks

EpistemeLinks.com
www.epistemelinks.com/Main/MainTopi.aspx

Policy Library: John Rawls
www.policylibrary.com/rawls

Stanford Encyclopaedia of Philosophy: Liberalism
http://plato.stanford.edu/entries/liberalism

CHAPTER 6

RADICAL POLITICS

Objectives

SANDRA REIN

Just the mention of the terms *radical* and *ideological* will raise eyebrows and cause the exchange of knowing looks. After all, in today's political parlance, to be radical is to be ideological and suspect—at least in the eyes of the mainstream media and those offering political commentary. Rather than exercise this same tendency to discredit "radicals" and "ideologues," this chapter will introduce **ideology** as a critical concept in political science and discuss key radical political ideologies of the past two centuries. Finally, the chapter will conclude with an overview of the ways in which these radical ideas continue to influence politics today.

Introduction

The concept of *ideology* has been a constant theme in the study of social and political life. Terry Eagleton's survey of a legion of definitions reveals that more than 16 different uses are commonly invoked by scholars. So, how is a student to understand ideology? Generally, we must understand that the history of ideology as a concept is essentially the competition between negative and more neutral connotations of the term. Negative representations define ideology as myth, illusion, or false consciousness. More neutral approaches see ideology as the study of the role of ideas in social and political life. Terry Eagleton argues that we can straddle these two approaches by viewing ideology as both "lived relations" and an "organizing social force" (Eagleton, 1990, 2, 30, 222). We can think about ideology as key sets of both those beliefs and values that serve to legitimate a certain social order, the so-called dominant ideology, and those values and beliefs that may be said to oppose or challenge that dominant ideology. There are several important implications that result from using such an approach to ideology. First, people promote and contest dominant ideologies. Second, Eagleton's definition accepts that ideologies have interested parties who stand to benefit from the adoption of their ideas and that the individuals adopting these ideas may be misled. Finally, this definition of ideology focuses attention on the contestable nature of social ideas. Although we recognize that ideologies play an important role in organizing social stability, they are also the primary midwives of social change. The combination of these implications means that ideology—the study of ideas as they inform society and construct the means for social change—are at the core of how we practise politics.

Modern Radical Political Ideologies

TRADITIONALLY, POLITICAL SCIENCE HAS TREATED MAJOR THEORIES THAT challenge the *status quo* as radical political ideologies. Specifically, we will review Marxism, socialism, anarchism, and communism. Each can be considered a radical political ideology and a political movement. Each offers an analysis of the ideas that organize social relations as well as a program of change. In Eagleton's words, each political ideology under discussion here has something to say about "lived relations" and "organizing social forces." However, before proceeding to a discussion of Marxism, a word or two needs to be said about why these particular ideologies are termed "radical."

Much like *ideology*, the term *radical* often suffers from a pejorative connotation. The very use of the word signals to one's audience that whatever follows is extreme and should, in the name of reasonableness, be discounted. However, radical has a more nuanced meaning. Rather than beginning our analysis by prejudging radical ideologies as extreme, we are better served by looking at radical thought as critical social theory. The Latin origin of the term radical is *radic*, meaning root. Radical critiques, thus, are those that propose to go to the root of the problem. All four ideologies under consideration offer fundamental and thorough critiques of various forms of social organization. In this sense, to be radical means to significantly challenge the *status quo*. Social scientists today who draw their analyses from *radical* political thought, particularly from the Marxist tradition, tend to avoid the pejorative title radical and instead opt for the general name *critical theory*. Nevertheless, the key consideration is always a critique of the *status quo* or in the words of Marx—"a ruthless criticism of everything existing" (Marx, 1978, 12–15).

Marxism

Marxism is often one of the most difficult "schools of political thought" to reduce to an essential core. The association of Marxism with the failed Soviet Union often causes confusion—what is Marxism? For our purposes, Marxism is drawn primarily from the works of Karl Marx (1818–1883), such as his famous *Das Kapital*. Marx's writings include both a theoretical analysis of capitalism and a commitment to radical political change. As he noted in his well-known eleventh thesis on Fuerebach: "The philosophers have only *interpreted* the world, in various ways; the point, however, is to *change* it" (Marx, 1978, 145). Although Marx's own writings are expansive (*Das Kapital* alone spans three volumes and thousands of pages), his major contributions can be seen as the development of a materialist conception of history, a critique of capitalist social relations, and a program for revolutionary change.

Method

For Marx, human history can be understood by looking at the way production is organized. In other words, the ways that land, labour, and resources (the **means of production**) come together to make things creates unique forms of social organization. Marx called this the **mode of production** and identified several historical modes as a result: slavery, feudalism, and capitalism. Each of these historical modes, or epochs, in human history is defined by a specific social antagonism or conflict. Slavery sees the struggle between owner and slave, feudalism sees the conflict between lord and serf, and capitalism is defined primarily by the struggle between the **bourgeoisie** (capitalists or owners) and the **proletariat** (the workers). It is the capitalist period of human history that Marx is most interested in, and he names the conflict between the bourgeoisie and the proletariat **class struggle**. By using a materialist approach as his method of inquiry, Marx reveals the essential elements of class society as defined by the capitalist mode of production.

Before examining Marx's critique of capitalism, it is important to stress that Marx's analysis focuses on antagonistic relations caused by a particular mode of production, but this focus should not be read as an indication that history itself must unfold in predetermined ways. His method instead revealed that history is about real struggles taking place within real historical societies with real historical consequences. However, as we have already noted, Marx believed philosophy needed to go beyond understanding history to changing history. In his analysis of capitalism, Marx's end goal was to outline the conditions under which the proletariat may overcome the bourgeoisie and end class struggle through the formation of communist (what he calls human) society. Let us turn now to an examination of Marx's critique of capitalism.

A Critique of Capitalism

Marx's life's work was focused on understanding the capitalist system "as a whole"—that is, the type of social relations a capitalist mode of production creates. Marx argued that the transformation from feudal and merchant societies to capitalist society created a new relationship between the labouring class (the proletariat) and those who owned the productive means of capital (the bourgeoisie). Capitalism established the conditions in which the only way for the labourer to survive was by selling her labour power (for a wage) to the bourgeoisie. This **wage–capital relationship** created two important social outcomes for the worker. First, the proletariat was **alienated** from the items being produced because of the factory division of labour. Second, the proletariat was vulnerable to **exploitation** by the owner because she relied on a paid wage to procure the necessities of life.

Although Marx was viewing the early days of the development of industrial capitalism dominated by the new factory system, his basic analysis of the working classes' reliance on wage labour continues to hold true. One need only reflect on Michael Moore's well-known documentaries, such as *Roger and Me* or *The Big One*, to know that workers continue to be vulnerable to plant closures, economic recessions, and capital relocation. However, it is not simply Marx's point that workers *can be* exploited under capitalism; rather, it is his point that worker exploitation *is* the *raison d'être* for capitalism. Why? Because by exploiting the worker (lowering wages, increasing working hours, and/or maintaining a "reserve army of labour" or "casual labour pool"), capitalists are able to realize what Marx termed **surplus value**, the value over and above the costs associated with production. Although it is slightly more complicated, we can think of surplus value as the ability of the bourgeoisie to realize a profit. And one may be further inclined to ask, what is wrong with profit? For Marx, two key problems arise from concentrating capital and pursing surplus value. First, workers are treated like any other piece of machinery or commodity. They are exploited and often treated as expendable. Marx says that even in situations where standards of living and wages improve for the workers, they continue to be exploited because they are always ulnerable to the whims of the owners. Second, the owners are able to use their wealth and social position to ensure that they maintain political power in capitalist societies. Today, we are familiar with the sayings "money talks" and "money makes the world go around." These truisms embody the essence of Marx's assessment of capitalist social relations—those responsible for actual production (the workers) are disenfranchised politically by those possessing wealth (the owners).

For Marx, the great irony of capitalism was that it held the potential to eradicate human want. Poverty, hunger, and scarcity could be ended through the technological innovations that present themselves in capitalism. Because of increasing concentration of capital (and the tendency toward monopoly), however, these technological innovations that could end scarcity merely serve to further impoverish the worker. A fair and equitable distribution of wealth, Marx argued, would first require the working class to become conscious of their exploitation.

Revolutionary Change

A fundamental question for us to put to Marx, then, is how do workers become conscious of their class position under capitalism? His answer was that modern capitalism produces fundamental contradictions in the lives of the working class that leads the worker to realize and ultimately contest her exploitation. The first contradiction workers experience is that the pursuit of profit leads to the ongoing attempt to decrease labour costs (through decreasing wages and imposing automation). So, even when capitalists are making huge profits and realizing surplus value, they are inclined to cut their labour forces or institute automation technology to replace human labourers. The second contradiction experienced by workers (and capitalists), according to Marx's analysis, is that the capitalist system is inherently unstable, frequently following periods of high growth rates (boom) with deep recessions (bust). These cycles of crises leave wage-dependent workers increasingly vulnerable to the dictates of a social system that they do not control.

Workers become conscious of their exploitation by their very lived experiences under the capitalist system. The factory model, in particular, brings workers together and increases the possibility for their collective political organization. Moreover, Marx believed that there is no simple reform that could be initiated to improve capitalism. Instead, he argued that these organized workers must overthrow the system and through their **revolution** create a new society. Thus, the end to the alienation, exploitation, and disenfranchisement of the working class is a revolutionary movement led by the proletariat that first establishes socialism and then communism. Communist society would embody the principle that "the free development of each is the condition for the free development of all" (Marx, 1978, 491).

Socialism

Historically, socialism as a political ideology predates Marxism, although it is impossible to deny that Marx's writings irrevocably changed socialism. The intellectual heritage of the key ideas of socialism are traced to Rousseau's critique of differences in property ownership, the concept of organic society, and the belief that individuals can aspire to the greater good (Baradat, 1988, 170). Rousseau's ideas were felt throughout revolutionary France. Another important early socialist who found inspiration in the French Revolution was Francis Babeuf (1760–1797). Babeuf advocated an extreme socialism that called for revolutionary transformation and the existence of an elite corps to lead the masses to revolution (Baradat, 1988, 171). Typically, we can delineate utopian, scientific, and social democtratic forms of socialism.

Utopian Socialism

Breaking from its revolutionary roots, socialism coalesced into a coherent set of ideas in the form of what has been termed utopian socialism. This form of socialist thought advocated the public ownership of the means of production, democratic social organizations, and the eradication of all want in society. Robert Owen (1771–1858) is identified as the "father" of utopian socialism. Ironically, Owen was a successful industrial capitalist who embarked on realizing his utopian vision after retiring from business. He was convinced that his factories had been productive because of his ethical treatment of employees. To prove his point, Owen participated in setting up communes on the principles of economic self-sufficiency and democratic decision making. The New Harmony commune, established in 1825 in Indiana, is recognized as one of Owen's most successful attempts at communal living. New Harmony, like all of the communal experiments of the time, ultimately failed because of an inability to be economically independent and to sustain democratic group decision making.

Scientific Socialism

Following utopian socialism, socialist thought was dominated by Marx's influence. Marx proposed that his form of socialism was scientific—drawing on Enlightenment notions of rationality and science. Marx argued that socialism is merely a stage of economic and social development following the demise of capitalism. Although scientific socialism had tremendous impact on the organizational forms of the working class (most notably in the case of the formation of the International Workingmen's Association, known as the First International), Marx's theories quickly became subject to debate leading to significant revision by subsequent socialist thinkers. Two areas of Marxist thought were most hotly contested—(1) the commitment to change through revolution only; and (2) what was perceived as the overemphasis on economic relationships (economic determinism). The resulting revisionist movement argued that social change could be achieved through evolution, rather than revolution. The revisionists also stressed the moral/social values of socialism, rather than economics. This was the position taken by Canada's most influential social democratic party—the Co-operative Commonwealth Federation (CCF)—which emerged from the depths of the Great Depression of the 1930s.

Social Democracy

Today, socialism remains a vibrant political ideology. While some movements still maintain a link to historical scientific socialism, the more prevalent legacy is apparent among the social democratic parties found in Western Europe. Social democracy is characterized by a commitment to universal social programs for citizens, a mixed economy of public and private enterprise, and public taxation to decrease income disparities. In the European Union, social democratic parties continue to have a significant presence on Europe's political landscape. The success of these parties has sustained interest in social democracy, and socialist thinking more generally, proving the ongoing relevance of this ideology.

Anarchism

Defined most simply, anarchism is the rejection of hierarchical forms of governance. Yet, this definition fails to capture the rich history of anarchist thought. Anarchism as a political ideology became popular in the early nineteenth century in response to the Industrial Revolution. Since that time, subscribers to anarchist thought have organized in most industrialized countries and have had a significant impact on developing political regimes, particularly in Africa. Generally, anarchist thinking can be divided into two distinct categories: social or collectivist versus individualist anarchism. We will examine each in turn.

Social Anarchism

Pierre Joseph Proudhon (1809–1865) was the first political thinker to call himself an anarchist. Proudhon is best remembered for his answer to the question "What is property?" He replied, "Property is theft." Proudhon outlined the key elements of anarchism that would see the eradication of the state and the free and harmonious association of individuals. Specifically, Proudhon advocated the organization of workers into syndicates that would collectively make all decisions about production and collectively share ownership. Proudhon's form of anarchism is often referred to as anarcho-syndicalism. Anarchist syndicate experiments did enjoy some short-lived success in Spain between 1936 and 1939. However, these syndicates obtained worker control through violent means, in contrast to Proudhon's non-violent prescription.

One of the best-known anarchists, Mikhail Bakunin (1814–1876), believed that violence was necessary to achieve an anarchist society. Closely associated with social (or communist) anarchism, Bakunin argued that revolution would be achieved by arming the most undesirable elements of the population. Clearly one of the most radical anarchists, Bakunin left a legacy of his strong belief in the necessary role of violence in effecting social change. Another well-known anarchist who subscribed to Bakunin's radicalism is Emma Goldman (1869–1940), who carried her anarchist message throughout the United States, the Soviet Union, and Canada. A tireless radical, Goldman was also outspoken on issues concerning women's rights and was particularly active in working for the legalization of contraception for women.

In her later years, however, Goldman became less committed to violent overthrow, largely because of the influence of Peter Kropotkin's (1842–1921) thinking. Kropotkin argued that society was more likely to progress through cooperation than aggression. Also a communist anarchist, Kropotkin believed that the modern state was "the personification of injustice, oppression, and monopoly." Kropotkin's vision of anarchist society was one of harmony and cooperation, rejecting the idea that revolutions were the best way to change social organization. He believed that industrial progress and technology would eventually eradicate human want. Once this level of technological advancement had occurred, Kropotkin believed that society would evolve to communism.

Individualist Anarchism

Both anarcho-syndicalism and communist anarchism share a belief that government prevents the free association among individuals and, therefore, limits personal autonomy and the possibility of cooperative and harmonious social organization. However, there is another strain of anarchist thinking that asserts that individuals should be completely free of social responsibility. Lyman Sargent notes that "[t]he individualist anarchist recognizes nothing above his ego and rebels against all discipline and all authority" (Sargent, 1996, 177). Individualist anarchist thought is historically associated with Max Stirner (1806–1856), who nicely summarizes his political ideology with the slogan "The people are dead. Up with me!"

Stirner represents individualist anarchism at its most extreme. Libertarianism, in many ways, represents a softer variant of Stirner's philosophy and continues to have a significant impact on contemporary politics, especially in the United States. Libertarianism is closely associated with the work of Robert Nozick, who asserts the "pre-eminent right" of private property. Libertarians reject government intervention in areas of social life and economic markets, although conceding the need for a very limited government. Threads of libertarian thought run through the rhetoric of political movements and political parties that promise to "down-size government" and to guarantee the "free market." For example, during the 2000 American presidential campaign, George W. Bush frequently asserted that he believed in "the people" and not "government." Indeed, a handful of libertarians typically compete in Canadian federal elections in order to deliver this message.

Communism

Communism, of all the ideologies discussed here, is the most difficult to define. We all have a sense that we know what communism is. We have seen it in its application in the former Soviet Union, China, Cuba, and the former Yugoslavia. With the demise of the communist regimes in many of these countries, we are also left with the sense that communism is a failed experiment, a political ideology that was "good in theory" but did not work in practice. However, this is a far too simplistic dismissal of the question of what communist ideology consists of and means in application. The "failure" of avowedly communist regimes and the more recent movement toward "democratization" and market liberalization does not speak to the theoretical and ideological concepts that underpin communist theory. In fact, many traditional Marxists were highly critical of the Soviet experiment. As with all political ideologies, there is often a large gap between political ideas and their concrete expression in political actions and institutions.

Marx argued that communism could only be achieved after capitalism and socialism, but he actually wrote very little about what communist society would look like. Some ideas, however, are found in his theoretical work. Communist society would involve the public ownership of the means of production (factories and so on), absolute social equality (that is, a classless society), and the "withering away" of the state. In this sense, communism is very much the melding of scientific socialism and social anarchism. For Marx, the communist ethic was embodied in the statement "from each according to his abilities, to each according to his needs." From Marx's original work on the question of communist society, other Marxists began to develop a more defined picture of communism. Most notable among these thinkers is Lenin (1870–1924). Lenin's concern was to take the theories that Marx espoused and to put them into action. As one of the key leaders of the Russian Revolution, Lenin was in a unique position to further develop communist political thought. Lenin was consumed by two concerns: how capitalism worked internationally, and how to organize a successful revolution. With regard to the latter concern, Lenin developed the notion of the party vanguard. Lenin argued that in order to successfully organize a revolution, it would be necessary to have a well-trained cadre of dedicated individuals who would work tirelessly for the success of the revolution. Following the revolution, the vanguard would ensure the nationalization of industry and the dictatorship of the proletariat.

Following Lenin's death in 1924, Joseph Stalin came to power in the Soviet Union. Stalin consolidated his personal authority in the Union of Soviet Socialist Republics (USSR) through bloody purges and political intrigue and challenged one of the fundamental precepts of Marxist thought. Marx believed that socialism had to be an international project. Stalin, in contrast, contended that "socialism in one country" was not only possible but also desirable. To this end, Stalin implemented intense industrialization and centralized planning. Some argue that his policies led inevitably to the demise of the Soviet economy in the 1990s. However, Stalin was not alone in attempting to offer significant revision to Marx's work. In China, Mao Tse-tung, leader of the Chinese revolution, argued that mobilization of the peasants, not workers, was the key to revolutionary success. This also represented a significant shift away from Marxist reliance on the working class as the focal point of revolution. Mao's communist reforms focused on the collectivization of farming as opposed to the Soviet model of speedy industrial development.

This very brief overview of communism leads us to two general conclusions. The first is that communist ideology need not be tied to the projects of the formerly communist countries. In fact, the basic tenets of communism—classless society and public ownership and direction of production—can be separated from those movements that have named themselves communist. Second, a political ideology can espouse a quite different view of social organization in theory than what is achieved in the application. The Soviet Union, Yugoslavia, China, and Cuba each had to adapt and change their political ideologies to face changing domestic and international circumstances.

The Intellectual Heritage of Radical Politics

As you were reading these overviews of radical political movements and theories, it is likely that you could think of current organizations that still espouse these ideas. For example, the Communist Party of Canada (Marxist-Leninist) still exists and even occasionally contests elections. However, the intellectual heritage of these ideas should be identified much more broadly than by looking for the names to reappear in modern political parties. This section will briefly trace the ongoing legacy of radical politics, particularly as these critiques reassert their salience in an era of globalization.

The Birth of the New Left

In May 1968, students in Paris organized a sustained revolt that was supported by industrial workers who went on strike across the French provinces. Although there are many interpretations of the events and those conditions that fostered them; what is clear is that the student protestors were drawing on critiques of capitalist society and calling for revolutionary change. These protests were not exclusive to France and, in fact, took place worldwide. In the United States, opposition to the Vietnam war was a major catalyst for organizing protest groups, which engaged in critiquing American society and challenging American imperialism around the globe. These movements took hold of the intellectual ideas presented in critical academic publications, such as the *New Left Review,* that published works strongly influenced by such radical thinkers as Karl Marx, Frederich Engels, and Vladimir Lenin. Rather than succumbing to anti-communist/Cold War propaganda, these types of scholarly publications attempted to preserve the critical nature of Marxism, Leninism, and socialist thought more generally. What is particularly significant is that these modern radical movements and political critiques, like those radicals that preceded them in history, were calling for an overthrow of the dominant power structures under which they lived in favour of a new vision of society. In order to sustain their radical critique, these varied movements drew on Marx's critique of capitalist society and the anarchist tendency toward open, non-hierarchical forms of social organization. The commune movement within "hippie culture" was itself an attempt to practise a form of communist social organization. In short, the radical politics of the nineteenth century had been adapted to the emerging critical practices of the mid-twentieth century.

Anti-Colonialism and National Liberation Movements

Radicalized politics were not restricted to North America or Western Europe. The 1960s were also a period of radicalization for colonized peoples, particularly those on the African continent. Often drawing on such ideas as Lenin's analysis of capitalist imperialism and "uneven development," as well as notions of justice and democracy, resistance groups formed and eventually won their independence in such places as Algeria, Gambia, and Tanzania. Although, the movements, experiences, and outcomes of independence movements varied across the continent of Africa, the leaders, activists, and outside supporters did draw on the analysis and critiques, as well as organizational forms, presented in earlier radical movements. Outside of Africa's experience, we can also see the social democratic legacy in Nehru's India or the socialist lineage of Allende's rise to power in Chile (1970).

Anti-Globalization

Lest we should begin to think that radical political ideas disappeared after the 1970s, it is important to recognize that the intellectual heritage is preserved and further enhanced in today's "anti-globalization" movements. The tens of thousands of protestors that converged on a World Trade Organization meeting in Seattle in 1999 were not unified by a single political program. They were, however, drawing on critiques of capitalism and questioning the logic of economic globalization that privileges corporations and trade over people. Present at the protests were anarchists, socialists, communists, environmentalists, anti-racism groups, feminists, trade union and labour activists, students, academics, farmers, and "average" citizens—to name just a few! What drew together these disparate groups was the sense that we need a radical critique of the nature of the global distribution of political and economic power.

Whether one is looking at the "people of '68" or "anti-colonial movements" or "anti-globalization protests," it is possible to see the common thread of radicalism that draws each of these together in a historical relationship. Each of these groups may have had a different political platform or series of demands, but all were drawing on Marx's call to ruthlessly critique "all that is existing." For the "people of '68" the focus was necessarily on the ways in which "the Establishment" oppressed groups of people, either domestically or through imperialist practices globally. For the anti-colonial movements, radical ideas offered the promise of a self-determined, better future. And for today's anti-globlization movements, the very act of challenging the logic of global capitalism and its institutions draws on older, radical traditions. Each of these movements drew from the radical political ideologies covered in this chapter, added their own adaptations and lessons, and offer us the opportunity to continue the practice of radical criticism in ever-changing conditions.

Summary

Recently, some academics and political commentators have been trumpeting the "end of ideology," and by implication, the end of radical politics. They confidently declare that this has been achieved by the worldwide acceptance (or at least striving toward) and realization of American-styled liberal democracy. However, we should be suspect of this argument on at least two counts. In the first place, it implies that democratic governments, such as those found in Canada or the United States, are non-ideological, which, if we recall Eagleton's definition of ideology, is simply impossible. And in the second place, it denies the continuing influence of radical ideologies on political movements around the globe. As we have already noted, Western Europe seems to be witnessing a resurgence in socialist-influenced politics, and countries in parts of the developing world, such as Africa and Central America, continue to draw on the insights and programs of previous ideological movements.

Moreover, the end-of-ideology view tends to overlook the importance of new and emerging critical movements. Critical political projects, such as the varied anti-globalization movements, will continue to draw their organizational forms and critiques from the legacy of radical ideologies. Returning to Eagleton, for a moment, ideology's role of making sense of our lived experiences and helping us envision new forms of social organization is going to be a consistent feature of our social existence. To argue that ideology is no longer a relevant concept and that radical politics is dead is to deny our ability as human beings to contest current social conditions and to create alternative ways of living.

Discussion Questions

1. Do you find that your thinking about some issues could be considered ideological? In what ways? Do you engage in radical politics? How so?
2. Are radical political ideologies desirable? Why, or why not?
3. What do you think is the future of socialist or communist movements today?

References

Baradat, Leon. 1988. *Political Ideologies: Their Origins and Impact.* Scarborough: Prentice Hall.

Eagleton, Terry. 1991. *Ideology: an Introduction.* New York: Verso.

Marx, Karl. 1978. *The Marx-Engels Reader* edited by Robert C. Tucker. New York: Norton.

Sargent, Lyman Tower. 1996. *Contemporary Political Ideologies: A Comparative Analysis.* New York: ITP.

Further Readings

Anderson, Kevin. 1995. *Lenin, Hegel, and Western Marxism: A Critical Study.* Chicago: University of Illinois Press.

Dunayevskaya, Raya. 1991. *Women's Liberation, and Marx's Philosophy of Revolution,* 2nd edition. Chicago: University of Illinois Press.

Goldman, Emma. 1969. *Anarchism and Other Essays.* New York: Dover Publications.

Lenin, Vladimir Ilich. 1972. *Collected Work of V. I. Lenin* translated by Clemens Dutt. London: Lawrence and Wishart.

Weblinks

The Socialist International
www.socialistinternational.org

Institute for Anarchist Studies
www.anarchist-studies.org

World Socialist Web Site
www.wsws.org

The Communist Party of Canada
www.communist-party.ca

Marxists.org Internet Archive
www.marxists.org

World Social Forum
www.wsfindia.org

Foundations of Governance

PART II

Governance, simply defined, refers to the ways in which we organize our common affairs. Although the exercise of political power and authority is often informal, all modern societies are governed by formal rules and practices exercised through political institutions. In political science, institutions are defined as deliberate, formalized, and expected patterns of behaviour. Political institutions are the embodiment of a nation's history of conflict and compromise as well as sites of ongoing political struggles. In this section of the text, we will discover that different countries at different times have had different configurations of political institutions or regime types, ranging from monarchies to dictatorships to liberal democracies. Yet, central to all is the state, an amalgam of political institutions that claims sovereignty over a defined territory. All states tend to share common political institutions—perhaps most fundamentally, a constitution. Constitutions are the basic blueprint for the daily operation of the state, dividing powers among levels of government, across institutions, and among leaders, elected legislators, public administrators, and the bureaucracy, which is empowered to enforce state laws and regulations. Other foundations of politics exert their influence in play with the formal institutions of the national state. As the chapters in this section outline, political scientists have developed a number of competing perspectives on how political institutions impact on individuals as citizens and as members of a variety of political communities. Finally, this Part examines electoral systems. They embody the rules and procedures whereby leaders are chosen and citizens' choices are calculated. The core institutions of the modern state contain and manage political conflict, make and enforce public policies, and realize political ideas and visions. In other words, they are the bread and butter of political analysis.

CHAPTER 7

POLITICAL REGIMES

Objectives

Human society is organized into groups to secure the means to life, to ensure survival and reproduction, and to develop and transmit culture. However "primitive" or complex, there is a pattern of authority within which decisions are made regarding fundamental activities. The study of those patterns is the essence of political science. Power is the capacity to make decisions and **governance** is the organized exercise of that capacity. Political science examines power, usually focusing on government—that set of institutions and structures embodying power. One way it does so is by categorizing and comparing the variety of organized governance experiences that human society has had. While many political scientists use the term *state*, another term applied in the comparative study of governance is *regime*. Defining regime and categorizing its different types is the subject of this chapter. The chapter first explores the four spheres—the state, society, the market, and the globe—that comprise and inform different regime types. Next, the essential features of three kinds of regimes—authoritarian, democratic, and revolutionary are described. The chapter concludes with some projections about the nature of political regimes in the future.

FRED JUDSON

Introduction

Nearly a century ago, German social scientist Max Weber coined the term *ideal-type* as a way to categorize and understand politics and society. He was not the first to create mental models. Plato and Machiavelli helped establish the central place of such concepts as democracy, oligarchy, tyranny, and republic in political science. Like them, Weber insisted that specific experiences of governance would never precisely conform to such ideal-types. Another insight, shared by Karl Marx, was that while ideal-types and concepts appear to be static, what they capture is definitely not. Each considered human societies and organized governance structures to be evolving and changing. Weber delineated three broad types of authority that characterize power and governance—traditional, charismatic, and bureaucratic. And he sought to understand each type's developmental aspect—its "laws of motion," as Marx would have put it. Marx focused on how the inherent contradictions of the grand social models he studied—slavery, feudalism, and capitalism—generated social development and change. Despite their theoretical differences, both Weber and Marx agreed that regimes, as organized governance experiences, are developmental and dynamic. They can be analyzed and compared across societies, with themselves at different points in time, and with ideal-types.

The Four Spheres of Regime

HOW CAN *REGIME* BE DEFINED? THE LATIN STEM *REG-* REFERS TO "RULE," and so the basic meaning of *regime* is "form of rule" over given spheres of human activity. The concept of *regime* as "organized governance experience" contains four spheres, namely, **state**, **society**, **market**, and **global insertion**. Each sphere is very complex and relates to the other three and to the whole that together they form—in other words, each sphere's dynamics effect and are affected by the others.

State

To understand the *state*, we can think of regime in the way Marx thought of social formation. This term conveys the idea that a society is organized economically, socially, and politically, and develops its coherence over time. In this sense, a social formation is a system of interacting dimensions. Social formations and regimes can be understood as both abstract concepts and real collective experiences. Perhaps the notion of a country is closest to regime at such a general level. The world's land and population are currently contained in some 180 countries. When we think of countries, we are thinking of states as sovereign units in the international political system. This means, at least theoretically, that no external authority may prevail over domestic authority. No matter what regime type characterizes that sovereign domestic authority, all states share the attribute of **sovereignty**. Though many now question its meaning because of striking disparities among states and the impact of globalization, it remains critical to the state as a sphere of regimes.

FIGURE 7.1 *All regimes contain four spheres*

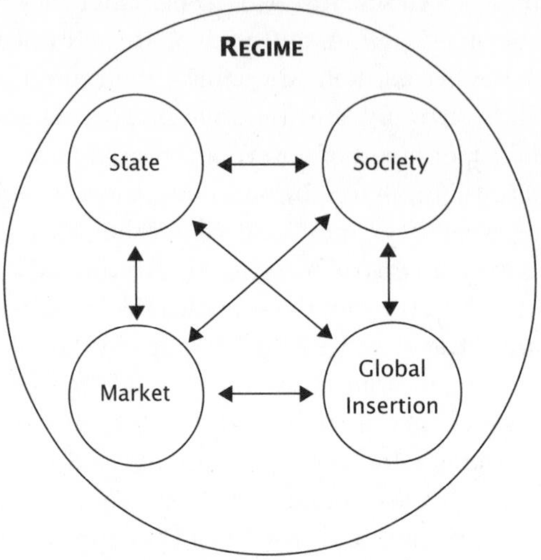

Arrows indicate dynamic interaction

The state also is the classic object of inquiry by political science: power and its sources; structures and practices of authority; and political institutions. Whatever the characteristics of a regime as dynamic interactions of the four spheres, it is mainly in the state that "who gets what, and how" is determined. Despite the disparities among states' capacities and today's border-ignoring globalization, for several centuries, it has been the domestic dimensions of states that most affect the lives of their citizens.

Society

We can deepen our understanding of the state and of regimes as dynamic interactions by considering the second sphere—*society*. Weber held that society's composition would determine the character of the state, structures of authority, and political institutions. In other words, the country shapes its state. His approach can be called **political sociology**. Using it, we can say that a society of "traditional" values and social classes, such as peasant, rural, and religious Russia before 1917, would most likely be a monarchy. A society in transition to an urban, secular, and capitalist society would likely be in revolt against state forms inherited from feudal, traditional, and aristocratic times. It would either develop a liberal democracy or an industrializing authoritarian state, possibly even a totalitarian police-state. In either case, Weber argued, a large bureaucracy would arise to administer the complexities of modern industrial society. Power contenders would almost always be elite groups, usually economic elites, but masses (peasants, industrial workers, small merchants and professionals, and the urban poor) could be volatile and decisive political actors.

Marx advocated another approach, called **historical materialism** or critical political economy. He argued that the primary organized human activity was economic, from hunting and gathering to agriculture to modern industrial production. The production of the means to life, for Marx, was logically prior to society and culture. Humanity's basic political aspect lay in the organization of the labour processes and material resources involved in that production and the distribution of what was produced. Social classes, such as serfs and landlords or capitalists and workers, derived from the relationship of people to the means of production (land, tools, machines, and capital) and their roles in production—the division of labour. For him, the state was the political expression and forceful guarantor of those basic relationships. In class societies, he argued, the dominant class, such as a landed aristocracy or an industrial bourgeoisie, controlled both the means of production and the state.

Market

After more than two centuries of capitalist economic development, with its prodigious increases in production and consumption, the importance of the economic dimension for understanding the modern state, society, and regimes is unquestioned. The triumph of capitalism over socialist experiments of the twentieth century and the acceleration of globalization also underline the centrality of the market. Weberian and Marxist approaches find common ground in our third sphere, the *market*. Considered broadly, the market sphere includes production, exchange, and distribution. Taking a cue from Marx, it includes relations of property and production, particularly who controls the means of production, finances the processes, and controls the profits. Following Weber's position that a society's composition shapes its state, we can characterize most of the world's societies as "market societies." In such societies, to a great degree, the social worth of individuals and groups is determined by "market principles," such as ownership, price, income, costs, and supply and demand.

Both Marxists and Weberians link wealth and political power to the market sphere. The market is where production and accumulation of wealth occurs, where the social contours of modern societies take shape, and where power focuses its attention. The market is the sphere in which a society's economic "mode of accumulation" operates, and from which states, like social classes, draw material resources for the exercise of power and the contention for power. Some political scientists use the phrase "regimes of accumulation" to capture these social, economic, and political aspects of the market sphere. The phrase conveys the sense that market decisions regarding such things as investment, production, and currency values are as important in influencing political decisions as are parliamentary, legislative, executive, and party activities or elections. Moreover, the link between market and political decisions is inherent. This link can be immediately grasped by noting the political significance, for example, of the Japanese recession of the 1990s or the North American Free Trade Agreement debates in the 1980s and 1990s.

Global Insertion

It is a short leap from observations about the market to the fourth sphere necessary for a critical conception of regime—*global insertion.* All countries, their respective societies, states, and markets occupy certain positions in larger international contexts. One context is the international state system. Another is the international economic system, comprising trade and financial transactions among states and firms, comparative economic development experiences, patterns of production and distribution, and, increasingly, globalization. These two international contexts—the modern state system and the international economy—have constituted a "world system" since the sixteenth century.

The state system has been shaped by a small number of "great powers" whose interests and exercise of power determine the "rules." The system has been conflictual—war, preparation for war, and national security concerns are constant elements. It is a hierarchical system, reflected in the twentieth century's experience of colonies, great and regional powers, client states, and superpowers with their alliance systems. World systems theorists divide the world's states into core, periphery, and semi-periphery. The familiar terms First World and Third World—with socialist countries, particularly China and the Soviet Union, until recently comprising the Second World—only partially convey the global structural analysis of world systems theory.

The economic dimension of the world system also has been hierarchical, often marked by domination and exploitation. Capitalist development also was accompanied by European colonial acquisition of much of the world. Simplifying greatly, capitalist economies in the core countries determined the patterns of economic development and underdevelopment in the rest of the world, in a system often called **imperialism**. The crucial political and economic decisions affecting the world's peoples were made by small numbers of people in the ruling classes of core countries. The relationship between core and periphery was characterized by unequal exchange, distorted development, and underdevelopment.

Countries able to improve their position, with some industrialization, increases in productivity, and improvements in quality of life, make up the semi-periphery. Recent cases are termed NICs (Newly Industrializing Countries). The rest, referred to as less-developed, developing, or underdeveloped countries, constitute the periphery. The three terms capture the political and economic "global insertion" of countries. Globalization constitutes the present manner of global insertion—our fourth sphere. With this change, the world system is evolving from the international state and economic systems toward an integrated global capitalist economy and some kind of post-sovereignty global politics.

Fundamental elements of the world system also define the processes of globalization, generating great social, political, and economic unevenness among and within countries. Capitalism creates extremes of wealth and poverty even as it includes more of the world's territory and population in a global market system. Politically, a wide variety of states and regime forms are present. Societies are affected by external influences and forces at unprecedented levels. Relationships of hierarchy and domination, between states and within societies, are present, but so are relations of civility, tolerance, cooperation, community, and solidarity. Altogether, they produce social forces of resistance and struggle, which contribute to change.

In sum, the four spheres allow us to define *regime*. A **regime** is a mode of governance over the organized activity of a social formation within and across its particular configuration of society, state, market, and global insertion. As organized governance across the four spheres, regimes are "modes of accumulation" for a social formation. Society's form and cohesion (its structure) are produced, enforced, and changed. The state is provided with its institutions and practices and is shaped, staffed, and managed. The market sphere maintains its means and relations of production, property, and distribution, provided that the conditions it needs to thrive are met. A social formation's global insertion defines and governs its economic and political relationships beyond its borders. A regime coordinates processes of accumulation within, between, and among the four spheres; in that sense a regime is a system-controller, a "hard drive" for a social formation.

A Classic Regime Typology

THE TWENTIETH CENTURY WAS WITNESS TO THE GREATEST VARIETY OF regimes humanity has known: developed societies lived alongside "Stone Age" communities; colonialism's end(s) generated disparate post-colonial regimes; state socialism engaged one-third of the globe; capitalism, science, and technology transformed whole societies, while the "development gap" widened; the planet's population and production surged explosively; hundreds of wars raged; and forceful ideologies shaped both domestic and international politics. The dominant *raison d'être* for regimes has been the pursuit of economic development within the dynamics of the world system. Power is dependent on it. Twentieth-century regimes fall under three broad categories: authoritarian, democratic, and revolutionary. They should be understood as ideal-types *and* as specific collective experiences. **Authoritarian** regimes are thought of as "rule by the few" or even the one, where force or the threat of force to maintain "order" is implicit or explicit. **Democratic** regimes are considered to be "rule by the many," where force is rarely necessary because the majority accept and support the particular "order" of the society, especially its economic and political arrangements. **Revolutionary** regimes are those where certain elites, groups, and/or the majority have overthrown the given socio-economic and political order and undertaken a radical transformation, usually in the name of a dominated and exploited majority.

Authoritarian Governance

By definition, absolutist monarchies are authoritarian, and few now persist. Examples include Saudi Arabia and Brunei, but most existing monarchies are constitutional, with greater or lesser degrees of authority and symbolic importance—they do not "rule." There is much more association of authoritarian regimes with "late" industrialization. Following Weber, analysts sought to explain ultra-authoritarian regimes, usually called *totalitarian*, in both capitalist and socialist countries, as deriving from the stresses of "late" and rapid industrial development. The two main cases are Nazi Germany, and the Soviet Union under Joseph Stalin. Japan, another "late-industrializing" country, also experienced a militarist authoritarian regime in the 1930s and 1940s. Some have deemed the People's Republic of China totalitarian, at least for various periods since its establishment in 1949. Also included are North Korea, and Cambodia under the Khmer Rouge.

A number of core countries have had fully authoritarian or semi-authoritarian regimes in the twentieth century, usually called *dictatorships*. Semi-peripheral countires, such as Portugal, Spain, Greece, and Turkey, all endured dictatorships of varying longevity in the twentieth century. Authoritarian socialist regimes ruled virtually all of Eastern and Central Europe from the 1940s until the 1990s. A number of authoritarian regimes, in Latin America, in West, Central, South, East, and Southeast Asia, in Africa, and in the Middle East/Persian Gulf, played roles in the global political, military, and economic strategy of the United States and other core states during the twentieth century. In many cases, American (and "allied") policy had a direct hand in the establishment and maintenance of "client" military-dominated authoritarian regimes. The term *bureaucratic-authoritarian* designates several such Latin American regimes of the 1960s to 1980s. But it is not sufficient to reduce these regimes to "sub-fascist client states" or "tools of multinational corporations," just as European and Third World authoritarian socialist regimes should not simply be considered Soviet "satellites." Authoritarian regimes are shaped not only by their global insertion but also by their respective spheres of state, society, and market.

TABLE 7.1 *The Three Regime Types*

	AUTHORITARIAN	DEMOCRATIC	REVOLUTIONARY
MAJOR CHARACTERISTICS	Rule by the few Concentration of power Use or threat of force State dominates civil society Usually social and economic inequality Class struggle controlled	Rule by the many through elections Constitutional separation of powers Consent of the majority Degrees of economic redistribution Class conflict managed Pluralist society	Radical transformation of social and political order Mass mobilization Socialist economic principles Class conflict is "official"
EXAMPLES	Latin American dictatorships, 1960s–1980s Indonesia, 1965–1998 Nazi Germany	Germany Costa Rica Canada	Cuba Vietnam Early Soviet Union

Post-Colonial Authoritarian Regimes

Decolonization after World War II transformed most of Africa, the Middle East, and much of Asia. Authoritarian regimes have abounded in these post-colonial social formations, though democratic and revolutionary regimes have also been prominent. Various explanations are offered for the high incidence of authoritarian regimes in post-colonial countries. For example, they have been considered "artificial" creations of colonial powers or elites created under colonialism as well as products of ethnic, cultural, and religious divisions that are more pronounced and less manageable than in core countries. It also is argued that the political culture of democracy either does not exist, is underdeveloped, or cannot compete with tradition, religion, ethnic politics, or ideology. Some suggest that authoritarianism is convenient for former colonial powers or international capitalism. For others, capitalism in the periphery is incomplete, distorted, and externally oriented and, thus, cannot support civil society and liberal democracy as they developed in the West. Finally, it is argued that authoritarian regimes are a predictable stage in the modernization process leading to democratic regimes.

As in most broad explanations, each of the above has some applicability. A deeper understanding of Third World authoritarian regimes results from considering each regime's specificity of state, society, market, and global insertion. What we can assert is that just as patterns of economic dependency and U.S. power are necessary but not sufficient bases for understanding Latin American authoritarian regimes, the historical experiences of colonialism, insertion into the state system, and international division of labour in the twentieth century are necessary but not sufficient for understanding post-colonial regimes in Africa, the Middle East, and Asia. We also can suggest that post-colonial regimes manifest more "traditional" affinities, values, and identities than do core countries. But we must be careful here not to fall into "othering" and patronizing because the same can be found in core countries as well. Aboriginal peoples, women, ethnic minorities and disadvantaged social classes have experienced as much (or more) marginalization and repression under Western liberal democracies as have their counterparts under Third World authoritarian regimes.

Many post-colonial social formations lack a capitalist "ruling class" with the material substance and social cohesion of its counterparts in the core and semi-periphery. Various factions contend for control of the state apparatus more from a patrimonial perspective than from an inclusive national "regime of accumulation" perspective. Such post-colonial elites have been vulnerable to military coups, external intervention, or revolutionary social forces. In cases where oil or another commodity is important to the international economy or the country has strategic traditional, nationalist, or military importance, authoritarian elites have had regime alliances with multinational corporations and/or core states.

The variety of post-colonial authoritarian regimes is striking. In Africa, personalist semi-authoritarian regimes often followed initial experiences of democracy.

TABLE 7.2 *Variety of Authoritarian Regimes in the Twentieth Century*

TYPE	EXAMPLE
Totalitarian	Nazi Germany, Stalinist USSR
Military dictatorship	Chile under Pinochet, Indonesia under Suharto, Myanmar
Authoritarian socialist	Eastern Europe during the Cold War
Bureaucratic authoritarian	Brazil 1964–1985, Argentina 1976–1982
Personalist	Zaire under Mobutu

Charismatic figures of the independence movement headed presidential and single-party regimes. There were instances in Asia and the Middle East as well. In some African countries experiencing wars of national liberation won by revolutionary movements, the regimes have had personalist, single-party, and authoritarian elements. Other personalist regimes were more identified with foreign patrons, corruption, an opulent life-style, and varying degrees of repression. In cases lacking a charismatic figure, a series of military individuals or groups managed varieties of authoritarian regimes in some of Africa's richest and poorest countries.

In the Middle East, several forceful leaders (Nasser, Qaddafi, Assad) in the 1950s and '60s articulated a mix of populist, nationalist, pan-Arab anti-imperialist, and anti-Israeli messages while promoting economic development and state social responsibility. Their regimes were semi-authoritarian, with varying degrees of repression, culminating in a fully authoritarian Iraq. Most Gulf states were semi-authoritarian monarchies or oligarchies dominating the oil wealth. At present, several countries have self-denominated Islamic regimes (Iran, Saudi Arabia, Sudan); their authoritarianism varies (it should be said that Islam is not inherently authoritarian).

Authoritarian regimes have characterized South and Southeast Asia, though not exclusively. More than half of Pakistan's political history and much of Bangladesh's have been military. Even democratic India has experienced periods of semi-authoritarian governance. Indonesia has emerged from decades of personalist, military-backed semi-authoritarianism, while the military has played central roles in Myanmar and Thailand. The Cold War's global dynamics greatly influenced regime formation in much of the region, ranging from the semi-authoritarian Marcos regime in the Philippines and the pro-U.S. dictatorships of Indochina to the authoritarian socialist regimes that followed, reaching the tragic extreme of the Khmer Rouge in Cambodia.

Democratic Regimes

Just as a continuum of authoritarian regime types reflects diverse experiences across the four spheres, there also is considerable variation among democratic regimes.

In order to have "governance by the many" in the liberal democracy ideal-type, citizens must have "inalienable" rights amounting to freedom. These rights should generate political and civic sensibilities and participation. In practice, liberal democratic regimes are more representative than participatory, with elected officials and with appointed and merit-based bureaucracies. Together, these bodies manage the state and exercise actual governance, embodying power in and over civil and market society. The inclusiveness and pluralism of such societies is ostensibly reflected in these regimes.

Liberal democratic regimes, which exist in consolidated form in over 30 countries, currently are the dominant regime type. Many formerly authoritarian regimes are in transition to liberal democracies, lending support to what some call "the globalization of democracy." A premise of this celebration is that capitalism and democracy are natural and necessary partners. Authoritarian regimes, however, have coexisted with capitalism, in every part of the world. As a harsh judgment puts it, "for capitalism, democracy if possible, but not necessarily." This polemic highlights a basic tension in liberal democracies. There may be formal political democracy and citizen equality in such regimes, but there is not an equivalent economic democracy and market equality. Market societies are characterized by the concentration and centralization of property and wealth in private hands, and their regimes tend to prioritize "ruling class" interests. Historically, this tension has been managed either by force or by the state's appropriation and redistribution of some of the wealth generated by the "operation of the free market." Thus, liberal democracies have taken a social democratic form. The state acts to bring the citizenry's social and economic status closer to the political equality all formally enjoy.

The term **corporatism** is applied to the state-directed arrangements between business and labour, and between organized civil society and government that social democratic policy agendas seem to require. Critics point to the political functions of such policy and arrangements. In short, the majority accept the "undemocratic" market as legitimate in exchange for a "social share" of the wealth that the "market" produces. Theoretically, the electorate could choose to establish a socialist democracy, as in the 1970 election of Allende in Chile. Such a regime would "resolve" the basic tension by "socializing" the capitalist economy/market (Allende's government acquired significant sectors of the economy, compensating the owners), just as liberal democracy had "socialized" political authority.

Critics consider liberal democracies in the core to be fundamentally "ruling class regimes," and they are sceptical regarding newly democratizing regimes in former "authoritarian capitalist" countries in the Third World and "post-socialist" countries in the Second World. Usually, critics associate neo-liberal policy and globalization, which favour core economies and periphery/semi-periphery elites, with those post-authoritarian regimes. They argue that formal democracy is accompanied by "savage capitalism" and a deterioration in living standards. Some argue that "oligarchic," "limited," or "dependent democracy" better describe these regimes. They insist that working-class, peasant, and leftist movements were crushed or severely weakened by decades of repression and now have no significant role in competitive electoral politics, making post-authoritarian regimes less democratic. Some view the political conditionality of international financial institutions' debt-restructuring policies as an imposition of vacuous democratic processes and institutions. As with authoritarian regimes, however, we should consider "democracies-in-transition" across all four spheres of the regime, acknowledging multiple sources of democratic impulses.

An illustration of this latter point is the rapid transformations of authoritarian socialist regimes into liberal democracies. It was not only "flawed" global insertion that brought their demise; the other three spheres need explanatory inclusion. Transitional regimes are characterized according to emphasis on one or another sphere. For example, some term Russia's successive economic crises and the impoverishment of the majority its "Third Worldization." Others focus on patterns of capital accumulation and certain business successes as "primitive capitalist accumulation" or "gangster capitalism." In the formal political realm, the assessment of democracy seems to follow the electoral fortunes of particular individuals, such as Yeltsin and Putin, as much as it does "efficiency" in governance or public opinion poll results. Fears are expressed about a "return to socialism," virulent nationalism, Russian imperial designs, instability, and even fascism.

Clearly, the transition from authoritarian socialist regimes is fraught with uncertainties. The composite modes of accumulation that comprise post-socialist regimes across the four spheres have been profoundly altered. It is not clear who constitutes the "ruling class," and the state is often incoherent. The majority's exposure to the non-democratic aspects of the capitalist market has been abrupt, and society has been thrown into decomposition and fragmentation. Global reinsertion, overall, has led to political and economic decline.

Revolutionary Regimes

Transitions underway in post-socialist regimes resemble the transformational dynamics of revolutionary regimes. A number of core countries have had democratic (state sphere), bourgeois/middle class (society sphere), and capitalist (market sphere) revolutions, though not socialist revolutions. Some early twentieth-century

TABLE 7.3 *Liberal Democratic Regimes*

TYPE	EXAMPLE
Representative	Canada, United States, India
Social democratic	Sweden
New democratizing	Nigeria
Corporatist	Germany, France, Japan
Socialist	Chile 1970–73
Oligarchic	Columbia

revolutions (Mexico 1910, China 1949) combined nationalism with a partial socialism. But generally, we associate twentieth-century revolutions with Marxism, centrally planned economy and suppression of capitalism, Communist Party monopoly, and commitment to the interests of the working class over others.

Failed socialist revolutionary efforts significantly outnumber actual revolutionary regimes, but two sets of circumstances seem to favour the latter—international wars and national liberation struggles. The Bolshevik (Russian) and Chinese Revolutions emerged from World Wars I and II, respectively. From the 1930s to the 1970s, anti-colonial and anti-imperialist struggles in Asia and Africa assumed a Marxist revolutionary character. Dozens of attempts to replicate the Cuban Revolution of 1959 took place throughout Latin America, all considering themselves anti-imperialist and anti-capitalist. Only one achieved state power—the 1979 Sandinista Revolution in Nicaragua. Few revolutionary movements have been able to gain power through formal democratic means. A rare example is the Popular Unity coalition that elected Salvador Allende in Chile in 1970, only to be overthrown by an American-backed military coup in 1973.

Given that most revolutionary regimes are born in violence, it is not surprising that many have had strong militaristic, security, and disciplinary elements. Defending the revolution, confronting capitalist and other domestic opposition, launching massive projects of "socialist economic accumulation," especially socialization of commerce, collectivization of agriculture, and rapid industrialization—all these tasks seemed to require authoritarian regimes. Democratic procedures were considered dangerous opportunities for the class enemy—unaffordable luxuries that impeded central planning and the creation of socialist values—or to be postponed until socialism matured into communism.

World War II's destructive impact on state, society, and economy, along with strategic dispositions at its end, combined with the Cold War in Europe and Asia to cast countries into opposing regime types. Liberal democracies were established in Germany and Japan. Dual authoritarian regimes divided Korea, while socialist regimes prevailed in Eastern Europe, experiencing authoritarian patterns as well as surges of liberalization. Their experiments in "market socialism" foreshadowed a hybrid of social democracy and socialism. Such an "evolutionary socialist" regime would combine the political processes and institutions of liberal democracy with a majority political culture of socialist values. The command economy model would become much more responsive to market principles, permitting small private enterprise, large worker-controlled cooperatives, and engagement with fully capitalist economies through trade and investment.

Marxist political strategy, centrally planned industrialization, and agricultural collectivization held strong appeal for many independence movements in Asia and Africa. The Soviet Union's rapid industrialization provided an example. After its 1949 revolution, China also provided an example, especially because of its official anti-colonial and anti-imperialist idealogy. Both communist countries, thus, became "natural allies" for national liberation movements. A number of those movements came to power and affiliated with the "socialist community," with trade and aid, arms, and advisors becoming integral to their regimes.

TABLE 7.4 *Selected Revolutionary Regimes*

Classic Communist	Russia (1917)
Nationalist-Reformist	Mexico (1910)
Nationalist-Marxist	Cuba (1959)
Marxist-Nationalist Liberationist	Angola (1975)
Marxist-Nationalist, Anti-imperialist	Vietnam (1975)
Islamic-Nationalist	Iran (1979)
Nationalist, Socialist Anti-imperialist	Nicaragua (1979)

While Marxist revolutionary ideology certainly emphasized internationalism and solidarity, most Third World revolutionary regimes concentrated on the spheres of state, society, and market. Replacing the previous regime, trying to transform social and class relations, and creating a national identity and a viable socialist economy absorbed the energy of people undertaking those tasks. These transitions would not have been easy in the best of global circumstances. Yet, the achievements, measured by increased equality, reduced exploitation, and marked improvements in quality-of-life indices for many Third World revolutionary regimes cannot be discounted.

Future Trends

THE HISTORICAL PREPONDERANCE OF AUTHORITARIAN REGIMES IS NOW strongly contrasted by consolidated and transitional liberal democratic regimes. Neither type is guaranteed, though revolutions are more likely to issue from authoritarian than from democratic regimes. All four spheres should be considered in determining whether transitional regimes in both Third and Second Worlds become consolidated democracies. People are more likely to adopt a revolutionary stance against a repressive authoritarian regime than a democratic one, even if the democracy is limited or corrupt. The expected stresses of democratic transitions, when exacerbated by the unevenness of globalizing capitalist accumulation, are more likely to lead to renewed authoritarian forms than to revolution. But the circumstances become more volatile, even for liberal democracies, when economic recession/depression increases marginalization and immiseration, especially when the wealth of the privileged is evident.

War, of course, introduces other factors prompting regime change. Both Marxists and Weberians would agree on that point, but we are already witnessing other outcomes. In parts of Western Africa and in Somalia, it is possible to speak of failed states, vacated states, or non-regimes. In some situations of humanitarian disasters, such as war, genocide, and famine, there have been temporary but functional United Nations peacekeeping regimes, non-governmental organization aid regimes, or proxy regimes operated by a militarily intervening neighbour. Since the events of September 11, 2001, there are American occupation regimes in Afghanistan and Iraq. In a certain sense, these are all forms of transnationalized regimes.

The manifold processes we call economic globalization also hold regime implications. Whether in Export Processing Zones or in countries where global corporations are the most important economic and political actors, there is a semblance of corporate feudalism, much like the "banana republics" of the early twentieth century, which operated as fruit company fiefdoms. And with the evident power of finance capital, currency markets, banks, and international financial institutions to affect governments' borrowing, debt-restructuring, and budgets, we have in effect yet another realm of transnationalized governance.

None of these transnationalized forms amounts to a full regime across the four spheres, yet clearly sovereignty is affected. In many instances, we could speak of "layered" regimes, some exercising governance over single spheres, some operating at local, regional, and national levels, and others transnationalized. Layered experiences, in fact, are not limited to poor, peripheral, or transitional regimes. Richer or larger countries, however, are generally better able to resist the transnationalization and layering of governance across their four spheres.

Summary

This chapter provided a definition of *regime* for comparative studies of governance. The four spheres that regimes control and coordinate are state, society, market, and global insertion. In surveying regimes of the twentieth century, it is clear that attributes of one regime type are often found in another. Democratic aspects of authoritarian regimes, for example, should not be ignored. Similarly, many democratic regimes have manifested authoritarian features. It is helpful to think of concrete regimes as composites or hybrids, both unique and comparable within a typology. We have seen, for example, that both authoritarian and liberal democratic regimes in capitalist countries employ corporatist arrangements to manage business/labour relations and public policy. We have also seen some convergence of social democracy and democratic socialism, though perhaps more in theory than in practice. And some revolutionary regimes have engaged with democratic pluralism and experimented with "market socialism." As the processes of globalization accelerate, variations in contemporary political regimes are both expanding and contracting. In this century as in the last, we should expect regime diversity and more regime composites.

Discussion Questions

1. What do you think will be the impact of globalization on our current typology of regimes?
2. Why were authoritarian regimes so common in the twentieth century?

3. Where are revolutions possible in the twenty-first century? Why?
4. What kind of regime or combination of regimes best suits the problems of governance in the current era of intensifying globalization?

Further Readings

Hobsbawm, E. J. 1994. *The Age of Extremes: A History of the World, 1914–1991.* New York: Pantheon Books.

Marx, Karl. 1967. *The Communist Manifesto* with an introduction and notes by A. J. P. Taylor. Harmondsworth: Penguin Books.

Weber, Max. 1949. *Max Weber on the Methodology of the Social Sciences* translated and edited by Edward A. Shils and Henry A. Finch; foreword by Edward A. Shils. Glencoe: Free Press.

Weblinks

Comparative Politics Online: Internet Resources
http://classweb.gmu.edu/chauss/cponline/links.htm

Comparative Politics
www.psr.keele.ac.uk/area.htm

U.S. State Department Background Notes
www.state.gov/www/background_notes/index.html

CHAPTER 8

THE MODERN STATE

LOIS HARDER

Objectives

The state is the core concept in political science that identifies where the formal and institutional terrain of politics begins and ends. There have been many different kinds of states in recorded history, ranging from the early Greek city state to the modern liberal democratic state. All states, however, perform similar tasks, such as making and implementing political decisions and protecting communities from internal and external threats. This chapter explores the role of the modern state that traces its origin to sixteenth-century western Europe. We will discuss the primary roles performed by the modern state as well as three different variations of the liberal-democratic state that have prevailed in western societies for the past two centuries. Finally, we will explore the future of the national state in the contemporary global era.

Introduction

All societies, from the most simple to the most complex, have organized some way to govern themselves. History has witnessed many experiments in government and many different kinds of states. Some have been efficient and enduring while others have been decided disasters. States have been a pervasive fact of our collective political history. Their sheer number and variety, however, evade a simple definition. The famous political sociologist, Max Weber, described the state as a distinct entity that can "successfully claim the monopoly of the legitimate use of physical force within a given territory" (1947, 154). Others make the rather circular argument that the state is the other side of civil society. Liberals tend to define the state as the public sector and contrast it to the private realm of the economy and the family. The state is, thus, contrasted to those areas of social life—the domestic world; the economic sphere; and cultural activities—organized by private and voluntary arrangements, individuals, and groups. (Held, 1996, 57).

Sometimes, the terms *state* and *government* are used interchangeably, but it is important to draw a distinction between the two terms. One way to think about the difference between state and government is to imagine a car and its driver. The car is analogous to the state, while the driver is analogous to government. All cars have certain components that are required for them to run and that distinguish them from other modes of transportation. These components may be organized in a variety of ways and may be more or less powerful depending on the car's design. Similarly, all states perform certain basic functions, such as maintaining the rules through which people interact, though some states may do this more actively than others. Obviously, a driver is essential if the car is to move, but there is no requirement that the driver always be the same. Different drivers may treat the car differently and may choose to steer the vehicle in different paths. They may be more active or passive, but there are limits as to what the machine itself will bear.

Consider the replacement of one political party by another within a modern liberal democracy. A **liberal democracy** is the system of government in which citizens elect representatives in periodic elections. When a new party is elected to form the government, voters have chosen to alter the leadership or policy orientation of the government by selecting a party that will drive the state differently. The offices of the state remain largely the same. The positions of president or prime minister remains, as do general institutions and constitutions. In other words, the offices of the state persist despite the change in government, although the policies pursued by these departments may be altered.

Political Scientists generally trace the origins of the modern state to the Treaty of Westphalia of 1648. The treaty brought an end to almost 150 years of religious and territorial conflicts and settled the Thirty Years' War, the first pan-European war. In one sense, the Treaty of Westphalia was simply an agreement to cease hostilities and impose specific terms of settlement. But it also laid the foundations for the elaboration of what we now understand as the modern state, as well as articulating the rules that govern interstate relations, even to the present day (Valaskis, 2001, 49–55).

Contributions of the Treaty of Westphalia to the Modern State System are as follows:

- Recognition of the primacy of sovereignty. Each state exercises absolute authority over the fixed geographic territory it governs, and the national state is recognized as the ultimate power in international relations.
- Emergence of international law based on treaties between sovereign countries. All states are regarded as equal before the law (Held, 1996, 70).
- War is retained as a recognized instrument of international relations and the ultimate expression of sovereignty (Valaskis, 2001).

What States Do

After recognizing the modern state's territoriality and sovereignty, political scientists typically study the state in terms of what it does. The most important among these are its legislative, executive, administrative, and judicial functions. It is important to recognize that while all states perform these roles, the specific mechanisms or institutions that perform them vary from one country to another and across time. In the liberal democratic systems that are the focus of this chapter, for example, institutional configurations vary most sharply between presidential and parliamentary systems.

Generally speaking, the *legislative function* of the state is concerned with the making of laws. Who makes the laws, what areas of social life are open to law making, and how the process of law making will occur are all dimensions of the legislative function. The legislative function is undertaken by people formally elected as legislators, although the executive and the bureaucracy also play an influential role in law making. For the purposes of this discussion, however, we are concerned with two broad approaches to the role of legislatures. In a congressional model of government, such as that of the United States, the power of the legislature (or Congress) is separated from that of the executive (the president and the cabinet). In such a system, the legislature plays an active role in the legislative process. By contrast, in parliamentary systems of government, such as that of Canada, the United Kingdom, Australia, and New Zealand, there is a fusion of legislative and executive powers. Hence, the initiation and formulation of legislation is largely undertaken by the executive (the prime minister and the cabinet), while the legislature serves an overseeing and approval function.

The active role of legislatures in congressional systems results from the strict separation of power that characterizes this system. The architects of the American Constitution—the originators of the congressional model—were particularly concerned with limiting the powers of the state generally and also ensuring that no single branch of the state would dominate the others. As a result, they implemented a system of checks and balances through which the legislature (the House of Representatives and the Senate) and the executive (the President), while having unique responsibilities, also have the power to review each other's decisions. For example, executive choices for judges to sit on the U.S. Supreme Court are subject to confirmation by the Senate. Bills passed by Congress must receive the assent of the President before they become law. In both situations, the opportunity exists to overturn the desired action of the President or Congress, respectively.

Fixed terms of office (the American president serves four years, members of the House of Representatives two years, and Senators six years) and separate electoral contests for these branches of government further reinforce the separation, tension, and distinct powers of the legislature and executive. Although citizens of parliamentary democracies sometimes envy the degree of legislative autonomy built into the congressional model, it does have its drawbacks. The legislative process can be very drawn out and unwieldy with no guarantee that the platform of either the President or the majority party in either house of Congress will be realized. Indeed, if any legislative action is to occur, co-operation between the branches of government is essential. When the executive and legislature are controlled by different political parties, a situation that characterized most of Bill Clinton's presidency (Democrat president and Republican House and Senate) and the first two years of George W. Bush's presidency (Democrat majority in the Senate, Republican control of the House and the presidency), the process of law making can be especially challenging. Bush's initial efforts to pursue oil exploration in Alaska's Arctic National Wildlife Refuge, for example, were stymied by Senate resistance.

In contrast to the separation of powers in the congressional system, parliamentary systems of government are characterized by the fusion of the legislative and executive branches. Rather than holding separate elections for these branches, a single electoral process is undertaken. The leader of the party that gains the most seats in that election is then named as prime minister (PM). The PM then chooses the members of his/her cabinet (also known as ministers of government departments) generally from among the elected members of his/her party. The PM and the cabinet then constitute the executive, also known as the government. The remaining elected representatives serve as legislators.

Fixed terms of office are not a feature of the parliamentary system, although there is a maximum time limit that a government can remain in office before an election must be called. This creates a situation in which the government must maintain the confidence of the legislature in order to remain in office—a feature of parliamentary systems known as responsible government. If the executive is unable to maintain this confidence (that is, majority support of the elected members), the government must resign and, usually, an election will ensue. It has become accepted practice, however, that governments are only obliged to resign when they are defeated on a money bill—generally the budget.

Because of this uncertain tenure, party discipline is a key feature of parliamentary governments. It is only through the reliable support of all government party members, be the members of the executive (cabinet) or the legislature (backbenchers), which the government can be assured of its ongoing survival. Of course, this situation does not require that all members of the various opposition parties vote along party lines. Nonetheless, if they are to represent themselves as a potential alternative to the current government, a coherent voice of opposition is the logical stance to assume.

While legislatures form the heart of democratic representation and policy making, in recent years the growing complexity of law making has shifted the active process away from legislatures and toward the bureaucracy and the executive. The result has been a decline in parliament, with elected legislators serving an overseeing role and rubber-stamping initiatives taken elsewhere.

In both presidential and parliamentary systems, the formal role of a state's executive is to implement the laws passed by legislators. Presidents and prime ministers, assisted by members of the cabinet, oversee the implementation process within specific areas of jurisdiction. They set the policy agenda, determining which issues will command the most attention. This function has been referred to as steering (Osborne, 1992).

Obviously, it is the head of government—that is the president or prime minister—who is the most prominent member of the executive. But these positions are not synonymous, given the rather distinctive systems of government in which they operate. As we noted previously, in order for the president's agenda and decisions to be accepted, a high degree of co-operation with the legislature is required. As a result, a considerable portion of the president's staff and executive offices are engaged in this process of negotiation. The president does have a cabinet, but its members are selected by the president from the country at large, rather than from among the elected representatives. Cabinet members serve at the discretion of the president and are not responsible to either congress or voters.

The prime minister, as both the leader of the largest party in parliament and the head of the cabinet, has a great deal more control over the policy agenda than his presidential counterpart. Nonetheless, the prime minister does not simply proclaim her wishes to cabinet members and proceed to pass legislation through parliament. Instead, the cabinet works together to formulate the general principles of the government's legislative program, and cabinet members stand together to support this program.

An additional distinction that must be drawn between the roles of the chief executives in presidential and parliamentary systems is the designation *head of state.* The term "head of state" refers to the symbolic representation of a country's identity both to its own citizens and to the world. This symbolism is embodied in the person of the President in the United States, who also serves as the head of government. In Canada, the head of state is the Queen or, more practically, her representative, the Governor General, while the Prime Minister serves as the head of government. In functional terms, however, the president and the prime minister serve as the highest ranking decision maker for his/her country in international forums. Advocates of the separation of these executive functions observe that, under circumstances in which a government's reputation is sullied by scandal, the broader reputation of the country remains unblemished when it is represented by someone who is detached from the gritty world of politics. The example of the Watergate scandal that eventually forced President Nixon from the White House is generally offered as evidence for the benefits of a split executive.

Non-elected officials, however, undertake the majority of executive functions. In this regard, we might think of the offices and agencies we typically recognize as the bureaucracy. Unlike the elected politicians or political appointments that make up the cabinet and are expected to steer, the role of the bureaucracy is to row (Osborne, 1992). Their job is not to set the overall policy direction but to provide the means by which that policy direction can be achieved.

In simple terms, the act of administering is one of making distinct entities work toward a set of common goals. Co-ordination is central to successful administration. The governance of society is a highly complex administrative task, in terms of the relationships both among the state, citizens, organizations, and corporate entities and within the myriad offices of the state itself. It should not be surprising, then, that administration is a key function of the state. It is made more complex in a democratic society by the demand for accountability. As citizens, we want to know how decisions are made and why things are done as they are. This demand for knowledge requires that the trail of decision making be easily followed.

As Western democracies have attempted reduce the size of the state in recent years, many governments shifted some administrative functions to the private sphere. The delivery of some social services, for example, has been taken over by community groups, private agencies are contracted to undertake accounting functions and public utilities have been sold to private interests. Although selling off public services or contracting to private providers may reduce the size of the government's budget, the ability to ensure that these private entities work in the service of the public good is circumscribed, and hence the trail of decision making can be obscured. Further, the opportunity for governments to reward supporters through the granting of contracts can counter the cost-saving rationale of privatization and undermine the government's credibility. In Canada, the scandal surrounding fraudulent and/or overpayments under a federal sponsorship program to Quebec-based public relations firms with strong Liberal ties has been an ongoing embarrassment for the governing party.

The fourth function integral to the state is the judicial function. Laws are not always precise, and hence there may be differing views as to if and how they should be enforced. It is the state's role to undertake this process of determining whether actions fit within the purview of the law. The largest share of this function is undertaken by a country's court system, but judicial functions may also be undertaken in less formal settings with less punitive outcomes. The state is also responsible for ensuring that the "rule of law" is upheld. Effectively, the rule of law refers to the conditions that must exist for a law to be justified. Certain procedures must be followed in the development of law in order for it to be considered valid; the punishment for breaking a law must be the same for all people; and laws must apply to everyone equally, regardless of their position within society.

Since the implementation of the *Canadian Charter of Rights*, concerns have arisen regarding the degree to which the courts have extended their powers beyond adjudication and into the realm of making law. Some critics of the *Charter* argue that in usurping Parliament as the ultimate law-making authority, the Supreme Court enables social movements (dubbed "the Court Party" by their detractors) to bypass the democratic process of political debate and obliges society to recognize identities and practices that they would otherwise not support (Morton and Knopff, 2000). Gay and lesbian marriages are an example. On the other side of this debate, social movements argue that legal challenges are only one strategy in their struggle for recognition and that being granted a right is often more symbolic than substantive.

So far, we have outlined the basic functions of the state. However, knowing that all states fulfill legislative, executive, administrative, and judicial functions does not tell us much about how power operates within states or about how that operation of power may be altered over time. In order to begin exploring these questions, we can examine some of the different forms assumed by the liberal democratic state.

Variations on the Liberal Democratic State

EARLIER IN THIS CHAPTER, WE EXPLORED THE ANALOGY BETWEEN CAR AND state and between driver and government. Within the context of that discussion, it was asserted that drivers may change but the structure of the car remains more or less the same. Over time, however, the vehicle's structure is subject to innovation and redesign in response to new demands and conditions in which it must operate. Similarly, the form of the state has also undergone transformations. Revolutions represent the most dramatic method of altering the form of the state, shifting dictatorships to democracies, as in the case of the former Soviet republics, and democracies to dictatorships, as occurred in Guatemala in 1956 and Chile in 1973. Less radically, modern liberal-democratic states also evolve and transform. These changes in state form are significant because they reflect a reordering or rebalancing of power within society and, as such, indicate the parameters framing citizen participation in their own governance. For the purposes of this introduction we will examine three liberal democratic state forms that have been implemented in Western liberal democracies. These include the *night watchman* or *minimalist* state, which saw its most profound incarnation in Britain's industrial revolution; the welfare state, which prevailed, in varying degrees within all Western liberal democracies in the period between the 1930s and the early 1970s; and the neo-liberal state, which is currently in the process of being embraced, again with numerous variations, on a global scale.

The Night Watchman State

It is not surprising that Marx, writing in the mid-nineteenth century during Britain's industrial revolution, would assert that the state was nothing more than "an executive committee of the whole bourgeoisie." He was arguing that the state operated solely in the interests of capital. During this period, participation in elections and the holding of public office was limited to property owners who had little compulsion to consider the interests of the majority of the population. Due to the unprecedented level of technological development that was occurring during this period, the production of goods increased at an astounding rate and industrialists were enriched accordingly. Agents of the state and elected representatives, most of whom were part-time politicians and full-time businessmen, saw their role as facilitating economic growth, primarily by allowing the market to function in as unencumbered a fashion as possible. In practice, this meant intervening as little as possible in the economy while upholding the laws of property, contract, weight and measurement, and the criminal code.

On the surface, the night watchman state, also termed the *laissez-faire* and minimalist state, appears passive, but its effects on the majority of people were profound. In the absence of any regulation of the conditions of work and the length of the working day, business owners required their employees to labour for long periods of time in dangerous environments. Further, poor laws were implemented, which, rather than providing a means of subsistence, subjected the jobless to increased misery and forced labour. The rationale behind this treatment was to make the condition of unemployment so terrible that people would be willing to labour under undesirable circumstances in order to avoid the even more horrendous conditions of the poor house. By refusing to play a role in regulating the workplace, the state appeared to be acting passively. However, for the majority of the population, this passivity had significant consequences in terms of their health and their independence. While business owners enjoyed an impressive level of personal liberty, such was not the case for workers who were the vast majority of the population.

This minimalist approach to the regulation of business—the distance between the rhetoric of equality, liberty, and solidarity that imbued the liberal democratic tradition and the real conditions of life for the majority of people—could not be maintained indefinitely. It became increasingly apparent that the long-term success of capitalism was not being well served through employment practices that regularly left workers debilitated and, hence, unable to provide for themselves. To persist with such practices would mean that either factories would run out of workers or that workers would become so disillusioned or angered by their ill-treatment that they would organize to overthrow their employers and perhaps the state as well. Moreover, as governments were increasingly pressured to broaden the electorate on the basis of the contribution that non–property-holders were making to the growth of the economy, politicians were compelled to address the demands of workers as well as owners in order to secure their re-election. It would take the Great Depression of the 1930s, however, before sufficient support for a more interventionist role for the liberal-democratic state was achieved.

The Welfare State

The economic crisis that gripped the world in the aftermath of the American stock market crash in October 1929 represented a dramatic challenge to the existing economic and political order. The breadth of the collapse cast so many workers into the ranks of the unemployed that it was no longer possible to blame individuals and their moral weaknesses for their inability to find work. It was clear that some action on the part of the state would have to be undertaken in order to prevent people from perishing and to salvage failing capitalist economies. It was during this period that social welfare and unemployment insurance programs began to be implemented and legislation that facilitated workplace organization by trade unions was put into place. It should be noted, however, that these initiatives, particularly in Canada and the United States, were rather tentative in their initial stages. In fact, it was only after World War II that most of the policies and programs of the welfare state were elaborated.

The devastation wrought by the war to the economies of Europe and Japan and the sacrifice of so many soldiers' and civilians' lives were powerful catalysts for a rethinking of the role of the state within society. It was clear that an active state would be necessary to rebuild wartorn countries. Further, the enfranchisement of virtually the entire adult population of most Western countries meant that the interests of a broad range of the population would have to be incorporated within the decision-making process. It was under these conditions that the welfare state realized its fullest expression.

Wanting to prevent further economic dislocations of such magnitude, governments in Western industrialized countries attempted to regulate their economies through the taxing and spending, or fiscal, policies first advocated by the British economist John Maynard Keynes. Keynes and the governments that took up his ideas wanted to balance out the boom-and-bust cycles that are characteristic of capitalist economies. Rather than leaving the market to sort itself out on its own, Keynesianism promoted state intervention through fiscal and monetary policy instruments. In times of economic downturn, governments would use their capacity to borrow as well as the revenues generated during times of growth to inject funds into the economy. Make-work projects, such as bridge and road construction and other public works initiatives, as well as unemployment insurance and social assistance payments would ensure that people had money to purchase goods, maintain demand, and fuel production. In order to offset the deficits created during these periods of economic downturn, the state would extract surplus funds during periods of economic growth, thereby creating a balanced budget over the long term.

The welfare state also is associated with a variety of universal social programs, including public education, health care, child care, and wage replacement programs, such as unemployment insurance, old age pensions, maternity benefits, and social assistance. Of course, not every country offered the same range of services. Neither were services equally generous across national borders. In the Anglo-American democracies of Canada, Great Britain, the United States, and Australia, for example, many social programs were not universally available to all citizens. Those with adequate incomes might be required to purchase services through the market, rather than relying on the state. Other services, particularly public education, would be available to all citizens regardless of income. With regard to services provided on an income, or means-tested, basis, citizens who could not afford to purchase services in the market were subject to the surveillance and regulations of state officials in order to prove their need and establish their worthiness. Often, this relationship between citizen and social worker could be quite paternalistic. It is not surprising, then, that as the economic interventionism of the welfare state came into question, so, too, did the interventionism of state agents in the lives of citizens.

Perhaps the greatest promise of the welfare state lay in its presumption that all citizens should be able to maintain a minimum standard of living—that there should be some rough equality, if not in terms of outcome, then certainly in terms of opportunity. Initially, this equality was to be realized among members of the working class. White male industrial workers and their families, in particular, was the object of these ambitions. Yet, many other groups were also interested in taking advantage of the opportunities promised by the welfare state. Hence, the post-war period is marked by the struggles of various groups. The Civil Rights movement, Aboriginal peoples, women, the disabled, and the youth demanded that the state include their concerns and perspectives within the policy-making process. These growing demands on state resources by groups previously marginalized within the economy and political process were perceived as a threat by the established order whose members had long benefited from those exclusionary practices. In addition to the economic crisis and the criticism of the welfare state's methods of service provision then, the welfare state was subject to criticism from groups that viewed the broadening of the welfare state's constituency as an unwarranted drain on increasingly limited resources, leading to demand overload and a crisis in governability. Others viewed them as a distraction from the more fundamental role of the state of ensuring the smooth functioning of the market.

As these criticisms intensified and various Western industrialized countries elected governments that reflected support for a rethinking of the welfare state, it underwent a profound crisis. Although certain elements of the welfare state persist in the state form prevalent in liberal democracies today, it would appear that a new arrangement between state and society is in the process of being consolidated. This new state form has been named the neo-liberal state.

The Neo-Liberal State

The central concern of the agencies of the neo-liberal state is to expand the terrain of the free market through cutbacks in social spending, the deregulation of industry and the privatization of public services (Yeatman, 1994). This objective is reminiscent of that of the night watchman state of nineteenth-century Britain. The current neo-liberal state, however, emerges amidst the increased complexity of contemporary societies, the historical experience of the welfare state, and popular expectations regarding the accountability of democratically elected governments. The welfare state both made the promise of equality and incorporated an ever-broadening circle of legitimate claims-makers within the purview of policy making. In the process, it created expectations of openness among those who wished to challenge the new state form. The neo-liberal state's emphasis on the primacy of the market, however, has closed many familiar avenues for groups to challenge its policy objectives. The political interventions of disadvantaged groups often are simply dismissed as reflecting "special interests" or as unwarranted impositions of "political correctness." It has become increasingly unpopular to make demands on the state. Instead, we, as individuals, are expected to look out for ourselves (Brodie, 1995).

The emergence of the neo-liberal state form reflects the belief that the power of the state has extended too far with deleterious consequences for the market and for individual freedom. According to its proponents, power would be better organized on the basis of the informal networks of the family, community, and market, with the state limiting its role to ensuring suitable conditions for economic growth. Neo-liberals assert that the national state should divest itself of those functions that impede the market's operation, particularly those that consume the greatest share of tax revenue, as well as state functions that attract political controversy. Governments at the regional level, but especially the local level, are viewed as more appropriate sites for political struggle, since the impact of such disputes can be confined within a limited geographic region (Kristol in Devigne, 1994).

Another significant motivation behind the push for the neo-liberal state is the desire to accommodate the global mobility of capital, particularly financial capital. In the attempt to address the problem of overproduction and declining profitability that contributed to the demise of the welfare state, large corporations began to shift their operations beyond their home countries. Subsequently, a global marketplace has been created, in which states compete with each other to attract and maintain increasingly mobile capital. In order to succeed in this process, many governments have chosen to reorient the state structures they administer so as to create an appealing environment for investors. While such an environment may be created through a highly educated and skilled workforce, a healthy population, a safe physical environment, and an efficient and effective infrastructure, such an approach requires high levels of public expenditure. Rather than making these investments, many governments have chosen, instead, to promote a low-wage workforce, minimum levels of regulation, and low taxes, especially for the corporate sector. Not surprisingly, levels of public service provision have been reduced accordingly. The degree of citizen participation in governance also has been reduced. International trade agreements, such as the North American Free Trade Agreement and the World Trade Organization, limit the range of policies available to governments. Proposals that might be perceived as infringing on profitability or protecting the domestic economy are open to challenge from other countries. The elevation of the economy and of trade liberalization as a primary organizing principle in public policy, in turn, gives financial managers and business interests inordinate influence in the policy-making process. The capacity of citizens to influence their national governments has been reduced, both in terms of opportunities and avenues of appeal and in terms of the social acceptability of organized dissent.

The State in a Globalizing Era

AS THE CONTEMPORARY PROCESS OF GLOBALIZATION HAS ADVANCED, SCHOLARS have engaged in lively debates concerning the ongoing relevance of the state. Reductions in barriers to the flow of goods, services, and finance capital and the promotion of production for global, rather than national, markets has created a situation in which economies no longer correspond to nation-states. In this context, it is asserted that the national state has been "hollowed out." Power has moved upward to international institutions, such as the WTO, outward to the market, and downward to sub-national levels of government, the family and the individual (Jessop 1993).

But as the effects of globalization become increasingly apparent, the voices of moderation are becoming louder. Even the most fervent supporters of the global market, from the World Bank to the World Economic Forum, now concede the need for a reinvigorated state and a renewed focus on the need for social cohesion and political stability. A "third way" between social democracy and neo-liberalism is being promoted in various liberal democracies, as a means to counter the alienating and exclusionary effects of competitive global markets (Brodie, 2003). Nonetheless, this third way does not represent a substantial reinvestment in social programs or an attempt to protect citizens from the market. Instead, the focus is on equipping populations to participate in the global marketplace and to ameliorate the worst effects of global capital on those most vulnerable (and, often, most likely to mobilize) to its operation.

The reassertion of a role for the national state is also evident in responses to the increased security concerns that have emerged after September 11, 2001. A raft of legislation has been passed in liberal democracies enabling national governments to infringe on democratic rights, including free speech, freedom of association, and the right to privacy. As these rights were enacted to protect citizens from the arbitrary use of state power, their diminishment is a clear representation of a perceived need for a strong state in the face of ambiguous but certain threats. The exercise of national-state power in areas ranging from security, disease, surveillance, immigration, and border controls aptly demonstrates that the national state continues to command considerable power.

Summary

This chapter demonstrates that the state is both constant in its enforcement and reflection of the power dynamics at work within a given society and adaptable to the historical circumstances in which it is situated. Although the state is often perceived as monolithic and impenetrable, a long-term view reveals that the institutions and functions of the state change considerably over time.

This introduction to the state has attempted to provide a sense of the breadth of this topic, an overview of the key functions of the state, a brief account of the various forms of the liberal democratic state and some consideration of contemporary challenges facing the state. In order to undertake this task, it was necessary to trace the origin of the concept of the state and clarify the distinction between state and government. All states—regardless of whether they are liberal democracies, dictatorships, or capitalist, command, or barter economies—must fulfill legislative, executive, administrative, and judicial functions. How these functions are fulfilled, however, depends on the specific political system and the character of a particular government.

Context also is central to the consideration of state forms. The transformation of the liberal democratic state from night watchman through welfare to a neo-liberal form demonstrates the dynamic character of the relationship between the state and the society it governs. The state is not fixed in time but is reformed through political struggle and altered circumstances. The study of the state should be viewed as a rich field of inquiry and one that, in all its complexity, is an essential component of the study of politics.

Discussion Questions

1. What are the primary functions of the state, and how do they relate to each other?
2. Assess the strengths and weaknesses of the congressional and parliamentary models of government.
3. Is it fair to say that Canada's national state is undergoing a change in its form? What evidence can you produce to support your claim?
4. What is the likelihood that international institutions will replace nation-states as the primary mechanisms for governance?

References

Brodie, Janine. 1995. *Politics at the Margins: Restructuring and the Canadian Women's Movement.* Halifax: Fernwood.

———. 2003. "Globalization, In/Security, and the Paradoxes of the Social" in Isabella Bakker and Stephen Gill. *Power, Production and Social Reproduction.* London: Palgrave.

Devigne, Robert. 1994. *Recasting Conservatism: Oakeshott, Strauss and the Response to Postmodernism.* New Haven: Yale University Press.

Held, David. 1996. "The Development of the Modern State" in Stuart Hall, David Held, Don Hubert and Kenneth Thompson, eds. *Modernity.* London: Blackwell.

Jessop, Bob. 1993. "Towards a Schumpeterian Workfare State? Preliminary Remarks on a Post-Fordist Political Economy." *Studies in Political Economy* 40: 7–39.

Morton, F.L. and Rainer Knopff. 2000. *The Charter Revolution and the Court Party.* Peterborough: Broadview Press.

Osborne, David. 1992. *Reinventing Government: How the Entrepreneurial Spirit is Transforming the Public Sector.* Reading, Mass.: Addison-Wesley Publishing.

Valaskakis, Kimon. 2001. "Long-term Trends in Global Governance: From 'Westphalia' to 'Seattle'" in *Organization for Economic Cooperation and Development, Governance in the 21st Century*. Paris: OECD. 45–66.

Weber, Max. 1947. *The Theory of Social and Economic Organization.* New York: Free Press.

Yeatman, Anna. 1994. *Postmodern Revisionings of the Political.* London: Routledge.

Further Readings

Pierson, Christopher. 1998. *The Modern State.* London: Routledge.

Held, David. 1989. *Political Theory and the Modern State: Essays on State, Power and Democracy.* Stanford: Stanford University Press.

McBride, Stephen. 2001. *Paradigm Shift: Globalization and the Canadian State.* Halifax: Fernwood Publishing.

Weblinks

Political Resources on the Net
www.sosig.ac.uk/politics

Government of Canada
www.gc.ca

United States Government
www.firstgov.gov

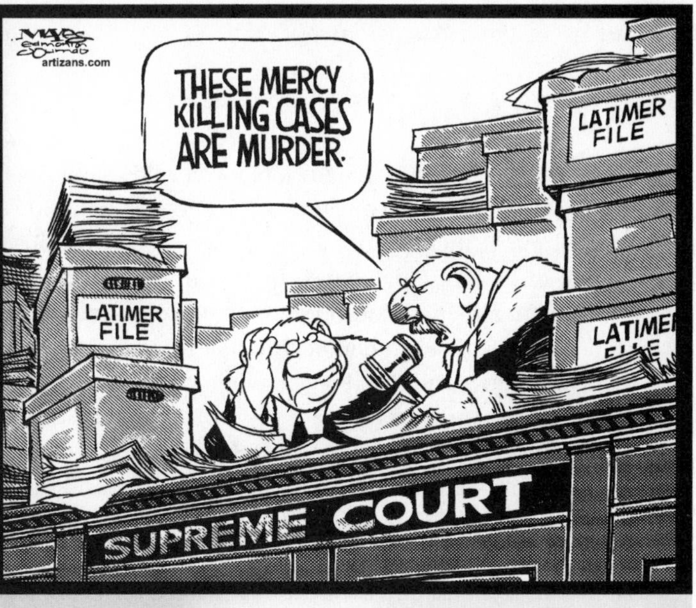

CHAPTER 9

CONSTITUTIONS AND THE RULE OF LAW

Objectives

Constitutions provide the blueprints for modern government. In this chapter, we examine the importance of the rule of law to governing in liberal democracies. We also will consider what constitutional provisions and change tell us about a country's politics. We will explore the difference between political systems governed by written and unwritten constitutions, as well as the critical importance of constitutional conventions or customs. We will discuss how constitutions may or may not divide sovereignty between national and regional governments, how constitutions are changed, and several features distinguishing parliamentary from presidential systems. We end by taking a critical look at the idea that written constitutions are crucial to the protection of the rights of citizens.

IAN URQUHART

Introduction

The capture of Saddam Hussein, former President Bill Clinton's sexual indiscretions, the arrests of drug squad officers in Toronto on corruption charges—other than high drama, what might these events share? How can they possibly be related to constitutions? The **rule of law**, a fundamental concept in democratic politics, is the thread joining these stories together and, through them, to constitutions. My appreciation of the importance of the rule of law to democratic politics came late in my student life, as a graduate student, when I read the 1985 language rights decision of the Supreme Court of Canada in *Reference re Manitoba Language Rights.* There, the Supreme Court said that the rule of law demanded at least two things. First, it required "that the law is supreme over officials of the government as well as private individuals, and thereby preclusive of the influence of arbitrary power." This statement outlines what will trap rogue drug squad officers who act "above the law." They exercise arbitrary, not legal, power. It will be up to a jury of their peers to decide whether the label "arbitrary" or "legal" should be attached to their actions. In Washington, those who dogged President Clinton for allegedly lying under oath and obstructing justice used the same rationale in response to the President's contention that he enjoyed absolute immunity from the ordinary criminal law process while in office. To his foes, this violated a fundamental premise of the rule of law: all citizens are subordinate to the law, regardless of wealth, social status, or political position.

Saddam Hussein's capture, more particularly his eventual trial, may be tied to the second condition demanded by the Supreme Court. Here, the rule of law "requires the creation and maintenance of an actual order of positive laws which preserves and embodies the more general principle of normative order. Law and order are indispensable elements of civilized life." Ensuring a fair trial for Hussein is essential to attempts to establish the legitimacy of overthrowing his government. Hussein's trial must respect these ideas in order to promote the Anglo-American notion of democratization in Iraq.

The principle of the rule of law, as Canada's Supreme Court argued, is implicit in the very nature of a constitution. The constitution stands out as the most important source of legal authority. Its overarching importance arises from the fact that constitutional provisions regulate the fundamental operations of the political system and the relationships between the system's key political institutions. Constitutions offer us basic information about the rules of the political game, who is allowed to play, and who is likely to play starring and supporting roles.

The United States Constitution illustrates this point well. Its first three Articles clearly delineate the separation of powers among the legislature, the executive, and the judiciary. The Article I locates the legislative power in the United States in the House of Representatives and the Senate. It goes on to outline the structure and powers of these institutions, the qualifications needed to run for electoral office, and the timing of elections. What powers does the president have? Who can run for president? Questions like these are answered in Article II's discussion of the executive powers of the presidency. Information about the responsibilities of the federal courts rests in Article III.

Not all written constitutions, however, offer good guidance to how a political system operates or the values it respects. In Zimbabwe, for example, government-orchestrated political violence and human rights abuses thrive despite the constitution's impressive written commitment to rights. In liberal democracies, too, political practice may stray—but in far less severe ways—from the expectations raised by written constitutional documents. Sometimes, as discussed later in this chapter, constitutional conventions are responsible for such departures. On other occasions, these departures are best seen not as the absolute rejection of core constitutional values (e.g., freedom of speech or equality) but, rather, as expressions of debates about the spheres of our lives in which these constitutional rights should govern behaviour.

Constitutions as Barometers of Political Conflict

CONSTITUTIONS SHOULD BE STUDIED FOR REASONS OTHER THAN FOR WHAT they tell us about how the political process operates. Constitutions bear examination for what they reveal about the nature of political conflict and the balance of political power in the countries we study. The evolution of constitutional documents and debates also tells us a great deal about the sorts of changes occurring in a society.

The drafting of the United States Constitution is instructive here. Shortly after the Declaration of Independence (1776) the 13 states drafted the Articles of Confederation. The Articles underlined emphatically that the War of Independence was a war against tyranny and for liberty. The revolutionaries had no desire to replace the British despot with a strong American central government that also could pose a threat to their liberty. In the Articles, the states guarded their sovereignty very jealously and ensured that the national government would be a weak and secondary level of government. Events during the subsequent decade suggested that hamstringing the national government was a serious constitutional error. An enfeebled national government was unable to maintain civil and economic order in the new Republic. Shays's Rebellion of 1786 supplies the exclamation mark for this observation. Disgruntled farmers, many of them veterans of the Revolutionary War, marched against a Massachusetts courthouse to stop farm foreclosures. When 12 of the 13 states refused to give Washington financial aid, the national government was powerless to respond. Although the Massachusetts militia ultimately quelled the rebellion, this event stood as an important sign that the United States government could not guarantee that it could preserve order or protect property.

These concerns provided the fuel for many of the debates during and following the Constitutional Convention of 1787. A strong national government was needed to ensure that the masses would not threaten the property of the rich or the order of America. The success of wealthy economic interests in securing a stronger national government is seen in various sections of the United States Constitution. Among other provisions, Article I outlines the military and commercial responsibilities entrusted to the national government. For example, Congress would issue all money in the United States, regulate interstate commerce, and raise an Army and Navy. The states could not pass laws excusing their citizens from paying their debts.

Canada's *Constitution Act* of 1867 provides a similar snapshot of the significant political conflicts that shaped Canada's formation. A number of the provisions in the *Constitution Act 1867* may be traced to the importance of the English/French tensions in the colonial politics of British North America. The political importance of "les Canadiens," the French-speaking population centred in Quebec, forced reluctant English-speaking politicians to accept a federal, rather than a unitary, political system. Such powers as education and property/civil rights were regarded as essential to the preservation of Catholicism and the French language and culture in Quebec. Consequently, they were entrusted to the provincial governments. Features of the Canadian parliamentary structure also testify to the importance of the French/English cleavage in the struggle to unite the British North-American colonies into one country. For example, Quebec was guaranteed 65 seats in the House of Commons, the same number of seats it claimed in the pre-Confederation legislative assembly. If Quebec's population fell, the province's political representation in the Commons would not fall below this minimum number.

The evolution of constitutions, like their creation, is also a valuable indicator of underlying political currents in societies. Throughout British history, constitutional developments, such as the *Reform Act* of 1832 or the *English Bill of Rights* of 1689 signalled the growth of Parliament's power, and of a growing middle class, at the expense of the monarchy. Since coming to power in 1997, Tony Blair's Labour government has pushed the United Kingdom onto a radical path of constitutional change. Devolution of power from Westminster to a Scottish Parliament, a Welsh National Assembly, and a Northern Ireland Assembly were significant changes to the British Constitution passed by the Blair government in 1998. Another significant constitutional change came in the shape of the *Human Rights Act*, a law incorporating the rights and freedoms outlined in the European Convention on Human Rights into British law. Finally, the Blair government has tackled the House of Lords. First, it eliminated the right of roughly 90 percent of the hereditary peers to sit and vote in the House of Lords. Then, after failing to generate a parliamentary consensus on change through a Royal Commission and a Joint Parliamentary Committee, the government proposed in the fall of 2003 to eliminate the remaining hereditary peers and to give the Appointments Commission (the independent body responsible for ensuring that appointments to the House of Lords are meritorious) a statutory basis. Taken together, these measures, which are responses to shifting balances in British politics and public opinion, have brought substantial constitutional change to Britain.

Amendments to the United States Constitution tell a similar story. They testify to how emerging political conflicts modified the political consensus forged in the Constitution. The American *Bill of Rights* of 1791—the first 10 amendments to the Constitution—harked back to the American Revolution's emphasis on individual liberty. The Constitution drafted at the Constitutional Convention of 1787 lacked an explicit commitment to protect individual freedoms. Those who feared that a strengthened national government would be emboldened enough to try on the robes of the English king demanded the addition of a list of guaranteed freedoms.

Some subsequent amendments to the Constitution testify to the importance of battles over the meaning of political equality to American politics. One of the consequences of the conflicts leading to the Civil War of the 1860s appeared as three constitutional amendments, the Thirteenth to the Fifteenth, amendments promoting black political equality. The Thirteenth Amendment abolished slavery. Part of the Fourteenth Amendment protected freed slaves. All persons born or naturalized in the United States—former slaves included—were citizens of the United States and the state they lived in. States were prohibited from abridging the privileges or immunities of citizens of the United States, from depriving any person of life, liberty, or property without due process, and from denying people the equal protection of the laws. The Fifteenth Amendment stipulated that the voting rights of American citizens could not be taken away or restricted due to "race, color, or previous condition of servitude." Expanding the boundaries of political equality also inspired several twentieth-century amendments, the most significant being the Seventeenth (popular election of Senators), the Nineteenth (extending the right to vote to women), and the Twenty-sixth (reducing the voting age to 18 years).

Written or Unwritten Constitutions and the Importance of Conventions

One of the key distinctions made in the study of constitutions is between written and unwritten constitutions. The United States Constitution is the longest living and a classic example of a written constitution. In that one document, you will find most of the information needed to understand the basic structure of political institutions and the logic of the American political process—in particular, the division of power among the three branches of government. A second defining feature of the written constitution, the type of constitution that most nations have adopted, is that it is an extraordinary legal document. It carries much more interpretive importance and weight than the ordinary laws that flow out of the corridors of Congress. Article VI outlines the Constitution's overarching importance. There, the Constitution is identified as "the supreme law of the land." As such, it takes precedence over any state constitution or state law. All law, federal or state, must correspond to the provisions and principles of the United States Constitution as interpreted by the Supreme Court.

When the written portion of the Canadian Constitution was enlarged in 1982, an even more explicit statement of the Constitution's importance was included. After following the American example by identifying the Constitution as "the supreme law of Canada" Section 52 of the *Constitution Act* (1982) went on to point out that "any law that is inconsistent with the provisions of the Constitution is, to the extent of the inconsistency, of no force or effect." This clause, as discussed later in the chapter, has been lamented by some critics for placing too much power in the hands of judges who interpret the constitution as opposed to elected representatives who make laws.

Britain is generally regarded as the classic example of a country guided by an unwritten constitution. But, the label "unwritten" is quite misleading. It really means that the British Constitution, unlike its American counterpart, cannot be found primarily within the confines of one document called "The Constitution." In fact, the unwritten British Constitution is made up, in part, of many written laws. Some, such as the aforementioned *Acts* of the Blair government, were passed by parliaments. Monarchs authored others before the dawn of parliamentary supremacy. The *Magna Carta,* signed by King John in 1215 and modified by Parliament in 1297, is one of the written pillars of Britain's unwritten Constitution. This constitutional document responded to a rebellion by English noblemen who believed King John was abusing his powers, especially by taxing them too severely. The *Magna Carta* limited the monarch's power and protected the English lords from royal authority. Its contemporary relevance to life in modern Anglo-American democracies may be found in such sections as the one guaranteeing that people may not lose their liberty or property without a trial by their peers.

The insistence on calling the British constitution "unwritten," rather than, say, uncodified, is best defended by pointing out that many of its most significant and well-accepted elements do not rest in written laws at all. They exist as constitutional conventions. **Constitutional conventions** may be regarded as extra-legal constitutional rules—rules without a foundation in the law. Because they lack a basis in law, they cannot be enforced by the courts. Their extra-legal nature does not mean, as one might think, that they are less important than laws. In 1981, for example, the Supreme Court of Canada was asked whether the Canadian government could ignore the constitutional convention that the approval of the national government and a substantial number of provinces was needed to amend the constitution. A majority of the Supreme Court answered that "some conventions may be more important than some laws. Their importance depends on that of the value or principle which they are meant to safeguard."

The most important conventions are ones that effectively transfer *de facto* power from one authority or one actor to another. In Britain, for example, the Queen has the legal prerogative to refuse to give Royal Assent to any legislation passed by her Parliament. Without Royal Assent, the bills passed by Parliament cannot become laws. Use your imagination for a moment. Suppose that the Queen had objected to the Labour government's *Scotland Act,* the law that gave some of the British Parliament's powers to a Scottish Parliament. She had the legal power to refuse to give the assent needed for this bill to become law. But, her refusal would have violated the British political convention that monarchs must sign legislation passed by a parliamentary majority.

What we have here is the type of clash identified above by the Supreme Court of Canada—a clash revolving around the importance of the value of representative democracy. In a country where the legitimacy of electoral politics is unshakable, it is unthinkable that a monarch who sits on the throne due to an accident of birth would frustrate an elected and publicly accountable Parliament. Because of its democratic pedigree, the convention that the Queen always grants her assent when it is requested trumps the legal possibility that Royal assent may be withheld. While the Queen continues to hold this ***de jure*** power, the ***de facto*** power to say yea or nay to legislation has been passed to the Prime Minister and a parliamentary majority.[1]

Constitutional Change

SHOULD YOU CARE ABOUT THIS DISTINCTION BETWEEN WRITTEN AND unwritten constitutions? One reason this distinction is valuable concerns the possibility of constitutional change. Written constitutions are notoriously difficult to amend. Since written constitutions are supposed to reflect the fundamental and enduring values of their host societies, constitutional amendments usually require extraordinary majorities. If a constitution is to be amended, the proposed change must be welcomed by a broad consensus in the society.

The United States Constitution and the Canadian *Constitution Act* (1982) illustrate this point about extraordinary majorities. Generally speaking, an amendment to the United States Constitution must be passed by a two-thirds majority in both the House of Representatives and the Senate. The amendment must also be passed by three-quarters of the states (38 of 50).[2] The Canadian amending formula is more complicated. Some items of the Canadian system of government, such as the composition of the Supreme Court or the amending formula itself, require the unanimous consent of the national Parliament and all of the provincial legislatures. According to the general amending formula, a formula that applies to such subjects as the powers of the Senate and the method of selecting senators a constitutional amendment requires the agreement of the national Parliament and the legislatures of at least two-thirds of the provinces (7 of 10) that have at least 50 percent of the total provincial population. The failures to add the Equal Rights Amendment to the United States Constitution and to incorporate the Meech Lake Accord to the Canadian Constitution demonstrate the substantial hurdles raised by the extraordinary majority requirement.

The situation with respect to unwritten constitutions is significantly different. Since the constitution does not live in one document, a formal amending formula does not exist. Without this formula, advocates of constitutional change face a far more flexible environment. For decades, this flexibility was "academic" in the pejorative sense of the word—it did not seem to have much bearing on daily life. However, the path taken by the Blair government in the United Kingdom changed that. Devolution, the *Human Rights Act*, and the reform of House of Lords led the *Times of London* to conclude: "Constitutional reform is changing the way Britain is governed in much more radical ways than is generally appreciated."[3] The flexibility of the unwritten constitution is key here. Without it, these radical changes would be much more difficult—perhaps impossible—to realize.

But should Canadians want that kind of flexibility? In the first place, since the Blair government's changes are all taking place through individual pieces of legislation, some worry that this approach to constitutional change is not as comprehensive or as well thought out as it should be. In other words, should constitutional change be a piecemeal process or a coherent and encompassing one? The flexibility afforded by unwritten constitutions also raises important democratic issues. If constitutions should reflect a political consensus in society, is it wise or desirable for the constitution to be changed only by the party that holds a parliamentary majority? Blair's Labour government, for example, only received 44 percent of the vote. Should fundamental changes to a constitution not be subject to a wide-ranging public debate—a more inclusive debate than these issues saw when they were debated in the British Parliament?

Unitary or Federal?

ANOTHER IMPORTANT FEATURE OF CONSTITUTIONS IS THAT THEY SPECIFY how jurisdictional power will be divided among national and sub-national governments, if at all. In other words, the constitution sets out the rules for both unitary and federal systems. What do we mean when we say that a constitution is federal? The term **federalism** refers to the division of sovereignty or ultimate governing authority between the different governments ruling over a shared territory. A federal constitution divides sovereignty between a national government and sub-national governments (states in the United States, provinces in Canada). In some policy areas, the national government will have the constitutional authority to act or to exercise sovereignty; in other areas, this sovereignty will rest with regional governments. In the United States, the Constitution assigns the powers to issue money, to regulate interstate commerce, or to sign foreign treaties to the national government. State laws intruding upon these areas are unconstitutional. In Canada, commercial fishing is vitally important to the people who live in the Atlantic provinces but the constitution assigns power over the fisheries to the national government. Therefore, the province of Newfoundland cannot pass legislation regarding who may fish or how many fish may be taken off its shores.

The idea of sovereignty offers a useful means to distinguish between federal and unitary constitutional systems. In a system governed by a **unitary constitution**, all governmental sovereignty rests in the national government. Although sub-national governments may exist in a unitary state, such as the United Kingdom, those governments are empowered to govern by the national government. Their authority comes from the national government; their authority is not constitutionally entrenched and protected. When the Scottish Parliament was elected in 1999, it was empowered to legislate on such matters as education, health, and local government. It was also allowed to vary the income tax that the Scots pay by a very small amount—a so-called "Tartan Tax." These powers were given to the Scottish Parliament by the British Parliament, not by the Constitution. The British Parliament retains the power to modify the Scottish Parliament's basket of powers in any way it wishes. Strong Scottish nationalists abhor this element of the devolution arrangement, for it underlines the fact that the face of constitutional government in Britain will still be a unitary one.

Separation or Union of Powers

We noted at the outset of this paper how the United States Constitution outlines the separation of powers among the legislative, executive, and judicial branches of government. To a significant extent, this choice underlined the Americans' rejection of the British system they had suffered under, a system featuring the union of executive and legislative powers. In Canada, emulation, not rejection, was the perspective taken toward the British model of parliamentary government. Consequently, the Canadian federation was established under "a Constitution similar in principle to that of the United Kingdom."

These constitutional choices have important consequences for the power and responsibilities of their respective legislatures and executives. The union of powers in Canada's parliamentary system enables the political executive (the Prime Minister and the cabinet) to dominate the legislature when the governing party holds the majority of seats in the House of Commons. Prime ministerial domination, enforced through strict **party discipline**, disempowers individual Members of Parliament when it comes to making laws. American Presidents, crucial political leaders that they are, nonetheless cannot dominate Congress in the same way. Members of Congress are powerful legislative players. Budgets, the lifeblood of governments, illustrate this difference well. No Canadian newspaper would describe the introduction of a Prime Minister's budget to Parliament in the way *The Washington Post* described the budget President Bush introduced to Congress in 2002—as "a recommendation." The *Post*'s language testifies to the crucial importance of Congress in the legislative process, reflected here in its power to challenge and amend Presidential spending priorities and plans. The public questioning of their spending priorities that Presidents regularly endure from Congressional members of their own parties is unheard of in Canadian politics. Parliamentary careers, governed as they are by the Prime Minister's wishes, would be ruined, rather than made, through this type of behaviour.

The Canadian system has come under increasing criticism. Advantages arguably delivered by a union of powers—such as stronger, more certain executive policy leadership and the Opposition's abilities to hold the government accountable through the daily question period—appear to carry less and less weight in public opinion. In February 2004, Prime Minister Paul Martin tabled a series reforms to parliamentary votes and committees designed to increase the ability of Members of Parliament (MPs) to shape policy and legislation. A "three-line voting" system was proposed to give individual MPs the freedom on "most votes" to offer their views and/or those of their constituents on policy matters. Party discipline only would be enforced on a "three-line" vote. It would apply "for votes of confidence and for a limited number of matters of fundamental importance to the government." Committees were promised greater resources, expanded authority, and greater independence.

Rights and Constitutions

JUST AS FEDERAL CONSTITUTIONS LIMIT THE LEGAL AUTHORITY OF GOVERNMENTS *vis-à-vis* each other, constitutions may also limit the legal authority of governments *vis-à-vis* their citizens. This is both an important and a controversial function of constitutions. In the United States, the sovereignty of the government over its citizens is limited by *The Bill of Rights* and other amendments to the Constitution. In Canada, the *Charter of Rights and Freedoms,* added to the Canadian Constitution in 1982, plays the same role. Part of the drive to incorporate the *Charter* into Canada's constitution developed out of a major shortcoming of the Canadian *Bill of Rights* (1960). While the Supreme Court decided in the case of *R. v. Drybones* that the *Bill of Rights* trumped other federal laws inconsistent with its provisions, the *Bill of Rights* was only an ordinary piece of federal legislation. Its guarantees, therefore, did not apply at all to the activities of provincial governments.

Viewers of American television crime dramas are familiar with the Miranda warning that American law enforcement officers are required to give to arrested suspects. The requirement to warn suspects that they have the right to remain silent and to consult a lawyer arose from the case of *Miranda v. Arizona.* In that case, the Supreme Court overturned the conviction of a confessed kidnapper and rapist because the police violated Miranda's Fifth Amendment right not to be compelled to make self-incriminating statements. This Fifth Amendment protection exemplifies **negative rights**—rights individuals have against being interfered with by other actors, such as the government. In the context of the government–citizen relationship, negative rights protect people from government interference.

The rights guarantees found in written constitutions may also exist as so-called **positive rights**—rights that require government intervention in order to be realized. The minority-language educational rights outlined in Section 23 of the Canadian *Charter of Rights and Freedoms* illustrate this alternative form of rights guarantee. This section stipulates that where the numbers of children warrant, Canadian citizens have the right to have minority language (English/French) education and educational facilities provided and paid for by the government.

Constitutional guarantees of rights are controversial for many reasons. The Miranda case raised one of the controversies associated with legal rights. Respecting individual rights occasionally may mean that the guilty escape punishment because their rights were violated somewhere in the criminal justice system. For some, constitutional rights are controversial because the job of interpreting what constitutionally appropriate behaviour looks like is turned over to the courts. Critics of **judicial review** on both sides of the United States–Canada border worry that judges will hijack the constitutions and fill its language with meanings that were never intended by the framers of the constitutions.

Courts and Legislatures

IMPORTANT AS THESE CONTROVERSIES ARE, I WOULD LIKE TO FOCUS ON A developing myth, particularly significant in Canada, about constitutional rights. The core of the myth is that judges, through judicial review, further rights while politicians and public servants, through their laws and actions, restrict rights. This is a dangerous caricature. It exaggerates the rights-protecting nature of the judiciary and undervalues the extent to which legislatures may also be important champions of the rights and well being of citizens.

There are several important fallacies in the conventional outlook on rights, courts, and legislatures. One fallacy lies in the message that the *Charter* simply protects the rights of individuals against the state. While this is sometimes true, it is also true that when the courts interpret the *Charter* they may instead protect the rights of some individuals at the expense of another category of individuals. In other words, individuals or groups of similar individuals both win and lose in some *Charter* decisions. Judicial review of the *Charter* may involve considerably more than upholding the rights of the individual against the government.

This general point that *Charter* cases may deal with intergroup conflict was illustrated dramatically in *R. v. Seaboyer*. This case struck down Canada's rape-shield law. This federal law sought to abolish some old common-law rules that permitted evidence of a rape victim's sexual conduct to be heard by a jury, irrespective of whether or not the evidence was relevant to the case at hand. Defence lawyers in rape trials grilled victims about their sexual history to try to convince juries they were unchaste, had probably consented to the alleged assault, and therefore were not credible witnesses. The rape-shield law, which permitted such evidence in only limited circumstances, also aimed to encourage the reporting of sexual assaults and to protect the victim's privacy.

The judge in Seaboyer's sexual assault trial followed the letter of the law. He refused to let the defence question the complainant about her sexual history. Seaboyer's lawyer argued that the judge's decision denied Seaboyer his Section 11(d) *Charter* right to a fair trial. A majority of the Supreme Court agreed. Justice Beverly McLachlin, writing for the majority, concluded that the law created "the real risk that an innocent person may be convicted." At one level, this decision fits the individual-versus-the state framework well. Government law treated Seaboyer harshly, and the Supreme Court vindicated his individual rights. However, if we peel the decision back to another level, we can also see that the state's law existed to protect the rights or the interests of a vulnerable group in society; the victims of sexual assault. At this level, the decision was one where the interests of one category of individuals (those accused of sexual assault) were protected at the expense of the interests of others (the victims of sexual assault). Court battles over whether laws violate the *Charter* may well be battles between classes of individuals and not simply battles between individuals and the state.

The Seaboyer case also allows us to argue that the core of the constitutional rights mythology—that courts further rights and legislatures restrict rights—is fallacious. The example of Seaboyer shows that the reality may be far more complicated. Government legislation actually protects or furthers the rights or interests of particular constituencies. Through legislation, such as the rape-shield law, governments may improve the position in our society of vulnerable or disadvantaged groups. This possibility also may be used to cast a more favourable light on the often criticized **notwithstanding clause**. This clause, Section 33 of the *Canadian Charter of Rights and Freedoms,* enables the federal and provincial governments to reinstate laws courts judge as unreasonable violations of the rights guaranteed under Sections 2 (fundamental freedoms) and 7 to 15 (legal and equality rights).

Summary

In this chapter, we have sketched out several roles constitutions play in liberal democracies. They establish the essential rules of political competition. They define the relationships among a country's key political actors. In this respect, they may or may not divide sovereignty among different levels of government and stipulate the sorts of protections and duties citizens can expect from their governments. We have also argued that constitutions are focal points for political conflict. For centuries, political actors have regarded constitutional provisions as key political resources, an outlook that is bound to flourish in the twenty-first century.

Endnotes

[1] The same relationship exists in Canada between the Prime Minister, Parliament, and the Governor General. Another important convention in Britain and Canada is that the leader of the party winning the most seats in an election is asked to form a government.

[2] There are two exceptions to this general formula. States may veto amendments depriving them of equal representation in the Senate; the Constitution also may be amended by a national constitutional convention.

[3] "The oracle of Westminster," *The Times (London)*, 27 July 1998.

Discussion Questions

1. If you were given the job of drafting a constitution for a new country, would you require extraordinary majorities in the constitutional amendment formula?
2. Would making the Canadian Parliament operate more like the United States Congress improve the Canadian system of government? What factors might complicate such a change?
3. "The notwithstanding clause is a valuable addition to Canada's Constitution." Would you agree with this statement? Why?

Further Readings

Cairns, Alan C. 1995. *Reconfigurations: Canadian Citizenship and Constutional Change.* Toronto: McClelland and Stewart.

Rossiter, Clinton, ed. 1961. *The Federalist Papers.* New York: Mentor.

Supreme Court of Canada, *Reference re Manitoba Language Rights,* [1985] 1 S.C.R. 721.

Weblinks

Judith Bowers Law Lists
www.cugini.net/law/reference.htm

Centre for Constitutional Studies
www.law.ualberta.ca/centres/ccs

Kingwood College Library: Constitutions of the World
http://kclibrary.nhmccd.edu/constitutions-subject.html

CHAPTER 10

CITIZENS AND CITIZENSHIP

Objectives

The political concept of **citizenship** can mean something as simple as legal membership in a country or a full menu of rights and obligations that define an individual's relationship with fellow citizens and with the state. In this chapter, we trace the origins of citizenship as a critical political concept. We explore the question of access to citizenship. Who historically has been included or excluded from citizenship status? Finally, we consider some of the tensions that underwrite recent uses of the term *citizenship* in contemporary politics. In particular, we focus on three primary tensions between rights and responsibilities, universality and difference, and the national and the global.

CHRISTINA GABRIEL

Introduction

In 1946, Secretary of State Paul Martin Sr. introduced Canada's first Citizenship Bill to the House of Commons. He declared that "citizenship is the right to full partnership in the fortunes and in the future of the nation" (Martin, Sr., 1993, 73). Despite this declaration, more than 50 years later, many of us find it difficult to describe what it means to be a "Canadian citizen" beyond a narrow legal definition or, indeed, to specify the content of "full partnership." Key political questions in Canada and elsewhere revolve around immigration as a source of potential citizens as well as the meaning of citizenship itself. These questions are particularly germane because the way we choose to answer them has implications for the kind of society and political community to which we aspire (Mouffe, 1992, 225).

Consequently, it is not surprising that citizenship, both in theory and in application, has been the source of ongoing debate. Some social theorists have characterized citizenship as a "slippery" concept whose meaning has shifted over time and as a contested concept that consistently generates political debate and conflict (Riley, 1992; Hall and Held, 1989). At the most general level, however, differing conceptions of citizenship are characterized by some common concerns, including the inclusions and exclusions that are constitutive of membership of a particular community; reciprocal rights in, and duties toward, the community; and full participation in practice (Hall and Held, 1989, 175).

Citizenship as a political concept has a long history. The classical ideal of citizenship can be traced to the ancient civilizations of Greece and Rome. In the Greek city state of Athens, for example, citizenship granted the privileges and obligations of self-government to a fortunate few. A citizen, according to the Aristotelian ideal, is one who both rules and is ruled. Political participation was regarded as a civic duty. The privileges of citizenship in these ancient times, however, were bestowed upon a select group: "A citizen must be a male of known genealogy, a patriarch, a warrior, and the master of the labor of others (normally slaves)" (Pocock, 1995, 30–31). Citizenship also was predicated on a strict division of the private from the public. The earliest citizen had slaves and women to satisfy his household needs, leaving him free to engage in politics. Such criteria excluded most of the Greek population, including women, slaves, foreigners, and resident aliens, from citizenship. In this respect, Athens's solution to potentially disruptive social inequality was to confine access and influence within the political process to a select few and "to limit the definition of citizenship" (Jenson, 1991, 198).

Although the origins of citizenship are ancient, many current conceptualizations of citizenship-as-rights are informed by the liberal political tradition dating back to the seventeenth century. The French Revolution's principles of liberty, equality, and fraternity were the grounds upon which French citizens claimed "universal recognition on the basis of common equality" (Hall and Held, 1989, 176). The American revolution of 1776 also revived and gave renewed energy and content to the concept of citizenship. These events were deeply influenced by the English philosopher John

Locke. His work "emphasized that the relationship betweem the people and their government was consensual and contractual" (Kaplan, 1993, 248). According to Locke's ideas, formal civil and political equality between citizens was guaranteed and protected by a limited state. Under the terms of Locke's "social contract," consent was the basis of authority. Locke was convinced that the business of government rested with the people and that they alone were responsible for their own good. They would "elect representatives, delegate powers, and agree to abide by majority decisions, but ultimately the representatives and officials hold their powers on trust and are responsible to the people" (Goodwin, 1992, 221). However, women and men without property did not figure into Locke's vision of sovereign people.

The ideal of equality, nonetheless, gives the concept of citizenship its radical emancipatory potential. Previously, citizenship had been underwritten by a range of exclusions. Take, for example, the basic political right of voting in Canada. In the years immediately following Confederation, income and property requirements, as well as the exclusion of all women, meant that only a small proportion of the population could vote. Most women won suffrage by the 1920s, but people of Chinese, East Indian, and Japanese origin were denied the vote until the late 1940s. Each of these groups contested their marginal status, using the language of citizenship, by making a claim for equality. In this respect, citizenship is a very powerful concept, implying that there should be no exclusion from the political community on the basis of, for example, gender or race.

Citizenship as Belonging

THIS SECTION CONSIDERS THE QUESTION OF CITIZENSHIP AS A LEGAL status—who is born a citizen and who can access the right to be a citizen. Some argue that for citizenship to be meaningful, it should be limited, granting rights to citizens not available to others. For example, recent American legislation has limited the right to benefits and services for legal immigrants who have not yet become legal citizens (Lister, 1997, 46). Others, in contrast, argue that citizenship should be freely available to all settled members of a community and that all individuals should be treated in the same way (Kaplan, 1993, 257). This debate has become particularly heated in the wake of the large-scale postwar migration to Western Europe and North America. These issues are a major challenge to conceptions of citizenship in modern liberal democracies.

Access to citizenship, in some ways, occurs along a spectrum. At one end are those born into citizenship. At the other end are groups of people resident in countries where their formal citizenship is in doubt or in question. The situation of Western European migrant workers (guest workers) is a good example. They were recruited under employment and residence permits in the post-war period. Today, they participate in the economic realm. They pay taxes, and many have children who were born in the host country. But many are excluded from political participation at both the local and national levels. This situation has led to questions about the representativeness of government when large segments of the population are disenfranchised. How long does a person have to live in a country before he or she can expect political representation? The dilemma of the guest worker is not limited to Western Europe. In Canada, the number of employment authorizations for temporary workers "matches or exceeds" the number of people applying for immigration to Canada (Stasiulis, 1997, 154). Foreign domestics, for example, enter Canada under the provisions of the Live-in-Caregiver program. These provisions include the granting of temporary "visitor" status and the condition that domestics live with their employers for a specified period. These conditions effectively render these workers "non-citizens" (Bakan and Stasiulis, 1997). In contrast to temporary visitors, people with Permanent Resident status share many of the same rights as Canadian citizens, but they are unable to vote or run for public office. They also may be barred from certain jobs in the public service.

Tensions Underlying Citizenship

THE POLITICAL APPLICATION OF THE CONCEPT OF CITIZENSHIP IS NOT LIMITED to legal definitions of access. It also addresses more substantive aspects of citizenship. Three are particularly noteworthy. First, the post-war conception of citizenship-as-rights is increasingly being challenged by "active" models of citizenship that stress responsibility. Second, the liberal conception of citizenship is being criticized for exclusions based on categories of difference. And last, conditions of globalization are giving rise to new forms of citizenship.

Rights versus Responsibilities

The work of British sociologist T.H. Marshall in *Citizenship and Social Class* is often taken as the starting point for thinking about the evolution of citizenship. Marshall's analysis addressed the meaning of citizenship within the context of class-based inequities characteristic of modern economies. Do rights have any relevance, asked Marshall, if people do not have the means or capacity to make citizenship meaningful in practice? Drawing specifically on the English example, Marshall mapped three elements of citizenship that had evolved in the modern liberal democratic state. The first element, **civil rights**, emerged in the eighteenth century and referred to rights necessary for individual freedom, including "liberty of person, freedom of speech, thought and faith, the right to own property . . . the right to justice." The second element encompasses **political rights**, such as the right to vote and run for political office. These rights date to the nineteenth century. According to Marshall, the twentieth century was associated with the **social rights** of citizenship. He defined this element as "the right to a modicum of economic welfare and security . . . according to the standards prevailing in society" (1950, 10). The law and Parliament were the institutions most closely associated with the first two elements of citizenship.

However, the welfare state was the institutional mechanism for social rights. Welfare state arrangements, such as public education, universal health care, public housing, and income security programs, were designed to counteract the insecurities generated by the market economy in which liberal democratic citizenship was embedded. In this respect, the welfare state added a social dimension to citizenship.

The specific configuration of national welfare states and the nature of social entitlements have varied from country to country in the post-war period. A host of factors including the level of national resources, differing capacities of groups to advance claims, institutional practices, and ideas about the state play a role in the degree to which countries have protected and advanced social rights. In Canada, social rights have also played an important role in fashioning post-war ideas about Canadian identity and citizenship. In a sense, social programs provided an important benchmark to assess our progress as a people. Some programs were "the standard by which Canadians could judge themselves vis-à-vis Americans. Canadians were more compassionate, more caring, and had a greater sense of social justice" (Taras, 1997, 2). Our health-care system offers a case in point. *Macleans* magazine recently reported that "medicare is a matter of enormous pride for Canadians, up there with the Maple Leaf flag as a symbol of what we are as a people" (Marshall, 2000/2001, 48).

Compared with Western Europe, social citizenship in Canada has been relatively limited and, unlike some Western countries, social rights are not protected in the Canadian Constitution. Despite differences among social welfare regimes, T.H. Marshall's key point was that citizens in need were entitled to welfare provisions not in the form of charity but as an entitlement of citizenship itself. In contrast to liberal ideas of citizenship, in which citizens figure as individual members of a state, Marshall's conception emphasizes collective membership in a community (Yuval-Davis, 1997, 69).

In recent times, this post-war idea about citizenship has sometimes been labelled "passive." This is because it emphasizes passive social entitlements "and the absence of any obligation to participate in public life" (Kymlicka and Norman, 1995, 286). New Right critics, such as the American social policy theorist Lawrence Mead, have argued that social and economic rights to collective public goods cannot be separated from moral obligations to society as a whole. Specifically, he emphasizes the obligation to work (Plant, 1991, 60). In the United Kingdom, Margaret Thatcher's Conservative government attacked the social dimensions of citizenship by praising the "active citizen." This individual discharges the duties of citizenship privately through neighbourliness, voluntary work, and charitable gifts. This notion detaches citizenship "from its modern roots in institutional reform, in the welfare state and community struggles" and rearticulates social welfare in the "Victorian concepts of charity, philanthropy and self-help" (Hall and Held, 1989, 174). This particular New Right construction of the "active citizen" marks an important shift in the way we experience citizenship. The social rights of the disadvantaged are transferred, in part, from publicly financed entitlements into the private sphere of charity and voluntary services (Yuval-Davis, 1997, 84).

Under the post-war social rights paradigm, basic entitlements were supported by tax dollars and available to all members of society. Current New Right thinking equates social citizenship rights and "entitlement" with the idea of dependency, privileges the better-off in society, and tends to reinforce existing social inequalities. "The work obligation is presented as one that unites all citizens in a contribution to the common good" but, as Lister further points out, the target of the active citizenship model is overwhelmingly the poor (Lister, 1997, 20). In the debate over rights versus responsibilities, the New Right's attempt to promote "responsible" citizenship has significantly eroded the social dimension of citizenship.

Universality versus Difference

The politics of citizenship, both in theory and practice, is also centred around the issues of "universality" and "difference." Within the concept of citizenship is an ideal premised on the basis of equality or universal status. This ideal of universality is found in such phrases as "everyone is equal before the law." Critiques by feminists, people of colour, and other disadvantaged groups, however, have raised concerns about the **universalism** attached to these concepts. These groups draw attention to the fact that formal citizenship rights have been no guarantee of full participation or full membership of everyone. We may be equal as citizens, yet may be "distinguished from other citizens by physical appearance, ethnicity, origin, culture or socio-economic position. Where such a separation gives rise to inequality, discrimination and racism, citizenship must be seen as incomplete" (Castles, 1994, 4). To some extent, Marshall's conception of citizenship tried to address this issue. Marshall's key preoccupation was how the working class was cut off from a common culture and prevented from accessing a common civilization (Kymlicka, 1992). Yet, exclusion can take many different forms. People of colour, women, people with disabilities, and gay men and lesbians have been excluded from full participation "not because of socio-economic status but because of their socio-cultural identity—their difference" (Kymlicka and Norma, 1995, 302).

The experiences of some groups of people following the attacks of September 11, 2001, offer a case in point. The focus on security and terrorism resulted in the introduction of various new pieces of legislation in Canada and the United States as well as regulatory changes in immigration and border control. Within the United States, Human Rights Watch—an independent monitoring organization that monitors rights in national and international law—reported that American officials targeted people on the basis of racial origin. It stated that more than 1000 people were detained on immigration charges allowing officials to deny them their basic civil rights and relatedly escape court scrutiny (Knox, 2002, A10). Additionally, American authorities announced that, as a security measure, they would fingerprint and interrogate nationals of Iran, Iraq, Syria, Libya, and the Sudan and reserve the right to do the same to visitors from other countries. Arab-Canadian permanent residents and dual citizens, in particular, were concerned by the spectre of racial profiling (Clark, 2002, A8), and the Canadian government issued a travel advisory to Canadians born in a number of Middle Eastern countries. Despite American assurances that additional measures would not be based on race or religion, a number of reported instances would appear to counter the claim. The award-winning author, Rohinton Mistry, an Indian-born Canadian, was prompted to cancel his book tours in the United States following his experiences in American airports (Freeze, 2002, A1). In these cases, despite claims to the contrary, people appear to be targeted because of their ethnic origins.

The recent experience of the Syrian-born Canadian citizen, Maher Arar, provides an additional insight into how people can have formal citizenship but whose experiences in the post-9/11 period belies this status. Mr. Arar was returning to Canada via New York following a family holiday in Tunisia. He was detained and questioned by the U.S. Immigration and Naturalization Service and accused of having links to terrorism. He was not allowed access to a lawyer. Despite Mr. Arar's Canadian passport and his request to be returned to Canada, American officials deported him to Syria, where he was imprisoned and tortured. After 10 months, Mr. Arar was returned to Canada; no charge had been levelled against him in any jurisdiction (Sallot, 2004, A9). In this case, Mr. Arar's Canadian passport was no protection in a national security environment that links some groups of people to terrorism. As Amnesty International wrote in the wake of the Arar case, "Governments claim that threats to public security require extraordinary measures . . . [but] the security of those swept into custody solely because of their place of birth, their ethnicity or religion—and the security of others who fear being targeted—has been drastically eroded (www.amnesty.ca/realsecurity/false.htm). In these cases, the failure to recognize citizenship status, due process, and international human rights renders some people, on the basis of group membership, "second-class" citizens.

The term "second-class citizens" is also used in reference to women's experiences. That is, they may claim formal citizenship rights, but this seeming parity is countered by the material aspects of their disadvantage as a group. What does citizenship mean in the context of the continuing gender division of labour or increasing feminization of poverty? Feminist accounts of citizenship have been instrumental in highlighting how this concept is deeply gendered. Noted political philosopher Carole Pateman, for example, has examined the ways in which women have been excluded or included in the category "citizen." Political theory, Pateman argues, despite its claim to universality, presupposes gender difference, and this, in turn, structures women's status as citizens. She argues that conceptions of citizenship are premised on a "patriarchal separation" between the public realm of politics and work and the private realm of gender relations and domestic life. Anything that happens in the private realm, the space traditionally associated with women, is treated as insignificant to citizenship (Pateman, 1989, 182-85). Moreover, the values citizens are expected to show, such as impartiality, rationality, independence, and political activism, are attached to men and the public realm (Lister, 1997, 70).

This public–private dichotomy, Pateman suggests, also informs the construction of the post-war welfare state. In "The Patriarchal Welfare State," Pateman takes exception to Marshall's theory of social citizenship. She argues that the very structure of the welfare state, Marshall's mechanism for the realization of social rights, far from ensuring full membership for women, casts them as "social exiles." The welfare state was constructed around the notion of a male "breadwinner/worker." It presumed that men are full-time wage earners who provide for dependent wives and children. Women, in contrast, were assumed to provide unpaid domestic care at home. They were the "dependent wives." The development of the welfare state was premised on the notion that certain aspects of care should be provided in the home by women's unpaid labour instead of through public provision (Pateman, 1989, 192). Pateman argues that these assumptions created a gendered two-tier structure in the welfare state. Men could claim "benefits available to individuals as 'public' persons" because they were paid employees. Women, however, were seen as "'dependents' of individuals in the first category" (Pateman, 1989, 188). Women's access to the rights of social citizenship was only partial. Through their unpaid labour, they could contribute to the welfare of men and society, but women's welfare and social citizenship rights were contingent upon their relationship to breadwinner-males. Explorations of citizenship, such as Pateman's, show how the emancipatory promise of citizenship's universal ideals—of full participation and membership—remain far from being realized by many.

Feminist theorist Iris Marion Young has argued that modern conceptions of citizenship can often serve to marginalize and oppress various groups of people. She begins from the point that a unitary conception of citizenship is unjust because, as she puts it: "In a society where some groups are privileged while others are oppressed, insisting that citizens, persons should leave behind their particular affiliations and experiences to adopt a general point of view, serves only to reinforce that privilege, for the perspectives and interests of the privileged will tend to dominate this unified public, marginalizing or silencing those of other groups." Young supports a democratic project that would incorporate people into the political community not only as individuals but as members of groups. Group representation becomes a method to "promote just outcomes within the democratic decision making process." Within this call is Young's conception of "differentiated citizenship," which requires the introduction of group-specific rights in order to confront oppression and disadvantage. She suggests that specific measures are necessary for effective recognition and representation of disadvantaged groups. Such measures would include, among other things, public support of group organizations, group representation in the generation and evaluation of relevant key policies, and veto power over specific policies that affect any one group directly (Young, 1990, 120, 124–125).

In the case of everyday politics there have been a number of examples where policies have been directed at specific groups, rather than at individuals. Many of these have proved very controversial. Multiculturalism policy in Canada, for example, has been the source of considerable debate. The policy has been criticized as "divisive" on the grounds that it emphasizes differences between citizens and produces "hyphenated Canadians." It has also been attacked on the basis that it grants "special status" and funding to ethno-cultural groups (Bissoondath, 1994). The notion of differentiated citizenship has been identified as a "radical development in citizenship theory" and one that constitutes a serious challenge to an understanding of citizenship premised on "treating people as individuals with equal rights under law" (Kymlicka and Norman, 1995, 302–3). Regardless of one's personal perspective, this growing debate about universality and difference is central to the politics of citizenship in the twenty-first century.

The National versus the Global

Various forms of globalization have challenged traditional understandings of citizenship. First and foremost, it is generally taken for granted that the nation-state provides the infrastructure for citizenship status and citizenship rights. Increasing global interconnectedness challenges this understanding. David Held sees a number of "disjunctures" in the areas of law, polity, security, identity, and economy between the sovereign power of the nation-state and the current process of globalization. Globalization effectively narrows the actions and decisions of governments. It blurs the boundaries of domestic politics, changes the administrative and legal environment in which decisions are taken, and effectively obscures "the lines of responsibility and accountability of national states themselves" (Held, 1995, 135).

How do these developments affect conceptualizations of citizenship that have been built upon the foundation of a sovereign nation-state? To what extent has citizenship been detached from particular states? Held, for one, draws attention to the "disjuncture" between citizenship, as a status with rights and duties stemming from an individual's membership in a national political community, and the growth of international law. The latter, he suggests "subjects individuals, governments and non-government organizations to new systems of regulations" (Held, 1989, 198). These emerging systems produce mixed consequences.

For example, membership in the European Union has created opportunities for individual citizens of member states to challenge their own governments in such forums as the European Court of Justice. This supraterritorial means for citizens to challenge their governments has already had some effect on national legislation (Held, 1989,199). The development of international legal regimes may contribute to the erosion of the nation-state to the extent that they constrain national sovereignty. Importantly, however, these regimes also provide opportunities for citizens who seek to protect their rights from national laws that may violate them.

Held also has focused on the development of new forms of transnational activities, highlighting the disjuncture between new forms of governance and the sovereign states (Held, 1995, 107–108). Nation-states have developed a host of international links in areas as diverse as trade, banking, and environmental regulation leading to profound changes in decision making and decision-making capacity. Canada is a member of numerous international organizations, such as the United Nations Organization (UNO). It participates in less formal but influential co-ordinating meetings, such as economic summits, by virtue of its membership in the G7. And, Canada is signatory to a number of trading agreements, of which the North American Free Trade Agreement (NAFTA) is the most encompassing. This matrix of international links affects the ability of nation-states to pursue policies that are truly national. This has potential consequences on the state's very ability to guarantee rights of citizenship. Regional trade agreements and rapid economic changes have led many companies to adopt drastic fiscal restraint measures and public sector retrenchment. Within this environment the fate of social citizenship rights is in question (Stewart-Toth, 1996, 271).

Within the matrix of international linkages, however, Lister also draws attention to the "unaccountable power" of institutions of global capital, transnational corporations, the World Bank, and the existing institutions of global citizenship. She argues that if the social and economic rights embodied in UN covenants are to be realized by countries that are less privileged, the asymmetrical power relations would need to be confronted. Citizenship "is tied to democracy and global citizenship should in some way be tied to global democracy" (Falk, 1994, 128 cited by Lister, 1997, 61). The implication here is that international institutions, such as the International Monetary Fund, should be reformed and made more democratically responsive to the people it regulates. There is a growing awareness among people that many political issues transcend national borders and, thus, cannot be addressed by national governments alone. This realization has led to transnational linkages among social movements and non-governmental organizations operating at an international level. The activities of such organizations as Amnesty International, women's groups, and environmental organizations are notable examples of transnational politics. These developments, it has been suggested, signal the "birth of an international global civil society" (Lister, 1997, 62).

Another reconceptualization of citizenship suggests that the trends highlighted above will require individuals to have "multiple citizenships." That is, people will be members not only of the nation-states they were born in or brought up in, but of wider regions and of the wider global order. This view of "cosmopolitan citizenship" is elaborated by Held in what he terms a "cosmopolitan project." He calls for a rethinking of democracy in terms of double democratization—"the deepening of democracy within a national community, involving the democratization of states and civil societies over time, combined with the extension of democratic forms and processes across territorial borders" (Held, 2000, 426).

Summary

The starting point of this chapter was an exploration of the concept of citizenship. Conceptualizations of citizenship are generally characterized by issues of inclusion and exclusion, rights and duties, and full participation. The nature of each of these issues, however, as this chapter tried to demonstrate, is historically specific, shifting, and the object of considerable political debate. Not surprisingly, citizenship as a concept has been rightly described as slippery.

While the roots of this concept are ancient, our current conceptualizations are largely informed by liberal understandings. Post-war conceptions of citizenship have been greatly influenced by T.H. Marshall's model of citizenship rights. His formulation

continued

has been the focus of considerable criticism by those who suggest that his account pays insufficient attention to the duties or obligations of citizenship. More recently, a number of diverse social groups have challenged the dominant assumptions of citizenship to argue that formal citizenship rights have not been a safeguard against socio-economic exclusion. Such groups have advocated for forms of "differentiated citizenship" to ensure full participation in the polity. In the early twenty-first centry, citizenship remains a highly relevant and politically charged concept and practice. New developments signal the emergence of the nascent concept of "global citizenship" that will further challenge many of our current ideas about citizenship. For these reasons, it is highly likely that citizenship will remain on the political agenda for some time to come.

Discussion Questions

1. To be a "Canadian citizen" is to enjoy the rights and privileges that flow from full membership of Canada as a nation-state. Discuss the ways in which some groups of people may feel excluded from the promise of full or effective citizenship in Canadian society. Are some groups in Canada "second-class" citizens?
2. How do processes of globalization challenge our understandings of citizenship? In the next century, will more and more Canadians come to see themselves as global citizens?
3. Many citizenship debates focus on rights and duties. What types of duties should be required of Canadian citizens? Is it possible to strike a balance between rights and duties?

References

Amnesty International, "False Security. Basic Human Rights Safeguards Under Threat." <http://www.amnesty.ca/realsecurity/false.htm> accessed 8 February 2004.

Bakan, A. and D. Stasiulis, 1997. "Foreign Domestic Worker Policy in Canada and the Social Boundaries of Modern Citizenship" in *Not One of the Family*. Toronto: University of Toronto Press, 29–51.

Bissoondath, N. 1994. *Selling Illusions*. Toronto: Penguin Books.

Clark, C. 2002. "Arab-Canadians fear 'persecution' at Border." *The Globe and Mail*, 10 September 2002, A8.

Freeze, Colin. 2002. "Mistry Cancels U.S. Tour Over Racial Profiling." *The Globe and Mail*, 2 November 2002, A1.

Goodwin, B. 1992. *Using Political Ideas*. 3rd ed. West Sussex, England: John Wiley & Sons.

Hall, S. and D. Held. 1989. "Citizens and Citizenship" in S. Hall & M. Jacques eds., *New Times*. London: Verso, 173–188.

Held, D. 1989. "Decline of the Nation-State" in S. Hall and M. Jacques, eds., *New Times.* London: Verso, 191–204.

———. 1995. *Democracy and the Global Order. From the Modern State to Cosmopolitan Governance.* London: Polity Press.

———. 2000. "Regulating Globalization?" in David Held and Anthony McGrew, eds., *The Global Transformations Reader.* Cambridge: Polity Press, 420–430.

Jenson, J. 1991. "Citizenship and Equity. Variations Across Time and in Space" in J. Hiebert, ed., *Political Ethics, a Canadian Perspective. Vol. 12,* Royal Commission on Electoral Reform and Party Financing. Toronto: Dundern Press, 195–228.

Kaplan, W. 1993. "Who Belongs? Changing Conceptions of Citizenship and Nationality" in W. Kaplan, ed., *Belonging: The Meaning and Future of Canadian Citizenship.* Kingston: McGill-Queens, 245–264.

Knox, P. 2002. "Rights Trampled in the U.S., Report Says." *The Globe and Mail,* 15 August 2002, A10.

Kymlicka, W. and W. Norman. 1995. "Return of the Citizen: A Survey of Recent Work on Citizenship Theory" in R. Beiner, ed., *Theorizing Citizenship.* Albany: State University Press New York, 283–322.

Lister, R. 1997. *Citizenship: Feminist Perspectives.* London: MacMillan Press.

Marshall, R. 2000–2001. "Paying the Price" in *Macleans* December 25/January 1, Vol. 113 No. 52, 48–50.

Marshall, T.H. 1950. *Citizenship and Social Class.* Cambridge: Cambridge University Press.

Martin Sr., P. 1993. "Citizenship in a People's World" in W. Kaplan, ed., Belonging. *The Meaning and Future of Canadian Citizenship.* Kingston: McGill-Queens, 64–78.

Mouffe, C. 1992. "Democratic Citizenship and the Political Community" in C. Mouffe, ed., *Dimensions of Radical Democracy.* London, England: Verso, 225–239.

Pateman, C. 1989. "The Patriarchal Welfare State" in C. Pateman, ed., *The Disorder of Women.* Stanford, California: Stanford University Press, 179–209.

Plant, R. 1991. "Social Rights and the Reconstruction of Welfare" in G. Andrews, ed., *Citizenship.* London, England: Lawrence & Wishart, 50–64.

Pocock, J. 1995. "The Ideal of Citizenship Since Classical Times" in R. Beiner, ed., *Theorizing Citizenship.* Albany: State University Press New York, 29–52.

Riley, D. 1992. "Citizenship and the Welfare State" in J. Allen, P. Braham & P. Lewis, eds., *Political and Economic Forms of Modernity.* Cambridge, England: Polity Press, 180–211.

Sallot, J. 2004. "Judicial Inquiry Set Into Arar Affair." *The Globe and Mail,* 29 January, A9.

Stasiulis, D. 1997. "The Political Economy of Race, Ethnicity and Migration" in W. Clement, ed., *Understanding Canada. Building on the New Canadian Political Economy.* Kingston-Montreal: McGill-Queens, 141–171.

Stewart-Toth, J. 1996. "Ideologies, Identity and Citizenship" in R. Gibbons & L. Youngman, eds. *Mindscapes. Political Ideologies Towards the 21st Century.* Toronto: McGraw-Hill Ryerson, 266–288.

Taras, D. 1997. "Introduction" in D. Taras & B. Rasporich, eds. *A Passion for Identity. An Introduction to Canadian Studies (3rd ed.)* Toronto: Nelson Canada, 1–5.

Young, I. 1990. "Polity and Group Difference" in *Throwing Like a Girl and Other Essays in Feminist Philosophy and Social Theory.* Bloomington: Indiana University Press, 114–137.

Yuval-Davis, N. 1997. *Gender and Nation.* London: Sage.

Further Readings

Aleinikoff, T. and Douglas Klusmeyer, eds., 2001. *Citizenship Today. Global Perspectives and Practices.* Washington: Carnegie Endowment for International Peace.

Hobson, B. 2000. *Gender and Citizenship in Transition.* New York: Routledge.

Lister, R. 1997. *Citizenship: Feminist Perspectives.* London: MacMillan Press.

Shafir, Gershon, ed. 1998. *The Citizenship Debates.* Minnesota: University of Minnesota.

Weblinks

Canadian government site for citizenship and immigration
www.cic.gc.ca

Environment Canada's Primer on Environmental Citizenship
www.ms.ec.gc.ca/udo/primer1.html

A network of individuals and institutions working in the area of citizenship, political education, and democracy in Europe
www.politeia.net

CHAPTER 11

COMMUNITY

Objectives

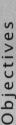

This chapter investigates various notions of political community arising in popular discussion and political science by addressing these questions: What is community? How do communities shape politics? Is community good (and for what)? Although we may have the sense that everyone lives in some geographic community, community can mean considerably more than one's place of residence. To draw a complete picture of community, this chapter distinguishes among three bases for communities, discusses the sentiment of community, and presents the powerful but controversial political discourses of communitarianism and cosmopolitanism. Liberal and feminist views on community are reviewed. Finally, the chapter suggests how community is a political strategy and a springboard for political participation.

JUDITH GARBER

Introduction

Few political concepts are employed more frequently in public discourse than community. What is truly fascinating, though, is the array of uses to which community is put. A week's *Globe and Mail* newspaper turns up stories about the anxiety caused by a contaminated community water supply; a community's demands that police identify pedophiles living in its midst; efforts throughout Canada to keep the peace between two communities supporting their warring brothers and sisters halfway around the world; a joint community–government–business drive to raise funds for playground equipment; a mayoral candidate campaigning as a member of various of the city's communities; and a woman seeking community in a neighbourhood of imposing homes and empty streets. For a word used so often, and so offhandedly, community turns out to be a surprisingly elusive concept.

Community always refers loosely to a group of individuals who recognize themselves, or whom others view, as holding something significant in common. This general description, however, does not produce an air-tight, universal definition. To begin with, it remains to be specified what that "something significant" is or why it is significant. The most helpful way to approach community is to recognize it not as one single thing, but as a collection of related ideas revolving around unity, connectedness, or sharing within groups of people. Unsurprisingly, listing the "essential elements" of "true communities" tells us little about politics, since how we define community depends on the context (Wood and Judikis, 2002, 12, 21). Political claims made about communal ties—about their influences upon political actions, identities, alliances, and values—are far more useful to explore.

Community in the Study of Politics

POLITICAL SCIENTISTS STUDY COMMUNITY BECAUSE IT HAS A STRONG POLITICAL core. The term *community* is sometimes used in ways that are not particularly political, such as in "entering an interfaith spiritual community" or "the physics community's prestigious award." The concept of community, however, is inherently political because of the built-in assumption that people have a natural capacity to act publicly, together, for common purposes. Community does not require that people's political interests and participation always be oriented toward the outlets provided by governments, such as elections and law making. The concept of community, nonetheless, conjures up the profoundly political notion of collective self-governance, as well as related issues concerning setting goals, distributing privileges and powers, enforcing rules, facing conflict, and reaching agreement within groups of individuals who hold something significant in common.

Political theorists have contemplated community ever since the invention of political theory. In fourth century B.C.E., Greece, Aristotle praised community as the foundation of a healthy *polis* (political society). The centrality of communal structures (village, monarchy, clan, church) was not seriously challenged until seventeenth century Enlightenment thinkers, such as John Locke, began arguing that political communities exist only to secure the life, liberty, and property of individuals. After liberalism became dominant in Britain, France, and America, influential political philosophers, including Jean-Jacques Rousseau, rediscovered community, insisting, as Aristotle did, that people are naturally political animals (Sabine and Thorson, 1973, 529). As we shall see, by the late twentieth century, this community versus individual debate expanded to include feminists who question the impact of community on minority groups, as well as cosmopolitans who envision community in global terms.

At the level of practices, political scientists study community because it is a live issue. In Canadian politics, at least four visions of community compete for dominance. One promotes a national community of distinct sub-communities, including francophones, Aboriginal peoples, and cultural minorities. Another proposes self-governing communities that exist totally (Quebec) or partly (First Nations) apart from "the Canadian community." The third seeks a dominant community guided by "traditional" anglophone-British-Christian culture and values. The fourth envisions Canada as a leader among a community of humanitarian, peaceful countries. Worldwide, both nationalist political leaders and fundamentalist religious leaders strive to cultivate communities that are homogeneous, assertive, and closed to outside influences. More commonly, people's conduct in the home, at work and school, over channels of communication, and on the streets is governed by rules that supposedly reflect the "community standards" and "community values" of one or more authoritative communities.

Three Foundations of Community

COMMUNITY FUNDAMENTALLY CONCERNS GROUPS OF PEOPLE WHO HAVE something in common. To make this concept specific and tangible, we can identify three major commonalities that underlie communities: place, identity, and interest. While these categories overlap, they capture distinct types of communities.

Place-Based Communities

Place-based community is a general term for a real territorial settlement. Here, community refers to geographical, usually local, places with identifiable boundaries, such as city limits. Community is often a synonym for municipality. Traditionally, community is associated with villages and towns, but the concept has been extended to the diversity of modern urban communities" (Gusfield, 1975, 32–33). Thus, we come across inner-city neighbourhoods, mobile home parks, gated housing developments, and Native reserves being called communities. What people primarily hold in common in these communities is shared space. This may cause shared interests and feelings of closeness that did not previously exist, and it frequently results from identifiable groups—for example, gays, retirees, the rich, Ukrainians—concentrating themselves in a location. Placed-based community does not necessarily go any deeper than geographic proximity. It may not even exist in the eyes of all those considered to be community members. Laws or group rules set out conditions for belonging to place-based communities, such as property ownership (for membership in condominium associations), citizenship (for voting), an address (for attending schools), or dues payment (for using the facilities of community leagues).

Place-based community is especially useful for contrasting localities with larger, more anonymous political jurisdictions. For many people, localities are communities precisely because they are not provinces, countries, or continental trading blocs. In an important sense, this form of community emphasizes the perceived grassroots or democratic character of local places, as opposed to more distant, "higher" levels of government. Local places are seen as communities because they are believed able to facilitate people's awareness of and participation in the decisions that affect their immediate, everyday lives in common. Mexico City, Toronto, and New York, with millions of residents each, are hardly intimate places, but they are often seen as more politically accessible and, thus, more like communities than Mexico, Canada, or the United States, which are also geographical places. More recently, some have argued that the virtual world of the Internet has rendered place-based communities increasingly irrelevant as people can communicate as quickly with people on the other side of the globe as with their next-door neighbour. Although there is conflicting opinion about the effect of the Internet on local communities like neighbourhoods (and on communal tendencies in general), evidence exists that "wired" communities actually "facilitate neighborhood based interactions," including helping organize political action on place-based issues (Hampton and Wellman, 2003).

Identity-Based Communities

Groups whose members share at least one identifiable characteristic make up another significant form of community. National origin, language, religion, gender, sexual orientation, skin colour, or physical ability may underlie people's personal and, thus, collective identities, as well as their political interests and claims. This is how we come to hear so much about "the francophone (or Somali or hearing-impaired or Jewish) community."

Identity-based communities can facilitate groups' self-awareness, appreciation of their culture and history, and organization for political action. Communities whose core is their identity may succeed in gaining official recognition, citizenship rights, inclusion in (or autonomy from) mainstream politics, or even the creation of a nation-state. In recent decades, in various countries, indigenous peoples' communities have sought each of these things. In peaceful democracies, the ordinary disagreements and negotiations among identity-based communities whose practices or political claims are at odds may become pressing issues. Identity-based community conflict, however, also has a history of violence and bloodshed. In the 1990s, in Bosnia and Rwanda, for example, systematic violence by powerful identity-based communities against disfavoured identity-based communities resulted in mass murder, ethnic cleansing, and other war crimes.

Interestingly, certain politically potent group characteristics are rarely identified as motivating identity-based communities. Compare how infrequently we hear about the "white community" with how regularly the "black (or Sikh) community" is mentioned, as if racial or ethnic visibility is politically noteworthy only for certain groups. Moreover, identity-based communities may get labelled from the outside, especially by politicians and the media. The result may be an inaccurate portrait of the group and its members' interests. The "Hispanic community," for example, homogenizes Spanish-speakers with roots in various continents and whose politics are shaped by distinctions in ethnicity, colour, class, gender, and citizenship status.

Even when viewed from within, identity-based communities may turn on constructed identities. Nationalism is a belief that there is a community of people bound by ethnicity—in effect, by blood ties and their manifestation in shared language, religion, culture, or territory. Calls for loyalty to the nation and for national sovereignty have political potency. However, Benedict Anderson (1991) calls nations "imagined communities." In this view, national identity is largely mythical—more the product of a political desire for community than actual relationships among people.

Interest-Based Communities

Interest-based communities exist to benefit their members, whether the ultimate benefits are recreational, economic, or political. In business and environmental communities, for instance, organizations provide their members with an array of benefits, such as affinity credit cards and group discounts. Nevertheless, they can reasonably be called political communities because they are bound by a set of interests that bear directly on the members' (selfish or selfless) political goals. Members tend to carry their shared interests into the political process, and the communities try to benefit their members by forming interest groups to influence elections and policy making. Indeed, the popular identification of many interest groups as communities (e.g., the gun-owning community, the medical community) is tied to their inserting their common interests (freedom to use firearms, health-care funding) into the political sphere.

The label "community" makes political sense only when applied to groups whose common interests include political goals—politically, goldfish owners are not a community. Non-political interests may become politicized, though, as happened with two well-publicized interest-based communities: divorced fathers and women with breast cancer. These communities began by providing emotional support and information to their members but are now demanding favourable child custody rules and funding for breast cancer research, respectively.

There are objections to using the term *communities* for interest-based groups. Increasingly, people with common interests meet and communicate entirely online.

Whether these "virtual communities" are genuine communities is a matter of intense debate because some observers judge online interactions as shallow and temporary. Similarly, joining Greenpeace, the Chamber of Commerce, or Students Against Drunk Drivers does not necessarily create profound communities—most members of interest-based communities merely pay dues and are not active in the lives of the organizations (Putnam, 2000, 155–60).

Community Sentiment and Social Capital

IT IS EASY TO NAME DOZENS OF EXAMPLES OF COMMUNITIES BASED ON CONCRETE commonalities among people; more abstractly, community is also a shared sentiment or feeling. Community, as a sentiment, emphasizes the quality or character of human relationships (Gusfield, 1975, xvi). Just as one could argue that political relationships should be grounded in honesty or courage, some people insist that these relationships should rest upon community. Here, community is a sentiment that endorses shared values, common goals, participation in public life, and ongoing relationships. People bound by sentiment trust and help one another. Communal sentiment is typically attributed to people who end up feeling like a community because they start out sharing territory, whether local (Downtown Eastside Vancouver) or national (Japan). In either case, community may go beyond describing some shared characteristic to defining a whole way of life.

Political scientists and sociologists increasingly refer to these communal sentiments—and our willingness to act on them—as **social capital**. Like other forms of capital, social capital adds value wherever it is expended. Thus, society and the political system are believed to be enriched if numerous people are community minded and feel impoverished if they do not have these attachments. Among other specific benefits, social capital "allows citizens to resolve collective problems more easily" and "widen[s] our awareness of the many ways in which our fates are linked" (Putnam, 2000, 288).

On a day-to-day basis, volunteer work by community groups and philanthropy by local community foundations convey communal feelings, as does the formation of neighbourhood watches as a community policing initiative. Community justice programs try to instill feelings of attachment and responsibility in people who have committed crimes by sentencing them to make amends to their victims or to the whole community, instead of imposing jail sentences that isolate offenders from the community (Karp, 1998). Voting, aiding someone in distress, and even joining bowling leagues are deemed significantly communal acts by some commentators (Putnam, 2000).

We also hear about the **international community**, typically in association with the United Nations and other organizations that act on the global stage to solve problems. Here, the international community is more a group of governments than a sentiment-based community. However, the international community can also symbolize shared sentiments of people in different countries, as when it "expresses outrage" at governments that take unilateral military action, permit the hunting of endangered species, or oppress political opponents. We can imagine a global public that shares moral values and common purposes—justice, health, safety, and peace—and extends empathy toward people around the world. The relationship between international community and cosmopolitanism is discussed below.

Communitarianism

COMMUNITY HAS LONG APPEARED TO SOME PEOPLE AS A SUPERIOR ALTERNATIVE TO pervasive individualism, social and geographic fragmentation, and civic and moral impoverishment. Throughout the twentieth century, community was championed in reaction to capitalism, urbanization, and secularization; in this century, globalized economies and cultures, suburban sprawl, and the transformation of the family are spawning new political demands for revitalizing communal structures. The call for community may take the form of a set of ideas about politics and society called **communitarianism**. Communitarians are a diverse lot, including religious conservatives and social democrats, philosophers and governmental policy advisors. Some communitarians envision strong relationships within the public sphere of collective self-governance, while others focus on the private sphere (Swift, 2001, 133-136). However, the one defining feature of communitarianism is a belief in the moral claim of "we–identities as against . . . I–identities" (Taylor, quoted in Etzioni, 1996, 26).

The Civic Tradition

Communitarians speak of "the public good" and "the good society," and often develop detailed plans for realizing these goals. This is civic language, or the language of citizenship. In communitarianism, a citizen's moral and political development is rooted in rich communal frameworks, rather than in economic competition or quests for self-discovery. Individual acts and achievements gain meaning when they enhance the goals of the group. Just as athletes generally earn respect when they perform as "team players" and superior teams function well as a unit, the health of society is judged by how well it inspires political and moral commitment on the part of its citizens or how much social capital it produces. Generally, "the public good is that which benefits society as a whole and leads to . . . public happiness" (Bellah et al., 1985, 335).

This approach to community is largely American in origin. Communitarians, who are preoccupied with identifying and faithfully following a community's "tradition," draw inspiration from the lengthy American tradition of localism existing alongside its evident liberalism. Many other countries claim vital, intact communal traditions. Indeed, how often is Canada (peace, order, and good government) associated with community and the United States (life, liberty, and the pursuit of happiness) with individualism? Whether or not this is an accurate picture of either country, there are plenty of Canadians worried about Canada moving away from its communitarian roots and toward an "Americanized" tradition of individual rights and freedoms.

Civic republicans recognize that, whether the United States, Canada, or elsewhere, each society has a "pattern" of values and practices supporting healthy community life. Thus, "communitarian societies do not all exhibit the same combination of order and autonomy," and some expect subgroups to commit only to selected "core values" (Etzioni, 1996, 92–93). Philosopher Charles Taylor (1993) has argued that a type of community-of-communities model is appropriate to Canadian traditions. Within individual sub-communities, whether these are based on language, culture, or another commonality, communal ties are very important. Such a diversity of strong communities is key to the public good of the larger Canadian national community.

Public and Private

Communitarians are more concerned with public, civic relationships than are liberals and many other people who think about politics, but the position of the private sphere within communitarianism is important. Depending on the communitarian vision, private sphere settings may receive more attention than the public sphere. Some communitarians, who are conservative by any North American standard, recommend taming individualism and social change by strengthening private-sector structures and intimate relations, such as marriage, family, religion, and neighbourhood. Public life is important if it upholds these private communal structures. Nevertheless, religious and "pro-family" organizations and their members may participate in electoral and legislative politics, lobbying for such policies as government funding for parent-controlled charter schools and tax deductions for parent-provided childcare or demanding that governments enforce law, order, and what they deem traditional moral values. This communitarianism is conservative in its conception of community itself because it rarely promotes equality or individual choice within the structures of intimate relationships, especially gender relations. In contrast, communitarians who are most concerned with civic life are generally receptive to openness and equality in families and other private relationships.

Yet another version of communitarianism, however, is directed toward equality in workplaces, unions, co-operatives, fraternities, communes, and other (semi-) private settings. This is a social democratic view of community. It encourages full, equal participation and discussion in decision making, substitutes equality-producing structures for hierarchical (corporate or bureaucratic) ones, and teaches habits of equal treatment and equal responsibility. It is also consistent with a type of feminist belief in the so-called "feminine" qualities of caring and co-operation, rather than competition for power and status (Gilligan, 1982).

These more private sites link with the fully public, political sphere in that participation in factories or housing co-operatives accustoms people to active, committed citizenship. As a way of governing entire countries, this communitarian framework would still require small-scale decision-making units so that everyone would have an opportunity to be heard. Although quite a few communitarians regard the Internet as a force of alienation from communal relations, electronic forums, such as "virtual dialogue," might support the communitarian goal of broader participation in national politics (Etzioni, 1996) as well as in neighbourhoods or interest- and identity-based "virtual communities" (Hampton and Wellman, 2003).

Cosmopolitanism

IN A WORLD WHERE COMMUNITY AND INDIVIDUAL LIBERTY ARE BOTH HIGHLY prized elements of democracy, they will always be in tension. However, liberals increasingly acknowledge that community priorities may actually enhance individual autonomy, if the will of the community is expressed through democratic procedures and if there are protections for fundamental liberties. For instance, censoring "hard-core pornography . . . harmful to the interests of members of the community" (Gutmann, 1993, 135–136) is acceptable to many liberals. Similarly, communitarians may work at "finding an equilibrium between universal individual rights and the common good . . . between self and community" (Etzioni, 1996, xviii). In practice, this might mean that the community refrains from heavily regulating or severely punishing individual lifestyle choices, unless they clash with core community values or endanger others.

Some liberals and communitarians agree that people's shared identity of "free and equal citizen" overrides both group identities and individual self-interest. Still, the basic "importance of people identifying with *their* particular community," for communitarians, does limit the scope of the community to something smaller than the entire world (Swift, 2001, 168). This limitation is a great concern in **cosmopolitanism**. Cosmopolitans "think that principles of justice, and conceptions of community, must apply globally" (Swift, 2001, 169). They ask "why must . . . democracy stop at the borders of a local or national community?" (Archibugi, 200, 28) Cosmopolitanism, thus, rests on the argument that because the contemporary world is so interconnected, most political issues transcend national boundaries. They, thus, promote the idea of a singular global community governed by common transnational and democratic structures of political action (Held, 1999, 104–105).

The two senses of "international community" presented earlier are, thus, highly relevant to cosmopolitanism, although the major international organizations, such as NATO and the International Monetary Fund, do not now operate in ways that represent all of the peoples and countries of the world, whether poor or rich, marginal or powerful. Neither do contemporary international organizations provide mechanisms for inclusive democratic decision making.

It also is evident that cosmopolitan ideas and values challenge communitarianism. In particular, cosmopolitanism appears to have a more contemporary understanding of globalization, which makes it unrealistic and unjust for each community to "pursue its internal happiness in its own way" (Archibugi, 2001, 28).

Difference, Conformity, and Community

LIBERALISM AND COMMUNITARIANISM, WHILE STILL DOMINANT VOICES, DO not define the entire debate about community. The demands of commonality that exist within communities may clash with the need to respect the great diversity among groups in society. Feminist and other criticisms of the impact of community on groups apparently "different" from the norm present a major challenge to communitarianism.

In nostalgic pictures of small-town life, people trust and identify with each other and can come to a consensus about matters of mutual concern. This scenario comes more from myth than from the real world, however. Communities invariably contain subcultures, outliers, and outright dissidents, but conflicting desires and needs go against the idea of the "sameness" of a community. The presence of poor people, disabled people, people of colour, immigrants, gays and lesbians, or strangers can so threaten a community's perceived identity that they may be shunned, threatened, or expelled, especially if they actually voice dissenting opinions (Rayside, 1989). And women "found that if they challenged communal traditions, be they in the Greek *polis,* Old Quebec, or the New England village, they risked being cast out of the community as traitors, whores, or even witches" (Sypnowich, 1993, 493).

Exclusion can happen in any community. The "feminist community" appeared in the 1960s and 1970s to share a unified set of goals (liberation from the nuclear family, economic and political equality with men). Unfortunately, this notion of a single community allowed major feminist organizations to ignore or silence working-class women who were already in the labour force, women of colour who faced discrimination from white women as well as from men, and lesbians who wanted access to the legal and social benefits of heterosexual women. These differences looked disruptive or irrelevant to a feminist community that wanted to preserve the illusion of common goals.

Communities may also have expectations for civic action that disadvantage some groups. Recall the assumption, built into the sentiment of community, that people are instinctually political, public creatures. Extensive, often face-to-face, interactions within the public sphere are one ideal of communitarianism. However, political practices that are heavily oriented toward public interactions favour the most assertive, verbal, and credible members of the group. Gender, class, culture, and other characteristics affect the outcome of group interactions and even the desire to participate (Mansbridge, 1983).

Summary

This chapter has shown how community is a multi-dimensional political concept. It encompasses communities based on various kinds of commonalities as well as sentiments about the goodness of human relationships, whether among citizens of a country or people around the world. Community supplies a framework for discussing, naming, and evaluating human relationships, including political ones. The term says as much about how we choose to characterize people's commonalities as about the commonalities themselves. It also indicates a lot about how we imagine that various kinds of people interact. On the one hand, ugly or pathological examples of community, such as white supremacist colonies or street gangs, rarely get called community. On the other hand, we persist in calling some places community, even where neighbours detest neighbours because of who they are or what opinions they hold.

But community is also an important political strategy. Strategically, people use community to build support for their preferred solutions to political and social problems. The success of community as a political strategy depends on placing community in a flattering light. This can be done by contrasting it with things that are clearly bad, such as social chaos, or using it so vaguely as to discourage scrutiny. In the typical North American city, far more people would rally to support a new stadium for "our community's football team" than for "the billionaire media mogul's team," even if it is the same team. Politicians routinely profess to be most sincerely committed to heartwarming proposals, such as resources for rebuilding communities or promoting voluntary community service.

Still, we should not conclude that *community* is a "glittering and nearly empty term" (Fowler, 1991, 150). A better assessment is that the term *community* provides a relatively familiar and easy route into politics for a wide range of citizens, including people who are not politically experienced or powerful. What community politics means in people's minds may begin with a public debate among city council candidates, but it does not end there. Community also applies to residents of a Native reserve protesting against a hazardous waste facility that pollutes their air, a coalition of mothers from both sides of a divided nation searching for solutions to civil war, parents organizing to take control of their troubled neighbourhood school, immigrant women starting a self-help program to combat domestic violence, or a virtual dialogue among farmers in different countries about genetically modified crops. Clearly, community persuades people to act on shared interests and values in many, diverse ways. Community's versatility comes from the fact that it is a flexible concept and strategy, not a rigid thing. Perhaps, then, the most interesting fact about communities is whether and why they exist in the eye of the beholder and for what purposes.

Discussion Questions

1. What are some differences between communities that people are born into and communities that people choose to enter into?
2. What are the points of convergence and divergence between communitarianism and cosmopolitanism?
3. How is community used as a political strategy by politicians, the media, and citizens?

References

Anderson, Benedict. 1991. *Imagined Communities: Reflections on the Origin and Spread of Nationalism.* London: Verso.

Archibugi, Daniele. 2002. "Demos and cosmopolis." *New Left Review* 12 (January–February), 24–38.

Bellah, Robert N., Richard Madsen, William M. Sullivan, Ann Swidler, and Steven M. Tipton. 1985. *Habits of the Heart: Individualism and Commitment in American Life.* Berkeley: University of California Press.

Etzioni, Amitai. 1996. *The New Golden Rule: Community and Morality in a Democratic Society.* New York: Basic Books.

Fowler, Robert B. 1991. *The Dance with Community: The Contemporary Debate in American Political Thought.* Lawrence: University Press of Kansas.

Gilligan, Carol. 1982. *In a Different Voice: Psychological Theory and Women's Development.* Cambridge, MA: Harvard University Press.

Gusfield, Joseph R. 1975. *Community: A Critical Response.* New York: Harper Colophon Books.

Gutmann, Amy. 1993. "The Disharmony of Democracy" in John W. Chapman and Ian Shapiro, eds., *Democratic Community,* Nomos XXXV. New York: New York University Press, 126–160.

Hampton, Keith and Barry Wellman. 2003. Neighboring in Netville: How the Internet support community and social capital in a wired suburb," *City and Community* 2 (December), 277–311.

Held, David. 1999. "The Transformation of Political Community" in Ian Shapiro and Casiano Hacker-Cordon, eds., *Democracy's Edges.* Cambridge, U.K.: Cambridge University Press.

Karp, David R., ed. 1998. *Community Justice.* Lanham, MD: Rowman and Littlefield.

Putnam, Robert. 2000. *Bowling Alone: The Collapse and Revival of American Community.* New York: Simon and Schuster.

Rayside, David. 1989. "Small Town Fragmentation and the Politics of Community," *Journal of Canadian Studies* 24, 103–120.

Sabine, George H. and Thomas L. Thorson. 1973. *A History of Political Theory,* 4th ed. Hinsdale, IL: Dryden Press.

Swift, Adam. 2001. *Political Philosophy: A Beginners' Guide for Students and Politicians.* Cambridge: Polity.

Sypnowich, Christine. 1993. "Justice, Community, and the Antinomies of Feminist Theory," *Political Theory* 21, 484–506.

Taylor, Charles. 1993. *Reconciling the Solitudes: Essays on Canadian Federalism and Nationalism.* Montreal and Kingston: McGill-Queen's University Press.

Wood, George S., Jr. and Juan C. Judikis. 2002. *Conversations on Community Theory.* West Lafayette: Purdue University Press.

Further Readings

Delanty, Gerard. 2003. *Community.* London: Routledge.

Low, Setha. 2003. *Behind the Gates: Life, Security, and the Pursuit of Happiness in Fortress America.* New York: Routledge.

Rheingold, Howard. 2000. *The Virtual Community: Homesteading on the Electronic Frontier.* Cambridge: MIT Press.

Weblinks

The Communitarian Network
www.gwu.edu/~ccps

Global Community Initiatives
www.global-community.org

Intentional Communities
www.ic.org

CHAPTER 12

PUBLIC BUREAUCRACY

MARCIA NELSON and STEVE PATTEN

Objectives

The form, structure, and functioning of the administrative machinery of the state is an essential part of the changing character of contemporary politics and government. This chapter offers an introduction to the administrative state. It introduces students to the public bureaucracy and examines the character of that bureaucracy. Readers will be encouraged to reflect on the ways in which politics and administration intersect within the public bureaucracy. There also will be an examination of the many different organizational forms that are found within the state. The overriding objective of the chapter is to encourage students to think critically and ask the tough questions about public bureaucracy. To what extent is the work of the bureaucracy actually "political"? To what extent can we, as citizens, be confident that there are mechanisms for limiting the power of the public bureaucracy? What should our opinion be of the recent preference for adopting private sector management techniques within the public bureaucracy?

Introduction

The bureaucratic structures of the state touch our lives in innumerable ways. As citizens, we pay taxes, work in regulated industries, utilize public services, and receive public benefits. All of our lives will, at some point, be affected by the character of the public bureaucracy. For this reason, each of us has a stake in the ongoing transformation of the character of public bureaucracy. In the political realm, a neo-liberal governing paradigm has been embraced as successor to the twentieth century welfare state. A new paradigm of administration known as "the new public management" is altering the character of administrative institutions and processes. This chapter works toward a discussion of the new public management and its impact on public bureaucracy. However, to understand the changing character of public bureaucracy, we must first tackle matters of definition. The chapter, therefore, begins by exploring the nature of public bureaucracy and the character of the various organizational forms found within it. Attention subsequently turns to an examination of the various checks and balances that are intended to ensure that the power of the administrative state is wielded in the public interest. The chapter concludes with a discussion of the ways in which the new public management departs from traditional notions of public administration.

Public Bureaucracy: Administration and Politics

THE PUBLIC BUREAUCRACY IS THE SET OF INSTITUTIONS AND PEOPLE WHO form the administrative machinery of the state. Sometimes called the civil service, the **public bureaucracy** is the coterie of administrative officials who take responsibility for policy implementation. They transform government policy into the concrete programs that enable elected governments to deliver on their political promises and agendas.

The fact that state bureaucrats are often called "civil servants" suggests that the administrative officials of the public bureaucracy exist to serve their elected political masters. By tradition, the civil service has been portrayed as the neutral implementers of politically determined policy directions, as if administration was purely technical and value-free. Policy making, by contrast, is understood to be an inherently political and value-laden process requiring politicians to make choices among competing interests. Thus, policy making and administration have been viewed as distinctive roles, as though a clear division of labour existed between the political work of our elected governments and the apolitical work of appointed civil servants. This notion of the separation between politics and administration is known as the **politics–administration dichotomy**. It was first popularized in the late nineteenth century when students of government were concerned about excessive patronage and extensive political manipulation of what was then only a very small public bureaucracy (Mellon, 1999).

Today, few observers consider the politics/administration dichotomy to be a realistic portrayal of the relationship between policy making and public administration (Whitaker, 2000). Almost everyone would agree that the public bureaucracy should remain strictly **non-partisan**—civil servants, in other words, should not be motivated by the interests associated with party politics. But few observers would accept the view that all aspects of public administration are entirely apolitical. For civil servants to serve their political masters, they must act in accordance with the government's agenda, and they must give advice that involves making choices among competing interests—and these are inherently political activities.

While we have long expected public bureaucrats to be non-partisan, it is usually recognized that the various tasks of civil servants are arrayed along a continuum, from relatively apolitical to obviously political. Particularly, the most senior bureaucrats are expected to give politically sensitive policy advice to their political masters (Sutherland, 1993, 86). But the political nature of administration does not stop with the giving of policy advice. Program administrators who have no contact with politicians are often required to use their discretion as they carry out their tasks and serve the clients of government programs. These discretionary decisions have policy consequences. From decisions taken by civil servants reviewing contracts for highway repairs to the judgments of case workers reviewing social assistance applications, administrative discretion is shaping the way that policies and programs are played out in real-life situations. There is little doubt that granting administrative discretion to civil servants involves bureaucrats in making policy decisions with political implications.

Recognizing the political nature of administrative discretion and policy advice, newly elected governments often worry about the extent to which they can trust and rely on civil servants who served the previous party in government. Highly professional bureaucrats are truly non-partisan, but—given that modern democratic principles assume governments are elected with a mandate to act on their campaign pledges—it is commonly accepted that a number of senior civil servants (such as the Deputy Ministers who head government departments in the Canadian system) hold their positions at the pleasure of the government. Similarly, Canada's most senior bureaucrat, the Clerk of the Privy Council, will remain in that office only so as long as she or he has the trust and confidence of the Prime Minister.

In the United States, the notion that the administration serves at the discretion of the President reaches even further into the public bureaucracy. There are a large number of important administrative posts and politically sensitive positions that are held by presidential appointees. In the twenty-first century, there is much less of the partisan political manipulation of hiring of mere functionaries that troubled nineteenth century advocates of the politics/administration dichotomy. Still, the power of political appointment at more senior levels remains extensive. Today, it is justified with the understanding that some dimensions of administration are political.

Organizational Forms of the Public Bureaucracy

IT IS EASY TO THINK ABOUT THE PUBLIC BUREAUCRACY AS A LARGE AND undifferentiated monolith—"the government bureaucracy." We all have contact with the administrative state. The bureaucracy processes our income tax, bureaucrats license our child care programs, administrative officials ensure restaurants meet public health standards, civil servants issue our marriage licenses, and so on. However, to understand public bureaucracy, we must recognize that there are, in fact, a number of organizational forms that have been used to accomplish the tasks associated with delivering programs and pursuing policy objectives. The language used to identify various organizational forms of public bureaucracy varies from country to country. Our discussion will highlight some of the more common labels in current use, with a particular focus on the Canadian experience.

At the core of what is known in Canada as the civil service are central agencies and operating departments. Central agencies are the "big picture" agencies that sit at the top of the bureaucratic hierarchy. These agencies—which include the Privy Council Office, Treasury Board Secretariat, and the Department of Finance—work closely with the Prime Minister and the Cabinet to co-ordinate the government's agenda (Thomas, 1999). They have considerable administrative, fiscal, and policy power. Their role is to test policy proposals for compatibility with the overall government agenda and analyze the potential costs, economic impacts, and legal and constitutional implications. The Privy Council Office (PCO) is an agency designed to serve the Prime Minister and the Cabinet. The most senior official in the PCO, the Clerk of the Privy Council, is deeply involved with providing non-partisan policy advice to the Prime Minister, as well as with appointing and supervising the Deputy Ministers who serve as the senior civil servants in government departments. With a staff of several hundred, the PCO helps the government set, control, and manage its policy agenda across the various departments. The Treasury Board acts as the manager and employer for government, setting the rules and administrative practices for departments in such areas as staff recruitment, budgeting, and reporting. Organizationally, the Department of Finance appears to be a regular department of government, but the power the department has to carry out economic assessments of government initiatives, shape fiscal policy through the annual budget, and influence monetary policy are, in combination, enough to elevate the Department of Finance to the status of a central agency. In recent years, the co-ordinative power of central agencies, such as the PCO and the Department of Finance, has increased quite significantly, not only in Canada, but throughout the world (Savoie, 1999).

In the first instance, the administrative state is organized around a number of operating departments with functional program and policy responsibilities. In Canada, for example, citizens would be familiar with such departments as Environment Canada, the Department of Social Development, the Department of Justice, and the Department of Human Resources and Skills Development. Government departments, such as these, are directly controlled by Cabinet Ministers who provide political direction to the civil servants who are responsible for delivering government programs and services, such as Employment Insurance. Of course, the role of departmental bureaucrats is not confined to service delivery. Ministers rely on civil servants to provide policy advice on a wide array of issues. Moreover, as the administrative state has grown in size and complexity, public bureaucrats have begun to serve as key points of contact for interest groups and public stakeholders who are working to influence policy development or program delivery. Indeed, Cabinet Ministers now expect their senior civil servants to play a role in managing relations within the various policy communities that impinge on the responsibilities of their departments.

The many other organizational forms constituting the public bureaucracy have been created to replace the traditional operating department when governments have, for one reason or another, preferred "arms length" service delivery or the removal of critical policy decisions from the realm of partisan politics. This is the case, for example, with regulatory agencies, state-owned corporations, and independent advisory bodies (Thomas and Zajcew, 1993). Regulatory agencies, such as Canada's National Energy Board or the Canadian Radio-television and Telecommunications Commission (CRTC), were created to administer and enforce policies and regulations set by Parliament. These policies could be administered by an operating department, but a decision has been made to delegate considerable administrative and policy discretion to an agency that, being independent of the Minister, is free from partisan influence. Similarly, the advice given by advisory bodies, such as the Royal Commission of Aboriginal Peoples or the Law Reform Commission, could have been generated within an operating department under the supervision of a Cabinet Minister. But a decision was made to create a non-departmental entity that would be considerably more independent.

State-owned, or crown, corporations are enterprises that take a corporate form but exist for public purposes. Some, such as Petro Canada and the Canada Development Corporation, were created to compete in the market place with the goal of influencing developments in particular economic sectors. Others, such as Ontario Hydro, were created to deliver goods that were not being delivered satisfactorily through private enterprises. Still others, such as Canada Post Corporation, exist to deliver a government service but to do so on a private sector model. These public enterprises represent examples of the government competing in the private sector. But, interestingly, they are also an example of private sector organizational forms being adopted by the public bureaucracy.

In recent years, there have been a number of innovations in terms of the organizational forms of the public bureaucracy. One fairly recent development has been the creation of special operating agencies, such as the Canadian Passport Office, that exist as separate "business units" within operating departments. While control continues to rest with the Minister, these agencies are exempted from many of the administrative rules that ordinarily curtail management flexibility. Indeed, one such agency, Consulting and Audit Canada, has been authorized to compete with the private sector for contracts as a way of funding the services it provides to government. Another recent innovation has been for government to establish and endow independent foundations, such as the Canadian Foundation for Innovation and the Canadian Millennium Scholarship Foundation. These foundations are independent, non-profit corporate entities, with multi-billion dollar endowments to invest, manage, and allocate. While the mandates of these foundations are established in the legislation that brought them into existence, they function as independent granting agencies outside traditional bureaucratic accountability networks.

Being aware of the various organizational forms of the public bureaucracy allows for a more sophisticated understanding of government administration. It is important, for example, to understand the unique power of central agencies, such as the Department of Finance and the PCO. Citizens also should be aware that the trend toward creating and assigning responsibility to non-departmental organizations—such as foundations, special operating agencies, and regulatory agencies—means, for both good and bad, less direct ministerial control of certain administrative functions of the state. Now that non-departmental organizational forms are increasingly common, students of public bureaucracy should give some serious attention to the issue of which organizational forms are most appropriate for which purposes.

Checks, Balances, and Accountability

GIVEN THE UBIQUITY OF PUBLIC BUREAUCRACY AND THE SIGNIFICANT responsibility of the administrative agencies that transform government policies into programs and services, a core issue of modern government is the question of whether adequate checks and balances exist to ensure that the power of the administrative state is wielded in the public interest. In the context of the British parliamentary system that has been adopted in Canada, there are four broad categories of checks on the power of the public bureaucracy: (1) the principles of ministerial responsibility and responsible government; (2) statutory and constitutional protections of rights; (3) formal administrative audit procedures; and (4) the informal political audit of members of the policy community (Inwood, 1999, 344-361). It is useful to examine each of these, if only briefly.

In Canada, the principle of **responsible government** confers upon the Prime Minister and Cabinet—sometimes called the government of the day—the power to establish the legislative and governing agenda and oversee the administrative machinery of government, but only so long as they maintain the support and confidence of the House of Commons. In other words, while the Prime Minister and

Cabinet are empowered to govern, they are responsible to Parliament for the way in which they govern. Cabinet Ministers, in the parliamentary system, are the direct political masters of operating departments, and ultimately responsible for the functioning of any arms length agencies for which they have legislative responsibility. The principle of **ministerial responsibility** also demands that ministers answer to Parliament for the activities and omissions of officials within the public bureaucracy. As an operating principle, ministerial responsibility is meant to shield civil servants from public blame and to simultaneously establish clear lines of accountability through the responsible Minister. This ensures that the parliamentary opposition can use the political process to address problems associated with the misuse of power by public servants. Significant bureaucratic indiscretions can, in principle, lead to the forced resignation of the Minister and political pressure to address problems within the public bureaucracy.

In practice, however, the principle of ministerial responsibility has been significantly watered down. While this parliamentary principle ensures that government ministers are "answerable" to Parliament, it is increasingly rare for the government of the day to take full and meaningful "responsibility" for the actions and omissions of the public bureaucracy. Ministerial resignations due to the indiscretions of public servants are almost unheard of in Canada (Sutherland, 1991). Particularly since the mid-twentieth century, when the size and complexity of government increased so dramatically, it has been accepted that ministerial responsibility exists only in a diluted form. While Parliament and its operating principles serve as a useful vehicle for opposition parties to draw attention to problems within the public bureaucracy, the constitutional principle of ministerial responsibility is no longer operative in its purest form.

Most liberal democracies now have legal and constitutional protections of citizens' rights that act as a check on the power of the public bureaucracy. In Canada, for example, the *Privacy Act*, the *Access to Information Act*, and the constitutionally entrenched *Charter of Rights and Freedoms* serve to curtail bureaucratic power by defining rights the state must respect. The *Charter of Rights* is the most far-reaching. It details a wide range of rights and freedoms and empowers the courts to protect citizens from violations of rights by the state. The *Privacy Act* outlines clear limits on the collection, use, and disclosure of personal information by government departments and agencies, and empowers a Privacy Commissioner to investigate complaints and carry out periodic privacy audits. The *Access to Information Act* ensures that individual citizens, advocacy groups, and journalists can request and secure the information necessary to hold civil servants to account. Taken together, the *Charter*, privacy protection, and rights to access information have served to empower citizens and place important limits on the public bureaucracy.

The office of the Auditor General plays an important surveillance role in the process of holding the public bureaucracy to account. The Auditor General reports to the public directly through Parliament and, as such, is independent of control by the Cabinet Ministers who serve as the political masters of the public bureaucracy. While initially established to carry out traditional audits of the government's financial statements, the Auditor General now engages in broad assessments of decision making and management in the public bureaucracy. With a mandate to (1) ensure proper management and accountability structures, (2) examine the utilization of human, physical and financial resources, and (3) verify that the operation of government programs is in compliance with the legislation and regulations establishing such programs, the Auditor General's reports have become a tool for opposition politicians, journalists, and citizens intent on identifying and addressing misuses of bureaucratic power. The political scandal that came with the Auditor General's exposure, in early 2004, of serious misuses of public funds through a federal sponsorship program is an obvious example.

A final, informal, but often powerful check on the power of the public bureaucracy is the ongoing political audit carried out by members of relevant policy communities. A **policy community** includes all the public and private actors with an active interest in an issue or area of public policy. These informal communities take their shape as interest groups, lobbyists, private think tanks, social movement organizations, and citizen stakeholders work to influence the character of public policies and programs. While the first order of business of members of a policy community may be influencing policy making, many of those affected by policies, programs and regulations have a desire to ensure that bureaucratic power is exercised fairly and within the limits specified by established policies. When there is a lack of progress on key government initiatives or when unexpected or unfair negative results occur, members of the policy community act as pubic watchdogs, bringing their concerns to the attention of appropriate civil servants, politicians and the media. Using the media focuses public attention on policy and program issues that politicians and senior officials need to address.

There was a time when the work of political scientists suggested that the bureaucracy could be held accountable through the operation of responsible government and ministerial responsibility. Today, less faith is placed in these formal operating principles of Parliament. Still, parliamentary principles ensure that the opposition parties are able to put political pressure on the government to address bureaucratic indiscretions. At the same time, citizens, activists, and politicians can now use statutory and constitutional protections of rights, reports of the Auditor General and pressure politics to help ensure that the power of the administrative state is wielded in the public interest.

From Public Administration to Public Management

PUBLIC BUREAUCRACIES ARE NOT STATIC AND UNCHANGING INSTITUTIONS. Their form, structure, and functioning evolve with national political cultures, economic conditions, and broader trends in governing paradigms. Over the past quarter century, for example, public bureaucracies throughout the liberal democratic world have been transformed by a new set of ideas and values regarding the organization and management of public service bureaucracies. This new paradigm had been labelled the **new public management** (NPM). For most of the twentieth century, particularly during the era of the Keynesian welfare state, the values of traditional public administration guided public bureaucracies. In recent years, however, as neo-liberal approaches to governance have been reshaping the accepted goals and purposes of the state, NPM values have reshaped the structure and culture of the civil service. The contrast between traditional public administration and the NPM provides a unique vantage from which to consider the changing character of public bureaucracy.

Traditional Public Administration

Careful academic examinations of the character of public bureaucracy and the administrative functions of the state began in the late nineteenth century. This was the era of the minimalist state. Government intervention in the economy and society was extremely limited. The civil service was small, with only the most basic administrative structures. The embryonic character of the public service limited the organizational distance between politicians and front-line public servants and increased the likelihood of hands-on political control and patronage.

In Canada, Cabinet Ministers micro-managed departmental affairs and regularly intervened in funding and hiring decisions to reward their political allies. This led to considerable public distaste of politicians meddling in and "politicizing" the bureaucracy. Influenced by a public sector reform movement that began in the United States in the late nineteenth century, Canada moved to reform its civil service in the early twentieth century. Embracing the ideals associated with the politics/administration dichotomy, the government established a Civil Service Commission, formalized the merit principle in federal government hiring, and adopted what are now considered traditional public administration values.

The principles of traditional public administration can be summed up as follows. First, professionalism in civil service employment is best demonstrated through a dedication to administrative prudence and a commitment to achieving equity and fairness through impartial and standardized approaches to the provision of public services. Second, administration is distinct from politics because the integrity of civil servants flows from their impartiality and non-partisanship. Third, public bureaucracies are, quite properly, rule-governed and process-oriented hierarchies. Centralized bureaucratic command and upward accountability are embraced, both as the essence of rational management and as a means of facilitating the functioning of ministerial responsibility.

In Canada, these principles were embraced in the era of the minimalist state, but they also guided the rapid expansion of public bureaucracies in the context of Canada's post-war welfare state. In contrast to the minimalist state, the welfare state was an activist state, prepared to intervene in the economy and society. Indeed, in the context of the post-war governing paradigm, it was commonplace to assume that state interventions were the solution to emerging social and economic problems. As such, the number and range of government regulations and programs expanded, the public bureaucracy grew ever larger, and process-oriented bureaucratic hierarchies became increasingly complex. By the early 1970s, Canada's welfare state was at its zenith, as a massive corps of civil servants administered and enforced an unprecedented number of programs and regulations.

New Public Management

When the conditions that had maintained the post-war economic boom began to unravel in the 1970s, economists, politicians, bureaucrats, and, finally, the public lost much of their faith in the welfare state governing paradigm. Thus began a period of struggle for new models of governance. Increasingly, state intervention was rejected as inherently ineffective, and market-oriented ideologies that championed non-government solutions to social and economic problems gained ascendancy. The ideas with the most political currency were ideologically neo-liberal—they placed faith in markets and rejected the activist state as a source of problems, not solutions. In this ideological context, the values and principles of traditional public administration were also under attack. Critics argued that the traditional paradigm had misunderstood the character of human organizations, placed too much emphasis on standardization, hierarchy of command, and due process. Public bureaucracies were criticized by neo-liberals for chasing abstract notions of the broad public interest while ignoring individual client satisfaction. In time, this anti-bureaucratic critique of the welfare state spawned a paradigm of public bureaucracy that insisted that government should be run more like a business—this was the new public management (Charih and Rouillard, 1997).

Over the past quarter century, the core principles of the NPM have increasingly displaced those associated with traditional public administration. First, innovation and risk taking are promoted over administrative prudence. Public bureaucracies are now expected to be flexible and creative institutions that place emphasis on individual "customer" satisfaction over the old values of impartiality and standardization. Second, there is a renewed commitment to the politics/administration dichotomy. Cabinet Ministers and their most senior bureaucratic advisors are expected to focus on policy making, not administration—or, in the NPM lexicon, on "steering not rowing." They are, in other words, expected to "let the managers manage." This has resulted in the dismantling of the hierarchical processes that facilitate direct political oversight. Instead, the trend is toward establishing organizational forms that give public bureaucrats more independence from ministerial control. Third, the NPM demands a commitment to flatter and more flexible organizational structures in which hierarchical process-oriented accountability is replaced by the establishment performance measures and accountability by results.

On the ground, inside public bureaucracies, there is considerable evidence of the influence of the NPM paradigm. There has, for example, been a measurable trend toward the use of **alternative service delivery** (ASD), which involves the transfer of responsibility for program and service delivery to private-sector providers, non-profit organizations, or new public-sector organizational forms, such as special operating agencies or foundations. Another important example of ASD has been the use of public–private partnerships in which contractual arrangements are established to allow the government and the private sector—either voluntary sector organizations or private corporations—to share authority and responsibility for the delivery of particular programs or the achievement of specific public policy objectives. As an extension of the neo-liberal critique of public bureaucracy, ASD moves responsibility for public administration from traditional operating departments to non-traditional organizational forms and the private sector.

At the same time, inside traditional operating departments, the rise of the NPM has meant the importation of private sector management techniques. For example, government departments now establish annual "business plans" to departmental operations. Performance measures are established and monitored to hold senior managers accountable for specific results and outcomes. These private sector management tools are a major departure from the traditional public administration's reliance on hierarchical rule structures and process accountability.

The benefits and drawbacks of the NPM are the subject of much debate (Savoie, 1995; Borins, 1995). Proponents of the NPM tend to be critical of the size, cost, and rigid character of the administrative machinery of the post-war welfare state. As such, their watchwords are efficiency, responsiveness, and flexibility. Indeed, they claim that program efficiencies achieved in the context of the NPM are partially responsible for the decreasing size of government and the trend away from the tradition of deficit financing. They argue, further, that NPM management techniques have unleashed the innovative capacity of staff, that operating departments have achieved a new clarity of purpose through the process of developing and implementing "business plans," and that client satisfaction has risen as program administrators embrace the NPM emphasis on service and responsiveness.

Of course, advocates of the traditional public administration paradigm remain critical of the NPM. Canada's Task Force on Public Service Values and Ethics summarized the traditional critique of NPM, noting that "[the new] public management pays too little attention to the democratic, parliamentary, political and public context, treats public goods as if they were private, ignores the complexities and trade-offs that characterize the public sphere, and downplays the importance of due process, vertical accountability, and the ultimate importance of the public interest or the common good" (cited in Gow and Hodgetts, 2003, 193).

Part of the critique of NPM is ideological. Many observers note that the NPM is associated with the rise of neo-liberal governance. They are concerned that it is really just an attack on government and public bureaucracy, nothing more than a management paradigm designed to reduce departmental staff, lower operating costs, and privatize services once located in the public sector. Those who are concerned about the neo-liberal privatization agenda, point out that the NPM's enthusiasm for ASD often removes government activities from traditional methods of accountability, such as investigations by the Auditor General and parliamentary oversight. While a new emphasis may be placed on responsiveness to individual "customers" of government programs, there is concern that this atomistic approach, when combined with outsourcing and ASD, actually undermines the traditional public administration's holistic approach to democratic accountability and transparency. There is, then, an ongoing debate not only regarding the wisdom of assuming that public bureaucracies can be managed like businesses but also concerning the core values and approach to governance that are associated with the NPM.

Summary

The purpose of this chapter has been to introduce students to public bureaucracy and some issues that are relevant to citizens whose lives are touched by the programs, regulations, and policies public servants administer. The chapter began with a discussion of the character of public bureaucracy, including the extent to which the work of public servants is, in fact, political. There was also a discussion of the different organizational forms of the public bureaucracy. But the issues of greatest political importance came in the latter half of the chapter. How effective are the existing mechanisms for limiting the power of the public bureaucracy? How should citizens react to the new public management and its preference for adopting private sector management techniques within the public bureaucracy? These are issues that go to the heart of democratic governance. They deserve our attention.

Discussion Questions

1. In what ways is the work of civil servants "political"?
2. Can the shortcomings of massive modern public bureaucracies be overcome by demanding that the civil service is run more like a business?
3. Are you satisfied with existing checks and balances on the power of the public bureaucracy?

References

Borins, Sandford. 1995. "The New Public Management Is Here to Stay." *Canadian Public Administration* 38(1), 122–132.

Charih, Mohamed and Lucie Rouillard. 1997. "The New Public Management" in Mahomed Charih and Arthur Daniels, eds. *New Public Management and Public Administration in Canada.* Toronto: The Institute of Public Administration of Canada.

Gow, J.I. and J.E. Hodgetts. 2003. "Where are we coming from? Are there any useful lessons from our administrative history?" *Canadian Public Administration* 46(2), 178–201.

Inwood, Gregory J. 1999. *Understanding Canadian Public Administration: An Introduction to Theory and Practice.* Toronto: Prentice Hall.

Mellon, Hugh. 1999. "Politics and Administration: Separate, Connected, or Integrated? Looking at Possibilities" in Martin W. Westmacott and Hugh P. Mellon, eds., *Public Administration and Policy: Governing in Challenging Times.* Toronto: Prentice Hall.

Savoie, Donald J. 1995. "What is wrong with the new public management?" *Canadian Public Administration* 38(1), 112–121.

———. 1999. *Governing from the Centre: The Concentration of Power in Canadian Politics.* Toronto: University of Toronto Press.

Sutherland, S.L. 1991. "Responsible Government and Ministerial Responsibility: Every Reform Is Its Own Problem." *Canadian Journal of Political Science, XXIV: 1,* 91–120.

Sutherland, Sharon L. 1993. "The Public Service and Policy Development" in Michael M. Atkinson, ed., *Governing Canada: Institutions and Public Policy.* Toronto: Harcourt Brace Jovanovich Canada Inc.

Thomas, Paul G. 1999. "The Role of Central Agencies: Making a Mesh of Things" in James Bickerton and Alain-G. Gagnon, eds., *Canadian Politics,* 3rd edition. Peterborough: Broadview Press.

Thomas, Paul G. and Orest W. Zajcew. 1993. "Structural Heretics: Crown Corporations and Regulatory Agencies" in Michael M. Atkinson, ed., *Governing Canada: Institutions and Public Policy.* Toronto: Harcourt Brace Jovanovich Canada Inc.

Whitaker, Reg. 2000. "Politics versus Administration: Politicians and Bureaucrats" in Michael Whittington and Glen Williams, eds., *Canadian Politics in the 21st Century,* 5th edition. Toronto: Nelson Canada.

Further Readings

Dwivedi, O.P. and James Iain Gow. 1999. *From Bureaucracy to Public Management: The Administrative Culture of Canada.* Peterborough: Broadview Press.

Johnson, David. 2002. *Thinking Government: Public Sector Management in Canada.* Peterborough: Broadview Press.

Shields, John and B. Mitchell Evans. 1998. *Shrinking the State: Globalization and Public Administration 'Reform'.* Halifax: Fernwood Publishing.

Weblinks

Public Policy Forum
www.ppforum.ca

The Institute of Public Administration of Canada
www.ipaciapc.ca

Treasury Board of Canada Secretariat
www.tbs-sct.gc.ca/index_e.asp

CHAPTER 13

ELECTIONS AND ELECTORAL SYSTEMS

J. PAUL JOHNSTON and HAROLD J. JANSEN

Objectives

The formal conduct of elections is often not well understood by citizens. In this chapter, we first consider the role elections play in modern politics, noting how they have been differently employed in constitutions to implement democratic principles of governance. Next, we set out the notion of an electoral system and describe its basic components and purposes. This is followed by a discussion that contrasts the two main kinds of electoral systems in use—those based on majority rule and those based on the proportional representation (PR) of different groups and interests in a society. The strengths and weaknesses of these two systems are assessed, and a brief discussion of an increasingly popular alternative to them—"mixed" electoral systems—follows. Finally, we consider the properties that seem most desirable in electoral systems and the general issue of electoral reforms aimed at achieving the promise that democratic politics hold out to citizens everywhere.

Introduction

When people think about politics, elections come immediately to mind. Richard Katz (1997, 3) tells us that elections are "the defining institutions of modern democracy." Indeed, among the different mechanisms that link citizens to the governing process in democracies, elections are the most prominent and most extensive in impact. Yet, many citizens misunderstand the role elections play in establishing and maintaining representative democracy. As a result, they become frustrated at what they view as ineffective performance of that role. Voter turnout rates are falling in a number of countries, and cynicism about the electoral process has shown a startling rise. The contrast between democratic theory and actual practice seems striking. How can we better understand its sources, and what is needed to remedy that situation, restoring the electoral process to the stature it holds in democratic theory?

The primary function of elections is to provide a means of selecting those who will hold high public office and exercise the authority attached to such positions. While we can do this in a number of ways, elections extend participation in that task to the citizenry at large. They also transfer control over such offices in a peaceful manner. And in doing so, they invest those who win office, the policies they formulate, the governments of which they are members, and, indeed, the entire electoral process, with legitimate authority grounded in the "consent of the governed." Popularly elected public officials become the agents of the electors, both individually and collectively; and elections serve as a means for holding them accountable to those they represent. To acquire office, they must persuade voters that they are the best choice, and to continue in office they must face the electorate again, adorned with their performance record, to renew their authorization. Authorization and accountability are both key goals sought by using elections to choose representatives and governments.

But, elections only provide a context here. The extent to which these functions are served rests also on the degree to which political elites organize such a competition, candidates and other officials submit to the accountability demands arising there, and electors require such conduct. One cannot force an evasive candidate or leader to make known their views or policy proposals. Nor can citizens be forced to learn the relevant information and acquire the necessary skills to monitor, evaluate, and critique those views and proposals or even to participate in the electoral process itself. Similarly, one cannot force an incumbent to run again or, if he or she does run, to account for what he or she did while in office, though one can withhold one's vote or support for his or her party and, in doing so, exert leverage unavailable in the absence of elections.

Constitutional Design and the Electoral Process

CONSTITUTIONS FORMALLY RECOGNIZE AND PROTECT THE POLITICAL rights citizens are seen to have; create a system of offices and agencies through which governance takes place; distribute power, jurisdiction, and obligations across these offices and agencies; and specify the basis on which particular public officials occupy these positions and exercise the powers attached to them. In all these respects, constitutions affect the role that elections play in democratic government and their outcomes, both in form and extent. Moreover, they do so in different ways in different nations and settings with differing consequences (see Table 13.1).

Consider the following differences between Canada and the United States. The American President is directly elected; Canada's Prime Minister is not. Canada's Prime Minister must be an elected member of its House of Commons and, by convention, so must those holding Cabinet positions. In the United States, the President appoints the members of the Cabinet and both they and the President are expressly precluded from being simultaneously members of the Congress. American voters can hold their President directly responsible for his or her performance, whereas Canadian voters can exercise popular control over their Prime Minister only by threatening the majority standing of his or her party in the Commons. And while Canadian Cabinet Ministers are directly accountable through the electoral process, unlike their American counterparts, it is only the local constituents of a Canadian Cabinet Minister who can exercise that popular control. By making executive offices differently elective, institutional arrangements in the two nations also make the task of holding their incumbents popularly accountable more complicated than democratic rhetoric suggests.

That effort also is made more difficult in presidential/congressional systems by the ways in which the separation of powers between the executive and legislative branches force those controlling one branch to share control over the policy process with those controlling the other. If opposing partisan camps control the two branches, competition develops. This often leads to what the Americans call "gridlock," wherein one popularly elected branch of government can block the policy agenda of the other branch, whose members can claim equal legitimacy to set policy based on their elective status. This makes it difficult to hold those in either branch responsible for failing to fulfill their promises. Such situations do not arise in parliamentary systems. However, the exercise of popular control is so indirect and requires such complex nationwide co-ordination that the elective status of officials offers little leverage over them.

TABLE 13.1 *Regional Differences in the Scope of the Elective Principle [N = 173 nations]*

REGION	NUMBER OF NATIONS	DEMOCRACY: POLITICAL RIGHTS		FORM OF GOVERNMENT (%)		DIRECTLY ELECTED PRESIDENT		BICAMERAL NATIONAL ASEMBLY	ELECTED UPPER CHAMBER	
		FREE	NOT FREE	MONARCHIES	REPUBLICS	%	N	N	%	N
Anglo-America	6	6	0	67	33	100	2	5	40	5
Caribbean	13	9	2	63	37	40	5	9	22	9
Central America	8	5	0	13	87	100	7	2	50	2
South America	12	7	0	0	100	83	12	7	100	7
Scandinavia	5	5	0	60	40	100	2	0	—	—
Western Europe	16	16	0	44	56	37	8	8	50	8
Eastern Europe	11	8	0	0	100	73	11	4	75	4
Former USSR[1]	15	3	6	0	100	73	15	5	40	5
Middle East[2]	10	2	5	20	80	50	6	2	50	2
Africa	47	11	15	6	94	87	37	15	20	15
Asia	18	7	5	33	67	50	12	8	38	8
Pacific Oceania	12	9	0	42	58	29	7	2	50	2
Totals	173	83	33	23	77	76	116	76	35	82

SOURCE: Information extracted from the Inter-Parliamentary Union PARLINE Database, www.ipu.org. Data include all nations the IPU lists as having a functioning assembly, where available. Information about forms of government and direct election of presidents taken from Blais, Massicotte, and Dobrzynska (1997), Appendix: 453–55. Freedom House Ratings of Democracy: Political Rights taken from Blais and Massicotte (1997) Appendix A: 118–24. Three categories are used: free, partly free, and not free. Data on government structure, presidential systems, and upper chambers also taken from the CIA World fact Book [online version].

[1] The "Former USSR" grouping includes Armenia, Azerbaijan, Belarus, Estonia, Georgia, Kazakhstan, Kyrgzystan, Latvia, Lithuania, Moldova, Russian Federation, Tajikistan, Turkmenistan, Ukraine, and Uzbekistan.

[2] Cyprus, Egypt, and Israel are included in the Middle East grouping with Iran, Iraq, Jordan, Kuwait, Lebanon, Syria, Turkey, and Yemen.

Similar problems of constitutional design arise in the structuring of national assemblies. All nations that claim to be democratic vest both the legislative powers and the power of consent to legislation primarily in an elected national assembly or parliament, which can be either **unicameral** or **bicameral**. The latter option reflects another application of the "separation of powers" principle, typically intended to establish some limit or "brake" on the actions taken by the "lower" chamber, which is taken to represent "the people" at large. Members of the "upper" chamber of a bicameral assembly can be elected to office either directly or indirectly or can be simply appointed. Appointment and indirect election, of course, limit or complicate popular control of such officials. Even when members of a second chamber are directly elected, the two chambers may differ in the procedures used to elect them, the constituencies each represents, and the jurisdiction each exercises. For example, lower chambers typically extend representation to persons as individual citizens on an equal basis, though taken collectively as embodying "majority consent," while representation in upper chambers might reflect regional interests or those of particular economic, cultural, ethnic, or linguistic segments of the population.

Election Laws and Electoral Systems

CONTEMPORARY ELECTIONS ARE LARGE-SCALE, HIGHLY COMPLEX, COLLECTIVE events, but many smaller, more specific interactions take place within their purview. To ensure that these activities conform to prevailing ethical standards, laws govern almost every aspect of organizing and conducting an election, from constitutional provisions that require the election of public officials to regulations that set voting hours. For our purposes, we can group these laws around four broad concerns—constituencies, participation, voting procedures, and electoral formulas. The entire set of rules, procedures, and institutional arrangements that governs how the electoral process is organized and conducted and shapes its outcomes is known as an **electoral system**.

Defining **constituencies** involves extending representation in the governmental process to specific segments of the citizenry as well as the citizenry at large. Broadly speaking, a constituency is a group of citizens whose policy interests are of relevant concern to those who govern and, hence, warrant attention by public officials. Making public offices elective gives citizens leverage over officials, inasmuch as they are, as a group, able to determine who holds the office in question. Thus, constituents also are those persons on whose behalf an elected official acts and to whom that official is, at least in theory, held accountable in elections. Different kinds of elective officeholders serve different constituencies, which, in turn, may be defined and formed differently. Executive officers in national governments typically act on behalf of all citizens of a country. Elections to fill such offices are generally conducted "at large" across the nation. Representation in a national assembly, in contrast, is usually extended to separate groups of citizens by dividing the nation into several territorial districts or "ridings," then assigning each district one or more elected representatives. Only those members of the assembly assigned to a particular electoral district formally represent residents in that district, and only electors in that district can vote to choose them.

The number of districts one creates, their geographic area and population size, varies widely in practice. At one extreme are electoral systems that treat the entire nation as one district. For example, Israelis elect their 120-member *Knesset* to represent the nation as a whole, with the entire country serving as one district. At the other extreme are those nations that create single-member districts (SMDs), electing one representative for each district. Canada, the United States, the United Kingdom, and several Commonwealth countries are examples. The first approach recognizes the national focus of policy made by members of the assembly, whereas the second one stresses the need to accommodate local interests in arriving at such policies. The former often reflects a consensual notion of national politics that attempts to accommodate diverse interests in the nation at large or through multi-member districts by adopting proportional representation. The latter sees politics as a competition among local interests, uses SMDs to capture that diversity, and resolves differences within and among local constituencies by the majority-rule principle.

Deciding which groups of citizens should be represented in legislative bodies, on what basis, and by how many elected representatives is invariably a controversial matter. The process used is called *apportionment.* A formal procedure for allocating representation is adopted to ensure fairness in extending representation to different groups of citizens. Various criteria can be applied in making such allocations. Seats are sometimes reserved for a group whose members warrant special arrangements to guarantee representation, as is done for New Zealand's Aboriginal Maori people. More frequently, geography plays an important role in apportionment. People have to reside somewhere, and so that becomes a convenient basis for grouping them together. All nations use territorially defined districts at some level in representing citizens, if only for administrative reasons. Often, doing so reflects a regional division of governmental authority as well. For example, seats in the Canadian House of Commons are first allocated to the different provinces and territories in numbers that are roughly proportional to their population. This practice is known as "representation by population" (or "rep by pop"). When followed strictly, it ensures the formal equal representation of individual citizens, another important apportionment criterion. Where single-member territorial districts are used to distribute representation within such jurisdictions, formal equality is achieved by creating districts that contain roughly equal numbers of people. Malapportionment is the unfair overrepresentation of one interest or group at the expense of another. Its most common form involves the overrepresentation of rural populations at the expense of urban ones, though other forms are possible.

A second broad set of election laws defines who can participate in the electoral process, their capacities, and activities. One subset indicates the criteria persons must meet in order to be eligible to vote in elections. Such suffrage laws govern the extension of the **franchise** to wider segments of the citizenry. Another subset of laws included here specify candidacy criteria that one must satisfy to stand for election, plus those rules and administrative procedures to be followed in declaring and pursuing their candidacy. These include regulations about nomination procedures and endorsements, campaign finance and expenditures, access to and use of the mass media, and ensuring fair campaign practices. Broadly speaking, these laws address access to and participation in the electoral process by candidates, voters, and campaign activists.

Voting involves making choices among alternatives. An important set of election laws focuses on how such preferences are to be expressed and recorded and the kinds of choice voters can make. Voting procedures, and the forms ballots can take, are primary concerns here. The former range from "open" voting procedures using "voice votes," a show of hands, or a "standing vote," to the latest kind of "touch sensitive" electronic voting machines. Each has its advantages and liabilities, and all have the potential for controversy and unfair practices, as the debacle surrounding the 2000 presidential election in Florida indicates clearly. Ballot form issues are less dramatic and controversial, though they are just as important. Laws regarding ballot structure indicate what kinds of choices voters can make in an election and what information they are to supply about their preferences among those alternatives. Are voters to choose between political parties or among candidates? If the latter, do they choose among individual candidates or lists of candidates in some fixed order of priority (slates) set out by party leaders? If party list ballots are used, do they allow voters to indicate preferences within a given list or to distribute votes over several different lists?

Our final theme deals with laws specifying **electoral formulas**. These rules indicate how individual votes are to be combined and weighted in determining the magnitude of support for a given candidate or party. They also note what decision criterion should be used to determine who won an office or how many seats should be assigned a given party in a legislative body. In short, they provide the details of how to translate the vote totals for a set of candidates or parties into a distribution of elected positions. Typically, the standard used specifies a quota of votes or some proportion of the valid vote cast that one must amass in order to win a position. The decision rule applied may require one to win more votes than any other competitor (a *plurality rule*) or at least one vote more than the sum of the votes that other competitors won (a *simple majority rule*). These rules stress the importance of clearly and decisively indicating who has won the right to govern. Alternatively, *proportional representation* is designed to distribute seats in an assembly to parties in shares that approximate as closely as possible the share of the total valid vote each party gained. Various rules are used to do this, typically involving some vote quota that "sets the price" of a seat in amount of support required. These basic distinctions have served to divide the different formulas into two broad families: **majoritarian electoral systems** and **proportional representation systems**. How winners are determined provides a way of classifying electoral systems. Recently, a third family has been added that combines aspects of both previous ones. These are known as **mixed electoral systems**.

Choosing an Electoral System

Majoritarian Electoral Systems

In *majoritarian* systems, elections are primarily meant to provide popular support for governments and legitimize their claim to govern. This is best accomplished when they can claim support from a majority of the voters—that is, when "majority rule" prevails. However, when more than two candidates or parties compete for a position, it is possible, even likely, that none will gain a majority of the votes, leaving the election indecisive. One option here is to hold a second, "run-off" election a short time later between the top two candidates in the earlier election, thus ensuring a majority decision.

A more common remedy is to adopt a **plurality decision rule** instead. Here, the winner is that candidate or party that receives more votes than any other opponent does. Usually, a plurality rule is combined with single member districts and a **simple candidate ballot**, creating the *first-past-the-post* electoral system (FPTP). Originating in Britain and still employed there, the FPTP system is mainly used in those countries sharing the British political tradition, such as Canada and the United States. FPTP is commonly also used to elect members of upper chambers and is almost invariably the choice for electing those members from the SMDs in mixed systems. The plurality rule is also regularly used in presidential elections (Blais, Massicotte, and Dobrzynska, 1997, 447).

Proponents claim that FPTP systems have several features that recommend their use. Adopting a plurality rule solves the problem of decisiveness, though at the expense of abandoning the majority principle at the district level. And, though that principle is given up locally, under FPTP systems, the most dominant party typically wins a majority of the seats at contest over the nation, ensuring a strong, stable government. Using simple candidate ballots offer an easy, straightforward choice and voting procedure. Moreover, since each district has only one representative, it is clear who serves in that capacity and can be held accountable in subsequent elections. This is often cited as FPTP's strongest and most attractive feature. Finally, FPTP systems are thought to produce two-party competition over time, as minor parties in a district have little chance of winning, eventually causing supporters to defect to one of the two largest parties ("Duverger's Law"). And two-party competition serves to structure political affairs in clear, easily understood terms. Together, these features present a strong case for adopting an FPTP system.

Critics of FPTP systems note that majority governments produced in FPTP systems are actually "manufactured" ones in the sense that a majority of seats may be won by a party with less than a majority of the valid votes having been cast for that party. On some such occasions, its vote share is even less than that gained by its main opponent. This undercuts the claim to "majority rule." Moreover, rather than encouraging stable two-party competition, recent research has shown that FPTP systems regularly overshoot their mark, producing one-party dominated competition with a fragmented opposition, a situation all to familiar to Canadians. And, the "tactical" voting that leads to the Duverger phenomenon is said to give a misleading sense of voters' true preferences, in the long run reducing the choices available to two very similar, centrist parties or candidates. Critics also argue that a plurality formula discriminates against minorities or small parties, unless their vote is concentrated in a few districts. Yet, such concentrations can create striking regional discrepancies between vote shares and seat shares, giving a misleading impression of the degree to which regional differences divide a country. Indeed, rewarding them FPTP encourages regional divisions. Canada offers a graphic and long-standing example of this kind of negative impact. Finally, the one-party dominance FPTP systems create reduced voter turnout.

Proportional Representation Systems

Advocates of proportional representation systems usually believe that the main purpose of elections is to represent accurately the diverse interests and opinions in the electorate. They argue that the share of seats a party wins should be as closely equal to the share of votes it won as is mathematically possible. Proportional representation systems come in two forms. One uses relatively large district magnitudes and a **party-list ballot**. In each district, every party supplies a slate of candidates, and voters choose among the several party lists. Seats won by a party are assigned to individual candidates in the order they appear on their party's list, and so the party officials decide who will be chosen to represent its supporters. Critics see this as a failing. Candidates ranked high on the party elite's list are virtually assured election. But that need not be so. In most cases, voters simply do vote for a pre-set party list, but in several nations they can also choose among candidates on that list and, by so doing, alter the rankings party officials set out. In Switzerland, voters can even choose candidates from different parties' lists, thereby making the process more candidate centred.

The second type of PR, the **single transferable vote** (STV) or Hare System, is used to elect the Irish Dail, the Australian Senate, Malta's House of Representatives, and the Belfast Assembly in Northern Ireland. It is currently of renewed interest to American advocates of electoral reform under a new label—*choice voting*. In contrast to party-list PR systems, voters choose among candidates, not parties. They rank the candidates in preference, and votes are then transferred among candidates on the basis of these rankings. The counting and vote transfer procedure is rather complex and can involve many rounds of transfers and new counts when the number of seats allocated is large. Following World War I, it was used for local elections in several cities and towns in western Canada and in various parts of the United States (Johnston and Koene, 2000). It is still used for municipal elections in Cambridge, Massachusetts. From the early 1920s to 1955, the members of the provincial assemblies in Alberta and Manitoba who represented Calgary/Edmonton and Winnipeg, respectively, were also chosen by STV (Johnston, 1992; Jansen, 1998). More recently, some have suggested using it to elect members of the Canadian Senate.

Opinions are mixed on the benefits of achieving such accuracy of representation. Women and members of minorities who tend to get fairer representation under PR

(Rule, 1987) see it as correcting a bias that generally works against them. Opponents of PR argue that it encourages a proliferation of minor parties by granting representation to parties that gain only minuscule support from the electorate; they view it as source of political instability, especially when it awards positions to fringe or extremist parties. They believe that it also encourages a splintering of party support, rather than moderating the partisan divisions already present, thus yielding unstable coalition governments. They cite the former Weimar Republic, post-war Italy, and Israel as examples. These are extreme cases, though. In rebuttal, one can cite Switzerland, the Scandinavian countries, and Germany (where PR is used in a mixed system) as nations that have successfully used PR. One can also use minimal vote share thresholds and manipulate district magnitudes to raise the standard that splinter parties must meet to win seats.

Critics of PR point out that using multi-member districts makes it difficult to single out specific elected officials as one's representative and hold them accountable. They see closed party-list ballots as taking choice away from voters. Even more importantly, they maintain that since seats are shared over a number of parties, a single party rarely gains a majority of the seats to form a government and that this leads to political instability. Coalition governments are, in fact, the rule in most PR systems, but contrary to popular assumptions, coalition governments are not necessarily unstable. Often, such governments are broadly inclusive, offer better policy-based representation, and are very stable (Powell, 2000). Moreover, PR systems *do* seem to increase citizen participation in elections. Cross-national studies show that countries using PR report higher levels of voter turnout than those using a plurality system do. There are three reasons why this happens. By improving the fit between vote shares and seat shares, PR systems make voters feel that their votes make a difference. This makes elections more competitive under PR systems, leading parties to campaign more widely, which, in turn, increases voter turnout. Finally, proportional representation also encourages more parties to compete, since every vote they gain increases the share of seats they might win. This, in turn, increases the likelihood that voters will find parties with which they can agree and representation will become more inclusive (Blais and Carty, 1990, 167).

Mixed Electoral Systems

In recent decades, the debate over the merits of majoritarian versus PR systems has led electoral reform advocates to combine elements of both plurality and proportional representation systems in the hope of achieving the best features of each, thereby creating **mixed-member proportional systems (MMP)**. The most commonly used MMP design employs two tiers of districts—one consisting of single-member primary districts chosen by a plurality or majority formula and a secondary tier composed of either a single national pool of seats or several regionally defined pools, which are allocated by a PR formula. How many seats are allocated under each formula is seemingly a crucial factor in how such systems work, but the relative proportions vary quite widely in existing systems (Massicotte and Blais, 1999). With such variation, any attempt to predict or generalize about the performance of such systems is quite risky (Shugart and Wattenberg, 2001). The intent behind their adoption seems to be to combine "the accountability strengths of plurality rule in single-member constituencies with the offsetting proportional qualities of regional and national lists" (Dunleavy and Margetts, 1995, 27). However, they also combine the FPTP tendency to reward territorially concentrated minorities disproportionately with PR's tendency to encourage splinter parties where a large-magnitude, nationwide district is employed. New Zealand, Italy, and Japan adopted variants of this model in the early 1990s. Later, the Plant Report and the Jenkins Commission on electoral reform in Britain drew on that experience in proposing that the newly formed Scottish Parliament and Welsh National Assembly be elected through MMP. Several other nations have adopted MMP systems since then, principally in the former USSR, Central America, Asia, and Africa. Thirty-one nations now use MMP schemes in electing their national assembly (Massicotte and Blais, 1999, 345).

Electoral Reform

ELECTORAL REFORM EFFORTS COME IN PERIODIC WAVES. WE ARE CURRENTLY caught up in such a period of change, one initiated by the collapse of communism and the USSR. The task of setting up free elections in communist bloc countries, where even a memory of such events was missing, led to much research on institutional design and "engineering" electoral systems. "Third-wave democratization" in other countries in Africa, Asia, and Latin America added to this dynamic. The move toward replacing FPTP systems with mixed electoral systems extended the effort to long-established democracies. Much of the effort dealt with issues raised in the previous section, but the opening of the twenty-first century has brought them to North America with force, and other events there have broadened their focus.

The debacle surrounding the American presidential election of 2000 has brought issues concerning ballot structure voting methods to public attention there. The *"Help America Vote" Act* (*HAVA*) was recently passed to fund research into improving the transparency, ease, accuracy, and reliability of voting technologies and procedures. On another front, the decennial exercise in redrawing electoral district boundaries, completed with little controversy in Canada, has drawn its usual flurry of litigation in the United States and continues to do so. This has left many Americans thinking that a better, fairer means of doing that task is urgently needed. And, on both sides of the 49th parallel, concern about the huge tide of money that has swamped electoral campaign efforts, creating unfairness in many forms and settings, has led to reform legislation, most controversially in the form of the *Bipartisan Campaign Reform Act* (*BCRA*)—or *McCain-Feingold Act*—in the United States.

In both nations, there has been discussion of abandoning FPTP for some form of proportional representation or a mixed system. This effort has progressed farthest in Canada, where official commissions or inquiries have been undertaken in Prince

Edward Island, Quebec, New Brunswick, and Ontario in 2003. British Columbia has gone the farthest with respect to reform. A Citizen Assembly for Electoral Reform has been struck, its members—ordinary citizens, one male and one female elector chosen in each riding—selected, and its "studies" begun. Should it recommend that reforms be proposed, these are to be put to a referendum in the May 17, 2005, provincial election. That date is significant in another sense, too. Its certainty reflects that provincial government's having adopted another far-reaching electoral reform: fixed election dates at regular four-year intervals. Efforts in these directions have also been undertaken at the federal level in Canada. The opposition parties unsuccessfully put forward a bill in 2003 calling for a referendum on adopting proportional representation. And, the Law Commission of Canada conducted a series of public hearings across the nation and will issue a report in mid-2004. These efforts have been spearheaded by the organization Fair Vote Canada.

The issues raised in electoral reform efforts are always contentious ones. Andre Blais has offered a set of criteria by which we can judge existing electoral arrangements and those being proposed as reforms. He argues that a well-functioning electoral system should ensure that the voting system is simple enough for voters to understand, yet capable of accurately reflecting their preferences. It should also ensure that each person's vote counts equally. It should produce elected officials and governments that are broadly representative of the electorate's interests and concerns and not systematically biased against certain groups or interests. And, finally, it should produce public officials and governments that are accommodating to citizens, effective in governing, and easily accountable to voters (Blais, 1999).

Summary

Heralded by some and battered by the criticism of others, elections remain a vital part of modern politics. Above all alternative mechanisms, they provide the critical linkage between citizens and the political elite. In turn, electoral systems shape the conduct of elections and the focus of electoral competition in a number of important respects. The basic choice remains that between majoritarian and proportional representation schemes. However, research on the workings of electoral systems in different societies and competitive circumstances has yielded a better understanding of those features that can be most easily manipulated to produce specific desired results. Similarly, greater insight into how constitutional design and other aspects of the legal and institutional framework in modern governments shape the role that the electoral process plays provides a basis for more prudent reforms in the future. Still, the differences in basic political philosophy that divide proponents of the two main forms of electoral systems will likely remain. As we have noted throughout this chapter, many other factors influence the degree to which these criteria are met. Still, if we can achieve electoral rules and procedures that produce elections that are fairly conducted and representative of the voters' preferences, we will be well on our way to confirming that elections are, indeed, the defining institutions of modern democracy.

Discussion Questions

1. Discuss the role that constitutions play in the electoral process.
2. Are there political contexts in which the strong control provided to a dominant plurality or majority by majoritarian electoral institutions is potentially harmful?
3. Discuss the impact that the adoption of a mixed-member proportional (MMP) electoral system for choosing the members of the Canadian House of Commons might have on the current regional fragmentation of party competition in Canada.

References

Blais, Andre. 1999. "Criteria for Assessing Electoral Systems." *Electoral Insight, 1,* 3–6.

Blais, Andre and Ken Carty. 1990. "Does Proportional Representation Foster Voter Turnout?" *European Journal of Political Research, 18,* 167–181.

Blais, Andre, Louis Massicotte, and Agnieszka Dobrzynska. 1997. "Direct Presidential Elections: A World Summary." *Electoral Studies, 16,* 441–55.

Dunleavy, Patrick and Helen Margetts. 1995. "Understanding the Dynamics of Electoral Reforms." *International Political Science Review,* 16, 9: 9–29.

Jansen, Harold J. 1998. *The Single Transferable Vote in Alberta and Manitoba.* Unpublished doctoral dissertation. University of Alberta. Edmonton, Alberta.

Johnston, J. Paul. 1992. *The Use of the Single Transferable Vote in Alberta Provincial Elections, 1924–1955.* Paper presented at the Annual Meeting of the American Political Science Association, Chicago, IL.

Johnston, J. Paul and Miriam Koene. 2000. "Learning History's Lessons Anew: The Use of STV in Canadian Municipal Elections," in Shaun Bowler and Bernard Grofman, eds. *Elections in Australia, Ireland, and Malta under the Single Transferable Vote.* Ann Arbor, Mich.: The University of Michigan Press.

Johnston, J. Paul and Harvey E. Pasis, eds. 1990. *Representation and Electoral Systems: Canadian Perspectives.* Scarborough, ON: Prentice-Hall Canada.

Katz, Richard S. 1997. *Democracy and Elections.* Oxford: Oxford University Press.

Massicotte, Louis and Andre Blais. "Mixed Electoral Systems: A Conceptual and Empirical Survey." *Electoral Studies, 18,* 341–366.

Powell, G. Bingham, Jr. 2000. *Elections as Instruments of Democracy.* New Haven, Conn.: Yale University Press.

Rule, Wilma. 1987. "Electoral Systems, Contextual Factors and Women's Opportunity for Election to Parliament in Twenty-Three Democracies." *Western Political Quarterly, 40,* 477–498.

Further Readings

Cox, Gary W. 1997. *Making Votes Count: Strategic Coordination in the World's Electoral Systems.* Cambridge: Cambridge University Press.

Johnston, J. Paul and Harvey E. Pasis, eds.1990. *Representation and Electoral Systems: Canadian Perspectives.* Scarborough, ON: Prentice-Hall.

LeDuc, Lawrence, Richard G. Niemi, and Pippa Norris, eds. 1996. *Comparing Democracies: Elections and Voting in Global Perspective.* Thousand Oaks, CA: Sage Publications.

Lijphart, Arend. 1994. *Electoral Systems and Party Systems.* Oxford: Oxford University Press.

Weblinks

Elections Canada
www.elections.ca

Inter-Parliamentary Union
www.ipu.org

Proportional Representation Library
http://mtholyoke.edu/acad/polit/damy/prlib.htm

Elections Around the World
www.aceproject.org

International Foundation for Election Systems
www.ifes.org

Fair Vote Canada
www.fairvotecanada.org

Arenas of Politics

PART III

This section examines some of the most important spaces and actors, outside the formal institutions of the state, that influence the course of political events. The play of power and influence is ubiquitous, occurring both inside and outside of the formal boundaries of the state and taking on many different forms. Perhaps the most familiar arenas of politics involve the formation and representation of political identities and interests and linking them to democratic institutions and the policy process. Political parties, interest groups, and social movements all act as transmission belts in contemporary politics. Nevertheless, political interests are forged in a variety of settings, including the broader political culture, civil society, local politics, and gendered spaces. Each of these arenas demonstrates that the informal and the personal often are very political. Citizens mobilize behind many vehicles of political influence, but not all citizens share the same capacity to influence political affairs. The chapters in this section also show that contemporary politics, especially in liberal democratic systems, is marked by a growing democratic deficit. Individual actors are choosing different models of political action that focus on the local or the global, rather than the national. They are also choosing to lend their political energies to non-governmental organizations and social movements, rather than to the formal institutions of liberal democratic politics and associated organizations, such as political parties. Finally, this section examines violence, from the singular act of a terrorist to war, as the means to and an arena for political action. Although violence always has been part of the toolkit of political actors, its heightened significance in the contemporary period speaks loudly to the failure of more familiar political arenas to represent political interests and to resolve social conflicts on local and global scales.

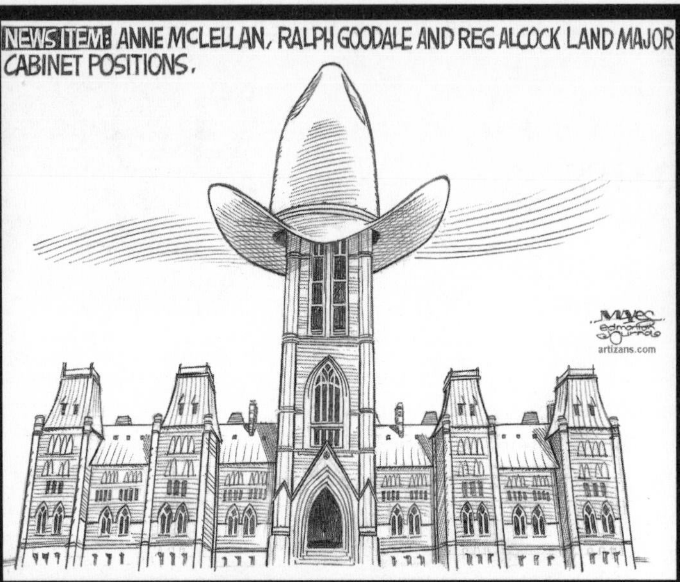
NEWS ITEM: ANNE MCLELLAN, RALPH GOODALE AND REG ALCOCK LAND MAJOR CABINET POSITIONS.
artizans.com

CHAPTER 14

REPRESENTATION

Objectives

Political representation is at the core of modern democratic politics. Indeed, representation is such a taken-for-granted aspect of political life that few people ever pause to explore what it means. As such, the initial objective of this chapter is to encourage the sort of critical reflection that will ensure that students appreciate the complexity of political representation. A second objective is to illuminate the ways that the institutions of political representation—including electoral systems, legislatures, political parties, interest groups and social movements—shape the character of political representation due to their "institutional biases." Finally, students will be pressed to consider the claim that representation is an active and formative relationship that shapes our political identities and the character of politics.

STEVE PATTEN

Introduction

Liberal democratic political regimes, such as the United States, Canada, and the United Kingdom are, by design, representative democracies. The people, it is said, govern themselves through their elected representatives. In fact, one of the chambers of the United States Congress is called the House of Representatives. In Canada and other parliamentary systems, the House of Commons is considered a representative chamber, and Members of Parliament are expected to serve as representatives of their constituents. But what does it mean to identify an elected governing body as representative? What is meant by the concept of political representation? These apparently simple questions do not have simple answers. Political representation is a multi-faceted and evolving concept. Even among the academic experts there is only limited agreement on what constitutes political representation. This chapter begins with an examination of the concept of political representation; then turns to an examination of the core institutions, mechanisms, and processes of political representation; and concludes with a discussion of the ways in which the processes of representation serve to constitute our political identities and shape the character of politics.

The Concept of Political Representation

POLITICAL REPRESENTATION IS A CONCEPT OF THE MODERN AGE. IN THE medieval era, the concept of representation had but one meaning: to represent was to "symbolize" or be the concrete embodiment of that which was represented. Thus, to say that the medieval monarch "represented the realm" was to suggest that the queen or king embodied, in their very person, the essence of the realm. Obviously, this notion of representation as **symbolic representation** was depoliticized and pre-democratic; there was no notion that consent had to be established through political arrangements, such as electoral democracy. In the era of the absolutist monarchs, it was commonly thought that sovereignty—or supreme and final governing authority—rested with the monarch by divine right, not political authority.

In Britain, France, and America, the liberal revolutions of the seventeenth and eighteenth centuries established parliamentary and republican systems of representative government, and the modern concept of political representation was born. With the establishment of freer and fairer elections rules and the extension of the vote during the nineteenth and early twentieth centuries, these governing systems were progressively democratized. This spawned considerable debate about the defining characteristics of political representation in a representative democracy. Leading liberal thinkers of the time offered a perspective that has come to be known as **descriptive representation**. From this perspective, the condition of representation is met only to the extent that our legislatures are a representative microcosm of the broader society. But conservative thinkers insisted on more formalistic notions of representation that were rooted in the assumption that representation merely requires that legislative bodies are authorized and/or held accountable by regular elections. As long as our law-making bodies are elected, the condition of **formalistic representation** is fully met.

Today, both descriptive and formalistic notions of political representation fail to capture popular thinking because it is now more common to conceive of representation as a process or activity, rather than a state of affairs. Since the 1960s, the most influential academic interpretation of political representation has been Hannah Pitkin's claim that representation involves representatives "acting in the interest of the represented in a manner that is responsive to them" (Pitkin, 1967, 209). By construing representation as an active, or instrumental, relationship, our attention shifts from the adjective "representative" to the verb "to represent." This marks a shift to what is known as **instrumental representation**. The defining feature of instrumental representation is the commitment to take action and speak for the represented.

But the concept's evolution does not stop there. Since the 1980s, a growing number of scholars have begun to argue that the essence of political representation can never be fully captured by instrumental notions of representatives acting for the represented (Dobrowolsky, 1998). Arguing that it is a mistake to assume that there are clear and already existing interests waiting to be represented, students of representation now argue that representation is never merely a matter of "acting for" a particular interest or community. Instead, representation is, by its nature, a formative relationship that actually serves to define the character of the political identities and interests that are being represented.

The point being made here is somewhat abstract, but it can be reformulated in fairly straightforward terms. According to one definition, a representation is a portrayal of something. Because individual citizens and communities are complex and multi-faceted, there can be many different portrayals of the political interests of a particular citizen or community. To represent a community of interest—such as agricultural workers, Atlantic Canadians, hard working taxpayers, or New Yorkers—is to act for this community of interest. But action cannot be taken without making assumptions about the proper portrayal of that community's core identity and political interests. To make and then act on such assumptions is to offer a portrayal that serves to define the community, once it is accepted in the collective imagination. In other words, the act of representing feeds back on the represented, defining who and what their political interests are. Representation, then, is a "formative relationship"—it "forms," "constitutes," or "gives meaning to" the interests that are represented.

There are, then, two dimensions to contemporary political representation. The instrumental dimension involves acting for a particular segment of the population or political interest. The constitutive dimension involves giving meaning to that interest by defining who it is that is being represented—this is known as **constitutive representation**. To understand political representation, it is necessary to explore both its instrumental and its constitutive dimensions (Jenson, 1992).

Instrumental Representation in Contemporary Political Institutions

PITKIN'S READING OF THE MEANING OF POLITICAL REPRESENTATION ACTUALLY signifies an attempt to steer a course between two views on the proper role and responsibilities of modern political representatives. The debate Pitkin attempts to navigate pits delegate against trustee models of instrumental representation. At the bottom, the **delegate model** stresses the importance of responsiveness, mirroring as best as possible the interests of the represented. The delegate model's first premise is that representative democracy is a necessary, but highly imperfect, substitute for direct democracy. The goal, therefore, should to maximize responsiveness in an effort to approximate the outcomes that would result from direct democracy. The actions of representatives should not be found to be at odds with the wishes of the represented.

The more conservative **trustee model** rejects the suggestion that good political representation is merely responsive representation. Representative democracy, according to the trustee model, is not merely a second-rate alternative to direct democracy. Instead, the virtue of representative democracy is that it provides a unique opportunity for a select group of trustees of the public interest to meet and thoughtfully discuss issues of governance in the deliberative chambers of congress or parliament. The trustee does not necessarily mirror specific community interests but, instead, works together with other elected representatives to find solutions for the common good. Representative democracy is, moreover, an opportunity to make wise decisions that are not constrained by the short term—and perhaps ill-informed—wishes of the population. The eighteenth century political theorist and Member of the British Parliament, Edmund Burke, was known for his advocacy of the trustee model of political representation. In a famous public speech, Burke argued that political representatives should never be bound by the inclinations of those they represent. Parliament, he stressed, is a deliberative assembly, and the first obligation of Members of Parliament is to employ their reason and judgment in deliberations regarding the national interest.

Today, the Burkean trustee model of political representation is inconsistent with the trend toward emphasizing responsiveness. Indeed, enthusiasm for the principles of direct democracy not only has informed the popularization of the delegate model of representation but also calls for a form of **plebiscitarian democracy**. Plebiscitarianism combines a delegate model of representation with the regular use of referenda—the people voting directly on key policy issues—and mechanisms of recall that allow citizens to, in essence, fire their elected representative if that representative is unresponsive and fails to accurately reflect public opinion.

At first glance, most students will assume that the delegate model and plebiscitarianism are preferable because they appear to have a greater claim to the mantle of democracy. Indeed, the democratic principle of majority rule is often invoked to defend the use of referenda and justify binding representatives to act as delegates of the dominant opinion within the community they represent. But the supporters of a trustee model argue that the overuse of referenda and treating representatives as mere delegates will not allow for the protection of minority interests. Nor will it ensure that representatives have the freedom to use their judgment to rise above local interests in favour of the national interest. Perhaps that is why Pitkin advocated an understanding of political representation that demands that representatives use their judgment to act in the broad interests of citizens but do so in a manner that is responsive to them. In considering the design and functioning of our political institutions, there is reason to follow Pitkin in trying to find a balance between the delegate and trustee models of instrumental representation. Students will note, however, that in Canada, our political institutions are biased in favour of the trustee model.

Institutions and Processes of Political Representation

WHEN EVALUATING THE PROCESSES OF INSTRUMENTAL REPRESENTATION IN liberal democratic political regimes, political scientists have tended to focus on the role played by political parties and the elected members of legislative bodies, including members of the United State Congress and the House of Commons in the United Kingdom and Canada. It is useful to extend our gaze slightly to also consider the role of the electoral system and some less formal institutions of political representation, specifically interest groups and social movement organizations.

Electoral Systems

The electoral system is the legal framework for transforming citizens' votes into legislative seats. Students often assume that electoral systems are representationally neutral. But this is not the case. The representational consequences of the electoral system are quite significant. In Canada, the United Kingdom, and the United States, for example, a **single-member plurality** electoral system has the effect of limiting the number and range of truly competitive political parties and increasing the likelihood that party politicians will adopt a stance consistent with the trustee model of political representation. The reasons for this are not complex. In a single-member plurality electoral system, the voters in each constituency elect just one member, and that election is determined by a simple plurality—that is, the candidate with the most votes wins. This is a winner-take-all system that disadvantages smaller political parties because if a party's candidates cannot win the most votes, they do not win anything at all. The result is that when the distribution of votes is contrasted with the distribution of seats in the legislature, the larger parties are overrepresented and the small parties without unique regional concentrations of support are underrepresented.

There are many examples of the single-member plurality system overrepresenting the dominant party. Take, for example, the province of Ontario in the 2000 Canadian general election. In that province, the Liberal Party won 51.5 percent of the vote but fully 97.1 percent of the seats. The Canadian Alliance, with almost 24 percent of the vote won less than 2 percent of the seats. Such results as these have a dampening effect on voters and activists who might have a desire to support or organize small parties that are committed to actively representing the views and interests of a particular segment of the population, such as Canada's Green Party or Christian Heritage Party. By contrast, large parties will be rewarded for downplaying particular differences of political interest in favour of offering vague *status quo* policy platforms that promise little more than to be effective trustees of the public interest.

By contrast, a multiple-member **proportional representation** electoral system encourages smaller parties by guaranteeing that the proportion of legislative seats will more closely reflect the party's proportion of the popular vote. Voters and activists can throw their support behind small parties that will represent their particular political interests and know that their votes and efforts will pay off.

Clearly, there are many other factors that also influence the number and character of political parties. However, there is considerable evidence of the relationship between the dominant political parties championing a Burkean trustee model of representation and the functioning of the single-member plurality electoral system. In fact, this relationship flows both ways—Canada's governing parties have, on several occasions, used essentially Burkean arguments regarding the value of having a small number of particularly strong political parties that are capable of forming majority governments to forestall the adoption of proportional representation.

Legislatures

As the branch of government responsible for law making, the legislature—the Parliament in Canada, the Congress in the United States—is a primary institution in the process of political representation. This is not the place for a detailed examination of legislative systems, but a few comments contrasting the American congressional system and Canada's parliamentary system will be helpful. The Canadian parliamentary system is structured by two core principles: executive dominance and strong **party discipline**. Parliamentary systems are characterized by what is called the **fusion of powers**. This is a reference to the fact that the political executive—the Prime Minister and the Cabinet—is responsible for both the executive function of state administration and law implementation *and* guiding the legislative function of law making. The Prime Minister and the Cabinet are members of the House of Commons. Indeed, the principle of **responsible government** demands that the Cabinet sets the legislative and governing agenda; the House of Commons exists merely to approve or reject that agenda. Major policy initiatives and new laws are introduced into Parliament by Cabinet Ministers, and the role played by elected members of the House is to scrutinize and then approve or reject these initiatives and laws. The role that the Cabinet plays in this system of responsible government ensures continued executive dominance in the parliamentary system.

Executive dominance is then reinforced by the principle of strong party discipline, particularly in Canada. Given that almost all members of the House of Commons were elected as candidates who offered themselves under particular party banners, the thrust and parry of parliamentary politics is shaped by the informal rules of the parliamentary party system. Paramount among these informal rules is the injunction that MPs support their party's line on all important issues. Each party speaks with one voice, and elected representatives are expected to accept the Burkean notion that when their sense of the local interests they represent conflict with the party's view on what is in the broader interest, they shall espouse the party line.

In combination, executive dominance and party discipline undermine the efforts of elected Members of Parliament who wish to act in accordance with the delegate model of representation. MPs can introduce private members legislation in response to the expressed wishes of their constituents. But the executive-centred system sidelines this legislation, while privileging legislative initiatives emanating from the Cabinet. Certainly, there are politicians who champion local interests and causes, and since the 1980s, there has been growing support for parliamentary reform to empower MPs to act in accordance with a delegate model of representation. But change has come slowly because the system of responsible government and the parliamentary party system are biased in favour of the trustee model of political representation.

In the United States, by contrast, the **separation of powers** eliminates the possibility of direct executive dominance and weakens party discipline. Under the American congressional system, there is a clear separation of the Congress, with its legislative powers, from the Presidency, with its executive powers. The President works hard to influence the legislative process in Congress, and he has some levers to influence Congress—including the threat of using the presidential legislative veto power—but the power to initiate and approve legislation rests, in the end, with the Congress. Moreover, while members of the Congress tend to vote along party lines, the notion of party discipline is considerably weaker in the congressional system. American legislators are much more likely than their Canadian counterparts to embrace a perspective on political representation that is in keeping with the principles of a delegate model of representation. In the Congress, legislative politics is as much about accommodating conflicting regional and local concerns as it is about broader party interests. Regional and local concerns are not absent from legislative debate in Canada, but they feature much more prominently in the United States Congress. The institutional bias in the congressional system is, then, toward the delegate model of representation.

Political Parties

Electoral politics and political parties are central to the processes of political representation in modern liberal democracies. Mainstream political science has, for its part, tended to characterize political parties as the institution most responsible for articulating societal interests to the state. This has assured parties considerable legitimacy; in fact, political scientists often assume political parties are uniquely responsible for setting the public policy agenda and guiding the processes of governance. Parties, from this perspective, are the primary representative institution in a democracy. Even during the late 1980s and early 1990s, when Canadian public opinion was most sceptical about the legitimacy of political parties, a major Royal Commission examining electoral reform issues—the Royal Commission on Electoral Reform and Party Financing—concluded that parties are the key to effective political representation because "only political parties can reconcile and accommodate diverse and competing interests to reach agreement on public policy" (cited in Dobrowolsky & Jenson, 1993, 65).

The Commission's conclusions regarding the unique capacities of political parties are not surprising. What is particularly interesting, from the perspective of theories of representation, was the Commission's implicit assumptions about the preferred character of political parties. Reflecting a perspective that is widespread in Canada, the Commission implied that parties are, ideally, large integrative institutions that work to accommodate diverse and competing interests. In Canada, parties of this sort are known as **brokerage parties**. Elsewhere, they are often called "catch all parties." Rather than committing themselves to the representation of particular societal interests, brokerage parties present themselves as champions of the broader public interest. They privilege pragmatism over policy consistency, and they tend not to challenge dominant policy paradigms. In campaigns, the leader's public image and the party's commitment to act as a trustee of the public interest overshadow unique or bold policy platforms. Brokerage parties strive to make a virtue out of being non-doctrinaire. Typically, these parties will have a particular base of support to which they feel some obligations, and like all modern political parties, brokerage parties do promise to be responsive. But in terms of models of representation, they are quite Burkean—they promise, first and foremost, to be accommodative trustees of the national interest.

Not everyone would accept the suggestion that the ideal political party acts as a broker of a variety of competing social demands. Brokerage politics, indeed, requires a certain responsiveness to reconcile competing interests, but one consequence of the accommodative politics of brokering is that many voices, particularly those associated with minority interests, are not heard. That is why supporters of a delegate model of representation often prefer more programmatic **doctrinal parties** that commit themselves to steadfastly articulating the views of particular ideological currents or political interests within society. In a single-member plurality electoral system, non-brokerage doctrinal parties have little chance of electoral success, but their commitment to articulating an alternative ideological vision, or representing a particular interest, overrides any pragmatic tendency to focus simply on winning elections. In a proportional representation electoral system, small parties win more seats, and as a result, there are more opportunities for doctrinal parties to serve as delegates of their supporters.

Groups and Movements

While political parties operating through the electoral system and within legislatures are at the core of representative democracy, interest groups and social movement organizations are also active mechanisms of political representation. Interest groups are organizations that act to influence the content and direction of public policy without seeking to hold formal legislative or executive power. They represent particular interests directly to government policy makers. Broad social movements, such as feminism and environmentalism, are informal networks of individuals and groups primarily interested in bringing about societal change by influencing our ideas and behaviour (Phillips, 1996). But many social movement organizations direct a portion of their energies into influencing government policy and, by doing so, they play a role similar to interest groups.

Groups and movements are sometimes criticized for subverting electoral democracy and the representative role of political parties. But this criticism emanates from the logic of the trustee model. Proponents of interest group politics tend to embrace the delegate model of political representation. From their perspective, brokerage-style party politics fails to represent a sufficient diversity of voices, and it is not good enough to just assume that governments are public trustees governing in the national interest. Interest groups and social movement organizations provide additional representational opportunities and alternative avenues for political representation. As representatives of particular interests, they ensure that more voices are heard and a wider range of issues is addressed. There is good reason, then, to assume that the political activity of groups and movements has the potential to enhance democracy.

For many observers, however, the question of the whether groups and movements have a positive impact on representative democracy depends on the types of voices that are heard through group politics. Historically, interest group politics was characterized as the realm of covert "backroom politics"—or elite accommodation—in which the social and economic elite interacted with the political and bureaucratic elite to shape public policy in their own self-interest (Presthus, 1973). Obviously the processes of elite accommodation do little to enhance democracy. But since the 1960s, the range of groups and movements involved in interest group politics has increased. There are now many highly visible citizens' action groups advocating for policies in the interest of non-elite segments of society. Unfortunately, while these groups have a public profile, the most visible groups are often the least powerful. Interest groups with real power—business interests, in particular—are quietly working the corridors of power. Thus, while groups and movements provide an alternative mechanism of political representation, it is a mechanism that is not equally effective for all segments of society.

Constitutive Representation: Defining the Content and Character of Politics

POLITICAL SCIENTISTS WITH AN INTEREST IN GOVERNANCE AND PUBLIC POLICY have, for obvious reasons, been very interested in the institutions, mechanisms, and processes of instrumental representation. Unfortunately, focusing on instrumental representation to the exclusion of constitutive representation hides the fact that representation is about more than advocating on behalf of pre-existing political interests. It is important, therefore, to consider the constitutive dimension of political representation. The starting point for understanding constitutive representation is the observation that political identities and interests are "socially constructed" and the discursive processes of political representation play a role in their social construction.

What does it mean to say that political identities are socially constructed? Essentially, it means that our political identities do not flow naturally from some objective facts about the communities we live in or about ourselves. Instead, there are social processes of debate, dialogue, and sharing of ideas that give meaning to things. These are called "discursive processes" because they involve the sharing of language, or discourse, that is imbued with meaning. We can probe this further by reflecting on our personal characteristics and places within the social structure. Clearly, there are many factors we can identify as potentially important to how we understand our political identities and interests. These factors include our gender, employment status, wealth, race, ethnic background, sexual orientation, religion, region of residence, and status as taxpayers or, perhaps, recipients of government social assistance. The discursive processes of constitutive representation play a role in determining which of these factors will be most politically salient and, therefore, central to our political interests. Does it matter politically that you are white, gay, a taxpayer, or resident of the province of Alberta? Historically, in Canada, regional and national political identities have been most salient. In the early 1990s, this was reinforced by the emergence of two non-brokerage parties—the Reform Party and the Bloc Québécois—that highlighted differences of regional and national political interest. Under the banner "The West Wants In," the Reform Party claimed to speak for western Canadian political interests. But the party's policies were shaped by a particular brand of conservative populism. Thus, through its representational discourse, the Reform Party called Albertans into politics as westerners, and then defined their interests in terms of populist conservatism. This is what Stuart Hall meant when he explained that representation "has to be understood as an active and formative relationship" that forges and gives meaning to interests by discursively defining *who* it is that is being represented (Hall, 1983, 26).

To argue that the constitutive dimension of political representation is, at the bottom, a process of identity formation is to make a point of considerable political consequence. Political identities serve to orient political action. We are all called into the world of politics on the basis of our political identities. We find political allies, understand and navigate salient political cleavages, and define the norms and values of politics from the perspective of our political identities. It can, thus, be said that the politics of representation helps shape who we are and what politics is all about. How important is the politics of race? Are our interests defined by our class position or our status as taxpayers? The representational activities of groups, movements, and parties shape the range of identities and interests that are considered politically relevant and, therefore, taken into account in the processes of governance. Political representation, from this vantage, is an exercise of profound power; it defines the content and character of politics (Jenson, 1999, 44).

In discussions of constitutive representation and the discursive processes of identity formation, one is likely to come across the idea of *identity politics*, which is a term reserved for the conscious pursuit of group-based identities by movements of, for example, women, Aboriginal peoples, and gays and lesbians. Since the 1960s, numerous progressive social movements have struggled to transform oppressive social relations. In the process, they have altered the landscape of salient political interests and identities in ways that have allowed new types of politics to emerge. As Barry Adam argued in his study of gay liberation and the gay and lesbian rights movement, it was only by embracing and articulating a collective political identity that homosexuals could be organized as a movement capable of representing and defending its interests (Adam, 1987, 107–108). Gay-positive political advocacy groups, such Equality for Gays and Lesbians Everywhere (EGALE), actively represent the political interests of gay men and lesbians in Canada. At the same time, however, they legitimize queer political identities and alter the landscape of political cleavages that define Canadian politics.

Summary

The preceding discussion has been quite wide ranging. The chapter began with an exploration of the concept of representation that identified instrumental and constitutive dimensions to political representation. This was followed by an outline of the delegate and trustee models of the proper role and responsibilities of political representatives. An examination of the core institutions, mechanisms, and processes of political representation—electoral systems, legislatures, political parties, interests groups, and social movements—revealed the extent to which institutional biases favour particular models of representation. In Canada, despite a popular trend toward embracing the delegate model, the existing institutions of political representation are biased in favour of the trustee model. Finally, after this detailed examination of instrumental representation, the chapter concluded with a brief discussion of constitutive representation that aimed to show how the discursive politics of representation shapes our political identities and the character of politics.

Discussion Questions

1. Which model of instrumental representation are you most comfortable with, the delegate or trustee model? Why?
2. In what ways do the institutional structures, mechanisms, and processes of political representation influence the extent to which a delegate or trustee model of representation will predominate?
3. How would you explain the claim that political representation is an active and formative—or "constitutive"—relationship? How is this important to the character of politics?

References

Adam, Barry D. 1987. *The Rise of a Gay and Lesbian Movement.* Boston: Twayne Publishers.

Dobrowolsky, Alexandra and Jane Jenson. 1993. "Reforming the Parties: Prescriptions for Democracy" in Susan D. Phillips, ed. *How Ottawa Spends 1993–1994: A More Democratic Canada . . . ?* Ottawa: Carleton University Press.

Dobrowolsky, Alexandra. 1998. "Of 'Special Interest': Interest, Identity and Feminist Constitutional Activism in Canada," *Canadian Journal of Political Science* XXXI:4, 707–742.

Jenson, Jane. 1999. "Understanding Politics: Concepts of Identity in Political Science" in James Bickerton and Alain-G Gagnon, eds. *Canadian Politics.* 3rd edition. Peterborough: Broadview Press.

Jenson, Jane. 1992. "A Political Economy Approach to Interest Representation" in Alain G. Gagnon and A. Brian Tanguay, eds. *Democracy with Justice/La juste démocratie: Essays in Honour of Khayyam Zev Paltiel.* Ottawa: Carleton University Press.

Phillips, Susan D. 1996. "Competing, Connecting, and Complementing: Parties, Interest Groups, and New Social Movements" in A. Brian Tanguay and Alain-G. Gagnon, eds. *Canadian Parties in Transition.* 2nd edition. Toronto: Nelson Canada.

Pitkin, Hannah. 1967. *The Concept of Representation.* Berkeley: The University of California Press.

Presthus, Robert. 1973. *Elite Accommodation in Canadian Politics.* Cambridge, UK: Cambridge University Press.

Further Readings

Carroll, William K., ed. 1997. *Organizing Dissent: Contemporary Social Movements in Theory and Practice: Studies in the Politics of Counter-Hegemony.* 2nd edition. Toronto: Garamond Press.

Pross, A. Paul. 1992. *Group Politics and Public Policy.* 2nd edition. Toronto: Oxford University Press.

Thorburn, Hugh G. and Alan Whitehorn, ed. 2001. *Party Politics in Canada.* 8th edition. Scarborough: Prentice-Hall.

Weblinks

Council of Canadians
www.canadians.org

Democracy Watch
www.dwatch.ca

Elections Canada
www.elections.ca

CHAPTER 15

POLITICAL CULTURES

Objectives

The purpose of this chapter is to explore why culture is important in the study of politics. Culture involves a shared way of life and, therefore, provides a collective frame of understanding that may influence and even potentially explain different political outcomes. Yet, culture is also a contentious and critical political concept. This chapter provides an overview of three distinct approaches to the study of culture and politics. These are the *political culture, cultural studies*, and *cultural identities* approaches. Each of these approaches traditionally examines politics and culture within the boundaries of a given state or country. However, the current period of globalization, coupled with the increasing diversity of national populations, suggests that we develop a new perspective on culture. In order to come to grips with the relationship between culture and politics in the twenty-first century, political scientists increasingly need to consider the implications of ideas, images, and especially people rapidly criss-crossing national borders.

YASMEEN ABU-LABAN

Introduction

The term "culture" is often used to refer to art, music, literature, and painting. Some distinguish between the "high culture" of classical composers, such as Mozart, or the plays of William Shakespeare, and today's "popular culture" forms, such as the rap music of Eminem or the television show "The Osbornes." Yet, culture is also sometimes used more broadly to talk about language, religion, sports, advertising, and even collectivities of varied sizes, as seen in such phrases as "Western culture," "American culture," and "youth culture." Consequently, culture has been a notoriously contentious concept, and hundreds of definitions have been offered for the term. How then should we understand what culture means?

Political scientists and social scientists generally agree that culture is something broader than just the arts and define **culture** simply as a shared way of life. Culture is not the property of an individual but, rather, is collective. Culture includes language, customs and manners, dress, rituals, behavioural conventions, and religion and other systems of belief. Precisely because culture is collective, a human creation, and inherited, it has long been of interest to those who study human social and political life.

The Significance of Culture to the Study of Politics

IN THE POST-WORLD WAR II PERIOD, CULTURE HAS BEEN VIEWED AS significant to the study of politics for three reasons. One reason has been that culture helps describe and explain the differences between states, including the kinds of policies they may adopt. For example, Canada has a universal health-care program and the United States does not. It has been argued that such contrasting characteristics can be explained by cultural differences. Seymour Martin Lipset (1990) argues that Canadians are more trusting of government, have a more collective orientation, and are less individualistic than their neighbours below the 49th parallel.

A second reason that those studying politics are interested in culture relates to the question of power. Culture has been used to explain why some groups hold power and how and why subordinate groups do, or do not, challenge those in power. For example, in Western countries, education is linked with one's life chances, including the kind of job and income one is able to acquire. Pierre Bourdieu has focused on the educational system in Western industrialized countries to examine why children of middle-class parents tend to excel more than children of working-class parents (1973). Bordieu finds that although schools may seem neutral, in fact, meeting the classroom expectations and doing well in assessments require certain cultural understandings. Bourdieu argues that in contrast to working-class parents, middle-class parents are able to endow their children with what he calls **cultural capital**. Just as money gives one the power to purchase consumer goods, cultural capital gives middle-class children the required language and cultural tools to succeed in education, to secure prestigious and well-paying jobs, and, ultimately, to perpetuate class inequalities generation after generation.

A third reason that culture is significant to the study of politics relates to the question of democratic justice. Is it enough to say that equality is achieved when all the laws in a country treat everyone the same? Or should there be distinct rights, treatment, or recognition for some groups on the basis of cultural difference? Whether indigenous peoples and ethnic, racial, and religious minorities should have distinct recognition in the law has been the source of ongoing debate. Consider the still unresolved question in Canada over whether the province of Quebec, which contains a majority of people whose first language is French, should actually be recognized as a "distinct society" in the Canadian constitution.

In sum, culture is highly relevant to the study of politics because it pertains to differences between countries; relations of power and challenges to the *status quo*; and questions of democracy and justice. Each of these reasons, in turn, is associated with a particular approach to the study of culture. As outlined below, the question of explaining cultural differences between countries is tied to the approach to the study of culture known as **political culture**. The question of power relations is key to a **cultural studies** approach. And, last, the focus on questions of culture, democracy, and justice is central to examining **cultural identity**.

Major Themes and Debates

Political Culture

The term *political culture* was first employed by political scientist Gabriel Almond in the 1950s when he attempted to distinguish political culture from culture generally. Almond drew on the influential political system framework established in the work of David Easton (1957), who suggested that the study of politics should be approached as a system of behaviour and institutions. For Easton, any country's political system consisted of institutions (such as political parties and legislatures). The political system, according to this model, was like a giant machine that would process inputs in the form of demands (what people want) and supports (how much support those making demands can obtain from other people) into specific outputs (decisions or policies). Easton's views are represented schematically in Figure 15.1. This depiction of the "political system" was an influential part of an attempt to build a "science of politics" in the twentieth century. Political scientists aspired to have a general theory that could be applied everywhere.

FIGURE 15.1 *Liberalism: The Art of Separation in Public Policy*

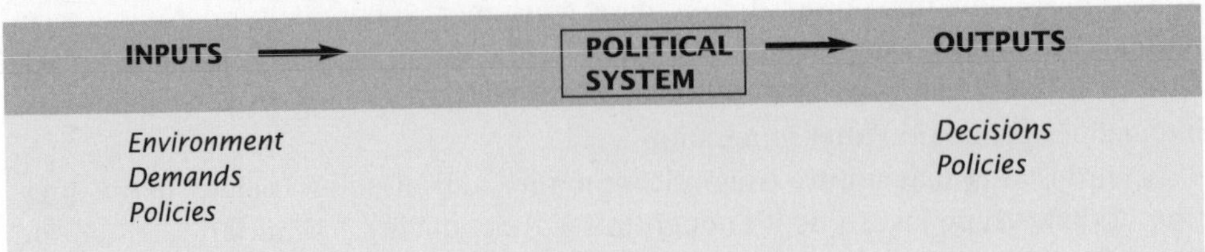

SOURCE: Adapted from David Easton, "An Approach to the Analysis of Political Systems," *World Politics* 9, 3 (1957), p. 384. Center of International Studies, Princeton University.

But what is political culture? According to Almond, the population of any given political system is characterized by a distinct pattern of attitudes about political participation—this is called political culture. Political culture was further elaborated in Gabriel Almond and Sidney Verba's well-known book entitled *The Civic Culture*, which examined the political cultures of Mexico, the United States, the United Kingdom, and Germany in order to explain their comparative political stability. For each country, the authors surveyed a **representative sample** of 1000 people. Almond and Verba argued that their evidence indicated that it is generally possible to speak of "attitudes that are characteristic of a nation" and, moreover, that political culture is key to explaining stability (1963, 51). They identified three distinct types of attitudes people have about their own role in the political process:

- *parochial*—people do not expect to participate and do not make any demands;
- *subject*—people have no expectation of being politically active, but they do expect that the system will provide them with the goods and services they want; and
- *participant*—people feel they can play an active role, and expect that the political system will deliver in return.

Almond and Verba's book argues that the best kind of political system has a "civic culture" that embodies a balance between democracy, as opposed to authoritarianism, and stability, as opposed to instability. The civic culture, demonstrating both democracy *and* stability is based on limited participation. The authors of *The Civic Culture* presumed that too much citizen activism creates instability. From their analysis, the countries that best characterize this ideal civic culture were the United Kingdom, and, especially, the United States. For the record, both Almond and Verba were American.

One major criticism is that *The Civic Culture* served as a justification for the *status quo*. The emphasis in this work was on the desirability of stability, as opposed to change. Indeed, for Almond and Verba, the limited participation of people was positive, precisely because it ensured stability. *The Civic Culture* also has been criticized for being *ethnocentric* and *ahistorical*. The book actually assessed the political culture of other countries in terms of how closely they resembled the American political culture. Moreover, the work did not address the historical differences between countries. Such historical differences are not captured by a "snapshot" glance at culture gleaned from administering a survey to a population at one particular point in time.

Finally, and not the least, *The Civic Culture* has been criticized for its exclusive focus on national political cultures to the exclusion of relevant subcultures within countries. This criticism emphasizes the idea of diversity because a **subculture** refers to a different, or distinctive, shared way of life within the national cultural setting, characterizing a smaller grouping of people within a country. For example, in the case of the United States, African Americans, who often hold specific attitudes toward politics, might be described as a subculture.

These criticisms of *The Civic Culture* did not dissuade other political scientists from employing the concept of political culture to study the attitudes, beliefs, and rules that guide a political system and, in some cases, to look at the question of subcultures within any given country. In addition, political scientists turned their attention to the process of **political socialization** or the way individuals actually internalized political values. Many studies have focused on the **agents of political socialization**, which include the family, the media, educational institutions, and political parties.

Cultural Studies

In contrast to the political culture approach, the *cultural studies* approach is premised on the desirability of transforming power relations. Also emerging in the post-war period, the cultural studies approach is interdisciplinary. This means that analysts working in this tradition draw on a number of theories and methods from disciplines both in the social sciences and in the humanities. These disciplines include literary criticism, linguistics, philosophy, art history, sociology, and political science.

Nonetheless, cultural studies is united by a core concern—to expose power relations and how these shape cultural practices, with a view toward challenging relations of subordination, especially in capitalist societies. Cultural studies analysts do not present their work as objective and value-free, in contrast to the stance taken by analysts seeking to develop a "science of politics" through the political culture approach. Cultural Studies has been profoundly influenced by the work of Karl Marx (1818–1883), and his understanding of the importance of ideology. While the concept of ideology was used as far back as the French Revolution, in the post-World War II period, the concept was largely associated with the writings and philosophy of Marx. Marx used the term to refer to those ideas which masked the uneven distribution of power between the workers (the proletariat) and the owners of the means of production (the bourgeoisie) in a capitalist system. Louis Althusser and Antonio Gramsci, two important twentieth century thinkers inspired by Marx, elaborated upon the factors that keep "bourgeois ideology" in place.

The French Marxist thinker Louis Althusser argued that under capitalism, people are conditioned through ideology that is passed on to them by what he termed "ideological state apparatuses" (ISAs) (1971). For Althusser, the ISAs include churches, schools, parties, unions, communications, literature, arts, and the family.

All, in complementary ways, encourage people to believe in the value of capitalism. The ISAs identified by Althusser bear a striking resemblance to the agents of political socialization in political culture accounts. For Marxists, however, the specific problem with Althusser's account was that the ideological conditioning seemed so complete that it was impossible to imagine change—in particular, how a working-class revolution would ever happen.

In much work in the Marxist tradition, culture is seen to be determined by economic relations. Antonio Gramsci (1891–1937), however, argued that culture was relevant in its own right and a key to understanding the possibility of change and revolution. Gramsci, one of the founders of the Italian Communist Party, was arrested by Mussolini's Fascists in 1926. While in prison, he wrote on the role of culture (Gramsci, 1971). Gramsci believed that social stability could not be achieved through state coercion or force. Instead, social support for capitalism, he argued, was the result of cultural consensus or **hegemony**. For Gramsci, the persistence of the capitalist system was largely achieved by the bourgeoisie's ideological domination (hegemony) of the working class. Gramsci suggested that because hegemony was never total, or static, but ever-changing, there was always a potential for revolutionary consciousness in the working classes.

The influence of Marx and Marxist accounts of ideology/culture through such figures as Althusser and Gramsci are evident in cultural studies work. Most thinkers agree that cultural studies began with the publication of Richard Hoggart's 1957 book *The Uses of Literacy* (During, 1993, 1). This book describes changes in working-class life in post-war Britain, compared with the beginning of the century. It details how just one practice—reading mass publications—has profound consequences on morals and attitudes. Hoggart was dismayed by the cultural changes brought to everyday working-class life by the ever-widening number and reach of popular newspapers and magazines. He argued that "they make their audience less likely to arrive at a wisdom derived from an inner, felt discrimination in their sense of people and their attitude toward experience" (Hoggart, 1957, 339).

In 1964, Hoggart, along with other British Marxist-inspired thinkers established the Centre for Contemporary Cultural Studies (CCCS) at the University of Birmingham. Here, culture was defined broadly as "the entire range of a society's arts, beliefs, institutions, and communicative practices" and, therefore, explicitly considered both "high culture" and "popular culture" (Nelson et al., 1992, 4). Analyses done at the CCCS tended to see culture as contested and as a modern site of class struggle. In this context, the stress was on "how groups with least power practically develop their own readings of, and uses for, cultural products—in fun, resistance, or to articulate their own identity" (During, 1993, 7).

While cultural studies developed first in the United Kingdom, it has had considerable influence in countries as diverse as Canada, the United States, and France. In the process, it has become institutionalized within many universities, and taken on issues and concerns sometimes different from the original goals of the CCCS at the University of Birmingham. Given that cultural studies was originally identified as a movement committed to bringing about change, especially socialism, its institutionalization has in itself brought about one of the major criticisms of cultural studies. It has been argued that the increasing institutionalization of cultural studies has led to the "[Walt] Disneyfication of the left," that its linkage with the working class has been muted and abandoned (Davies, 1995, 159–160).

A second major criticism of cultural studies is that it pays little attention to Third World countries that experienced colonialism and to diverse groups other than the working class that might experience disadvantage in advanced capitalist countries (such as women and ethnic and racial minorities). The importance of thinking about culture in broader terms than class and Western industrialized countries is clear when considering acts of cultural resistance, such as that of celebrated Kenyan writer Ngugi wa Thiong'o. In 1986, Thiong'o wrote *Decolonizing the Mind: The Politics of Language in African Literature.* As an act of resistance against a historical past marked by British colonialism, this book was expressly the last book he wrote in English. Since then, Thiong'o has written his novels and plays in his first language, Kikuyu. For Thiong'o, the imposition of the colonial language of English was aimed at undervaluing indigenous culture. It was also central to the maintenance of colonial power. As Thiong'o puts it, "Economic and political control can never be complete or effective without mental control. To control a people's culture is to control their tools of self-definition in relationship to others" (1995, 443).

Cultural Identity

The third approach to the study of culture, the *cultural identity* approach, stems from the branch of political science known as political philosophy. Political philosophers are interested in the normative question of "what ought to be," as opposed to the empirical question of "what is." A central normative question in political philosophy concerns identifying the best forms of government and establishing the standards by which such a judgment can be made. Political philosophy is characteristically **deductive** in its method. That is, political philosophers start from an axiom (or principle) and then deduce from this principle.

Today, a central issue for many political philosophers concerns the nature of equality that the states deliver to their citizens. Contemporary political philosophers generally agree that discrimination against individuals on the basis of membership in a cultural group is wrong because such discrimination contravenes the principle of equality. However, there remains considerable debate over how equality is actually best achieved, particularly in Western industrialized countries where distinct cultural groups may experience discrimination, disadvantage, and inequality despite formal laws that provide for equal treatment.

Consider the case of Canada as an example. Canada is a settler-colony founded on French and British immigration, and the expropriation of land from Aboriginal peoples. Prior to European settler-colonization in the early seventeenth century, Aboriginal societies themselves were characterized by a rich range of cultural, linguistic, social, and political practices. As such, ethnic, linguistic, religious, and cultural diversity is a hallmark feature of this country's experience. According to the 2001 Census, immigrants constitute 18.4 percent of the Canadian national population (Canada, 2003, 1–3). Since the 1970s, there has been a steady decline of immigrants arriving from the countries of Europe and an increase of immigrants arriving from countries in the Caribbean, Central and South America, Africa, the Middle East, and Asia. For much of Canada's history, state laws and policies explicitly limited the ability of racial minorities to access education, housing, and employment. Today, overtly discriminatory laws and policies have been eradicated. Yet, there is considerable evidence that racial minorities and Aboriginal peoples encounter subtle forms of discrimination and are, therefore, still disadvantaged in such areas as education, relations with the police, social services, and the justice system (Henry et al., 2000, 383–389).

The question of cultural groups and equality has also become pertinent as a result of the emergence and demands of what are termed "new social movements." During the 1960s, a variety of new social movements emerged, coalescing around the idea of identity. Feminism, linguistic rights for minorities, Aboriginal rights, disability rights, and gay rights are examples. This emphasis on identity often takes a cultural form. The increasing relevance of cultural identity in Western liberal democratic countries, as Charles Taylor notes, raises the obvious question of whether equality is best guaranteed by principles of **universalism** and difference blindness or whether true equality requires special recognition and valuing of difference (1992, 37–44).

Difference blindness holds that through the policies and laws of the state, everyone should be treated equally and exactly the same, no matter what differences may exist among them—whether in terms of gender, religion, ethnicity, or past history of oppression. The value attached to difference blindness is seen in many constitutions of liberal democratic countries. For example, the French *Declaration of the Rights of Man and Citizens*, the American *Bill of Rights*, and the Canadian *Charter of Rights and Freedoms* all include universal individual rights, based on the principle that the constitution should not draw any distinction among citizens because of their cultural, social, religious, or linguistic background. The rule of law holds that the basic laws of the land should be "difference blind."

An alternative perspective holds that real equality can not be achieved without recognition and valuing of difference and even according differential rights on the basis of group membership. Within a liberal democratic state, group-differentiated rights in the form of language rights in education, a veto power in constitutional amendments, or territorial autonomy are rights that may enable minority cultural groups to overcome potential vulnerability and disadvantage from majorities (Kymlicka, 1995). For proponents of this perspective, if everyone is treated exactly the same, without regard to their special or unique context, inequality may actually be the result. Along with Charles Taylor, two other contemporary political philosophers, Iris Marion Young and Will Kymlicka (1995), are associated with passionate criticisms of difference blindness as the sole approach to equality. For example, Iris Marion Young has argued that "strict adherence to a principle of equal treatment tends to perpetuate oppression or disadvantage" (1989, 251). Young argues that special rights need to be given to groups defined as different in order to actually overcome oppression and disadvantage.

The critique of difference blindness—the advocacy of special rights and recognition—has generated its own criticism. Some argue that the official recognition of group rights on the basis of cultural identity might allow grounds to violate the rights of the individual (Fierlbeck, 1996, 21). Many continue to say that the best protection of the individual is difference-blind laws and rights only. Critics of differentiated rights on the basis of cultural identity also raise concerns about national stability, arguing that any recognition or emphasis on diversity is destabilizing. If minority cultures are accorded separate rights and recognition, can there still be a uniting national culture, or will there be unending fragmentation and disorder? These questions have particular pertinence in a country, such as Canada, where the issue of national unity has been recurring and is still salient in the early twenty-first century.

The Challenge of Globalization

THE TERM *GLOBALIZATION* IS USED TO REFER TO THE INTENSIFICATION of a world-scale reorientation of economic, technological, and cultural processes and activities that transcend state boundaries. Today, capital rapidly crosses state borders, and markets have been enlarged and extended. Modern forms of transportation mean that people, too, can rapidly cross state boundaries. Contemporary communication systems, such as satellite television, cellular phones, fax machines, and the World Wide Web allow information to quickly pass around the globe. The processes associated with contemporary globalization may affect specific countries differently. Nonetheless, as a package, these processes suggest that culture must also be considered in a context larger than the national state. Yet, many analysts feel that in the absence of a world state, it is inappropriate to talk about "a global culture" as something akin to the national culture of a country. It is quite possible, however, to refer to the globalization of culture (Featherstone, 1990, 1).

Currently, many kinds of cultural flows—including ideas, images, and people—quickly transcend state boundaries (Appadurai, 1990, 295–310). The power of such ideas as democracy or human rights, the worldwide television images of the September 11, 2001, attacks on the World Trade Centre in New York, and the movement of tourists, immigrants, refugees, guest workers, and exiles suggest how there has been a globalization of culture. Indeed, global migration has become a central form of globalization and one which serves to contribute to the internal diversity of nation-states. Given this, it would seem that the study of culture would be best approached by combining a sensitivity to diversity within states, with a sensitivity to forms of political participation, power relations, forms of resistance, and identities that transcend national borders.

Evidence of political participation at levels larger than the national state challenges the traditional study of political culture that has emphasized peoples' attitudes toward national participation. One of the things that has coincided with globalization is the deepening of regional integration, as seen in the 1993 North American Free Trade Agreement between Canada, the United States, and Mexico and especially developments in the 15 European countries now making up the European Union. Along with a European Parliament, whose members have been elected Europe-wide since 1979, there is now a European passport, a European flag, and a European anthem. These were expressly designed to create a European (as opposed to a simply national) cultural identity. The European Union illustrates how political symbols, forms of identity, and even opportunities for electoral participation have transcended the national state.

Globalization also raises important issues from the cultural studies perspective. It has been suggested that in many ways national governments are unable to exert control over global economic and technological processes. The Internet, for instance, has made it virtually impossible for governments to regulate or control the flow of information, particularly in the context of ever-changing technological developments. Given the economic and technological processes which challenge the national state, there are new ways less powerful groups (e.g., women, workers, minorities) may try to resist the spread of capital globally. Adequately addressing how resistance is demonstrated increasingly requires looking at how groups may join together across state boundaries. A variety of examples suggest how such organizing is occurring. For instance, the "battle of Seattle" saw an array of students, labour groups, and other non-governmental organizations from the United States and around the world protesting the meeting of the World Trade Organization (WTO) in Seattle in December 1999. The WTO consists of the governments of over 130 countries (including Canada) committed to reducing trade barriers between countries; protesters were critical of trade liberalization for its impact on the environment, labour standards, poverty, as well as the perceived lack of democracy in the WTO. More recently, the decision by the United Staes to wage war on Iraq in 2003 spawned a number of simultaneously timed massive peace demonstrations in countries around the world.

Finally, globalization spells changes for culture and cultural identity—the key concerns in much contemporary political philosophy. As one example at the level of the arts, consider world music, which has been described as music without borders. World music is characterized as coming from parts of the developing world (Cuba, Brazil, Algeria, Senegal, South Africa, India, and Pakistan), drawing from sounds the world over and making its way to Western markets. As noted by one musician, "When artists come out of their culturally bound musical traditions and start using modern instruments, they mutate the sound, they make a new stew, a new blend. This is what is called world music. There is no pure music in the world. Everything is a fusion because that's the way it is intended" (Mickey Hart as quoted in "Music," 1998, 76).

Just as world music reflects a fusion of a variety of sounds from across the globe, contemporary globalization creates a host of new opportunities for cultural intermixing, as people, images, and ideas traverse state boundaries. What results from such fusions? The case of France suggests some distinct possibilities as to how the globalization of culture creates new cultural identities and political claims. During the 1950s and 1960s, predominantly Muslim migrants from Algeria, Tunisia, and Morocco came to France to work—typically in such areas as manufacturing and construction. The second-generation children of these migrant workers, born and raised in France, are popularly referred to as *les beurs*. This name is Parisian slang for "Arab" and signifies the sense of a distinct cultural identity among the second generation that is simultaneously neither and both North African and French. Notably, the second generation has also made unique claims on the French state for recognition and equality (Wihtol de Wenden, 1994).

The reality of cultural intermixing is especially important to consider, given some recent discussions. Since the September 11, 2001, attacks in the United States, there has been a renewed popularity in presenting the world as marked by a "clash of civilizations" between Muslim and Christian societies (Abu-Laban, 2002). Yet, in reality, both Christianity and Islam are marked by diverse traditions. Moreover, there is no "purely" Muslim or Christian country, since national populations are themselves characterized by religious and cultural diversity (Abu-Laban, 2001). Indeed, today, Islam is the largest religion represented in countries of Western Europe after Christianity, a feature arising from historical processes, such as colonialism, as well as to contemporary migration flows (Abu-Laban, 2001). Accounting for globalization challenges those that study culture to rework overly simplified representations of "culture" that rest on treating any given population or society as homogeneous.

Summary

This chapter has addressed three ways that the study of culture and politics has been approached in the period following World War II. The political culture approach places an emphasis on peoples' attitudes toward political institutions and participation. In contrast, the cultural studies approach draws from Marxism to highlight power relations and how these shape cultural practices. Cultural studies, as an approach, has traditionally been concerned with transforming relations of power. Finally, many contemporary political philosophers examine the implications of cultural identity claims made by groups in liberal democracies, for equality, democracy, and justice. While each of these approaches is distinct, they share in common a tendency to look at culture and politics within the confines of a state. In this era of globalization, there are new themes and concerns related to culture that transcend state boundaries, suggesting the need to balance a state focus on politics and culture that is sensitive to diversity, with a more global focus on culture and politics.

Discussion Questions

1. Is there a distinct political culture to the place you live in now? If so, how would you describe it?

2. Discuss whether popular culture forms (e.g., television programs, music, the popular press) serve to help maintain or challenge the *status quo*.
3. Why do so many groups seek special recognition or rights? Can we expect such demands to grow or lessen, given contemporary patterns of globalization?

References

Abu-Laban, Yasmeen. 2001. "Humanizing the Oriental: Edward Said and Western Scholarly Discourse" in Naseer Aruri and Muhammad A. Shuraydi, eds., *Revising Culture: Reinventing Peace: The Influence of Edward Said.* New York and Northampton: Interlink Publishing. 74–85.

———. 2002. "Liberalism, Multiculturalism and the Problem of Essentialism," *Citizenship Studies* 6, 4 (December): 459–482.

Almond, Gabriel and Sidney Verba. 1963. *The Civic Culture.* Princeton: Princeton University Press.

Althusser, Louis. 1971. *Lenin and Philosophy and Other Essays.* New York: Monthly Review Press.

Appadurai, Arjun. 1990. "Disjuncture and Difference in the Global Cultural Economy" in Mike Featherstone, ed., *Global Culture: Nationalism, Globalization and Modernity.* London: Sage. 295–310.

Bourdieu, Pierre. 1973. "Cultural Reproduction and Social Reproduction" in R. Brown, ed., *Knowledge, Education and Cultural Change.* London: Tavistock. 71–112.

Canada, Statistics Canada. 2003. "Census of Population: Immigration, birthplace and birthplace of parents, citizenship, ethnic origin, visible minorities and Aboriginal peoples." *The Daily,* January 23. Available at: <http://www.statcan.ca/Daily/English/030121/d030121a.htm>. (Accessed September 29, 2003).

Davies, Ian. 1995. *Cultural Studies and Beyond.* London: Routledge.

During, Simon. 1993. "Introduction" in Simon During, ed., *The Cultural Studies Reader.* London and New York: Routledge. 1–25.

Easton, David. 1957. "An Approach to the Analysis of Political Systems." *World Politics* 9, 3, 383–400.

Featherstone, Mike. 1990. "Global Culture: An Introduction" in Mike Featherstone, ed. *Global Culture: Nationalism, Globalization and Modernity.* London: Sage. 1–14.

Fierlbeck, Katherine. 1996. "The Ambivalent Potential of Cultural Identity." *The Canadian Journal of Political Science.* XXIX, 1 (March), 3–22.

Gramsci, Antonio. 1971. *Selections from the Prison Notebooks.* London: New Left Books.

Henry, Frances, Carol Tator, Winston Mattis, and Tim Rees. 2000. *The Colour of Democracy: Racism in Canadian Society.* Toronto: Harcourt Brace.

Hoggart, Richard. 1957. *The Uses of Literarcy.* Middlesex, UK: Penguin.

Kymlicka, Will. 1995. *Multicultural Citizenship: A Liberal Theory of Minority Rights.* New York: Oxford University Press.

Lipset, Seymour Martin. 1990. *Continental Divide.* New York: Routledge.

"Music without Borders: Mickey Hart Charts World Beat's Sonic Boom."1998. *Shift Magazine* (August), 76.

Nelson, Cary, Paula A. Treichler, and Lawrence Grossberg. 1992. "Cultural Studies: An Introduction" in Lawrence Grossberg, Carly Nelson and Paula Treichler, eds., *Cultural Studies.* New York: Routledge. 1–14.

Taylor, Charles. 1992. "The Politics of Recognition" in Amy Gutmann, ed., *Multiculturalism and The Politics of Recognition.* Princeton: Princeton University Press.

Thiong'o, Ngugi wa. 1995. "Decolonising the Mind" in Stuart Hirschberg, ed., *One World, Many Cultures.* Boston: Allyn and Bacon. 428–437.

Wihtol de Wenden, Catherine. 1994. "Immigrants as Political Actors in France." *West European Politics* 17, 2 (April), 91–109.

Young, Iris Marion. 1989. "Polity and Group Difference: A Critique of the Ideal of Universal Citizenship." *Ethics* 99, 250–274.

Further Readings

Political Culture

Nevitte, Neil. 1996. *The Decline of Deference: Canadian Value Change in Cross-National Perspective.* Peterborough: Broadview Press.

Cultural Studies

Sardar, Ziauddin, and Borin Van Loon. 1997. *Cultural Studies for Beginners.* London: Icon Books.

Cultural Identity

Kymlicka, Will. 1995. *Multicultural Citizenship: A Liberal Theory of Minority Rights.* New York: Oxford University Press.

Weblinks

Citizenship, Democracy and Ethnocultural Diversity Newsletters
http://qsilver.queensu.ca/~philform/newsletter.html

Cultural Studies Central
http://home.earthlink.net/~rmarkowitz

Cultural Studies Resources
www.is.bham.ac.uk/resources/Cultural/res.htm

CHAPTER 16

CIVIL SOCIETY

Objectives

The arenas of political interests and competition stretch far beyond the highly visible institutions of liberal democracies, such as political parties and legislatures. The voluntary groups, religious institutions, and the many organizations that champion social issues or social interests on a local, national, and international scale also play key roles in the practice of politics. These kinds of activities usually are not directly attached to government but, instead, occupy a political space located between governments and citizens or between the public sphere of the state and the private sphere of the family. This space is generally referred to as "civil society," although as this chapter explains, there is considerable debate about both the boundaries and nature of civil society.

LAURIE ADKIN

When Mahatma Gandhi was asked his opinion about Western civilization, he replied, somewhat sarcastically, that it would be a good idea. The same could be said about civil society. Civil society is a complicated and contested concept that is deployed in different ways by different and often antagonistic political actors. Sometimes, it is used as a description of a space for political action and, at other times, as a theory prescribing an idealized vision of state–society relations. This chapter untangles the various uses of civil society and reviews some of the key criticisms of civil society theory. Lastly, it identifies the links between civil society and social movements, especially the growing importance of global social movements.

Introduction

The concept of civil society draws our attention to the many and complex relationships between state and society, formal and informal political practices, and the public and private spheres. As a *concept*, civil society refers to the arenas, relationships, practices, and interests that are directly or indirectly political, but which lie outside the formal boundaries of the state. As a *theory*, civil society is often used to portray an opposition between an oppressive state and democratic and inclusive social activism.

Until the end of the eighteenth century, the meaning of "civil society" was derived from similar terms used by ancient Greek and Roman philosophers. For Aristotle, *koinônia politiké*, or political society, was roughly equivalent to the idea of a community governed by a state, as opposed to some kind of "state of nature." Thus, the term implied a human society that had attained a certain level of "civilization," in the sense of norms and rules for collective decision making, or governance. It implied a society whose members played an active role in political decision making. Both society and state were encompassed by this concept. With the development of capitalism and the bourgeois revolutions of the seventeenth and eighteenth centuries, the term *civil society* took on a different meaning, while retaining an association with the idea of citizenship. In the thought of such philosophers as John Locke, Thomas Paine, and Adam Ferguson, there emerged a distinction between civil society and the state. Civil society was viewed as the sphere of citizen-organized struggles against despotism, through the formation of associations, use of the press, assertion of democratic rights, and other political activities.

For Marx, however, civil society meant something much closer to "bourgeois society," encompassing as well as expressing market and production relations. The emergence of the civil society/state opposition was, for Marx, the outcome of a historical stage of development in which the bourgeoisie could establish an "economy" distinct from the state. The entrenchment of property rights protected from monarchical power or from state political regulation is the foundation of liberal economic and political institutions. Thus, wrote Marx and Engels in *The German Ideology* (1845): "The word 'civil society' emerged in the eighteenth century, when property relationships already had extricated themselves from the ancient and medieval communal society. Civil society as such only develops with the bourgeoisie" (1963, 26–7). Viewed as a sphere *separate or distinct from the state*, then, civil society only arises with the development of capitalism and the modern state.

Although civil society is widely understood as a political space located outside of the state, sometimes, it is deployed as an idealized vision of democracy and as a prescription for state–society relations. As a *theory* about state–society relations, "civil society" entered the scene with the democratization movements in Eastern and Central Europe in the 1980s. The intellectuals of these movements depicted a conflict between burgeoning civil societies and totalitarian states, wherein civil society harbours democratic and pluralist values in opposition to oppressive states. Subsequently, anti-authoritarian movements in various parts of the world have been characterized as the resistance or renaissance of civil societies against undemocratic governments as well as powerful international institutions, such as the International Monetary Fund (IMF) or the World Bank.

International non-governmental organizations (INGOs) and development agencies now view civil society organizations (CSOs) as key actors in stabilizing liberal-democratic institutions and market economies in countries described as "transitional" (post-authoritarian) and/or "developing." Such CSOs include grassroots non-governmental organizations involved in educational work (literacy, primary health care), service provision (refugee centres, women's shelters), and economic activities, such as the organization of co-operatives or support for small businesses. Voluntary initiatives, such as community kitchens, foodbanks, or daycare centres, provide non-state and non-private sector resources for low-income communities. CSOs also may be involved in human rights work and other forms of political lobbying or organizing. The proliferation of these organizations and activities has generated considerable debate about the kinds of responsibilities that appropriately belong to the state, the private sector, the family, or civil society.

While the above examples of CSOs are mainly local and national in scale, many now argue that a global civil society is emerging. In this view, national boundaries no longer define or confine political space. Ideas, issues, and conflicts transcend the nation-state, and their communication and interchange have been greatly facilitated and accelerated by developments in information technology. Moreover, the idea of a global civil society retains the Enlightenment connotation of citizens' struggles against anti-democratic institutions or regimes and is often equated with opposition to the globalization of capitalism. CSOs are linked electronically; participate in common campaigns that establish connections between local, national, and global developments; and organize international gatherings, such as the World Social Forums. These organizations are largely critical of the culturally homogenizing effects, environmental costs, and social inequalities associated with the liberalization of trade and capital flows and with the power of transnational corporations. The same phenomena also are analyzed by other theoretical approaches that do not start with the premise of the opposition of civil society to the state or to the market. The rest of this chapter examines in greater detail the meanings of civil society, criticisms of civil society theory, and the relationships between civil society and other theories, including social movement theory.

Defining Civil Society

CIVIL SOCIETY IS GENERALLY DEFINED AS A *SPHERE*, OR *ARENA*, OF POLITICAL and associational activity located between the state and the family. This includes any kind of individual involvement in groups, clubs, or other associations—from soccer leagues, churches, and community theatres to explicitly political organizations, such as anti-war coalitions. Such organizations may be autonomous from the state, although many groups obtain funding from governments and international organizations. Participation in civil society organizations may be voluntary but, increasingly, this arena is occupied by paid employees. Civil society organizations may be organized around activities (e.g., sports), the defence of particular interests (e.g., community involvement in urban planning proposals), or the assertion of values (e.g., gender or racial equality, pacifism, community). Activities, interests, and values, of course, combine in innumerable ways.

Most definitions of civil society separate this realm from the state. There is less agreement about the relationship between civil society and other realms, such as the family or the economy. Some differentiate civil society from both the state and the economy (or private markets), defining civil society as the sphere of everyday life where individuals participate not as workers, employers, political representatives, or voters but as members of families, churches, neighbourhoods, or associations (Barber 1998). A narrower definition of civil society views it as a space of practices and struggles specifically related to the definition of *citizenship*—that is, to rights claims (Ku, 2002). The separation of civil society from the sphere of the family is identified as particularly problematic by feminists. The separation of civil society from the economy as well as from the state is rejected by Marxists and post-Marxists. We examine these perspectives in more detail in the next section.

Liberal-democratic "civic" norms and institutions, including the rule of law, guarantees of individual rights and freedoms, separation of church and state, political competition, and so on are widely viewed as the essential preconditions for the existence of a strong, active, civil society. Indeed, these are sometimes conflated with the idea of civil society itself so that civil society takes on a marked normative content. In the view of members of the CIVICUS Institute (World Alliance for Citizen Participation): "Civil society is linked both conceptually and practically to the promotion of democracy, to good governance, to a hybrid of the two (democratic governance), and ultimately to sustainable development." CIVICUS explicitly reserves for civil society "a set of civic norms and democratic practices that distinguish it from [the state and the market]," including the values of "trust, reciprocity, tolerance, and inclusion, that enable individuals to feel secure in entering into relationships of mutual benefit and collective action" (Naidoo and Tandon, 1999, 6–7, 11). Collaborative ethos, empathy, and consensus seeking are other values often attributed to civil society (Marschall, 1999, 171). Importantly, these definitions of civil society exclude any organizations, movements, or actors that do not meet the normative criteria of "tolerance, inclusion, non-violence, commitment to promoting the public good, and so on" (Naidoo and Tandon, 1999, 13). Civil society, however, harbours a plethora of groups advancing decidedly anti-democratic, exclusionary, and intolerant agendas.

Thus, we move from a view of civil society as a sphere of associational activity with significant autonomy from both state and economy, to a view of civil society as a realm of *citizenship* struggles. From here, it is a short step to a conception of civil society as a set of values that provides both the means and the ends of politics. As Robert Fine (1997, 8) points out, the meaning of "civil society" is inseparable from the theoretical approach, or perspective, within which it functions. While the liberal conceptions of civil society sketched in the above discussion have become very influential, since the 1980s, especially in the literatures on Third World development and globalization, they are strongly challenged by feminist, Marxist, and other critics. The following section clarifies the ways in which civil society as a *concept* is related to civil society as a theory.

Criticisms of Civil Society Theory

THE CRITICISMS OF CIVIL SOCIETY THEORY ARISE MAINLY FROM ITS ASSOCIATION with liberal ideology and liberalism's treatment of market, state, and society as separate spheres of human interaction. These "boundary problems" are further complicated when we try to define civil society in relation to distinctions between "private" (referring to the family or to the private sector of the economy) and "public" (referring to public life, political participation, or the public sector of the economy) spheres and in light of citizenship theory.

A number of classical liberal assumptions about the nature of society are embedded in the kind of civil society theory espoused by CIVICUS and similar organizations. The enabling conditions for a strong civil society are generally identified as a set of civil and political rights (freedoms of speech, association, security of the person, political competition, or pluralism, and so on). The social conditions required for the full exercise of citizenship receive little or no attention. Least among these are secure livelihoods, freedom from poverty, equitable and adequate education and health care, equitable distribution of domestic labour, work models that accommodate parenting, and other life-cycle needs. While CSOs are said to act in the interests of the "common good," there is little sense that society is characterized by profoundly conflicting interests, that all of these interests may be actively represented in civil society, or that the conditions of their struggles may be systematically unequal. Moreover, in liberal civil society theory, CSOs are generally viewed as "partners in governance" (Naidoo and Tandon, 1999, 10–11) or as organizations seeking to influence government. The question of the nature or role of the *state* in relation to class or other societal interests is largely sidestepped. From a Marxist perspective, in contrast, society is characterized by class, race, and gender divisions, and the state functions to maintain capitalist accumulation.

Critics of this kind of civil society theory argue that such representations of "strong," "robust," or "mature" civil society function, in prescriptions for Third World development, as a metaphor for Western liberalism. They are, therefore, not only ideologically laden but ethnocentric as well. As Seckinelgin argues, the "widely used language of civil society organisations is more about the entrenchment of an international liberal agenda based on a particular form of life in market-economy social relations than about engaging with people's expressed concerns"(2002, 375). The separation of civil society (encompassing the economy, the market, and the family), or private sphere, from the state, or public sphere, arises—as Marx observed—with the development of capitalism and bourgeois society. Unsurprisingly, international non-governmental organizations (NGOs) or development agencies based in the West have adopted this "ideal type" as a model for Third World (or Second World) societies. Some argue that civil society has become a "political slogan" that echoes the developmentalist discourse of the post-World War II era that sought to bring "modern" values to "traditional" societies (White, 1994, 376–378).

Neo-liberals and neo-conservatives draw a sharp dichotomy between the state and civil society to suggest that civil society (the economy and the family) is the realm of individual freedom and morality, to be defended against the encroachment and misrule of state bureaucracy and collectivism. Such a characterization of private and public spheres may be used to legitimate market liberalization in various contexts. It is perhaps not surprising that activists in the democratization movements of Eastern and Central Europe held a largely negative view of the state. Yet the dichotomy drawn by neo-liberals, while idealizing civil society, also neglects the ways in which states may act to defend democratic principles and institutions against undemocratic elements within civil society. Governments also may act to protect "public goods," such as health, education, water supply, or the environment, from forces seeking to privatize them or avoid government regulation cast in the public interest.

Idealized depictions of civil society leave out, of course, its decidedly undemocratic elements. Where should we locate, for example, patron–client networks, ethnic violence, white supremacist organizations, or gay bashing? Should the family be considered "an independent domain of free social life" (Barber, 1998, 4), when we know that it is also characterized by power inequalities grounded in gender, generational, and income-based differences? In other words, the liberal conceptualization of civil society tends to ignore the inequalities that mark the terrain of civil society and that are rooted in capitalism, patriarchy, and racism.

Finally, we come to the problem of "boundaries." First, the separation of civil society actors from the political realm, or from the state, raises the same objections as earlier characterizations of social movements as operating in the purely "cultural" realm, "outside" of the state. Social movements and other civil society actors practise a number of change-orientated strategies simultaneously. Jean Cohen (Cohen and Arato,1992, 526) characterizes these strategies as the politics of influence, identity, and reform. These actors try to change cultural values and norms, develop and mobilize the resources necessary for collective action and political influence, lobby governments around public policy, and reform institutions. Their resources and freedoms are significantly determined by political institutions and legal frameworks. Second, from a political economy perspective—as we will see in the discussion of Marxist, feminist, and post-Marxist approaches, below—the treatment of these realms as independent of one another is simply untenable.

Marxist and Feminist Perspectives on Civil Society

For theorists influenced by the Marxist tradition, "civil society" is not an ideal type of society but a concept rather closer to the idea of "society" itself. For Marx, civil society simply reflects, culturally and institutionally, the predominance of capitalist interests and ideology. For example, the bourgeois family, viewed here as a part of civil society, is seen by Marx and Engels as the ideological expression of "a mere money relation," in which the wife is "a mere instrument of production"(1985, 82, 101).

This tendency to equate civil society with bourgeois society reappears at times in the writing of the Italian Marxist, Antonio Gramsci (1891–1937). For example, in the section of the *Prison Notebooks* entitled "State and Civil Society," Gramsci treats civil society as the capitalist economic relations and cultural norms that must be suppressed by the revolutionary party-state so that a new proletarian order may be created. Gramsci also treats civil society as the crucial terrain of both economic and cultural struggle *against* capitalist **hegemony**. For Gramsci, the boundaries of state and civil society are less important than the exercise of hegemony by the forces and institutions that they encompass. Hegemony is exercised both by the state and by the institutions and associations of civil society. While military force is typically the monopoly of the state, Gramsci emphasizes the "educative" or "ethical" function of the state. At the same time, civil society and the economy (sometimes conflated in his usage) exercise their own forms of coercion as well as producing "consent." The "domain of civil society," Gramsci says, "operates without 'sanctions' or compulsory 'obligations' but nevertheless exerts a collective pressure and obtains objective results in the form of an evolution of customs, ways of thinking and acting, morality, etc." (1971, 242). While Gramsci viewed civil society as a terrain upon which hegemony is both reproduced and contested, he recognized that the terrain is not level. The ruling class has superior resources (including military) as well as positions within the state.

The concept of civil society faded from the work of late twentieth-century Marxists who were more concerned in the 1970s and 1980s with theorizing the capitalist state, ideology, changing class structure, the **new international division of labour**, and the crisis of the post-World War II model of capitalist development. In the late twentieth century, "post-Marxist" thinkers turned their attention to the new social movements and their importance for a project of "radical democratization." Post-Marxist **new social movement theory** (NSMT), focusing on questions of social and political changes in the advanced capitalist countries, thus proceeded more or less *parallel to* the later emergence of a "civil society" literature that was focused on anti-dictatorship struggles in the Soviet Union and its satellite states, Latin America, and elsewhere. In this stream of literature, civil society is idealized, in contrast to the state, as an "embodiment of social virtue confronting political vice: the realm of freedom versus the realm of coercion, of participation versus hierarchy, pluralism versus conformity, spontaneity versus manipulation, purity versus corruption" (White, 1994, 376–377). This constructed opposition between civil society and the state contrasts with Marxist-influenced analyses of civil society. For Marxists, civil society is an internally conflictual sphere, where the logic of market relations, property ownership, and social inequality conflict with the broader democratic ideas of public good and human solidarity. Rather than the last refuge of everything good, Marxist analyses view civil society as mirroring and reproducing the socio-economic inequalities characteristic of capitalist economies (Blakeley, 2002, 94).

For feminists, the liberal conception of civil society papers over not only class conflict but also gender oppression. Insofar as civil society is identified with the economic sphere (paid labour force participation, ownership of capital) or with the "public" sphere of participation in political life, it remains a predominantly male domain. The abstract *citizen* in liberal democracies is an economically independent male who enjoys the necessary resources to participate in public life. The sexual division of labour that operates in the "private" realm of the family—in which women bear children and, typically, do the lion's share of care giving and domestic labour—underpins women's exclusion from or marginalisation in civil society. The failure of employers and the state to adapt labour and social policies to the requirements of a typical female life-pattern (including periods of pregnancy and child rearing)—to allow both men and women the flexibility and security to take up care giving for children and elderly relatives—perpetuates these inequalities. Similarly, the women's movement has sought to put domestic violence on the public agenda. In sum, from a feminist perspective, civil society cannot be equated with democratic values and institutions or with democratizing social forces. Instead, civil society itself requires profound democratization. As Neera Chandhoke argues, "whereas we can with some legitimacy conceptualize civil society as a site where people associate in ways that are distinct from the way they associate in the economy or in the political sphere, we can hardly assume that civil society is either emancipated or abstracted from the ethos that permeates these two spheres" (2001, 8, 14).

Global Civil Society

MARXIST, GRAMSCIAN, AND POST-STRUCTURALIST UNDERSTANDINGS OF capitalist logic and of the bourgeois nature of the state and civil society underpin **post-Marxist** analyses of new social movements and labour movements (Adkin, 2002). Rooted in post-Marxist analyses of capitalist crisis in the West, NSMT has been extended and revised to examine emancipatory social movements in the "South" and the East. The focus of NSMT is counter-hegemonic struggles in a variety of national contexts. "Social movement theorists also are concerned to explain the origins and bases of support for "reactionary" movements—those characterized, for example, by authoritarian, patriarchal, and/or racist orientations.

More recently, attention has turned to the question of transnational social movements (TSMs), following the proliferation of "anti-globalization" protests around the world. An evening spent surfing the Internet opens a window to a seemingly infinite universe of citizen-based organizations and campaigns. Every new meeting of world leaders provokes a vast mobilization of NGO networks. For example, leading up to the Johannesburg Summit (or United Nations World Summit on Sustainable Development) in 2002, activists around the world organized educational events, petitions to governmental representatives, delegations, and demonstrations. "Social Forums" of citizens' organizations from around the world have been held in multiple locales, amassing thousands of people—all seeking to identify alternatives to the global hegemony of capitalism.

Atasoy and Carroll (2003) survey the resistance and alternatives to globalization without ever using the term *civil society*. Instead, these social movement theorists refer to NGOs, "NGO-led social movements," "transnational political movements," "local cultural projects," "popular movements," "transnational social movements (TSMs)," or particular collective actors (e.g., women in the Maquiladoras). Unlike the liberal-pluralist accounts (or "visions") of civil society as the site and agency of democratization, these analyses of the forces for social change begin with the political-economic context of capitalist globalization and a different understanding of democracy. The liberal theorists are concerned with the role of civil society in democratizing societies in transition from authoritarian regimes to liberal democracy (and to market liberalism in the cases of Eastern and Central Europe) or with "strengthening" civil society in various post-colonial contexts (leading to political and economic "development"). Although democratization is also the focus of social movement theory, it contemplates more radically egalitarian processes and outcomes. These theorists are concerned with the organization of democratic alternatives to the capitalist model of development. Radical democratization theory is anti-capitalist, anti-patriarchal, and anti-racist.

Interestingly, when civil society theory shifts to the global level, as in "global civil society," it tends to be assumed that diverse actors (social movement organizations, international research and advocacy networks, global policy bodies, INGOs, United Nations bodies) are mobilizing against the negative effects of capitalist globalization. Here, there is a convergence with the Marxist and post-Marxist work on TSMs. It has also been observed that both civil society theory and new social movement theory have preferred to study "progressive"anti-globalization actors while neglecting anti-democratic or defensive reactions to globalization. Notwithstanding these similarities, it should be emphasized that the concept of civil society—while often equated with new social movements—is not reducible to new social movements. Indeed, as a sphere, or arena, of political struggle, civil society encompasses new social movements along with many other actors. New social movements and other civil society organizations simultaneously operate and attempt to bring about change within the spheres of state, civil society, economy, and family.

Summary

This discussion has reviewed the meanings and uses of civil society as a concept as well as the criticisms of civil society theory. The latter focus on the tendency to equate civil society with an idealized model of liberalism and to reproduce an overly-simplified dichotomy between state and civil society. Specifically, liberal civil society theory is said to downplay the regulative and redistributive roles of political institutions that enable citizen activism; ignore the undemocratic elements of civil society; and minimize the ways in which society, economy, and state interrelate. The approach is further accused of ethnocentrism, insofar as its prescriptions for, and vision of, "mature democracy" or "development" simply mirror the Western model of societal development.

Marx's equation of civil society with bourgeois society, in contrast, reduces civil society to the mere expression of capitalist social relations. Marx did not envision the potential of democratic institutions to protect and extend workers' rights. Nevertheless, his speculation about the potential for "political" revolution in countries where workers were enfranchised suggests a more complex view of civil society as a terrain of political, cultural, and economic class struggles. Gramsci, with his theorization of capitalist hegemony in the West, helped lay the groundwork for later **post-structuralist** thinking about societal conflict and collective action.

The greatest distance is found between liberal civil society theory and post-Marxist new social movement theory [NSMT]. Civil society theory emerged in the late 1980s in association with anti-state socialist struggles in the East, while NSMT emerged in the 1970s in an attempt to theorize the new anti-capitalist and counter-hegemonic movements in the West. Both approaches were subsequently "exported" to other contexts. Their understandings of society, the state, and democracy are significantly different. The future of civil society theory—currently so influential, in its liberal variant, in various institutional contexts—is an interesting question. While some theorists are convinced of "the relevance of the concept of civil society to modern political theory" (Cohen and Arato,1992, vii), others have concluded that civil society is an archaic concept that evades the substantial political challenges of the contemporary period (Kumar, 1991, 392).

Discussion Questions

1. What distinguishes the term "civil society" as a concept from civil society as a theory?
2. Are the meanings of civil society and social movements the same?
3. Why is liberal civil society theory so influential in policy circles today?

References

Adkin, L. 2002. "The Rise and Fall of New Social Movement Theory?" in A. B. Bakan and E. MacDonald, eds., *Critical Political Studies: Debates and Dialogues from the Left.* Montreal and Kingston, ON: McGill-Queen's University Press. 281–318.

Atasoy, Y. and W.K. Carroll, eds. 2003. *Global Shaping and Its Alternatives.* Aurora, ON.: Garamond Press.

Barber, B. R. 1998. *A Place for Us.* New York: Hill and Wang.

Benthall, J. 2000. Civil Society's Need for De-deconstruction. *Anthropology Today,* 16, 2, 1–3.

Blakeley, G. 2002. "Civil Society" in Georgina Blakeley and Valerie Bryson, eds., *Contemporary Political Concepts: A Critical Introduction.* London: Pluto Press.

Chandhoke, N. 2001. "The 'Civil' and the 'Political' in Civil Society." *Democratization,* 8, 2, 1–24.

Cohen, J. and A. Arato. 1992. *Civil Society and Political Theory.* Cambridge, Mass; London, UK: The MIT Press.

Edelman, M. 2001. Social movements: changing paradigms and forms of politics. *Annual Review of Anthropology,* 30, 285–317.

Falk, R. 1993. "The Making of Global Citizenship" in J. B. Childs, J. Brecher, J. Cutler, eds. *Global Visions: Beyond the New World Order* (pp. 39–50). Boston: South End Press.

Fine, R. 1997. "Civil Society Theory, Enlightenment and Critique." *Democratization,* 4, 1, 7–28.

Gramsci, A. 1971. *Selections from the Prison Notebooks.* Q. Hoare & G. N. Smith, eds. New York: International Publishers.

Ku, A.S. 2002. "Beyond the Paradoxical Conception of 'Civil Society without Citizenship.'" *International Sociology,* 17, 4, 529–548.

Marschall, M. 1999. "From States to People: Civil Society and Its Role in Governance" in M. Akuhata-Brown et al., eds., *Civil Society at the Millennium.* West Hartford, Conn.: Kumarian Press; CIVICUS. 167–178.

Marx, K. and F. Engels. 1963. *The German Ideology (1845).*R. Pascal, ed. New York: International Publishers.

———. 1985. *The Communist Manifesto (1848).* Introduction by A.J.P. Taylor. Trans. by Samuel Moore (1888). Harmondsworth, Middlesex, UK: Penguin Books Ltd.

Naidoo, K. and R. Tandon. 1999. "The Promise of Civil Society" in M. Akuhata-Brown et al., eds., *Civil Society at the Millennium.* West Hartford, Conn.: Kumarian Press; CIVICUS. 1–16.

Seckinelgin, H. 2002. "Civil Society as a Metaphor for Western Liberalism." *Global Society,* 16, 4, 357–376.

White, G. 1994. "Civil Society, Democratization and Development (I): Clearing the Analytical Ground." *Democratization,* 1, 3, 375–390.

Further Readings

Ehrenberg, J. 1999. *Civil Society: The Critical History of an Idea.* New York; London: New York University Press.

Hall, B.L. 2000. "Global Civil Society: Theorizing a Changing World." *Convergence*, 33, 1–2, 10–33.

Keane, John, ed. 1988. *Civil Society and the State: New European Perspectives.* London: Verso.

Weblinks

CIVICUS World Alliance for Citizen Participation
www.civicus.org/new/default.asp

European Social Forum
www.fse-esf.org

Rio 10
www.rio10.dk

United Nations Division for Sustainable Development
www.un.org/esa/sustdev/index.html

World Social Forum
www.wsfindia.org

CHAPTER 17

LOCAL POLITICS

Objectives

JAMES LIGHTBODY

Even with global connectedness, the politics of local communities remain a priority to many. In this chapter, we explore critical issues that define local politics and political participation. Local politics—the governing of cities, villages, towns, and municipalities, and their school districts—is often considered of little importance. Local governments, however, directly deliver some of the most tangible public goods of the modern state. Politics and citizenship have little meaning unless citizens have water and sewerage, roads and walkways, fire and police, recreation, and the privacy that ensues from effective town planning. This is especially so since a general system of global city-regions is emerging, and in the process, traditional roots of policy problems in urban life like income inequality have been dramatically exacerbated.

In these generally prosperous global cities, the exceptionally well-heeled live right alongside the extremely poor. As local communities redefine their situation within the emerging world political economy, and seek international approval, they must confront this central paradox. An alleged decline in the importance of national governments coincident with the rise of world cities has led to renewed calls for a revitalized local democratic tradition. Local governments, initially conceived by some as the most appropriate site to nurture democracy in the relationship between citizens and government, are these days finding that the prospect of enhanced world status and subsequent economic growth may actually ease oppressive and non-democratic national state practices.

Introduction

During the age of the global, the import of the local ought not to be overlooked. Although the contemporary era seems fixed on questions of the global economy and global security, at the practical level, it is still the city's neighbourhoods that respond to poverty and housing the poor, basic consumption, urban transportation, and neighbourhood protection (Scott, 2002, 347–368). In America today, global trends have reinforced the legitimacy of a two-tiered urban society with restricted access to high-rise neighbourhoods and gated communities, defended on aesthetic grounds, and public spaces barricaded for privileged use. The **global city**'s two realities are noted by a critic from Chicago, Evan McKenzie (2001) who has observed that "for the have nots, who didn't catch a ride on the neo-liberal express, there is plenty of scarcity to go around. They are still dependent on public institutions."

These findings remind us that even as headlines capture the extremes of religious expression of citizenship, the real day-to-day struggle to live any identity is carried out in the daily fight to gain access to clean water, working sewers, reliable policing, and accessible buses. While few cities today are immune from the glossy pressures of high-level global comparison and internationally oriented policy networks, even in post-industrial societies, local politics is mostly about providing these same central necessities of life.

The Real Worlds of City Politics

THE BIG CITY EXPERIENCE IS A LIVING REALITY. BY 2001, TWO-THIRDS OF Canadians lived in 27 metropolitan areas, just under 80 percent lived in urban areas of over 10 000 people, and slightly over half lived in the four largest urban agglomerations of Toronto, Montreal, British Columbia's lower mainland and southern Vancouver Island, and the Calgary–Edmonton corridor. International immigration was the strongest single component of growth in Toronto and British Columbia. For Calgary–Edmonton, the two strongest factors were migration from other provinces and natural increase from a relatively youthful population. In contrast, Montreal had a net out-migration to other provinces that was moderately compensated for by immigration.

This reasonably small number of rather large centres has become increasingly cosmopolitan as measured by ethnically diverse populations. In the six largest centres, by 2001, Canada's historic charter groups comprised a slim majority only in Ottawa-Hull. Even by adding the new "Canadian" self-classification label, only Montreal joined Ottawa-Hull with 75 percent traditional group dominance. Elsewhere, diversity was the norm, with large settlements of persons (the East Asian community in British

Columbia, the Caribbean in Toronto or Montreal, and the South Asians in the west) who, in many instances, retained strong international linkages.

Arguably, the political sophistication of local politics has not grown apace. In international terms, western European countries, such as France and Italy, are marked by strongly partisan local elections: "The United States, Canada, and Australia are world outliers with their weak parties. In these three former British colonies, the Victorian tradition is alive and strong in institutions like nonpartisan elections and the professional city manager" (Clark, Hoffmann-Martinot, 1998, 111). What this means is that the non-party city council provides a political opportunity for senior administrators, and the policy communities which work in concert with them, to make and implement public policy. When councillors are absolute independents with a very high probability of re-election, each policy issue is "up for grabs." Councillors who are non-partisan have been found to be less able to just say "no" to coherent policy communities and new citizen movements working through the city administration than where local parties control the agenda as is usual in the United Kingdom and many large American cities. Indeed, Canadian councillors concede, when asked, that the greatest influences over their budgeting choices are their own finance staff, departmental heads, and chief administrative officers (Lightbody, 2003).

In American cities, the presence of strong party organizations at city hall has led to both lower expenditure levels and less expenditure growth when contrasted with those **non-partisan** cities whose policies are focused on citizens as clientele. The Canadian mayor has few formal powers beyond being head of council and, while not merely the symbolic head of council as in the United Kingdom, the office is certainly not the strong corporate chief which is, today, the American strong mayor system. In the absence of effective party leadership or a strong mayor, skilled individual administrators jockey behind the scenes to protect and serve their programs, build citizen alliances with clientele groups, and, not uncommonly, sabotage whatever policy damage they perceive council to have wreaked by either whimsy or neglect. In bigger cities, these political tendencies are magnified.

Mega-Cities, Global Cities

THE EMERGENCE OF WIDER-AREA CITY GOVERNMENTS WITH ROUGHLY THE same boundaries as the city-region's demographically defined space has proven difficult, especially when that approach would replace multiple local governments with their own councils and histories. Such a move requires either a tough partisan or ideological calculation by the central government. In the United Kingdom, the Conservative government finally abolished area-wide metropolitan government in London (and six other metropolitan centres) in 1986 for partisan reasons. In 1998, the Blair Labourites reinstated it with a claim that it would better position London for global economic competition.

For Canadian **city-regions**, the decade beginning in 1995 marked a period of city-region unification unparalleled in other countries. Halifax (1996) joined Winnipeg (1971) with "one government for one city." Toronto became the largest single-tier Canadian city by provincial law in 1998 when six cities plus an area-wide metro authority were amalgamated. Toronto, with a population of 2.5 million, is currently the fifth largest municipality in North America even though not among the largest 30 in the world. Its website boasts: "The city's governed population is actually more than all the Atlantic provinces combined and is twice that of Manitoba. Only the governments of Canada, British Columbia, Alberta, Ontario, and Quebec govern larger populations. . . ." Ottawa and Hamilton followed in 2001. Montreal (and four other Quebec city-regions) were unified in 2002, largely in emulation but also due to perceptions that economic development was endangered otherwise. Of the dozen largest Canadian city-regions, only Vancouver and Edmonton persist today with multiple municipalities.

Not only does Canada locate a high percentage of residents in a small number of very large city-regions, but these are more unitary in municipal institutions than is the comparable international experience. This differentiates the country's municipal system from the American urban tradition, in which multiple smaller municipalities, the average number being about 120, encourage small town politics within the larger socio-economic city. American city-regions are characterized by continuing segregation by social position, income, and race through the legal means of municipal borders. One major consequence is significant differences in both services provided and taxes levied.

Global city-regions, phenomena that were once known as "world cities," may be defined as a new regionalism, sub-national regional social formations, or "dense nodes of human labor and communal life." Urban Planner Sir Peter Hall was among the first to draw attention to "world cities" in 1966 and defines global cities as post-industrial production sites. They encompass international firms that provide and innovate in corporate services and finance. The inventory by the World Cities Study Group at the University of Loughborough ranks 122 sites as being either Alpha (10 cities, such as London and New York), Beta (10), or Gamma (35). In Canada, Toronto stands as a Beta, Montreal a low-ranking Gamma, and Vancouver embraces "some evidence" of world city formation akin to Brisbane, Cairo, and Montevideo but ahead of Hanoi and Tijuana (Scott, 2002, 69–72). The central thesis in all this is that a general system of global city-regions is emerging and, in the process, often traditional policy problems of urban life, such as income inequality, have been dramatically exacerbated.

The internationalized urban centres of Canada are based on a complex series of relationships. At a minimum, this includes a cosmopolitan population, international transportation and telecommunications links with their concomitant trading patterns, a local presence of world financial institutions (and such local institutions working abroad), significant social interactions with multiple foreign organizations and associations (students, tourism, cultural exchanges), and independently initiated formal public and private co-operative agreements with other world communities.

Such cities seek to host international sports events, cultural festivals, and exhibitions. They usually have established twinning agreements or strategic links with other countries' major cities and, in some instances, have begun to develop their own foreign policies (e.g., strategies as to where to invest and with whom to trade).

Place remains important. The concept of global city raises issues of power and inequality, however. Since it embraces a larger territory with a wider range of production capabilities and personal incomes, the idea of **city-region** permits broader questions about the impacts of urbanization (Sassen, 2000). Thus, the global-city paradox is this: in these wealthy agglomerations, the exceptionally wealthy live cheek-by-jowl with dense populations of the very poor. Yet, across multiple city-regions, there is a constant. The wealthy few have become wealthier, even as the poor have become poorer. Moreover, this constant has a racial element. Across all city-regions, "there is a correlation between low income and membership in marginal ethnic or racial groups" (Scott, 2002, 294).

Central–Local Relations

AS ARE PERSONS IN OTHER COUNTRIES, CANADIANS ARE CONCURRENTLY citizens of different official levels of authority. Conflict is built into this relationship when the policy objectives of national and sub-national governments have to be administered by municipalities. Over time, this may lead to heightened local sensitivity over the extent to which municipal citizens possess the defining authority when it is pitted against the national, regional, or provincial economic, social, and political agendas for which the same citizens, presumably, have also voted. When surveyed by Environics Research in early 2003, 63 percent of Canadians thought that municipal representatives showed most leadership on issues, compared with 59 for provincial, 56 for ethnic and religious leaders, and 53 percent for federal politicians. At the same time, 46 percent of those surveyed indicated that the provinces were responsible for the issues most important to them, while 32 percent identified the federal government. Only 13 percent of the respondents said that local governments were responsible for the political issues most important to them.

Centralized or unitary states (such as the United Kingdom and France) directly control local government while federal states (Canada, the United States, Australia) have such authority devolved to sub-national units of states, provinces, or regions. The harsh reality is that decentralization to the municipal is always subject to the greater or lesser authority of some central government. Senior governments impose rules for local administration that direct local expenditures, limit local revenues, and often restrain genuine local democracy. From time to time, structural reform in the recasting of boundaries may also be imposed. One lesson from the Canadian experience is that except in the rhetoric of ministerial speeches, the major city-region consolidations of the 1990s were far more about other policy issues (such as booster-style economic promotion, regional planning, modest redistributive policies) than with post-unification cost savings. For instance, the Toronto 2003 operating budget of

6.4 billion dollars had grown by a third after consolidation, even as the capital budget remained static. The new city does, however, employ a third fewer employees *per capita* than is the average for Canadian core cities.

Many Western nations responded to the twin forces of globalization and neo-liberalism by decentralizing central components of national welfare states to ostensibly more autonomous local officials. In a unique move, both Quebec and Ontario did this while also drastically reducing their total number of municipalities—Ontario from 815 to 447. Municipal employment for the two provinces dropped by about 35 000 people in the 1990s. As sustaining, *per capita*, general purpose grants to local governments were suspended, the complementary neo-liberal practice of downloading responsibilities onto local governments to meet redistributive demands without additional revenues established considerable stress as councils sought to respond to issues of existing economic inequities and of economic development opportunities missed.

Local governments were created to meet local needs with local revenues. The concept of a tax on real property for local spending purposes originated in the middle ages, and it has not grown in value to meet policy expectations of new times. Local own source revenues are simply insufficient to satisfy expenditures. To help sustain new services, central governments may transfer monies to their municipalities. In the United Kingdom today, for example, one-fifth of the local budget comes from fines, fees, licenses, and charges; two-fifths from central grants; and about one-third from property taxes. When money is transferred, it usually comes with strings attached. Specific, or conditional, grants from central governments constitute about half of local government revenues. By **conditional grants**, what is meant is that one level of government (with superior taxing powers) will support the programs of another if certain conditions are met. So, the programs of local governments are controlled through the regulations necessary to gain funds from the central government.

Of the more than $30 billion transferred to Canadian local governments, 98 percent is from the provinces and just under 90 percent of that has conditions attached. The idea of grants with program conditions was inherited from the nineteenth century (the United Kingdom has had such conditions since 1835) and will undoubtedly be sustained through the twenty-first. In practical terms, this means that local priorities are set elsewhere. Moreover, local choices often clash with external funding requirements. Just under two-thirds of federal funds are transferred with no conditions, but the ratio of tied funding to general grants, provincial to local, is nine to one. In Canada less than half of local revenues derive from the property tax. In western Canadian cities, in particular, reliance on the residential property tax has declined as a revenue stream to under 25 percent, at the same time as operating grants from senior governments has dried up. User fees and other revenues have been hiked to compensate for lost revenues. Other revenues usually constitute about one-third of today's city budgets. But it is the consistent reduction in operating support from the provinces for local functions that has created an "enormous financial strain" for city councils. In Vancouver, for example, a $90 *per capita* grant in 1990 became $15 in 2000. In Edmonton, a grant of about $100 fell to less than $50.

In short, like other industrial democracies, Canadian municipalities have experienced a time of severe **austerity** in their fiscal management over the past two decades. Citizen expectations of local government shifted considerably after the 1970s, benchmarked by the passage of Proposition 13 in California in 1978 and new tax limitations imposed by referenda in such states as Massachusetts and Michigan. Those elected to public office quickly took the cue from those they represented. Similar inclinations appeared in Canada. By the turn of the twentieth century, local governments employed almost 40 000 fewer people than at the start of the 1990s. Such a decrease represents ideology in action. It is the direct consequence of the neo-liberalism that emphasized a trend to privatizing service delivery, an off-loading of traditional soft service obligations to quasi-private agencies for such matters as recreation and community social supports, and to other, usually non-unionized, private operators for hard services, such as solid waste collection or snow removal.

Elsewhere in the world, genuine devolution in policy making from the centre to the local appears to have promoted innovation at the city-regional level. Especially at the municipal level, **fiscal innovation** is not ideologically restricted to participants of either the left or the right. Innovation in politics may partly be measured by new participants: Canadian cities with more educated residents have (statistically) significantly more women as mayors and councillors (Clark, Hoffman-Martinot, 1998, 156–157). Innovation also appears to be correlated with growth in the high-tech and service economies, and with a capacity for official municipal co-option of local social movements.

Councils and Their Cities

COUNCILS HAVE NEVER CLOSELY REFLECTED THE SOCIAL AND ECONOMIC composition of the communities they purport to represent. In Canadian cities, women remain heavily underrepresented, for instance, and visible minorities are almost invisible. New migrants have historically been spatially segregated as well, usually as virtual refugees to less desirable neighbourhoods just as Aboriginals have always been located in the more dilapidated housing districts. The difference between these two communities is that the former has, over time, at least been upwardly mobile in economic terms.

The idea of local democracy implies more than locally elected officials. Worldwide, it is associated with the more direct, open, free, and meaningful involvement of women and men in the ongoing resolution of policies directly impinging on daily lives. Seldom, however, does the reality measure up to the idea: studies in Britain suggest that only about 50 000 in the population of 44 million are actively involved in local *and* national governing (Lightbody, 1995, 19). Canadian studies consistently reveal that fewer than 5 percent of citizens are actively engaged in political life. This persistent distance between citizens and political authority reflects a widespread cynicism toward those who hold public office, those who report their activities, and any traditional hierarchy of authority be it public or private.

Over the years, institutionalized pressure groups, such as the local Chamber of Commerce, developers' cartels, and even well-established neighbourhood residents' groups, have become accepted as the legitimate voices for sectors in the population. These stable, polished, continuous professional lobbies are consulted in advance of policy change, work behind the scenes with bureaucrats to accomplish policy adaptation, and have their official members appointed to administrative boards and agencies. They polish their public pressures on elected office-holders through longer-term media management tactics. Effective administrators are frequently known to have sustained and encouraged these groups to lobby on behalf of their stake in local budgets. These are the traditional stakeholders whose longstanding control over city hall purse strings is now the frequent target for more issue-specific social movements.

The term "democratic deficit" has been used to describe the lack of trust shared by citizens in their politicians and traditional political institutions. Coincidentally, recent studies across the industrialized democracies have uncovered the growth of a new local political culture whose more policy innovative leaders have been called "fiscal populists" (Clark, Hoffmann-Martinot, 1998, 9–19). They have found that the classic left–right taxonomy has shifted in city politics, as the left now stands for social issues, rather than state economic intervention. Stands on social and fiscal issues are distinguished, and a political leader's position in one area cannot be inferred from positions in the other. In practical terms, Marxist mayors in France have privatized garbage collection, while tight-fisted conservatives in North America have supported same-sex benefits for civic employees and stringent privacy laws. With change in the public's policy awareness of social causes (such as environmental concerns), the appearance of new stakeholders leads to new social movements. More precise, short-term, dramatic, and demonstrable outcomes are demanded by educated citizens with the time and affluence to command the short attention spans of those in full-time public life.

Many of these newly informed agendas have been sculpted in the suburbs of city-regions. In the United States, where Democrats generally control central cities and Republicans the rural and small towns, the "Soccer Mom" becomes a metaphor for the crucial swing vote based on gender and located in the suburbs. In Canada, the new life-style voter in Ontario has been termed "the 905 vote" (for the area code of Toronto's suburban ring from Niagara Falls around to Oshawa). This new, urbane, upper middle class has emerged primarily throughout the First World, and it is not so concerned with "physical sustenance and safety" but with issues relating to "self-expression and the quality of life" (Clark, 1998, 9–36, 95–99). Consistently, these better-educated individuals with higher incomes are more tolerant of the culturally divergent than were their predecessors, even as they seek to live in those global city-regions with enriched societal amenities. This new world class is prepared to buy what they want and live where they wish.

This new political culture has been stronger in larger cities. One reason is that larger cities have more powerful print and electronic media that command officials' responsiveness to citizens. In a very important way, these media empower citizens by providing more information as well as more information about new ways of thinking about public policy issues and solutions (Clark, Hoffmann-Martinot, 1998, 159–160). In public policy struggles today, even well-informed and attuned managers in public institutions are seldom able to surpass the expertise of outside specialists on their own policy issues. In any event, this latter group exists, by definition, to fight any kind of establishment structure in public office or private space, and provides continuous breeding ground for new social movements and their leaders.

Curiously, the evidence suggests that the strength of the existing hierarchical organizations in large corporations or powerful centralized bureaucracies appears directly correlated with the likelihood that new social movements will emerge to challenge. New social movements emerge to demand innovation from institutions that are characterized by incremental and hierarchal patterns of decision making. The ensuing confrontation between the two types of organizations often leads to policy stalemates. In practical terms, more extreme neighbourhood activities have virtually balkanized cities. Neighbourhood planning controls and constraints exerted locally have fragmented wider decision possibilities. Since the 1960s, NIMBY (Not in My Back Yard) movements have frustrated booster activities designed to promote the city as a whole. NIMBY activities have highlighted citizen struggles with traditional hierarchical structures in North American city politics. Marginalized NIMBY extremists have also been labelled BANANA (Build Absolutely Nothing Anywhere Near Anyone). In Canada, similar behaviour found vivid expression in the heated arguments against the imposition of the mega-city. Under a new localism veneer, the traditional opposition of suburban councillors was joined by groups representing specific clientele in the city's centre who had established working arrangements with their own councils.

Genuine devolution in policy making from the centre to the local appears to have promoted innovation at the city-regional level elsewhere in the world. What this has meant in practical application is an increased salience of lifestyle policy issues relevant to the individual, many of which are not costly in economic terms (such as abortion, gay rights, employment equity, and environmental protection), rather than issues of importance to a socio-economic category. A new style of successful political leadership at the municipal level, where innovation is not ideologically constrained, is directly focused on reducing the influence of hierarchical organizations, measured by new participants drawn from more educated residents, and correlated with growth in the new high-tech and service economies.

New policy movements tend not to be individuals and groups pursuing wild imaginings. They are, instead, normally possessed of quite specific program objectives and, through comparison shopping practices, also know the price tags. Globalization of public policy communities has led to high levels of emulation from country to country. In the absence of hierarchical leaders (in church, union, corporation), complexity further builds as leadership patterns in policy networks have become less stable, less coherent, and less established in traditional clientele patterns. Fluctuating membership loyalties among these policy subsystems also leads to constant questions, even about the legitimacy of their own spokespersons. One pitfall is that, frequently, local policy elites will find that their common interests lie not at home with citizens without such education and access but with knowledge compatriots abroad. One consequence is that the locally focused, urban, political culture can become something quite different from that to which wider-area state or national leaders must appeal.

Establishing Priorities

THE CLASSIC LOCAL MANAGEMENT FORMAT FOR SMALL TOWNS AND RURAL municipalities in Canada, inherited from the British, is the council with standing committees headed up by a mayor or reeve with few powers beyond the symbolic chairing of meetings. Other countries, such as France, Spain, and Italy and some American cities, employ a strong mayor with the power to hire and fire and to control the budget and political agenda. The extreme council-manager form in Australia, Finland, and parts of the United States may replace the mayor with an appointed official. Local party caucuses provide political direction in the United Kingdom and some Scandinavian locales. With the committee form, each major department or area of municipal business (parks and recreation or public works) is to be "supervised" by a committee of the councillors themselves. In simpler times, this tended to be good enough. The larger urban municipalities in Canada today employ an Executive Committee, or a part of council, chaired by the mayor and sometimes including the heads of standing committees, to co-ordinate municipal operations in concert with a management team of department heads.

Local councillors have a tendency to short-term planning due to their short and fixed terms of office. This is reinforced by the apparent whimsy that attends the always variable size and condition of grants from other government levels. Many council budget decisions are partly dictated by largely independent agencies, such as school boards, police commissions, library boards, and parks and planning authorities, over whom they have little leverage. There is also an absence of political direction, let alone cohesion, which is directly attributable to anti-partyism in North America.

It is fair to say that elections under non-partisanship masquerade a really myopic political style. At the heart of the anti-party vision is a peppy **boosterism** that, in its essentials, requires unbridled support for a community's sustained growth as assessed in commercial terms. For those subscribing to this kind of fertility measure of success, the role of local government is clear. It is to support expansion of the community's entrepreneurs at the expense of any and all other objectives, be they social, cultural, or environmental. These advocates like to build things (arenas, convention centres, and roads) and tirelessly promote the community to external business leaders. Sometimes, "world status" is even believed to be conferred by the hosting of major athletic events or exhibitions.

Superficially, much of what local government undertakes may seem like a business operation, which has led some neo-liberal critics to argue for operational efficiencies by copying corporate methods (Osborne and Gaebler, 1993). Indeed, throughout the twentieth century, business-based reformers have tried to apply corporate models to city halls. Like a board of directors, councillors would devise "policy" and a professional city manager would provide "administration." But the reality is that it is not easy to separate out the business end of administration within politics and public policy choice. For instance, does the reasonable business expectation that users should pay for operating a public swimming pool not close its doors to residents with lower incomes? Business accepts that not everyone can afford to shop at The Gap, but the public policy for pools cannot. Successful municipal managers are sensitive to the expectations of their clienteles and mesh those with the political requirements of the elected.

Increasingly, these actors must respect a new world opportunity structure rooted in transportation, telecommunications, and financial institutions, in which city performance is measured not against other communities within the country but with international trading partners and competitors. Policies will be assessed as they affect a specific city-region's making it onto the New York CEO's short-list of investing locations. Seeking international trade, tourists, and investments, local management practices and political reputations have had to be burnished; bad social ecology is "out." In some developing countries, the prospect of enhanced world status (and the prospect for resulting economic growth) may mitigate oppressive state practices and open doors, at least municipally, for local citizens. Otherwise, knowledge networks can mobilize with the capability to assign targeted sanctions rapidly.

Local political leaders, fearful of being labelled "losers," have increasingly tried to showcase their cities as efficient operations that are internationally competitive. Terry Clark does note, though, that "new was the pressure to compare specific performances to others world wide, such as tax rates, travel times, and many quality-of-life measures increasingly published in popular magazines and used by consulting firms advising corporations about location decisions" (1998, 39). Sadly, it is still not usual to expect policies of assistance to the locally disempowered underclass (through housing, mental health, family supports) to compete well with economic promotion policies geared toward recreation and consumption, cosmopolitan entertainments, and educational opportunities of "world renown," all of which purportedly develop a connectedness to the global stage.

Summary

New social movement elites, the new populism for this new century, cut through social class divisions to focus on the individual. Individuals can mobilize very quickly around agenda items and lifestyle issues that directly affect them, often using the newest information technology. They are, thus, able to overwhelm the hierarchy and structured relationships of traditional lobbies and their self-perpetuating leadership cadres with resources gleaned globally. One consequence is that being out of the "policy loop" in this private sense, citizens come to think of themselves as being out of the public loop altogether. *Who* is in the traditional decision "loop" is irrelevant if only a small handful of the self-important perseveres and public participation is manipulative and reactive.

The actual shrinking of state activities so embraced by neo-liberalism has, of necessity, produced a growing sense of individual responsibility. Individuals now unwilling or unable to turn to state mechanisms for broader economic purposes may find a collective sense of community through involvement with issues that directly impinge on their choices for lifestyle. New movements are prepared and willing to enter, and quickly exit, government policy worlds, especially that which is most at first hand—the local.

Discussion Questions

1. Is the municipal government of the "global city" an appropriate agency with which to address redistributive policy issues?
2. For whom does the non-partisan nature of local elections in Canada, Australia, and the United States permit most influence over public policy decisions?
3. In what ways might central governments set limits to the democratic autonomy of local governments?

References

Clark, Terry Nichols. 1998. "The New Political Culture: Changing Dynamics of Support for the Welfare State and Other Policies in Postindustrial Societies" in Clark, Terry Nichols, Hoffmann-Martinot, eds. *The New Political Culture.* Boulder, CO: Westview, 9–72.

Clark, Terry Nichols, Hoffmann-Martinot, eds. 1998. *The New Political Culture.* Boulder, CO: Westview.

Lightbody, James. 2003. "Adventures in Adequacy: Recent Developments in the Quest for Better Management Practices in Canadian Municipal Government." *Public Performance & Management Review,* 27, 1 (September), 71–87.

Lightbody, James, ed. 1995. *Canadian Metropolitics: Governing Our City.* Toronto: Copp, Clark.

McKenzie, Evan. 2001. "Is the New Political Culture Only Middles Class?" *Chicago Journal,* December 3 (FAUINET@list.serv.nd.edu).

Sassen, Saskia. 2000. *The Global City: New York, London, Tokyo.* Revised edition. Original published 1991. Princeton: Princeton University Press.

Scott, Allen J., ed. 2002. *Global City-Regions: Trends, Theory, Policy.* New York: Oxford University Press.

Weblinks

Canadian Tax Foundation
www.ctf.ca

City of Toronto
www.city.toronto.on.ca/budget2003

Federation of Canadian Municipalities
www.fcm.ca

CHAPTER 18

GENDER POLITICS

Objectives

Biology determines a person's sex, but social, cultural, political, and economic forces shape what being male or female means in everyday life. **Gender**—the social construction of masculinity and femininity—reflects power relations and is a key feature of many political struggles. Although the feminist movement has challenged some of the most rigid sex stereotypes, gender continues to shape the life choices of women and to constrain their political involvement and impact. This chapter explains why gender is political and shows how the politics of gender factor into contemporary political realities for women.

LINDA TRIMBLE

Introduction

Most students in university-level political science courses would contest the notion that men are "better" at politics than are women and that political life should remain a male preserve. Yet, around the world, this message continues to be conveyed to women who step onto this traditionally male turf. In a few Gulf Arab states, women are denied the right to vote and sit in parliament. In Canada, where many women have enjoyed voting rights for 85 years, female party leaders remain a rarity. Commenting on Sheila Copps's bid for the leadership of the Liberal Party of Canada, columnist Don Martin wrote, "It would take many belts of tequila to view Sheila Copps as a prime minister. You'd probably be scraping the worm off an empty bottle's bottom before any such hallucination could take hold" (Martin, 2003). Copps was widely regarded as the most powerful woman in the federal Liberal Party and in the House of Commons. After Copps lost the Liberal leadership battle in late 2003, however, the victorious Martin both dumped her from the Cabinet and forced her to contest nomination in the very Hamilton constituency that she had represented successfully for many years. The 2004 media coverage of Magna International CEO Belinda Stronach's entry into the race for the leadership of the new Conservative party also is indicative of gender bias. Journalists highlighted the candidate's youth and appearance by calling her a "hot babe" and making reference to her "bodacious good looks" and "blonde ambition" (Trimble, 2004). One final example illustrates the continued division of labour between men and women and the distinction between public and private roles. In February 2003, the Speaker of the Victorian Legislative Assembly in Australia decided to eject a Member of Parliament, Kirstie Marshall, who was at the time breastfeeding her infant daughter. Breastfeeding, apparently, is not explicitly against the rules (indeed, there are no rules about that in Victoria's parliament). Rather, baby Charlotte was judged to constitute "a stranger in the house," and strangers are not allowed (Price, 2003).

These examples show that even though women are not formally excluded from political institutions, neither are they fully included. Political party elites, legislatures, and political leadership remain male territory, as men continue to dominate many aspects of political life. In most countries, women are as politically active as men in community politics, interest group and social movement activism, electoral activities, and everyday acts of political rebellion—activities which are sometimes called mass politics. In all but a few nations, women remain significantly underrepresented in formal arenas of political power, such as legislatures, city councils, the leadership ranks of bureaucracy, and the courts (Vickers, 1997, 66–69). The more difficult question is why men's control of political institutions, ideas, and decisions is still considered the natural order of things. The next section explains how male dominance of political life emerged as normal, or commonplace. But why is this understanding important? Why should we care that more men than women hold positions of political power?

Political decisions shape understandings about gender with significant consequences for everyone. Those who hold political power decide whether or not birth control, abortion, and new reproductive technologies are legal and available to women. Policies can shake up the traditional division of labour in the household by providing paid parental leave for fathers. Politicians can allow men who sexually assault women to claim an "honest though mistaken belief" that the victim consented to sexual activity; or they can make laws ensuring that no really does mean no. Political actors can provide economic supports, child care, and job training for mothers on social assistance, or they can force single moms into workfare programs. Employment opportunities for female immigrants can be enhanced or constricted on the basis of access to government-funded language training programs. Women (and men) with disabilities can enjoy more, or less, mobility and autonomy, depending on policy makers' decisions about funding accessible public spaces and government services. Politicians and judges decide whether lesbians can legally marry or adopt children. The list is endless. Political decision makers can challenge or uphold patriarchal structures, with very real effects on the everyday lives of men and women.

Gender, Patriarchy, and the Public–Private Divide

PATRIARCHY MEANS RULE BY MEN. IN PATRIARCHAL SOCIETIES, MEN have more power than do women and enjoy greater access to what is valued by the social group (Code, 1993, 19). **Patriarchy** conveys the core notion of systemic gender inequality, whether in the household or in the broader domains of economic and public life (Walby, 1996, 24).

Patriarchal thought prescribes power and authority to men, both as fathers in the household and as members of the legal profession, the business community, organized religion, and, of course, the political arena. Patriarchy has been constructed and maintained through political practices and public policy. Governments, from archaic state forms to complex modern regimes, have passed laws designed to uphold the patriarchal family and keep women in their assigned place within the household, performing domestic duties appropriate to chaste daughters or monogamous wives and mothers. For instance, Mesopotamian city states in the second and third millennium B.C.E. decreed that women, slaves, and children were legally the property of men. These ancient governments passed laws that allowed men to commit infanticide, pledge their children in marriage, and sell their wives, concubines, and children into slavery (Lerner, 1986, 88–91). In some feudal societies, political authorities upheld the so-called "rule of thumb." It decreed that a man could beat his wife, as long as he used a stick no thicker than his thumb. Control of women is a key feature of patriarchal power relations, and so laws have regulated and restricted women's sexual and public behaviours. Legal strictures and cultural practices, such as veiling, silencing, menstruation taboos, forced marriage, genital mutilation, and penalties of death for errant wives, ensured male domination of the female body (Miles, 1989, 103–123).

Patriarchal power relations construct sexual difference as political difference by giving legal form to the belief that women, because of their sex, are fit only to serve as wives and mothers in the domestic sphere, where they can be ruled by men. These presumptions are usually based on biological determinism and on the public–private dichotomy. **Biological determinism** is "the belief that a woman's nature and all of her possibilities are determined by her biology" (Code, 1993, 22–23). This perspective sees women as bodies governed by hormones and reproductive destiny, not as bearers of minds with the capacity for intelligence, rationality, and free will. Biological determinism holds that biology is destiny, that since women are "naturally" subservient and inferior to men, it is also natural for women to be ruled by men.

Social, economic, and political forces have structured these assumptions into a foundation for mutually exclusive gender roles, called the public–private dichotomy. Characteristics, roles, and standards are separated into two distinct spheres—the private sphere of family and domestic life and the public world of business, government, culture, sports, and organized religion. Women are regarded as emotional, family focused, irrational, dependent, other-regarding, nurturing, and therefore, "naturally" suited for private-sphere roles. Men, on the other hand, are believed to be rational, independent, competitive, self-regarding, civic minded individuals with the right stuff for engagement with public-sphere activities and duties. The division between public and private remains the foundation for gender codes—different roles, characteristics, resources, norms, and expectations based on the meanings ascribed to sex differences.

Patriarchal assumptions form the foundation for laws and policies that oppress women. **Oppression** is "a system of interrelated barriers and forces which reduce, immobilize and mould people who belong to a certain group, and effect their subordination to another group" (Frye, 1983, 33). Post-confederation Canadian law provides a good example of political efforts both to render women subordinate to men and to cast non-white women as subordinate to white women. Canada's earliest electoral legislation, for example, explicitly excluded women, children, and so-called "mental incompetents" from voting. The very notion of equality for women (and other marginalized groups, including poor, Aboriginal, black, Indo- and Asian-Canadians) was ridiculed as a dangerous and outlandish idea in Canada's early years. The vote was almost exclusively limited to white male property owners.

Patriarchal assumptions guided the law, denying women economic liberty in Western industrialized countries until at least the 1920s in most respects. Men were the legal heads of households, which gave them the exclusive right to control family finances (including their wives' wages), to own and sell property, to sign contracts, and to exercise guardianship rights over children (Burt, 1993, 213–214). Entry into prestigious professions, particularly medicine and law, was the exclusive privilege of men. Women who left, or were abandoned by, their husbands were not legally entitled to make any financial demands on their estranged spouses and were often left destitute as a result. Women did not have reproductive autonomy either. In Canada, criminal laws banned the sale, advertisement, or distribution of birth control information, procedures, and devices until 1969. In short, laws and policies forced and reinforced women's economic dependence on the male head of the household and their physical confinement to the domestic sphere.

Women have never been passive victims of patriarchal ideas and structures: indeed, they have been creative in claiming their fundamental rights as citizens. Politics has provided a key arena for women's citizenship claims because citizenship is at one and the same time a status (a set of rights) and a practice (involvement in civil and political lives, including informal and formal politics) (Lister, 1997,196). In other words, women practised citizenship before they were accorded citizenship rights, thereby challenging patriarchal thinking, the public–private divide, and oppressive laws and practices. For example, women's suffrage movements were interpreted as a grave threat to the sexual order. In Australia, opponents of women's voting rights argued that if granted political equality in law, women would neglect their duties as wives, mothers, and homemakers. Moreover, they accused suffragists of promoting polyandry and free love (Sawer and Simms, 1984, 2). In contrast to these patriarchal views, feminist thought provided the foundation for women's political activism, inspiring an enduring and increasingly international social movement.

Feminism

FEMINIST POLITICAL ACTION IS ABOUT THE PURSUIT OF WOMEN'S LIBERTY, justice, equality, and solidarity. Feminism seeks to change the gender order so women can enjoy autonomy and gain acceptance as socially valued members of the community. Yet, feminism truly defies a compact definition. The feminist literature is diverse, complex, full of internal debates, and constantly evolving through self-criticism and introspection. There is no feminist orthodoxy. Feminism, however, must mean something—otherwise how can we identify a feminist approach to understanding political life?

Feminism is woman centred. This does not mean that only women can be feminists or that feminists are only concerned with women. It means that feminism presents ways of understanding women's experiences and offers strategies for demanding changes that will improve the everyday lives of women. Feminists ask why patriarchy exists, how gender codes have been socially and politically constructed so that women are seen as subordinate to men, and what types of institutions and ideas maintain women's oppression. Feminist theories offer diverse interpretations of the nature and origins of gender-based oppression. Feminist theories also offer different ideas about how to challenge and change the discrimination and dependence women confront because of their sex and often also because of their ethnicity, sexual orientation, class, and physical or mental abilities.

Feminism is shaped by culture and, thus, differs from place to place. In North America, certain variants of feminism have been very active and have shaped women's social, cultural, and political movements. Radical, liberal, and socialist feminism are arguably the dominant threads, though postmodern feminism has made many important contributions to contemporary feminist thought and political practice. To briefly summarize these theoretical approaches is to grossly oversimplify complex and varied bodies of thought. Students seeking a more thorough account of feminist theories are encouraged to read further (see Tong, 1998).

To North Americans, who are accustomed to claims for equal rights, liberal feminism is the most familiar variant of feminist thought. Liberal feminists argue that inequality for women is the result of different treatment. Patriarchal assumptions, rooted in biological determinism and manifested in the public–private dichotomy, created a set of political, legal, and economic structures that denied women a place beyond the household. As discussed above, women lacked basic citizenship rights, such as equal access to education, politics, property, and employment. Liberal feminists argue that when women are denied the right to become free, self-actualizing individuals, they, not surprisingly, act like second-class citizens and form dependency relationships with men. Socialized and educated to be man's helpmate, women are unable to claim autonomy. The solution, for liberal feminists, is equal rights for women, accompanied by social cues and educational messages of liberty and equality. Women's subordination will end when discriminatory practices—such as denying women business loans, refusing to hire women on the grounds that they will take time off for child care, and barring women from certain professions—are eradicated. Women, then, should have the same opportunities, rights, and liberties as men.

Radical feminists, however, would point out that even though women have won equal rights and have entered the workforce, they continue to grapple with oppression. Radical feminism exposes the roots of the "sex/gender system," the set of rules, assumptions, institutions, and understandings that uphold women's subordination to men. Biological determinism, or the "biology is destiny" perspective, leads to narrowly constituted gender roles for women (as wife, caregiver, mother). At the same time, women's traditional roles are undervalued and even ridiculed. Consider the oft-used phrase "I'm just a housewife." Radical feminists show how patriarchal thinking is manifested in everyday practices, such as the traditional heterosexual family and expectations about gender roles. Radical feminists focus on the ways in which legal, social, and political control of women's bodies lead to sexual exploitation, promote economic dependency on men, and deny women a political voice. Women's lack of reproductive autonomy and their fear of sexual assault on the job, in the home, and in the streets maintain their subordination.

Early Canadian policies illustrate what radical feminists are talking about. Women did not have the right to control their bodies, and laws ensured their physical, emotional, and economic dependence on their fathers or husbands. For instance, until 1983, the law guaranteed a woman's consent to sexual activity with her husband. If she denied sex to her husband, he was legally entitled to force himself upon her, however violently, with no legal recourse available to her. In sum, radical feminists identify a key source of women's oppression as male control of women's bodies.

Liberal feminists reveal legal, social, and political practices that prevent women from making free choices and competing on a level playing field with men, and radical feminists show how sexual domination oppresses women in public and private spaces. Socialist feminists emphasize economic sources of oppression, arguing that capitalism and state patriarchy intersect to reinforce women's social marginalization and economic dependency. Women have been consigned to unpaid household duties because capitalism benefits from a sexual division of labour wherein women serve a nurturing and reproductive function. Increasingly, women are entering the workforce to take up underpaid casual or part-time jobs, acting as a cheap, exploitable, and disposable "reserve army of labour" for the private economic sector. Governments uphold patriarchy and capitalist gender exploitation by reinforcing women's dependence on men and on low-income work. For example, workfare programs coerce single mothers into insecure, minimum-wage jobs, and "spouse in the house" rules cut women off from social assistance when they form relationships with men. Liberal, radical, and socialist feminists alike point to the role of the state in maintaining women's dependency. All point out that governments have done little to promote women's autonomy. Socialist feminists contribute another layer to the analysis by revealing how the state often acts in the interests of capital, which relies on the unpaid or underpaid work of women.

Postmodern variants of feminism are not well known or understood, since they are based on theoretical premises that challenge the foundations of modern epistemology (ways of knowing). Postmodernism challenges the very existence of universal truths or common understandings about such things as justice, equality, citizenship, and democracy. Postmodern thinkers believe that such "meta-narratives" are part of a symbolic order that is socially constructed by discourse (ideas, words, text, and images). As a result, reality is not set but is continually being formed, challenged, deconstructed, and reformulated. In other words, there cannot be a single unassailable version of any event or communication. Postmodern feminists apply this thinking to social constructs, such as "gender" and "woman," arguing that there can be no universal, comprehensive understandings of these concepts. For instance, women's diversity challenges the very concept of "woman," as different women have different contexts, realities, and conceptions of their own identities. This idea—that there is no single, unifying woman's reality—has become very important within the contemporary women's movement, as early feminist thought and practice tended to ignore women's multiple, overlapping, realities and oppressions and to speak from the standpoint of the white, middle-class, able-bodied heterosexual woman. A quest for the unifying policy goals of the "universal woman" did not encompass the experiences, social positions, or political claims of many women who faced oppression on the basis of their sex and their ethnicity, sexual orientation, mental or physical ability, or class position. The willingness of postmodern feminists to fracture the category "woman" was reflected in a difficult, but necessary, struggle within women's groups to recognize women's diversity and confront women's oppression by other women.

Another contribution of postmodern feminism is attention to language and discourse. Postmodern feminists argue that language, not laws, represents the main instrument of patriarchy because discourse constructs a masculine symbolic order. In other words, dominant discourses underpin political decisions about laws and policies. Feminists are paying increased attention to the symbolic gender order evidenced in mass media and popular culture. In her film *Still Killing Us Softly III*, Jean Kilbourne (2000) deconstructs advertising, arguing that product ads construct "a mass media fantasy world populated by carefully crafted and highly restricted models of femininity." Advertising, she shows, sells values, images and concepts of normalcy, thus writing a cultural script for "who we are and who we should be." Women are told their worth is determined by how they look, and women's bodies are routinely scrutinized, criticized, objectified, and even dismembered by advertisements.

Gender and Political Representation

GENDER POLITICS IN CONTEMPORARY SOCIETIES REFLECTS BOTH THE impact of feminism and the persistence of patriarchy. Women were denied the right to vote and stand for political office until the late nineteenth and early twentieth centuries in most nations. In Canada, white women who were British subjects were granted the federal franchise in 1918, but Aboriginal, Asian, and East-Asian Canadians had to wait significantly longer to exercise this basic political right. The fact that women were seen as biologically destined for the domestic household, not the Houses of Parliament, is illustrated by the fact that a mere 18 women entered Canada's Parliament between 1921 and 1970. In Canada, Australia, and the United States, early female legislators commonly inherited the seats of their deceased husbands, indicating that women found acceptance not as politicians in their own right, but as political substitutes, grieving "wives of" male politicians. This path to political office was commonly referred to as "widow's succession." Politics was a man's game, and so the women brave enough to enter the fray without being marked as male appendages were regarded as anomalous, even deviant. New Zealand MP Mary Batchelor recalled: "At cocktail parties I was often asked: 'Whose wife or secretary are you?'" (Waring,1996: 6). "Are you a woman or a politician?" reporters asked Canadian Members of Parliament Flora MacDonald and Judy LaMarsh as late as the 1970s (Robinson and Saint-Jean, 1991:136).

Despite being formally excluded from participation in political life because of their sex, women's activism over decades secured political rights, and in most nations, women now participate at all levels of public life. But it was not until the contemporary women's movement gained force in the 1970s and 1980s that women's political representation increased beyond token levels. Canada's 1988 federal election brought 39 women into the House of Commons, a record 13 percent. In the United States, 1992 was hallmarked as the "year of the woman" when 24 female newcomers won office at the Congressional and Senate levels. The entry of 120 women MPs into House of Commons in 1997 in the United Kingdom represented a high-watermark for women in Westminster, with women holding 18 percent of the seats. Yet, these successes do not come close to the growing numbers of women in other legislative bodies, especially in the Nordic countries, where **gender parity**—representation proportionate to presence in the population, with a goal of roughly 50 percent representation for women—now seems possible.

On the other hand, a report by UNIFEM, the United Nations Development Fund for Women, revealed that a scant 14 percent of the members of parliament worldwide in 2002 were women. Only 11 nations reached a target of at least 30 percent representation for women in their national parliaments by the end of 2002, the target set at the 1995 Beijing World Conference on Women. Canada, the United States, and the United Kingdom were not among them. Canadian women's share of elected positions has increased slowly since the mid-1980s, and currently women comprise just over 20 percent of the legislators in national, provincial, and territorial legislatures (**http://stillcounting.athabascau.ca**). Canada is above the worldwide average, but ranks as thirty-sixth in the world for representing women in the national parliament (**www.ipu.org/wmn-e/world.htm**).

Why does it matter that women continued to be markedly underrepresented in the world's parliaments? Some say it is a measure of democracy, fairness, and equality. When women cannot be counted among the ranks of the politically powerful, it is assumed that their needs, interests, and goals do not matter. Moreover, to regard the underrepresentation of women in electoral politics as normal or acceptable is to assume that women have little of value to contribute. When a group is systematically excluded from, or underrepresented in, democratic institutions of governance, those institutions lack legitimacy. "The seed of democracy lies in the principle that the legitimacy of the power to make decisions about peoples' lives, their society and their country" is based on representation of all those who are affected by the decisions (Ginwala, 1998, 1). Women's underrepresentation in political life reflects an enduring democratic deficit and a gendered leadership gap (Trimble and Arscott, 2003, 3). Notwithstanding certain exceptional cases, such as Britain's Margaret Thatcher, "women have been largely absent from images of political leaders as well as from the set of practices involved with leadership and governance" (Duerst-Lahti and Verstegen, 1995:214). Perhaps this explains why the perception of politics and femininity as mutually exclusive persists. Former Canadian Prime Minister Kim Campbell maintains that "the qualities people ascribe to a leader overlap almost completely with the qualities they ascribe to men" (Powell, 2003). New Zealand's Prime Minister Helen Clark has endured criticisms of her appearance, insinuations about her sexual orientation, and such epithets as "Dragon Lady" and "Darth Vader in drag" (McGregor, 1996).

Most importantly, the presence of women in democratic political institutions can affect the everyday lives of women. As feminist scholars point out, when women are not equal partners in the political decision-making process, their experiences and concerns are not given equal, or even a modicum of, attention. When political institutions are shaped by unequal gender relations, the resulting policy decisions often fail to adequately address, or even recognize, the needs of women. Studies conducted in a variety of Western industrialized nations show that women politicians see the representation of women's interests as an important part of their representative role, and they tend to bring woman-centred priorities and ideas into the legislative arena and onto the policy agenda (Swers, 2001). Evidence suggests that women who are included in the institutions and practices of political decision making do make a difference to political discourse and policy outcomes (Trimble and Arscott, 2003, 138–146). When women constitute a critical mass, or at least 30 percent, of the legislators, they can alter the style, subject, options, and outcomes of political debate.

Summary

This chapter has argued that gender matters to politics because patriarchal assumptions and the public–private divide continue to shape social, political, and economic institutions and practices. Women have entered the public world of business and government but are not yet as visible or powerful as men. Former New Zealand Member of Parliament Marilyn Waring's (1988) thorough investigation of the United Nations system of national accounts revealed that women were not counted because they were regarded as "counting for nothing" when tallying a nations' economic productivity. It is only very recently that Statistics Canada decided to account for women's unpaid work in the home and community. Similarly, numerous studies have illustrated the "symbolic annihilation" of women by the mass media (Tuchman, 1978). Media treatment of women has been marked by omission, trivialization, and condemnation. Female politicians' looks and private lives are the subject of media scrutiny, while their issue positions are obscured or overlooked. Australian MP Carmen Lawrence recalls that when she became Premier of Western Australia, "the Sunday newspaper invited local fashion consultants to do a 'make-over' of my hair style, glasses, clothing . . . more attention was paid to my family circumstances than my professional qualifications" (Lawrence, 2002). Women are now starting to be counted among the powerful, but their scarcity in the top jobs, as company presidents, prime ministers, and parliamentarians alike, illustrates the continued impact of gendered assumptions and sex-specific barriers.

Discussion Questions

1. Describe some contemporary gender codes evident in daily life or in popular culture. How do such examples as the ways in which people dress or act or their depictions in music videos, sitcoms, or movies illustrate the social construction of gender?
2. Different approaches to feminism inspire different political analyses. Apply liberal, socialist, radical, and postmodern feminism to a contemporary political issue, such as pornography, pay equality, or child care.
3. Why is an analysis of gender politics key to understanding women's political representation?

References

Burt, Sandra. 1993. "The Changing Patterns of Public Policy" in Sandra Burt, Lorraine Code, and Lindsay Dorney, ed., *Changing Patterns: Women in Canada.* Toronto: McClelland & Stewart. 212–242.

Code, Lorraine. 1993. "Feminist Theory" in Sandra Burt, Lorraine Code, and Lindsay Dorney, ed., *Changing Patterns: Women in Canada.* Toronto: McClelland & Stewart. 19–58.

Duerst-Lahti, Georgia and Dayna Verstegen. 1995. "Making Something of Absence: The 'Year of the Woman' and Women's Representation" in Georgia Duerst-Lahti, and Rita Mae Kelly, ed., *Gender Power, Leadership and Governance.* Ann Arbor: University of Michigan Press. 213–238.

Frye, Marilyn. 1983. *The Politics of Reality: Essays in Feminist Theory.* Freedom, Calif: The Crossing Press.

Ginwala, Frene. 1998. "Forward" in Azza Karam, ed., *Women in Parliament: Beyond Numbers.* Stockholm: International IDEA. 1–4.

Kilbourne, Jean. 2000. *Still Killing Us Softly III.* (Video available from Media Education Foundation; see www.mediaed.org/videos).

Lawrence, Carmen. 2002. "Women Politicians and the Media." Retrieved March 12, 2003, from www.carmenlawrence.com/says/papers/wompol.htm.

Lerner, Gerda. 1986. *The Creation of Patriarchy.* New York and Oxford: Oxford University Press.

Lister, Ruth. 1997. *Citizenship: Feminist Perspectives.* New York: New York University Press.

McGregor, Judy. 1996. "Gender Politics and the News: The Search for a Beehive Bimbo-Boadicea" in Judy McGregor, ed., *News Media Politics in New Zealand*). Palmerston North, NZ: Dunmore Press. 181–196.

Martin, Don. 2003, February 14. "Even Tequila Won't Help Sheila's Odds." *Canada.com news* (accessed from www.canada.com).

Miles, Rosalind. 1989. *The Women's History of the World.* London: Paladin.

Powell, Alvin. 2003. "Former Canadian Leader Campbell Addresses Gender Bias." *Harvard University Gazette,* www.news.harvard.edu/gazette/2003/02.27/03-campbell.html

Price, Jenna. 2003, February 28. "Memo to the Speaker: Break a Few Rules." *Canberra Times,* p. A13.

Robinson, Gertrude J. and Armande Saint-Jean. 1991. "Women Politicians and Their Media Coverage: A Generational Analysis" in Kathy Megyery, ed., *Women in Canadian Politics: Toward Equity in Representation.* Toronto: Dundurn Press. 127–169.

Sawer, Marian and Marian Simms. 1984. *A Woman's Place: Women and Politics in Australia.* Sydney: George Allen & Unwin.

Swers, Michele. 2001. "Research on Women in Legislatures: What Have We Learned, Where Are We Going?" *Women & Politics* 23,1/2, 167–185.

Tong, Rosemarie Putnam. 1998. *Feminist Thought: A More Comprehensive Introduction*, 2nd edition. Westview Press.

Trimble, Linda. 2004, January 21. "Memo to Belinda Stronach: You're Being Framed." *The Globe and Mail*, p. A 15.

Trimble, Linda and Jane Arscott. 2003. *Still Counting: Women in Politics across Canada.* Peterborough: Broadview Press.

Tuchman, Gaye. 1978. "The Symbolic Annihilation of Women by the Mass Media" in G. Tuchman, A.K. Daniels, and J. Benet, ed., *Hearth and Home: Images of Women in the Mass Media.* New York: Oxford University Press. 3–38.

Vickers, Jill McCalla. 1997. *Reinventing Political Science: A Feminist Approach.* Halifax: Fernwood.

Walby, Sylvia. 1996. "The 'Declining Significance' of the 'Changing Forms of Patriarchy" in Valentine Moghadam, ed., *Patriarchy and Economic Development.* Oxford: Clarendon Press.

Waring, Marilyn. 1988. *Counting for Nothing: What Men Value and What Women Are Worth.* Wellington: Bridget Williams Books Ltd.

———. 1996. *Three Masquerades: Essays on Equality, Work and Human Rights.* Toronto: University of Toronto Press.

Further Readings

Trimble, Linda and Jane Arscott. 2003. *Still Counting: Women in Politics across Canada.* Peterborough: Broadview Press.

Brodie, Janine. 1995. *Politics on the Margins: Restructuring and the Canadian Women's Movement.* Halifax: Fernwood.

Karam, Azza. 1998. *Women in Parliament: Beyond Numbers.* Stockholm: International Institute for Democracy and Electoral Assistance.

Vickers, Jill. 1997. *Reinventing Political Science: A Feminist Approach.* Halifax: Fernwood.

Weblinks

Still Counting Website—companion to Trimble and Arscott book, with updated information on women's electoral representation in Canada
http://stillcounting.athabascau.ca

Feminist.com
www.feminist.com

National Organization for Women (NOW) Home Page
www.now.org

Status of Women Canada—Welcome
www.swc-cfc.gc.ca/direct.html

CHAPTER 19

POLITICAL VIOLENCE

SEAN McMAHON

Objectives

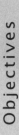

Violence has a longstanding relationship with politics. Wars have long been associated with politics. Less obvious is the fact that many of our most cherished political institutions, such as public assemblies, and even the modern state, resulted from the exercise of violence. The attacks of September 11, 2001, and their aftermath in Afghanistan and Iraq only served to highlight further the connections between violence and politics on a global scale. This chapter examines violence as an important correlate of politics. More specifically, it examines three types of violence: **political violence**, **terrorism**, and **war**. The chapter concludes with some observations about the changing face of political violence in the era of globalization.

Introduction

Major American cities are racked by gang violence. On September 11, 2001, four airplanes were crashed into the World Trade Center in New York, the Pentagon, and a field in Pennsylvania. On March 20, 2003, the United States invaded Iraq. All of these are acts of political violence. This chapter is an introduction to the concepts of violence and politics. More specifically, it examines the connections between *political violence*, *terrorism*, and *war* and the pursuit of political ends in the contemporary period. It does so by asking four questions: (1) What is political violence? (2) What is terrorism? (3) What is war? (4) What is the relationship between violence and globalization? Implicit in this examination is a distinction between political violence and terrorism. I make this distinction and caution against the all-too-frequent and loose use of the term *terrorism*. While the phrase *political violence* encourages inquiry into the histories and political motivations of those who use violence for political ends, *terrorism* is a term that often serves political purposes by obscuring questions of history and motivation.

What Is Political Violence?

Politics is about power. At its most basic, violence is the use of physical force to cause injury. Political violence is the use of physical force to affect power relations. People often treat power and violence as synonyms. They think that power is the ability to inflict violence and that a measure of power is the ability to cause massive injury. This is inaccurate. Violence is often combined with power in the practice of politics, but the two concepts are not the same. It is this combination that is of interest to such authors as Hannah Arendt and Charles Tilly. According to Arendt, violence has an instrumental relationship with power (Arendt, 1970, 46). In other words, violence is a tool. Physical force is used by power to repel foreign invaders. Moreover, violence is used as a tool to injure those in positions of power and/or to injure those who would challenge those in positions of power. Revolutionaries, such as Che Guevera and Nelson Mandela, used violence to challenge the prevailing corrupt and discriminatory governments that characterized pre-revolutionary Cuba and South Africa. These governments also used violence against these revolutionary figures and masses of citizens, many of whom were only indirectly involved in insurrection, if at all. Ultimately, however, what counts is the power supporting the violence, not violence alone. Arendt argues that violence unsupported by power will never accomplish political goals or serve as an effective means to a political end. Furthermore, violence cannot create power but only destroy it (Arendt, 1970, 49, 56).

Power is premised on the support of significant sectors of society. A lone man with a gun is not powerful. A man with a gun backed by social groups, such as wealthy classes, the military, or mass popular support, has the power to use violence successfully.

Similarly, even the most violent authoritarian governs because (s)he is supported by a certain social group or groups (Arendt, 1970, 50). The authoritarian can use violence because (s)he exercises power. Despite media representations to the contrary, this is true even of a dictator, such as Saddam Hussein. This violent regime rested on the implicit and explicit support of the United States, the Ba'ath Party, and Sunni Muslims in Iraq.

This said, no government can exist that is premised exclusively on violence (Arendt, 1970, 50). Governments can, however, use more or less violence against their own populations. It is generally understood, however, that governments are most likely to resort to violence against populations when they are losing their grip on power. The spectacle of tanks in the streets facing down protestors or the practice of making "missing" opposition leaders are signs that governments have lost their legitimacy and popular support. The more power that is lost, the more violence will be used. The substitution of violence for power will not reverse the government's loss of power because, as noted above, violence cannot build power (Arendt, 1970, 54). In fact, the use of violence may undermine popular support for the government and, thus, its legitimacy and power. This also means that a popularly supported group challenging the government has the power to successfully use violence against the government. For example, the Sandinista movement had popular support and as a result was able to use violence successfully to topple the Somoza regime in Nicaragua in 1979.

Arendt also considered the important question of when it is legitimate to use violence. For Arendt, violence is never legitimate but can be justifiable. Conversely, power requires no justification and is legitimate because people have come together to act in concert. The distinction is that violence relates to some future end, while power is based on the past act of coming together. The justification for violence comes from the promise of future changes brought about through the violent means (Arendt, 1970, 52). For Arendt violence is justifiable in easing human suffering.

The idea that violence can destroy power casts violence in a negative light. It must be recognized, however, that violence can also be understood as a productive and positive exercise. For example, Tilly argues that it was the control and subsequent use of violence by fledgling European states that lead to the consolidation of power and, more importantly, the making of the modern state (Tilly, 1990, 70). This is an essential feature of Weber's oft-cited definition of the modern national state. With the end of feudalism, regional powerholders and/or notables no longer controlled the means of violence in society or the capacity to wage private wars. The state disarmed the populations and made illegal private armies. Effectively, the state consolidated the means of violence and power at the expense of domestic rivals (Tilly, 1990, 76). This does not mean that the state eliminated violence. Instead, the state institutionalized and regulated its use in the form of domestic police forces and standing armies.

Standing armies became the essential feature of the state and their construction and maintenance, in turn, generated bureaucratic mechanisms for popular conscription and courts (Tilly, 1990, 70, 75). The ruler's use of political violence in the form of war expanded the structure of the state itself. For example, the need to supply and pay the army and rebuild after wars necessitated that the state collect and store revenue. This led to the development of state treasuries and state-wide systems of taxation. Public assemblies developed in much the same manner.

Toward the end of the eighteenth century, states stopped using mercenaries in their armies. Instead, the state conscripted its own citizenry into the army. As states taxed citizens and demanded that they fight for the state, the citizenry began to make demands of the state. One demand in particular was for popular working class franchise—if the citizens were good enough and old enough to die for the state they were good enough and old enough to vote. As electorates grew and elected assemblies became ever more central to the conduct of political life, lawmakers were pressured to appeal and be accountable to ordinary citizens (Tilly, 1990, 83). Many of the bureaucratic features of the modern state, such as state treasuries, systems of taxation, and public assemblies, were the by-products of war making.

What Is Terrorism?

At the 1972 Munich Olympics, 11 Israeli athletes were taken hostage and killed by a Palestinian splinter group called Black September. In 1985, Air India Flight 182 was bombed while en route from Montreal to New Delhi, killing all on board. Three years later, PanAm flight 747 was blown up over Lockerbee, Scotland. In 1995, Aum Shinrikyo unleashed sarin gas in the Tokyo subway system, killing 12 people. Most would agree that all of these examples are acts of terrorism and that the perpetrators of these acts are quite clearly terrorists. Of course, such easy and straightforward conclusions prompt important questions such as: What is terrorism? What is a terrorist?

The term "terrorism" was first applied during the French Revolution. British statesman Edmund Burke used the term to describe France's Jacobin government that, from 1793 to 1794, was dominated by Robespierre, the Reign of Terror, and the frequent use of the guillotine. Since then, definitions of the term have proliferated, not the least because of the highly contentious and politicized nature of this type of political violence. Defining terrorism has often faltered on the adage "One man's terrorist is another man's freedom fighter." Even the American government cannot agree on a definition of terrorism. For example, the State Department, the Federal Bureau of Investigation (FBI), the Central Intelligence Agency (CIA), and the Defense Department all define terrorism differently. In the wake of the September 11 attacks, the American government set about defining domestic terrorism in legislation. In Section 802 of the *Patriot Act* (2001), Congress defined domestic terrorism as acts dangerous to human life that are a violation of the criminal laws of the United States or any state; appear to be intended to intimidate or coerce a civilian population; to influence the policy of a government by intimidation or coercion; to affect the conduct of a government by mass destruction, assassination, or kidnapping; and occur primarily within the territorial jurisdiction of the United States (*Patriot Act*, 2001).

The contentious nature of defining terrorism also kept the Canadian government from offering a definition until the passage of the *Anti-terrorism Act* in 2001. There are four facets of this definition. First, terrorism is an act or omission committed for a political, religious, or ideological purpose. Second, the act must be intended to intimidate specific social groups or the public generally or to compel an individual or institution to do or to refrain from doing any act. Third, the act must intentionally endanger a life, cause death or serious injury, endanger the health or safety of the public, cause substantial property damage, or disrupt the delivery of essential services. Finally, a terrorist group is an entity that has as one of its purposes or activities facilitating or carrying out any terrorist activity (*Anti-terrorism Act*, 2001).

Similar to governments, the contemporary academe also has failed to develop a consensus about an acceptable definition of terrorism. Definitions vary from the use or threatened use of force designed to bring about a political change to the illegitimate use of force to achieve a political objective by targeting innocent people (White, 2002, 10). These are the most simple and imprecise definitions. Crenshaw offers a more developed definition. She sees terrorism as the systematic use of unorthodox political violence by small conspiratorial groups with the purpose of manipulating political attitudes, rather than physically defeating an enemy (Crenshaw, 1983, 2). She continues to argue that the intent of terrorist violence is psychological and symbolic. The violence is premeditated and purposeful, and employed in a struggle for political power (Crenshaw, 1983, 2).

Common Themes

All of these definitions pose problems of interpretation, including identification of non-combatants and victims, the illegitimate use of force, and the differences between an act of terrorism and an act of war. Despite these ambiguities, there are several characteristics or themes common to most definitions of terrorism. Four of the most frequently cited characteristics are (1) an act of terrorism is violent and uses force; (2) the act is intended to serve a political end or purpose; (3) the victims of the act are often random or arbitrary; and (4) the act is intended to instill fear in a larger audience. Schmid, however, has produced a composite definition that is the most inclusive of the broad range of activities often labelled as terrorism. First, Schmid states explicitly that both non-state and state actors practise terrorism. Terrorism is not practised exclusively by clandestine organizations. Second, the victims of terrorism are not the primary target of the violence. Third, terrorism is a communication process. The latter two points are closely related to the fourth characteristic: terrorism communicates a message far beyond the fate of the victims. In fact, the victims are not the intended recipients of the message. Instead, the message is conveyed to an audience that is the primary target of demands, intimidation, or coercion (Schmid and Jongman, 1988, 28).

Chomksy and Said add another important element to the definition of terrorism. It is premised on the idea that defining terrorism is dependent on the definer or, perhaps more accurately, on whoever has the power to define terrorism. Chomsky suggests that a terrorist act is one committed against "us"; it is terrorism when "we" are the victims. It is not the scale of the violent act or the body count that determines whether the act is labelled a terrorist act (Chomsky, 2002, 1). When "we" are bombed by "them," it is an act of terrorism, and "they" are the terrorists. When "we" bomb "them," it is a pacification campaign, or low-intensity warfare, and "they" are collateral damage (Booth and Dunne, 2002). "We" are never terrorists and, most certainly, never perpetrate acts of terrorism. In keeping with this idea, Said speaks to why the labels "terrorism" or "terrorist" are applied to the actions of others. He says that identifying someone as a terrorist isolates them from time, from causality, and from prior action and thereby portrays him or her as inherently and gratuitously interested in destruction for its own sake (Said and Hitchens, 1988, 154). A terrorist, according to this perspective, is someone who lives outside of history, who is without legitimate grievances, who has not suffered dispossession or deprivation, and who is only interested in killing for killing's sake.

The cry of "terrorism" should be used with considerable caution precisely because of the political function the term is made to serve. Labelling someone a terrorist all too easily precludes us from searching for the root causes of their violent actions. Instead, we come to simplistically reduce the root causes of terrorism to terrorists alone. We are encouraged to assume that the reason there is terrorism is that there are terrorists and not poverty or state repression or foreign occupation. Unfortunately, this reductionist gaze leads to equally simplistic policy responses. It suggests that the only way to be rid of terrorism is to eradicate the terrorists themselves, rather than the root causes. Without dealing with the larger issues, single-minded assaults on terrorists only succeed in creating more determined terrorists focused on changing unsustainable material and political circumstances.

State Terrorism

Examples of state terrorism abound, such as the well-publicized examples in the last century of Pinochet's death squads in Chile and the United States' Contras in Nicaragua. On September 11, 1973, the United States backed a coup that replaced Chile's democratically elected president Salvador Allende with Augusto Pinochet. Under Pinochet, state security services and death squads targeted all forms of political opposition—members of political parties (primarily leftists), union and religious leaders, agrarian reformers, and anyone else considered to be an opponent of the regime. These death squads were responsible for the disappearance, killing, and torture of thousands of people.

Similarly, in 1981, the United States initiated an aggression against the socialist Sandinista government of Nicaragua. The instrument of this aggression was a mercenary army, called the Contras, trained, funded, and supplied by the United States. Over the next five years, the Contras, working from their bases in Honduras, killed and tortured more than 11 000 Nicaraguan peasants and villagers. In both cases, the state used paramilitary groups to intimidate and kill both random and symbolic targets in order to convey messages of obedience (Chile) or opposition (Nicaragua) to larger segments of society. In fact, the former Director of the American Central Intelligence Agency, testifying before Congress, said as much when he called the American Contra war "state-sponsored terrorism" (Chomsky, 1988, 27).

It is commonly asserted that "terrorism is the weapon of the weak"—meaning that such acts as bus bombings and airplane hijackings are the only violent means available to non-state actors lacking resources and an organized state military. If we look at the historical record, however, we see that terrorism has often been used by militarily powerful states, rather than weak non-state actors. From the sixteenth to the nineteenth century, for example, colonial powers, such as Britain, Portugal, and Spain, used state terrorism to eradicate indigenous populations in Africa, Asia, and South America. In the past century, the United States has practised state terrorism in, among other places, Nicaragua, El Salvador, Vietnam, and Cambodia. Finally, Israel continues to use state terrorism in an attempt to subvert the Palestinians' quest for nationhood. Historically, militarily powerful state actors have made recourse to terrorism.

If we return to the relationship between violence and power suggested by Arendt, we see an interesting similarity between non-state and state terrorism. Recall that the successful use of violence requires political power that is embedded in other popular support. Al-Qaeda intimidated and bombed while Hussein tortured and killed. However, neither of these actors had significant popular support in Afghanistan or Iraq. In fact, these actors tried to compensate for their narrow power bases through the use of violence. While able to make use of violence, these non-state and state actors were politically weak. In this case, terrorism is, in fact, the weapon of the *politically* weak.

What Is War?

WAR IS AN INTEGRAL AND TIMELESS PART OF THE HUMAN CONDITION. The Greek city states fought the Peloponnesian War from 431 to 404 B.C.E. The Muslim and Ottoman empires fought wars from the seventh century up until the twentieth century. Europe experienced the Napoleonic Wars of the late eighteenth and early nineteenth centuries as well as World Wars I and II in the twentieth century. In the early twenty-first century, Project Ploughshares reported that there were 37 armed conflicts ongoing in 29 countries, as varied as Columbia, Sudan, Russia, and the Philippines. How should we understand this destructive force that is older than recorded history itself?

Clausewitz offers the standard three-fold conceptualization of war. First, war is a social and political activity of states. Second, says Clausewitz, "war is an act of force to compel our enemy to do our will." Third, "war is an act of policy" (Clausewitz, 1989, 75, 87). For Clausewitz, then, war is a military tool used by states that meets ends left unsatisfied by other political mechanisms, such as diplomacy. War, however, is not an autonomous activity; it is always linked to larger political imperatives, such as sovereignty, imperialism, territorial expansion, and hegemony. It is in this sense that Clausewitz most famously declared that "war is a political instrument, a continuation of political intercourse carried on with other means" (Clausewitz, 1989, 87).

Despite offering the standard conceptualization of war, Clausewitz was not the first to study this particular political activity. Greek historian Thucydides analyzed the Peloponnesian War between the Greek city states of Sparta and Athens. He analyzed this as a war in which Sparta defended its dominant position amongst the city states against the ascending power of Athens. Medieval religious scholars were the next to treat the issue of war. They did so in the form of "just war" theory. St. Augustine argued that one Christian could kill barbarians in the defence of another Christian. St. Aquinas developed and refined Augustine's thought further into the principles of justness of war (*jus as bellum*) and the just conduct of war (*jus in bello*). According to Aquinas, in order for a war to be just (*jus ad bellum*), it had to meet six standards: (1) war must be declared by legitimate authority, (2) the cause of the war must be just, (3) the party declaring war must have the right intention, (4) war must be the last resort, (5) war must be proportional, and (6) the war must have a good chance of succeeding. Once a just war is initiated, it must be conducted according to rules (*jus in bello*), including discrimination between combatants and non-combatants, and due proportion (parties should not use excessive means to achieve military goals).

The contemporary United Nations institutionalizes the tenets of "just war" theory. For example, echoing the tenet that war must be the last resort, Article 2.3 of the *Charter* states that all states shall settle their disputes by peaceful means. Furthermore, Article 41 states that members of the Security Council can use measures not involving force to realize its decisions, and Article 42 outlines forceful measures that can be taken if the Article 41 measures are inadequate. Moreover, the idea that the fighting of wars should be governed by some rules is expressed in such international institutions as the Rome Statute (which created the International Criminal Court) and the United Nations Convention on the Prevention and Punishment of Genocide. The Rome Statute, for example, identifies rape and sexual slavery as war crimes and, thus, forbidden for use as a weapon against the enemy.

The United Nations Convention confirms that **genocide** is a crime under international law under all circumstances during times of peace or war. The convention defines genocide to mean any of the acts committed with the intent to destroy, in whole or in part, a national, ethnic, racial, or religious group. Among the list of aggressive acts considered as genocidal are: killing members of the group, causing serious bodily or mental harm to members of the group, deliberately inflicting on the group conditions of life calculated to bring about its physical destruction in whole or in part, imposing measures intended to prevent births within the group, and forcibly transferring children of the group to another group (**www.unhchr.ch/html/menu3/b/p_genoci.htm**). Another rule of war is that the destruction of an entire group cannot be the intended outcome of the use of violence. Both the Rome Statute and the Convention on Genocide demonstrate conclusively that all is *not* fair in love and war.

War is politics by other means. Rather than the instrument being the ballot box (in the case of domestic politics) or diplomacy (in the case of international politics), the instrument is organized violence executed by a military. Attempts to regulate war, however, have not always been successful. The United Nations Convention did not prevent genocide in Rwanda or in the former Yugoslavia in the late twentieth century. Like any other political activity, be it the selection of party leaders, national elections, or international trade people, have instituted rules to govern the conduct of war.

Recently, steps have been taken to enforce these rules of war. The International Criminal Court came into effect in 2002. This permanent court takes the place of *ad hoc* international criminal tribunals. It enforces the rules of war by holding individuals responsible and accountable for the commission of war crimes, such as genocide. In addition to the enforcement of the rules of war through the punishment of perpetrators, the court also aims to deter future war criminals. After initially participating in the treaty creating the court, the United States has subsequently withdrawn from the treaty and declared that it will not be bound by the court.

Relationship between Violence and Globalization

SOME AUTHORS ARGUE THAT WAR HAS FUNDAMENTALLY CHANGED IN THE era of globalization. Mary Kaldor, for example, asserts that the violence in such places as Yugoslavia, Rwanda, and Sierra Leone are "new wars." These new wars blur traditional distinctions among war, organized crime, and large-scale violations of human rights (Kaldor, 1999, 2). New wars are bound up with the interconnectedness of globalization and its related processes that both integrate and fragment, homogenize and diversify, and globalize and localize (Kaldor, 1999, 3). What results is a reversal of the development of the modern state as conceptualized by Tilly. States in an era of globalization no longer exclusively consolidate power and do not monopolize the means of violence. Furthermore, these "new wars," in contrast to old wars, are about identity politics and not geopolitical or ideological goals (Kaldor, 1999, 6). The aim of "new wars" is to eliminate people of different identities, the Tutsis in Rwanda, for example. As a result, civilians, not soldiers, are the targets of violence in the "new wars." A century ago, the ratio of military to civilian casualties in wars was 8:1; now, the ratio is approximately 1:8 (Kaldor, 1999, 8). Increasingly, civilians suffer the violence that was historically reserved for soldiers.

Other authors, such as David Keen, have noted that in the era of globalization, the ends to which violence is directed have changed. Violence is often now used not with the intent of seizing control of the state, but of legitimizing actions that during times of peace would be criminal. Furthermore, violence is deployed as a means of restructuring economic relations (Keen, 1998, 11–12). In the case of Angola, for instance, the civil war has enabled the otherwise marginalized rebels to enrich themselves through control of the diamond mines in their territories. In the absence of war, these resources would be exploited or, indeed, redistributed by the Angolan ruling class. In both instances, the goal of winning a war in the traditional sense has been replaced by different objectives.

This idea that the end of violence may not be the seizure of state power is reflected in the September 11 attacks. Al-Qaeda did not have as its end control of the American state. Neither were the attacks followed by an invading force. The four hijacked planes did not fundamentally threaten the American state. Instead, Al-Qaeda used violence to strike a blow at the symbols of American economic and military might so readily associated with globalization. Among other things, the attacks were aimed at convincing the government of the United States to withdraw its forces from Saudi Arabia.

Al-Qaeda's actions were facilitated by many of the processes of globalization. In fact, much of contemporary violence is expedited or even promoted by globalization. The increasing ease, speed, and opacity of financial transactions facilitated Al-Qaeda fund raising and allowed for the strategic disposition of those funds, just as the globalized economy encourages the lucrative trade of Sierra Leone's diamonds, Cambodian timber and gems, and Columbian drugs and oil. The increased movement of peoples among states enabled the Al-Qaeda hijackers to move among Saudi Arabia, Afghanistan, Germany, and the United States with relative anonymity. Furthermore, the increasing transfer of goods globally means that Soviet-made small arms end up in the hands of child soldiers in Somalia, Uganda, and Burundi. Another important connection between violence and the processes of globalization involves modern communication technologies that bring wars into living rooms as the wars unfold in real time. However, these technologies come into play most spectacularly in the case of terrorism. The Internet and satellite television produce truly global audiences for such events as September 11, 2001.

Summary

This chapter has examined a few of the complex and unfolding relationships between violence and power and between terrorism and war. Violence is an important correlate of politics, and the strength of this relationship is not waning in the twenty-first century. Neither has it been diminished by the processes of globalization. The recent American aggression against Iraq highlights some of the ideas presented in this chapter. First, this war demonstrates that the use of violence, even by the world's dominant state, does not produce power or legitimacy. In fact, the use of violence begets more violence with unintended effects. Second, the accusation of terrorism is dependent on who has the power to define the term. The United States does not define aerial bombardment that randomly terrorizes, maims, and kills civilians as state terrorism. Rather than being defined as victims of terrorism, the civilians are defined as collateral damage. Third, the United Nations does have rules to govern the conduct of war. However, these rules are not always obeyed, and transgression of these rules can go unpunished. Fourth, war can be an effective means of securing valuable resources, such as oil.

This chapter's consideration of political violence, terrorism, and war prompts further questions such as: Under what conditions is violence justified? How does a legitimate

continued

regime emerge? What are the politics around using the term *terrorism*? To whom do the rules of war apply? How are the rules of war enforced? Finally, how will the processes of globalization continue to alter political violence? The politics of the early twenty-first century begs an open debate and action on these questions because they are increasingly critical to human security in a globalizing era.

Discussion Questions

1. What is the relationship Arendt establishes between violence and power? Critically assess this relationship.
2. In the fight against unjust regimes, such groups as Nelson Mandela's African National Congress employed acts of political violence that were characterized as terrorism. Is terrorism always morally reprehensible? Or does the justness of the end legitimize the use of terrorist means?
3. Will human societies always engage in war? What are the alternatives?

References

Anti-terrorism Act. Canada. December 18, 2001.

Arendt, H. 1970. *On Violence.* New York: Harcourt, Brace & World.

Booth, K. and T. Dunne, eds. 2002 *Worlds in Collision: Terror and the Future of Global Order.* New York: Palgrave.

Chomsky, N. 1988. *Culture of Terrorism.* Montreal: Black Rose Books.

———. 2002. *Pirates and Emperors, Old and New: International Terrorism in the Real World.* Cambridge: South End Press.

Clausewitz, C.V. 1989 *On War.* Edited by Howard, M. & Paret, P. Princeton: Princeton University Press.

Crenshaw, M. 1983. *Terrorism, Legitimacy, and Power: The Consequences of Political Violence.* Middleton, Conn.: Wesleyan University Press.

Kaldor, M. 1999. *New and Old Wars: Organized Violence in a Global Era.* Stanford: Stanford University Press.

Keen, David. 1998. *The Economic Functions of Violence in Civil Wars.* Oxford: Oxford University Press.

Patriot Act. United States of America. October 24, 2001.

Said, E. and C. Hitchens. 1988. *Blaming the Victims: Spurious Scholarship and the Palestinian Question.* London: Verso Books.

Schmid, A. and A.J. Jongman. 1988. *Political Terrorism: A New Guide to Actor, Authors, Concepts, Data Bases, Theories and Literature.* New York: North-Holland Publishing Company.

Tilly, C. 1990. *Coercion, Capital and European States, AD 900–1990.* Cambridge: Blackburn.

White, J. 2002. *Terrorism: An Introduction,* 3rd edition. Canada: Wadsworth.

UNHCR. Retrieved January 25, 2004, from **www.unhchr.ch/html/menu3/b/p_genoci.htm**

Further Readings

Chomsky, Noam. 2002. *Pirates and Emperors, Old and New: International Terrorism in the Real World.* Cambridge: South End Press.

Esposito, John L. 1995. *The Islamic Threat: Myth of Reality?* Oxford: Oxford University Press.

Worcester, K., S.A. Bermanzohn, and M. Ungar. 2002. *Violence and Politics: Globalization's Paradox.* New York: Routledge.

Weblinks

COW—Correlates of War Project
www.umich.edu/~cowproj

SIPRI—Stockholm International Peace Research Institute
www.sipri.se

Project Ploughshares
www.ploughshares.ca

Global Perspectives

PART

IV

The politics of the early twenty-first century are marked by a movement of power and capacity from the level of the national state to international and transnational scales. For centuries, the national state was the most significant unit in the study of politics. The state contained key political institutions and largely determined what happened within its boundaries. Relations between the states in the international system—international relations—were and are influenced by power inequalities among states, which, as the early chapters in this section describe, are increasingly characterized by turbulence, transformation, and instability. The contemporary era of global (dis)order and post-Cold War politics has been variously described as the end of history, a clash of civilizations, and a new anarchy. Another interpretation—the new imperialism—finds support in the emergence of the United States as a global hegemon that can exercise unilateral military power across the globe. Globalization also has collapsed geographic distances and discredited the idea that national populations can be protected from outside forces. The fates of the North and the South have been drawn closer together, exposing in stark relief the growing and indefensible disparities in well-being and life chances between the minority and the vast majority of the world's population. The current era has witnessed new roles for established international organizations and new agendas for multilateral action on a global scale. New transnational entities and international financial organizations hold increasing sway over politics within and between states. Driven by the promises of neo-liberalism, these organizations largely elude the democratic procedures that were incorporated into the practices of national political institutions. The final part of this text demonstrates that the sites of politics are rapidly shifting beyond the boundaries of the national state to the level of the transnational, where the possibilities of politics are opened to new ideas about equality, inclusion, and ethics. In this era of uncertainty, we once again are asked to contemplate the meanings and methods of good governance.

CHAPTER 20

GLOBAL GOVERNANCE AND WORLD (DIS)ORDERS

W. ANDY KNIGHT

Objectives

Global politics in the early twenty-first century has been shaken by rampant terrorism, multilateral and unilateral military reprisals, and mounting civil strife. These turbulent times reveal cracks, if not a breakdown, in the prevailing global order and have led to ever-louder demands for the creation of new norms and institutions of global governance. As this chapter describes, this is not the first time in world history when prevailing systems of global governance have eroded in the face of pronounced structural change. In past centuries, world citizens and leaders have been challenged to find new international mechanisms to tame the conflicts and disorders of their times.

To understand how such disorders have been dealt with in the past, the chapter provides a snapshot survey of both the breakdowns in past world orders and the subsequent attempts to govern the turbulence that was generated by periods of fundamental change. A cursory review of the structural changes from pre-Westphalian to Westphalian world order is undertaken followed by a brief discussion of the introduction of global governance systems aimed at reestablishing world order equilibrium amidst what appears to be another round of global disorder in contemporary times.

Introduction

The terrorist attacks in the United States on September 11, 2001, reminded us of the extent to which dominant theories in international relations are inadequate for explaining the world around us. Realism, a popular approach to the study of international politics, stresses the sovereignty and centrality of national states that act in their own interests in global politics. The realist approach may have been useful in providing an explanation for the precarious stability of the Cold War era but finds it hard to comprehend the relevance and force of transnational non-state actors in the contemporary world. International relations experts are known to disagree about the nature of our contemporary world order. Some argue that since the end of the Cold War and the intensification of globalization forces, we are witnessing a decided shift in the underlying structures of world order. Some describe the new world disorder with the term "turbulence."

The immediate post-Cold War period facilitated the removal of the structural and ideological underpinnings of superpower conflict that characterized the previous half century. Apart from relaxing global tensions, this changed structural condition ostensibly reduced the major security threat that the world faced during the Cold War, notably, the threat of nuclear war between two heavily armed military camps (Mutual Assured Destruction—MAD). But the face-off between the superpowers had provided a milieu in which many conflicts that were seething underneath the Cold War blanket were figuratively frozen. Lifting that blanket, in some cases, resulted not only in a thaw but also in a percolation of incipient conflicts, many of which became violent civil wars. What was even more significant about this period of global structural change was the opportunity it provided for American triumphalism, best exemplified by Krauthammer's claim of the emergence of "a **unipolar moment**" (1990–1991, 23).

The formidable position of the United States was aided by the fact that the formerly powerful Soviet Union disintegrated "into an unstable constellation of fifteen independent states" (Klare, 1998, 59). The initial thawing of the Cold War also seemed to unfreeze a number of seething conflicts around the globe, resulting in civil wars and internecine violence in such places as Afghanistan, Rwanda, Somalia, and the former Yugoslavia. In the aftermath of the collapse of the Soviet Union, it has been estimated that there were approximately 93 conflicts around the world, in which 5.5 million people were killed—75 percent of those being civilians (Keating and Knight, 2003, 1–4). Almost all of these were intra-state conflicts, thus explaining the disproportionate number of civilian casualties.

A culture of violence emerged in the latter part of the twentieth century as hypernationalism and long-suppressed ethnic conflicts reared their ugly heads. Some examples of this culture are the debacle in Somalia, the Rwandan genocide, the indiscriminate slaughter of civilians that occured in the Congo, Sierra Leone, Liberia, Mozambique, and the continued violence in other places, such as the Middle East, Asia, Chechnya, and Latin America. Other human tragedies and gross human rights violations occurred in so-called "failed states," where the total absence of governance structures meant that civilians were particularly vulnerable to futile violence. Millions of innocent people became refugees and displaced persons, fleeing the violence, and thousands of children were recruited as child soldiers by both government and rebel forces. The destruction of national infrastructures and of governmental and societal institutions worth billions was due to internecine violence and natural and man-made disasters during this immediate post-Cold War period. To this new dimension of insecurity was added the longstanding and continuing problems of unchecked population growth, crushing debt burdens, barriers to trade, drug trafficking, the trafficking in women and children, and a growing disparity between rich and poor. Poverty, disease, famine, natural and man-made disasters, oppression, and despair compounded the problems and led to a new preoccupation with what was labelled as "broadened and deepened" transnational security threats. One analyst, who had anticipated this scenario, predicted, "We will soon miss the Cold War" (Mearsheimer, 1990). This picture of the immediate post-Cold War period has been described as one of turbulence and global disorder, if not an emerging anarchy (Kaplan, 2000).

Toward a New World Order?

Other observers, while recognizing the tumultuous and significant events that accompanied the conclusion of the Cold War, insist that what seems like global disorder in the early phase of the post-Cold War era represents, in fact, a temporary adjustment period—a transitional period. Such a transition is to be expected when the world order undergoes change of the magnitude experienced since 1989. But, when one observes the trends in world politics over a relatively long period of time, one may be able to discern certain patterns of order within what seems to be disorder (Rosenau 1990). Stephen Gill calls this condition "patterned disorder" (Gill, 1994, 170). In fact, some politicians were convinced during the early 1990s that a New World order had emerged from amidst the turbulence of the immediate post-Cold War period.

The results of the 1990–91 Gulf War, which pitted Iraq against an insuperable U.S.-led coalition, lent credence to the notion that the United States was now the sole global superpower. It was in a position to bring order to the global disorder as the world's policeman or, more menacingly, to shape the global post-Cold War world order in its own likeness. Even American President George H.W. Bush got caught up in the headiness of the moment and prematurely declared, in 1991, the emergence of a "new world order." In his view, this was a new order in which American power could be wielded, in concert with "coalitions of the willing," to bring order and stability across the globe. Clearly, only the United States was in a position to do this, or so it was assumed by the Bush-senior administration. As it turned out, Bush lost the next election, and it did not take long before there was further evidence of the "new world disorder."

Critics suggested that the announcement of a "new world order" was premature, if not a chimera (Slaughter, 2001). Realists, in particular, have long argued that the essential features of the international system have not changed since the time of Thucydides. They are convinced that the international system always has been, and continues to be, anarchic. This is so, according to those who hold this position, because there are no supranational institutions that can impose order on national states—the dominant systemic actors in the world order. States have always been bent on survival and self-preservation. As a result, the international system is filled with security competitions and confrontations and what is generally referred to as "security dilemmas." Kenneth Waltz is one such supporter of this notion that the world has not been transformed since the end of the Cold War. His work stresses the continuities that are observable in world politics (Waltz, 2000, 39). Similarly, John Mearsheimer suggests that international anarchy did not change with the thawing of Cold War conditions. In his opinion, states are still the principle actors in world politics and, as long as that is the case, the future is likely to look very much like the past, with military competition between sovereign states as the distinguishing feature of world politics (1992, 214).

But there are others who disagree with the above position arguing that the underlying structure of the international system has shifted in recent years. They point to evidence of such change in technology-driven developments, such as the information revolution, the proliferation of telecommunications systems worldwide, and the evident shrinkage of the globe as a result of globalization and growing complex interdependence. The change is one in which states are losing their monopoly over instruments of power and regulation. Concurrently, non-state actors (some benign, others malign) are taking advantage of this vacuum of power and absence of regulatory ability to increase their power *vis-à-vis* the state. Jessica Matthews, for instance, argues that "the end of the Cold War has brought no mere adjustment among states but a novel redistribution of power among states, markets, and civil society." National governments are not simply losing autonomy in a globalized economy but, instead, are sharing powers, including political, social, and security roles at the core of sovereignty with non-state actors (1997, 55).

However, a more nuanced position holds that both continuity and change are exhibited during times of transition. James Rosenau, for instance, advances the notion that the contemporary era can be described as "a historical breakpoint." In his words, "Global life may have entered a period of turbulence the likes of which it has not known for three hundred years and the outcomes of which are still far from clear." He suggests further that today's changes are "so thoroughgoing as to render obsolete the rules and procedures by which politics are conducted, thereby leaving observers without any paradigms or theories that adequately explain the course of events." While some may dismiss these changes as mere anomalies, Rosenau is convinced that these "anomalies" are more pervasive than the recurrent patterns and that the discontinuities are more prominent than the continuities (Rosenau, 1990, 5–6).

Overwhelming evidence, particularly since 1989, points to systemic changes in world order. But there is also evidence that during times of systemic instability, political actors have risen to the challenge by proposing and adopting governance mechanisms to contain turbulence and bring equilibrium to the seeming disorder. The next section provides a survey of the evolution of global governance in response to transformative shifts in world orders since 1648. The innovative capacity of political action is ever present during moments of crisis, even though the prescriptive governance solutions have not always been adequate to meet the challenges of the times.

Global Governance and World Order

KIMON VALASKAKIS MAKES THE CASE THAT THROUGHOUT HISTORY, THERE HAVE been essentially three recognized systems of global governance. The first is illustrated by *pax romana*, or *pax britannica*, or *pax americana*—the exercise of authority by a hegemonic power. The second is tied to the notion of balance of power. In this case, countervailing forces bring a measure of order to a system. In the Westphalian world order, for instance, the balance of power system found root in national state sovereignty. In a sovereign states system, there is no overarching power to impose settlement from above. Therefore, sovereign states maintain some order in the system by negotiation, by forming alliances, or ultimately through war. The third is a system of governance obtained through a pre-arranged set of criteria. Valaskakis uses as one example of this form of governance federalism—a system of governance in which the jurisdictions of central government and those of subjugated units are clearly outlined in advance (2001, 46–47). A survey of world order over time reveals at various turbulent junctures the introduction of different types of global governance systems in an attempt to bring order to the disorder.

From Pre-Westphalian to Westphalian Order

Beginning with the early Modern Period, in pre-Westphalian Europe, one is struck by the extent to which the world order at the time exhibited a similar type of turbulence and structural change as our current world order is experiencing. This pre-Westphalian era was a period of declining empires, retreating feudal lords, and an emerging class of traders and capitalist entrepreneurs (Valaskakis, 2001, 48). The Holy Roman Catholic Church represented God's rule on earth and had established itself as the hegemonic power, an influential power that acted as an instrument of European governance. However, by the early 1600s, there were already signs of tremendous turbulence in this early world order. One indication of this was the first pan-European war, which severely weakened the influence of the Church and resulted in the hegemon being replaced by about 300 sovereign princes.

The old order disintegrated due to the disorder of the religious wars and was slowly replaced by a new pan-European order based on the equal sovereignty of newly created states. This European states system eventually expanded to encompass the entire globe, reaching its zenith around 1945 with the creation of the United Nations (UN) system—the only universal governance system of which 191 states today are members. So, one can safely label the period 1648 to 1945 as the Westphalian world order.

Sacrosanct claims of sovereignty characterized the Westphalian world order. This order consisted of a proliferating number of sovereign states, each supposedly in unchallenged control of its territory, resources, and population. With no overarching governance body to mediate between these sovereign entities, self-restraint gave way to numerous clashes among them in the 150 years following the signing of the Westphalian Treaty. It has been estimated that between 1650 and 1800, there were about 67 significant wars, many of which involved the "great powers" of the time. To address this problem, and to maintain a semblance of order, a system of international governance and law was created.

First came the codification of rules of diplomacy at the Vienna Congress in 1814–15, after the defeat of Napoleon by a coalition composed of Austria, Britain, Prussia, and Russia. These rules established a consensus about regular peaceful relationships between most European states. Out of this Congress also emerged a concert system of governance to deal with future threat to the system. In Article VI of the Treaty of Chaumont, the four great European powers agreed to "renew at fixed intervals . . . meetings for the examination of the measures which at each of these epochs shall be considered most salutary for the repose and propriety of the Nations and for the maintenance of the peace of Europe" (Hinsley, 1967, 195). The idea of preventing war through regular meetings of the states in the system was, indeed, novel. However, these Congress meetings also institutionalized the *status quo*, making it difficult for necessary systemic change to take hold. This tension between stability and change pitted Britain (sympathetic to the forces for change) against the Holy Alliance of reactionary rulers of Austria, Prussia, and Russia (bent on maintaining the *status quo*).

The importance of the control of territory to the European sovereign entities led to a rivalry over the so-called "new world"—a number of "ungoverned" territories in Africa, Asia, the Americas, and the Caribbean. The colonial expansionary period allowed some European states to amass great wealth as they acquired new territories and pillaged the wealth and resources of indigenous peoples through conquest. Britain became "great" during this colonial period, with France not too far behind. Great Britain rose to global pre-eminence by 1815. Aided by the industrial revolution, this country held a disproportionate share of the world's manufacturing production and of Europe's industrial growth. With a combination of growing wealth and an expanding colonial empire backed by a formidable Royal Navy, Britain became a global hegemon within the Westphalian world order.

That hegemon also became the "holder of the balance" in the balance of power system of the colonial period. As Hans Morgenthau put it: "The balancer is not permanently identified with the policies" of the other states in the system. In fact, "its only objective within the system is the maintenance of the balance, regardless of the concrete policies the balance will serve." It does so by throwing its weight on one scale or another to ensure a relative equilibrium of the system (2001, 147–148). Britain's role as balancer, or arbiter of the system, during the colonial phase of the Westphalian world order is generally described as *pax Britainnica*—a term reserved for the period of peace that resulted from Britain's tenure as the dominant global power.

Eventually, the Congress system of governance became a loose regime, labelled the Concert of Europe, that addressed problems reactively as they arose. It did not deal with those problems at regular meetings in a pre-emptive fashion—as was initially intended. The Paris Peace Conference was convened to bring an end to the Crimean War in 1856. The Congress of Vienna in 1864 addressed the Schleswig Holstein War, the conference at Prague brought an end to the Seven Weeks War in 1866 and the one at Frankfurt in 1871 similarly helped to end the Franco-Prussian War. The Concert of Europe also used its status to try to force a long-term settlement of the Balkan question in 1878 at the Berlin Congress. At a later Berlin Congress (1884–85), the Concert divvied up much of the African continent.

The Concert system proved effective at maintaining balance in the expanding international system by recognizing emerging powers and broadening the governance system beyond Europe. It thus internationalized the Westphalian order. The Concert granted recognition to the United States, an emerging power, in 1783 with the Treaty of Paris, and to several Latin American states in 1823. The Ottoman Empire and Rumania were granted admission to the Concert system in 1856 by the Treaty of Paris, and Japan was added in 1853. The expansion of the international governance system became even more evident in 1907 when the Hague Conference drew 44 states, including 18 from Latin America.

Turbulence in the Westphalian World Order

The Concert of Europe provided a governance framework for an expanding international system for almost a century. While small conflicts erupted from time to time, the Crimean War was the only major international war during that period. The Concert was, therefore, successful as long as it could maintain order within the international system. But once it was unable to facilitate the peaceful settlement of disputes between the European states, it quickly lost legitimacy and relevance. The Concert's demise was due, in large part, to the turbulence that accompanies shifts in the underlying structure of a world order. The Westphalian world order, as noted above, was initially a Pan-European order. As that European order became internationalized with the entrance of new states into the system, the resulting tensions called out for the creation of a new governance system—one that would be more relevant to the changing times.

Added to this governance problem was the need for functional agencies during the early phase of globalization, to manage the co-ordination of a number of transnational issues in the socio-economic sphere. The Convention of Octroi in 1804 created a centralized supranational administration to control navigation on the Rhine. An international commission for the Elbe was created in 1821. The Treaty of Paris in 1856 established a Commission for the European Danube in an attempt to supervise the free navigation of that river after national administration proved unable to deal with the modern world of shipping and international trade along that water system.

This trend in functional governance continued with the creation of the International Telegraphic Bureau (later named the International Telegraphic Union) in 1868, the General Postal Union (later renamed the Universal Postal Union) in 1874, the International Bureau of Weights and Measures in 1875, the International Union for the Publication of Customs Tariffs in 1890, and the Metric Union and international Health Offices in 1881 and 1901. A concurrent trend was the emergence of public international unions, private international associations, and hybrid bodies, such as the International Labour Organization (ILO), formed in 1919. Already, by the 1900s, there were clear signs that the Westphalian order, which had embedded the notion that states were the only actors of significance in world politics, was beginning to be challenged by the multiplication of actors on the world stage.

Functional co-operation proved insufficient for keeping the Westphalian world order from undergoing turbulence and change. Between 1914 and 1945, that world order seemed more like a world disorder that was shaken by two major world wars, the 1929 stock market collapse, the 1930s economic Depression, the rise of fascism, economic protectionism, and the League of Nations' demise.

Actually, the establishment of the League was an attempt at bringing order to the post-Concert disorder. During the course of World War I, several individuals and civil society groups worked with some governments to propose a plan the save the world from another major war. American President Woodrow Wilson was one of the world leaders who felt strongly that a new governance system was needed to bring a semblance of order back to the international system. At the Versailles Peace Conference, President Wilson chaired a special commission on the League of Nations. The blueprint for this new international governance body drew heavily on perpetual peace plans of earlier eras, the experience of the Congress and concert systems, and the experimentation with functional transnational regulatory instruments (Knight, 2000, 65–81).

The Covenant of the League of Nations became the governing constitution of this world body and reflected hope that a lawful, just, and peaceable world order would eventually be the outcome of international co-operation among the members of the states system. It adopted in the 1920s the *Geneva General Act for the Settlement of Disputes*, a Permanent Court of Arbitration, and a Permanent Court of Justice to provide the states with mechanisms for resolving conflicts. In forming a Financial Commission, the League made an attempt to regulate the expanding world economy and to "reconcile reparations with financial stability, reduce trade barriers, and reconstruct the international monetary system" (Tehranian, 2002, 12).

The League was plagued by several problems. First, it was not a truly global body because the colonized world was not a part of this arrangement. Second, despite President Wilson's efforts, the United States never became a member of the League. Third, the League was not flexible enough to accommodate the demands of the revisionist powers—the Soviet Union, Mussolini's Italy, Nazi Germany, and Imperial Japan. These powers disliked the global *status quo* and rejected extant institutions, including the League, treaties, diplomacy, international law, and the international economic order. Japan attacked China and occupied Manchuria in 1931. The League failed to respond to that act of aggression. Italy launched an attack on Ethiopia in 1935, and again the League proved impotent to act. In 1933, Hitler withdrew Germany from the League and began a series of aggressive measures that basically went unchecked by the League. Furthermore, the Westphalian "states system" world order, institutionalized in the League's Covenant, was being challenged in the 1930s by the emergence of NGOs that were filling voids of governance. Finally, and ultimately, the League was unable to prevent the outbreak of another World War in 1939.

In many respects, one can view World War II as a by-product of the dialectical current produced from the clash between continuity and change, as well as *status-quo* forces and upstarts. Germany had emerged out of World War I as a totally dissatisfied power. Not only was it defeated on the battlefield, its territorial ambitions were thwarted by the *status-quo* powers. In addition, the Versailles Treaty, which formally brought an end to the war, forced Germans to pay for the economic costs of the war through reparations. Widespread dissatisfaction in Germany over this "victor's justice" became fertile ground for a rearmed Adolf Hitler to sow his seeds of hatred and stir up the bed of domestic unrest and global disorder.

Since the League was unable to constrain Germany and Japan, the world was thrust into a cataclysmic war only 20 years after the conclusion of what was commonly referred to as the "war to end all wars." As distinguished historian E.H. Carr succinctly put it then: "The characteristic feature of the twenty years between 1919 and 1939 was the abrupt descent from the visionary hopes of the first decade to the grim despair of the second, from a utopia which took little account of reality to a reality from which every element of utopia was rigorously excluded" (1939, 224). This explains to a large extent the great pains taken in the closing days of World War II to construct a global governance system that would balance the utopian hopes of humanity for prolonged and sustained peace with the realism of state leaders who felt that deterrent and enforcement measures were required to keep delinquent actors in line.

In August 1941, just months before the United States entered World War II, President Franklin D. Roosevelt joined British Prime Minister Winston Churchill in putting together the Atlantic Charter. This Charter formed the basis for the Declaration of the United Nations, which was signed on January 1, 1942, by 26 governments. The premise of the Declaration was the need to establish a permanent governance system that would ensure general global security after the war was over. At the Yalta Conference in February 1945, Roosevelt, Churchill, and Stalin laid out the basis for the UN Charter, the constitutional document that would guide the operations of the United Nations—a new global governance institution—and lay out the parameters of the post-World War II world order.

Diplomatic negotiations at a conference in San Francisco on April 25, 1945, resulted in agreement on the UN Charter. This document enshrined veto power for five permanent members of the organization's apex body, the Security Council (the United Kingdom, China, France, the Soviet Union, and the United States). It also intimated that Japan, Germany, and Italy were "enemy states." Fifty states signed the Charter, representing all geographical areas of the globe. For the first time, the global governance institution demonstrated signs of becoming truly universal. Today, the UN membership stands at 191 states.

The Cold War climate stymied the UN's ability to perform as expected, according to the UN Charter. The animosity between the United States and the Soviet Union was played out in the UN Security Council and other organs of the world body. Excessive use of vetoes by both superpowers limited the UN's ability to maintain the peace. The post-Cold War era initially offered great promise of a more assertive UN. However, the expansion of the security concept, the prevalence of new security threats, including transnational terrorism and transnational crime, the agitation by non-governmental organizations to have a greater say in global governance, and the problems associated with unregulated globalization, all reveal the need for major transformations in the way the UN governs. Failure to do so could result in the organization being sidelined, as we witnessed recently in the cases of Kosovo and Iraq, or in the development of new systems of global governance.

Reform of the UN is critical to any discussion of ways to address the current global disorder. It is still the only universal governing framework for the globe, but it cannot function properly as an enforcer of the global rule of law unless its member states, particularly the most powerful ones, empower it to do so. The choices for dealing with the new world disorder are becoming clear. Either we choose to strengthen the UN and the multilateral system of governance or we allow a governance system of *pax americana* to take over the task. Unfortunately, the choice may not be entirely in our hands as citizens of the globe. It will take a combination of acquiescence on the part of the world's hegemonic power (the United States) and the development and acceptance of a post-hegemonic conceptualization of global governance to find an acceptable means of bringing equilibrium back to the international system.

Summary

The survey above indicates clearly that the world has undergone critical turning points and turbulent periods in the past. We are, today, living in one of those periods of turbulence and transition. Existing dominant theories of international relations fail to explain contemporary world politics. This causes us to consider the need for new approaches to understanding world politics and to develop new ways of thinking about the problem of transition, turbulence, and change in world order. Our current era exhibits signs of a structural disjuncture. While, on the one hand, there are tendencies toward global integration and global governance, there are, on the other, also propensities toward fragmentation and global disorder. While "old political, economic, and social structures are under stress or breaking down," we have only begun to imagine the foundations for a new global order (Gill, 1994, 170).

Discussion Questions

1. What evidence is there that we live in a new world disorder?
2. What are the differences of opinion within the scholarly and practitioner communities about the current state of world order?
3. How has human agency been instrumental in developing global governance mechanisms to address the turbulence of world disorders?

References

Carr, Edward Hallett. 1939. *The Twenty Years' Crisis, 1919–1939: An Introduction to the Study of International Relations.* New York: Harper Torchbooks.

Gill, Stephen. 1994. "Structural Change and Global Political Economy: Globalizing Elites and the Emerging World Order" in Yoshikazu Sakamoto, ed., *Global Transformation: Challenges to the State System.* Tokyo: United Nations University Press.

Hinsley, F.H. 1967. *Power and the Pursuit of Peace.* Cambridge: Cambridge University Press.

Kaplan, Robert D. 2000. *The Coming Anarchy: Shattering the Dreams of the Post Cold War World.* New York: Random House.

Keating, Tom, and W. Andy Knight, eds. 2004. *Building Sustainable Peace.* Edmonton: University of Alberta Press.

Klare, Michael. 1998. "The Era of Multiplying Schisms: World Security in the Twenty-First Century" in Michael T. Klare and Yogesh Chandrani, eds., *World Security: Challenges for the New Century,* 3rd edition. New York: St. Martin's Press.

Knight, W. Andy. 2000. *A Changing United Nations: Multilateral Evolution and the Quest for Global Governance* (Houndmills: Palgrave.

Krauthammer, Charles. 1990–91. "The Unipolar Moment." *Foreign Affairs,* 70.

Matthews, Jessica. 1997. "Power Shift." *Foreign Affairs,* (January–February), 76.

Mearsheimer, John. 1990. "Why We Will Soon Miss The Cold War." *The Atlantic Monthly,* Volume 266, No. 2 (August).

———. 1992. "Disorder Restored" in Graham Allison and Gregory F. Treverton, eds. *Rethinking America's Security: Beyond Cold War to New World Order.* New York: Norton.

Morgenthau, Hans. 2001. "Different Methods of the Balance of Power" in Karen Mingst and Jack Synder, eds., *Essential Readings in World* Politics. New York: W.W. Norton & Company.

Rosneau, James N. 1990. *Turbulence in World Politics: A Theory of Change and Continuity.* Princeton, New Jersey: Princeton University Press.

Slaughter, Anne-Marie. 2001. "The Real New World Order" in Karen Mingst and Jack Snyder, eds., *Essential Readings in World Politics.* New York: W.W. Norton & Company.

Tehranian, Majid. 2002. "Globalization and Governance: An Overview" in Eşref Aksu and Joseph A. Camilleri, eds., *Democratizing Global Governance.* Houndmills: Palgrave/Macmillan.

Valaskakis, Kimon. 2001. "Long-term Trends in Global Governance: From 'Westphalia' to 'Seattle'," in Organization of Economic Cooperation and Development, *Governance in the Twenty-first Century.* Paris: OECD.

Waltz, Kenneth. 2000. "Structural Realism after the Cold War." *International Security,* 25 (Summer).

Woolf, L. 1916. *International Government,* 2nd edition. London: Allen & Unwin.

Further Readings

Aksu, Eşref, and Joseph A. Camilleri. eds. 2002. *Democratizing Global Governance.* Houndmills: Palgrave Macmillan.

Archer, Clive. 1983. *International Organizations.* London: George Allen & Unwin.

Cox, Robert W. 2002. *The Political Economy of a Plural World.* London: Routledge.

Rosneau, James N. 1990. *Turbulence in World Politics: A Theory of Change and Continuity.* Princeton, New Jersey: Princeton University Press.

Weblinks

On the Concert of Europe
www.pvhs.chico.k12.ca.us/~bsilva/projects/concert/concessy.html

On the Treaty of Westphalia
www.hfac.uh.edu/gbrown/philosophers/leibniz/BritannicaPages/WestphaliaTreaty/WestphaliaTreaty.html

On the League of Nations and the United Nations
www.bbc.co.uk/history/state/nations/league_nations_01.shtml

CHAPTER 21

POST-COLD WAR POLITICS

Objectives

For nearly 50 years, the Cold War struggle between the superpowers—the United States of America and the Soviet Union—had a profound impact on political life among and within states and societies around the globe. The end of this rivalry in 1991 marked the onset of remarkable sea changes in political affairs. Many analysts predict even more dramatic future changes that will challenge the conventional political expectations and categories that dominated the Cold War era. In the aftermath of the September 11, 2001, (9/11) terrorist attacks on the United States, the uncertainties of the post-Cold War era have only intensified. This chapter outlines three distinct reasons why the Cold War began and ended. These focus on ideological struggle, domestic politics and leadership, and the international power structure. Next, we explore five competing visions of politics in the post-Cold War era: the end of history; McWorld versus Jihad; the Coming Anarchy; the Clash of Civilizations; and, in the most recent post-9/11 phase, the assertion of the American Empire.

ANTONIO FRANCESCHET

Introduction

The **Cold War** was the antagonistic political relationship between the United States and the Soviet Union between approximately 1946 and 1991. Although these two superpower states (and their allies) frequently clashed, open fighting never occurred between them. Most agree that dramatic change has occurred with the end of the Cold War but disagree on *what* has changed, *why*, and *how* things will look in the future as a result. Whether the post-Cold War era is something to celebrate, as citizens of Eastern Europe did when the Berlin Wall fell and the Soviet Empire crumbled, or something to lament and fear has been a central theme in political science since 1991. What is clear in the post-9/11 era, however, is that the bipolar nuclear stalemate between East and West is no longer perceived as the gravest threat to global peace and security, for reasons discussed below.

Why the Cold War Began and Ended

THE COLD WAR WAS GENERATED BY POLITICAL RELATIONS MARKEDLY DIFFERENT from those in today's world, and to understand the present, we need a basic grasp of the Cold War past. The Cold War was marked by important episodes, circumstances, and statements that either incited and perpetuated or moderated and dampened the tensions, suspicions, and antagonisms between the superpowers. Some important historical markers of the Cold War include Winston Churchill's famous "Iron Curtain" speech in Fulton, Missouri (March 5, 1946), the Korean War (1950–1953), the Cuban Missile Crisis (October 1962), and a seemingly insatiable nuclear arms race. But why did the Cold War break out? What forces sustained it? Ideology, domestics politics, and international military power, all have been identified as root causes of the Cold War.

Ideological Struggle

A popular and compelling explanation of the Cold War is that it was generated and sustained by profound ideological differences. The 1917 Bolshevik Revolution that formed the Soviet Union was based on communist ideology, while the United States was fashioned on the basis of liberal democratic ideology. Although the two countries co-operated to defeat Nazi Germany in World War II, without a common enemy the deep incompatibilities between each state's fundamental political ideas and institutions became apparent. The Cold War was, therefore, a contest over opposed visions of polity, society, and economy. Both superpowers engaged in a missionary attempt to convert other states around the globe to either liberal capitalism or communism and to prevent them from being influenced by the rival's ideology.

The United States meddled in the domestic politics of western European states to prevent the left—especially the strong communist parties of France and Italy—from gaining power. It also intervened in and subverted states throughout the Third World to guard against a perceived Soviet agenda of "taking over the world." American foreign policy makers frequently referred to a **domino effect**, through which a single communist state, such as Cuba, would infect neighbours until the entire "free" world fell to this ideology. The Soviets relentlessly maintained control over Eastern and Central Europe through the so-called Warsaw Pact alliance. Although the liberal capitalist and communist ideologies changed somewhat throughout the Cold War, the essential differences remained to drive the conflict until the Soviet Union abandoned the central features of its ideology. When Soviet leader Mikhail Gorbachev (1984–91) introduced liberalizing political reforms and market economics, there was eventually little left on which the two sides could disagree.

Domestic Politics and Leadership

Another explanation of the Cold War is that domestic politics in each superpower state started and then exacerbated it. This explanation stresses the unique role and interests of political elites and leaders in both the United States and the Soviet Union. In both societies, an external threat or enemy helped legitimate rule, consolidate power, and silence domestic dissent or opposition. Throughout the Cold War, leaders in both states depicted the enemy in mirror-like terms as evil, aggressive, expansionist, and unpredictable. Rather than being opposed because of ideological differences, leaders like American President Harry Truman and Soviet Chairman Joseph Stalin fostered conflict in order to promote cohesion in domestic politics.

According to this explanation, "the Cold War ended when Gorbachev shifted the basis of authority" within his state. Gorbachev "needed to reward a different set of constituencies whose interests required a shifting of resources away from defence" (Lebow, 1999, 23). The Soviet leadership became interested in domestic economic and political reforms and international accommodation as ways to overcome the crippling limits of a planned economy locked in a costly arms race.

International Structure

A school of International Relations known as **Realism** claims that the Cold War was simply the result of a "bipolar" international structure. Realists see conflict and antagonism among states as an essential and enduring reality, one that determines international events, such as those of the Cold War period. Unlike politics within states, there is no international political authority to settle conflicts—there is, instead, only **anarchy** defined as the absence of overarching authority. Realists argue that the unequal distribution of military power among states in anarchy will have an effect on the international structure. For example, if there are—as in the Cold War—only two states of roughly equal military power, there is a bipolar structure and with several, a multi-polar structure; and, when there is only one great power, as is currently the case, a unipolar structure emerges.

For Realists, the Cold War was a product of the bipolar international structure, inevitable after World War II had weakened Europe, dismembered the German state, and disempowered Japan. The pre-war multipolar structure of several great powers was displaced by a global political rivalry between the United States and the Soviet Union. This rivalry produced two blocks of allied states that either chose or were compelled to "choose" affiliation with the superpowers. "The root cause of the Cold War and its demise," for Realists, was the "rise and fall of the Soviet Union as a global power" (Lebow, 1999, 22).

The ideological, domestic–political, and international structure accounts of the Cold War and its ending provide partial perspectives on a complex phenomenon. To some extent, the first two can be synthesized to create a richer explanation of the conflict between the superpowers and the conduct in which they engaged. The third, Realist, account is set apart, however, by its stubborn rejection of the significance of ideological and domestic factors.

The Post-Cold War Era: From the "End of History" to the "American Empire"

THE END OF THE COLD WAR HAS LED TO CONTINUED SPECULATION ABOUT THE emerging contours of global political life. As James Richardson notes, "in groping for new landmarks, commentators have put forward a bewildering variety of diagnoses and prescriptions" (1992, 1). As the ideological and nuclear stalemate between the Soviet Union and the United States has receded, what are the prospects for, and threats to, fundamental values, such as peace, security, justice, and welfare? How should any threats to these values be managed or confronted? There have been five influential and widely debated visions of the post-Cold War order. The first four emerged prior to 9/11 but are still of some relevance to explaining and debating issues surrounding the current American-led campaign against the so-called global terrorism. The fifth vision, that of the American Empire, has emerged to characterize and debate the United States' foreign policy in the aftermath of 9/11. In particular, the so-called "war on terrorism," the "Bush Doctrine" (White House, 2002) on the pre-emptive use of force against rivals, and the regime change in Iraq are taken as important signs of a new phase in the post-Cold War order.

The End of History?

In 1989, Francis Fukuyama proclaimed that the end of the Cold War meant the "**end of history**" (1989; 1992). He did *not*, as sceptical critics charged, mean that history, as events or occurrences in time, would stop. That would be absurd. Rather, Fukuyama was making a more profound philosophical point. Fukuyama adapted the "end of history" notion from philosopher G.W.F. Hegel (1770–1831), for whom political progress was considered to end once the liberal state became fully established. Fukuyama claims that progress is now impossible, since the Soviet Union has collapsed and communism has been repudiated. The Soviet Union was the last great impediment to the universal recognition that liberal democracy and capitalist economics were the best of all possible regimes and systems, "free from . . . fundamental contradictions" (Fukuyama, 1992, xi). Consequently, Fukuyama predicts the democratization of all states, the flourishing of human potential, rights and liberties, greater peace and stability among states and peoples, and growing prosperity for all in the very long term.

Along with greater peace and prosperity, Fukuyama claims that cultural diversity and ideological disagreement have simply come to an end in the post-Cold War, post-historical era. "Rather than a thousand shoots blossoming into as many different flowering plants, mankind will come to seem like a long wagon train strung out along the road" (1992, 338). This incredible homogeneity may seem boring, he concedes, but it is better than living with the terrible conflicts of history. The only disagreements now are simply over the means of political life, not the ends. Politics now is simply about implementing liberal capitalism because, according to Fukuyama, all the "really big questions" have been settled (1992, xii).

How does Fukuyama account for the civil strife, bloodshed, and nationalist fervour that also emerged after the Cold War? There has been ethnic cleansing in the Balkans and genocide in Africa. Fukuyama is clear to distinguish between two worlds: the liberal capitalist "post-historical" world in which advanced, industrialized states, such as Canada and the United States, reside and the illiberal peripheral world that simply contains what he considers "irrational" peoples stuck in history, like the Yugoslavs and the Rwandan tribes (1992, 276). There may be short-term conflicts in the historical world and between the historical and post-historical worlds. Eventually, however, he argues, all humanity will be integrated into the post-historical world. In other words, although Fukuyama thinks the end of the Cold War is something to celebrate, residual and peripheral conflicts and discord will exist for the foreseeable future.

This last point is a major concession that weakens the power of Fukuyama's overall argument—the benefits and stability of the post-Cold War era are not evenly distributed. And the violence and poverty in the daily lives of the majority of the world's population have not been noticeably ameliorated since the triumph of liberal capitalism over communism. Other political scientists are, thus, rightly less confident or sanguine than Fukuyama about the prospects for peace, prosperity, and democracy in the post-Cold War era.

Certainly, in the aftermath of the 9/11 attacks, Fukuyama's claims about the inevitability of historic progress and the inherent universal appeal of liberal, Western, and capitalist values has been called into question. Indeed, it is obvious that American political and military leaders are now too impatient for history to vindicate the values they hold to be of global significance and appeal. The 2003 American-led invasion and occupation of Iraq has been justified as necessary to jump-start the democratization and the economic integration of the Middle East, the region held to be most resistant to the so-called "end of history."

McWorld versus Jihad?

Benjamin Barber (1995) argues that the great ideological contradiction between communism and liberal capitalism has simply been replaced by an even more dangerous collision of forces—*McWorld* and *Jihad*. Barber uses these terms to signify a global battle between two dangerous threats to democracy and human liberty worldwide.

McWorld refers to the forces of global capitalism, consumer greed, and the cultural homogeneity they breed when unchecked by democratic politics. **Jihad** refers to the forces of intolerance that lead a people or state to reject universal political values, rights, and freedoms. McWorld is, thus, a symbol of the planet being artificially unified and transformed by corporate power and American consumer desire, such as the global dominance of McDonald's fast food restaurants. For Barber, Jihad represents the world being torn apart by self-righteous, inward-looking, fanatical advocates of traditional religious, ethnic, national, cultural, historical, and political identities. These zealots spur on others to slaughter the threatening infidels from the outside world.

Barber does not draw a direct connection between the end of the Cold War and the eruption of the two conflicting McWorld and Jihad forces. However, he does suggest that Western states and publics have, in light of their victory over Soviet communism, become too complacent and accepting of free-market madness—that is, the unfettered and uncontrolled interests of global capitalism. McWorld has emerged as soulless corporations have emancipated themselves from the control of sovereign states. Barber claims that we are paying the price for this in two related ways. First, we in the West are now enduring a destruction of public or civic culture by the mindless consumer advertising and "branding" of McWorld. Second, we must now be on guard against the reactionary, mainly anti-Western Jihad forces that are provoked by the conformity, homogeneity, and cultural insensitivity of McWorld.

McWorld and Jihad may appear like contradictory forces. Yet Barber claims they actually reinforce and sustain each other: "Jihad not only revolts against but abets McWorld, while McWorld not only imperils but recreates and reinforces Jihad" (1995, 5). McWorld and Jihad are two sides of the same anti-democratic coin, creating chaos and anarchy, rather than reinforcing the popular control that a tolerant and respectful civil society ideally enjoys over the levers of government. "Antithetical in every detail," he adds, "Jihad and McWorld nonetheless conspire to undermine our hard-won (if only half-won) civil liberties and the possibility of a global democratic future" (1995, 19).

Certainly, the actions of terrorist networks, such as Al-Queda, can be read as a reaction against Western dominance and arrogance, thus seeming to confirm Barber's concerns. However, it is doubtful that the motives and grievances of anti-Western, Islamicist extremists can be reduced to anger over, or dealt with by simply curtailing, corporate power (for example, by closing down McDonald's restaurants throughout the world). Nonetheless, Barber's vision, unlike Fukuyama's, is one of divergence and struggle, rather than of convergence and harmony in the post-Cold War era.

The Coming Anarchy?

Realists assume that anarchy is an ever-present feature among sovereign states in the international system, in contrast to politics within states. Realists assume that in the domestic arena, governments authoritatively settle disputes and uphold common laws among citizens. According to journalist Robert Kaplan (1994; 2000), we can no longer take these assumptions for granted within states—anarchy is now emerging *within* them and will, in the future, undermine domestic political orders and the individual security that states are supposed to provide.

Kaplan's influential reportage from the Balkans and Africa during the 1990s made the broad claim that the lawlessness, ethnic enmity, and criminally irresponsible government he found there would, in the future, be reproduced in many more states and societies. He claims the causes of these terrible problems are "natural" disasters, rather than political and social breakdowns. What Kaplan means by "natural" is that resource scarcity, environmental degradation, overpopulation, migration, and squalid urbanization are creating a powder keg in the developing world—domestic violence and struggle over the basic resources needed to sustain life. Unable to cope, governments are collapsing, and states, particularly the former European colonies in Africa, are incapable of upholding the law, providing welfare, and preventing the gross abuse of human rights. The anarchy in such places as Sierra Leone and the Ivory Coast are, Kaplan claims, a part of our future simply because *all* humans depend upon scarce natural resources and are vulnerable to the limits of the physical environment. Moreover, the global population, particularly in the developing world, is exploding. But soon, Western governments will face the same problems, not least because refugee migrants from the Third World will arrive on the shores of the wealthy states, thus spreading the anarchy. In the wake of the 9/11 attacks, many have suggested that both migration and terrorism threaten to harm the West from the so-called unruly, failed states at the periphery.

How did the end of the Cold War unleash the coming anarchy? Kaplan explains that the end of European imperial control over the Third World left it populated with weak, ill-constituted states that could not independently cope with the challenges of governing. The Cold War provided a temporary stop-gap to the coming anarchy because the superpowers invested aid, trade, and support to these states to fight the battle against communism and/or capitalism. The end of the Cold War, thus, opened the flood gates to "a cruel process of natural selection among existing states," claims Kaplan. "No longer will these states be so firmly propped up by the West or Soviet Union" (2000, 40).

As the political geographer Simon Dalby has noted, Kaplan constructs a new and alarming threat, one that is even more unpredictable and ominous for the Western way of life than was communism (1996). Quite simply, the privilege, prosperity, and rule of law (that we simply assume is part and parcel of the West) will start to erode when too many people compete for decreasing natural resources. In this lifeboat depiction of the future, Kaplan fails to consider that Western colonialism, privilege, and economic interests have created many of the problems the developing world must now confront. Thus, the anarchy that undoubtedly arises from scarcity, overpopulation, and forced migration is not simply a product of natural limits, but also of political realities, many created by Western imperial powers. Finally, by highlighting allegedly "natural" factors, Kaplan's analysis detracts from the possibility of creative political and social solutions to the most pressing problems facing the world today.

The Clash of Civilizations?

The political scientist Samuel Huntington claims: "In the post-Cold War world, the most important distinctions among peoples are not ideological, political, or economic but, instead, are cultural (1996, 21). The bipolar international structure of the superpower rivalry has been eclipsed by a multipolar, multi-civilizational order, in which six to nine different civilizations have become distrustful rivals. These civilizations—Western, Islamic, Sinic (based principally in China), Hindu, Orthodox (principally Christians in East Europe and Russia), Japanese, Latin American, African—are based on different and, moreover, *incompatible* religious precepts and world views.

Huntington's argument contrasts with the others discussed above because he rejects the idea that the non-Western world will embrace liberal democratic values. Global harmony, Huntington argues, is an illusion because "enemies are essential" in creating political identities (1996, 19). Huntington assumes that the basic dynamics of global politics will shift with the rediscovery of cultural identities by differing peoples after the Cold War. It is time, he warns, for Westerners to recognize that they are not superior and that such values as individual freedom, the rule of law, and human rights will be rejected by other civilizations (1996, 51). It is also time to recognize that multiculturalism is a disastrous policy to adopt within Western domestic societies. Multiculturalism only weakens the sense of coherent identity required to meet the challenge of a multipolar world in which the interests of the American-led West must defend against "Rest" (1996, 306). Finally, Huntington alarms his readers about the relative decline of Western global power and influence when compared with other civilizations. Other civilizations are experiencing population and economic growth that will soon render the existing power of the West less impressive than ever—and these other civilizations will not necessarily show mercy when they perceive Western weakness. A dangerous clash of civilizations can be averted only by carefully strengthening Western power while not provoking the wrath of the non-Western world, particularly its core states—China, Iran, and India.

Huntington almost certainly exaggerates the incompatibility among civilizations and ignores the shared characteristics among them. For example, although human rights may be a Western concept, all cultures share in common a belief in the value of human life and a prohibition against cruelty. Also, the distinctions he draws between civilizations are arbitrary and difficult to sustain. For example, why is Latin America separate from the West, given that Catholicism is a common element in both cultures? If religion is not always the most important difference, why does Huntington separate Orthodox Christian civilization from Western Christendom? And so on. Finally, Huntington's clash of civilizations thesis may contain the seeds of a self-fulfilling prophecy, feeding distrust and enmity between the West and the Rest, rather than solving disputes that may arise in the future.

In the immediate aftermath of 9/11, there was much talk in the media about a global clash of civilizations along the lines Huntington had earlier described. In spite of this, the American political and military response has not been in line with his prescriptions. To the contrary, rather than following Huntington's advice and backing away from global hegemony into a more modest "civilizational" balance of power, there has been, according to many, the assertion of the American Empire.

The American Empire?

The most recent image of post-Cold War politics is the assertion of the American Empire. Whereas America was allegedly too tentative, confused, and inward looking during the 1990s, 9/11 provoked its leaders to reassert with a vengeance political, economic, and especially military power over the world. Although American political leaders have denied that the country either now controls or wishes to amass an empire (President Bush has said, "We do not seek an empire"), a major debate among pundits and scholars has emerged anyway. The debate is over what kind of empire, if any, America wields, in addition to the (alleged) benefits that such an empire brings to the world. As the *Economist* (2003) magazine notes, the "unfashionable" concept of imperialism "has been given a remarkably warm reception" in American think-tanks and in recent books and articles.

Imperialism is a policy in which one great power asserts control and dominance over other peoples and states. This is normally done through military means, although political, diplomatic, and legal tools are also important. Empires, such as the famous Roman Empire of past millennia and the British Empire less than a hundred years ago, are characterized by the formal rule over vast territorial holdings by the centre and for a long duration. Empires have historically been used to brutally dominate and suppress peoples around the world, but in each era of imperialism, there have been two dominant rationalizations or justifications to support them. First, that Empires bring civilization, laws, and culture to so-called "barbarian" or "backward" peoples; second, that Empires provide peace and order by supplying a credible, effective military to police and suppress the violent and unruly (an example in today's world would be Saddam Hussein).

The United States clearly has the military capacity to police the world. "What other country divides the world into five military commands with four-star generals to match, keeps several hundred thousand of its legionaries on activity duty in 137 countries—

and is now unafraid to use them? For, stung by the events of September 11th, America is no longer shy about spilling blood, even its own" (*Economist,* 2003). Michael Ignatieff, Niall Ferguson, and Max Boot have advocated that America use its unquestioned military power to enact a post-Cold War empire. All three acknowledge that an American Empire would be based on self-interest, yet contend that it has the potential to prove benign, even beneficial, by providing global peace, security, democracy, and human rights around the world. In Ignatieff's words, "Imperialism used to be the white man's burden. This gave it a bad reputation. But imperialism doesn't stop being necessary just because it becomes politically incorrect" (2002, 31). Ignatieff also claims that the American Empire is the "last hope for democracy and stability alike" (2003, 54). The American-led war on global terrorism and the invasions of Afghanistan and Iraq to overturn enemy regimes and install friendly governments are clearly "exercise[s] in imperialism," but, he claims, "[t]he moral evaluation of empire gets complicated when one of its benefits might be freedom for the oppressed" (2003, 28, 25).

There are some clear difficulties in the assertion of (a benign) American Empire. The first is acknowledged even by its advocates: after invading and occupying such countries as Afghanistan and Iraq, is America willing to stay the course and pay the costs of nation building? Ignatieff worries that America is building something he calls "Empire Lite" by simply using military force to destroy so-called rogue and barbarian governments and then withdrawing precipitously before a viable and stable democratic state is left behind. Ferguson describes this worry more bluntly: "The United States is acting like a colossus with an attention deficit disorder engaged in cut-price colonization" (2003, 66). For these commentators, too little, rather than too much, American imperialism is the problem with the post-Cold War era.

The more significant problem with the assertion of the American Empire is, quite simply, that the rest of the world does not want it. Indian author Arundhati Roy puts this forcefully: "Debating imperialism is a bit like debating the pros and cons of rape. What can we say? That we really miss it?" (2004, 11). Anti-imperialist and anti-colonial political norms, including national self-determination, have become widely accepted in the era of the United Nations (Jackson, 2000). If the United States were to continue to pursue imperialism, even the so-called "lite" version that Ignatieff worries is too little, it would cause only resistance and further conflict. Quite simply, "Imperialism and democracy are at odds with each other. People nowadays are not willing to bow down before an empire, even a benevolent one, in order to be democratized" (*Economist,* 2003).

At this stage, few believe that an American Empire is a sustainable future model for the post-Cold War era. This is not to say that American power and dominance will not be asserted as it has been since 9/11, often in defiance of international law and global public opinion. It is simply unlikely, that a single country can continue to translate its overwhelming military power into a widely accepted, legitimate agent of global governance.

Summary

Although there is substantial agreement in political science that the Cold War has ended, there is little agreement about what this means for current and future generations. This suggests that the so-called facts of global politics are highly conditioned by contradicting assumptions about the continuity or discontinuity of the key elements of the Cold War era. For example, scholars are divided over whether the post-Cold War era is likely to see greater peace or conflict and whether these basic trends will pertain equally to all states, societies, and other political identities or to only a particular subset of them.

The purpose of uncovering the main assumptions that different political scientists hold about the post-Cold War era is to develop a critical understanding of different trends in the discipline and in the larger realm of global politics. As the above analysis shows, clearly not all of these assumptions can be true: Fukuyama, Barber, Kaplan, Huntington, and the advocates of American Empire disagree and there is little chance of synthesizing their contrasting visions of the present and future. They cannot all be correct, can they? Students will likely be attracted to some or only one of these competing visions of the future; or they may find grounds for rejecting all of them.

The interests and alternative visions of the post-Cold War era presented in this chapter are also grounded in the central role of the most powerful state in the global political and economic system, the United States. Without exception, a concern of the most influential post-Cold War scenarios evaluated above has been the future of the United States' foreign policy. However, there is good reason not to simply follow slavishly a limited number of political alternatives that reflect the concerns, values, and interests of the American polity after the demise of the Soviet threat and the apparent emergence of global terrorism as a replacement.

Certainly, the material presented in this chapter does not exhaust all available options for the post-Cold War era—they may obscure more than they illuminate. One of the great difficulties of the Cold War period was the lack of choice and alternatives to the stark dichotomies of capitalism versus communism and the United States versus the Soviet Union. If we really have moved beyond the Cold War, our range of options concerning the future of politics ought to be much wider than is conventionally assumed. In the post-9/11 era, however, there has been a reassertion of stark dichotomies, evidenced by American foreign policy and Bush's statement, "Either you are with us, or you are with the terrorists" (2001). Similar to the efforts of the non-aligned states during the Cold War, Roy has responded to Bush's ultimatum as follows: "'No thank you.' . . . [T]he people of the world do not need to choose between a Malevolent Mickey Mouse and the Mad Mullahs" (2003, 16).

Discussion Questions

1. Did the United States "win" the Cold War? Can it "win" the so-called War on Terrorism in the post-9/11 era? Why, or why not?
2. In your opinion, which vision of the post-Cold War era presented in this chapter is most compelling, and why? How convincing are the End of History, McWorld versus Jihad, Coming Anarchy, and Clash of Civilization images in the post-9/11 era?

3. Is the so-called Western world really declining in influence in global politics as Huntington claims? If this is so, what are the implications?
4. Is maintaining an empire the best foreign policy for the United States after the Cold War? Why, or why not? What is the likely role for other Western countries in Europe or Canada in an era of American Empire?

References

Barber, Benjamin R. 1995. *Jihad versus McWorld.* Toronto: Random House Ltd.

Bush, George W. 2001. "Address to a Joint Session of Congress and the American People." September 20, 2001. www.whitehouse.gov/news/releases/2001/09/20010920-8.html (Accessed February 18, 2004).

Dalby, Simon. 1996. "Reading Robert Kaplan's 'Coming Anarchy.'" *Ecumene,* 3, 4.

Economist. 2003. "Special Report: Manifest Destiny Warmed Up? America and Empire" August 16, 19.

Ferguson, Niall. 2003. "The 'E' Word." *Wall Street Journal.* June 6, A10.

Fukuyama, Francis. 1989. "The End of History?" *The National Interest,* 16, 3–18.

———. 1992. *The End of History and the Last Man.* New York: Avon Books.

Huntington, Samuel P. 1996. *The Clash of Civilizations and the Remaking of World Order.* New York: Simon and Schuster.

Ignatieff, Michael. 2002. "Nation-building Lite." *New York Times Magazine.* July 28.

———. 2003. "The Burden." *New York Times Magazine.* January 5.

Jackson, Robert. 2000. *The Global Covenant: Human Conduct in a World of States.* Oxford: Oxford University Press.

Kaplan, Robert D. 1994. "The Coming Anarchy." *The Atlantic Monthly,* 273, 2, 44–76.

———. 2000. *The Coming Anarchy: Shattering the Dreams of the Post Cold War World.* New York: Random House.

Lebow, Richard Ned. 1999. "The Rise and Fall of the Cold War in Comparative Perspective." *Review of International Studies,* 25 (Special Issue), 21–39.

Richardson, James L. 1992. *Questions about a Post-Cold War International Order.* Working Paper 1992/3, Department of International Relations, Australian National University, Canberra.

Roy, Arundhati. 2003. "Confronting Empire." *The Nation* 276, 9, 16.

———. "The New American Century." *The Nation* 278, 5, 11–14.

White House. 2002. *The National Security Strategy of the United States of America.* www.whitehouse.gov/nsc/nss.html (Accessed February 20, 2004).

Further Readings

Fergusson, Niall. 2003. *Empire: The Rise and Demise of the British World Order and the Lessons for Global Power.* Toronto: HarperCollins.

Ignatieff, Michael. 2003. *Empire Lite: Nation-building in Bosnia, Kosovo, and Afghanistan.* Toronto: Penguin Books.

Ned Lebow, Richard and Thomas Risse-Kappen, eds. 1995. *International Relations Theory and The End of the Cold War.* New York: Columbia University Press.

New Lebow, Richard and Janice Gross Stein. 1994. *We All Lost the Cold War.* Princeton: Princeton University Press.

Weblinks

A version of Robert Kaplan's "The Coming Anarchy" is posted online
www.theatlantic.com/politics/foreign/anarchy.htm

A version of Benjamin Barber's "McWorld versus Jihad" is posted online
www.theatlantic.com/politics/foreign/barberf.htm

Cable News Network (CNN) Documentary Report on the Cold War
www.cnn.com/SPECIALS/cold.war

Council on Foreign Relations
www.cfr.org/index.php

CHAPTER 22

INTERNATIONAL RELATIONS

Objectives

Finding explanations for why national states act the way they do on the international stage has been a central preoccupation of the discipline of Political Science. This chapter uses the case of the 2003 War in Iraq to demonstrate the central premises of three dominant analytical models—realist, liberal, and radical—in the study of international relations. The chapter shows that each of these models of world affairs is grounded in quite different understandings of human nature, national states, and the contours of power in the international system. The War in Iraq demonstrates that explanations of international conflict and peace are complex, involving multiple levels of analysis, the divergent motivations of international actors, and systemic inequalities among national states.

JURIS LEJNIEKS

Introduction

American foreign policy in the immediate aftermath of the September 11, 2001, attacks on the World Trade Center and the Pentagon can be described as a policy success by almost any standard. The United States put together a global coalition to overthrow the Taliban regime in Afghanistan that had been harbouring Osama bin Laden and his Al Qaeda organization. The coalition included critical state actors, such as Russia, China, Pakistan, India, and Japan, along with the usual NATO government support. The Taliban regime was overthrown, and Afghanistan is in the process of being rebuilt. When the Bush administration went to war against Iraq and the Saddam Hussein regime in March of 2003, however, Washington's attempts to build another broad coalition ran into serious resistance. Many of the same states that had supported the war against the Taliban, such as France, Germany, and Russia, were now opposed. It was a major diplomatic defeat that continues to bedevil American foreign policy in its efforts to rebuild post-war Iraq. American allies are limited to the United Kingdom and a group of smaller states called "the coalition of the willing."

Why was there opposition to the War against Iraq? The regime of Saddam Hussein had displayed a flagrant disregard for the rights of its own citizens. It had a history of using Weapons of Mass Destruction (WMD) against the Kurds in northern Iraq and the Iranian troops during the war with Iran. Also, Iraq disregarded the wishes of the international community by ignoring a number of UN Security Council resolutions in the aftermath of the Gulf War. The regime of Saddam Hussein was an obvious target for international condemnation and action, including a decade of economic sanctions, but that condemnation did not extend to the use of force as proposed by the United States in 2003.

Again, why was there such a lack of a broader international support for America's determined policy of regime-change in Iraq? A number of possible reasons have been put forward. Among the reasons offered are the Bush administration's inability or reluctance to wait a few more weeks to achieve a second Security Council resolution; the overemphasis on a military, as opposed to a diplomatic, solution; and the Bush administration's strident rhetoric and uncompromising attitude toward its allies and the United Nations. The invasion of another state is never an easy proposition in today's world, especially when that state clearly has not instigated aggression, like Iraq had done in the early 1990s against Kuwait. Legitimizing that use of force is even more difficult. Underlying the legal issue of **legitimacy** is the question of the Bush administration's motives for pursuing the War on Iraq and whether or not Bush was willing to accept any alternative to the military solution and the deposing of Saddam Hussein. It appeared to the world that the United States was committed to overthrowing Hussein and that no level of Iraqi compliance with American and UN demands would suffice.

Analyzing International Relations

THE SPECULATIONS ABOUT THE BUSH ADMINISTRATION'S MOTIVATIONS ARE numerous and depend on public statements both by Bush and his supporters and by his critics and the more speculative arguments about the underlying and unstated Bush policy. Here are some possible "reasons" for the American commitment to war:

- the probability that Iraq had WMD that were an imminent security threat to the United States;
- the United States' obligation to uphold and enforce UN resolutions that the UN Security Council had been unable or unwilling to enforce as an organization;
- Iraq's support and harbouring elements of Al Qaeda. In other words, the attack on Iraq was part of the broader American-led "War on Terrorism";
- the pursuit of regional stability in the Middle East by democratizing Iraq; and
- the toppling of Saddam Hussein, which would put an end to a murderous regime.

Unstated reasons, because they have not been publicly voiced by the Bush administration, are

- the desire by Bush to finish the job that was started by Bush senior during the Gulf War;
- supporting Israel by eliminating a potential future threat to its security; and
- providing a long-term, secure, and cheap energy (oil) source for the American economy.

The problem for students of international relations and foreign policy is to choose which of the above explanations are the "correct" explanations for the invasion of Iraq. That problem has been addressed by the development of a number of tools in a search for appropriate explanations. It may be that it is impossible to determine the "correct" explanation because we may be missing critical facts and opinions on which to base our analysis. We, as well as decision makers, evaluate and act on incomplete data. Despite the often-noted lack of data, the task of explanation is assisted by our ability to structure our information in several different ways. The rest of this chapter explores two ways—the use of levels of analysis and the use of analytical models, particularly realist, liberal, and radical models.

First, we can organize our explanations according to three levels of analysis. (1) At the individual level, the focus is on the perceptions, personalities, and world views of key individual decision makers (George W. Bush and Saddam Hussein) or other important participants (Vice-President Cheney, for example). (2) At the state level, the focus is on state characteristics, such as type of government, political culture, economic structures (the military-industrial complex for example), or identifiable national interests, such as security needs. (3) At the systemic level, the focus is on the structure of the international system and the nature of the distribution of power among the actors that make up the system, especially whether it is anarchical (and thereby lacking in security) or co-operative, whether it is unipolar, bipolar, or multipolar. Levels of analysis are important because they help us categorize our empirical data and focus our attention on a range of possible explanations. We can ask such questions as: What is the effect of systemic or regional structures on state behaviour? What is the effect of individual (decision maker) behaviour on state behaviour?

A second major tool that we employ to explain war and peace are analytical models. An analytical model is a set of propositions that explain events by connecting relevant concepts. We generate propositions by positing a relationship between independent and dependent variables. The statement that the War on Iraq is caused by the Bush administration's insecurity based on the perception of immediate threat from Iraq's WMD is an example of such a proposition. The proposition, however, ultimately depends on the nature of the analytical model employed. In the study of foreign policy and international relations, we normally employ one of a number of available analytical models: realism and two of its variants, neo-realism and hegemony; liberalism and liberal institutionalism; and the radical model based on Marxism.

Realism

Realism rests upon a number of interrelated assumptions. Principal among these assumptions are that humans are egotistical and power seeking, that politics is a struggle for power in the pursuit of national interest, that the state is the pre-eminent actor in the international system, and that progressive change more often occurs in domestic politics than in international political life.

Realists are pessimistic about human nature—human beings are self-interested, egotistical, and power seeking, which results in aggression and conflict. The nature of humans is immutable, and that nature makes humans think and act in terms of power.

The second assumption addresses the key concept of power. There are a large number of definitions of power because of its controversial nature, but here I define power as "the capacity to act in global politics." The central preoccupation of international political activity is the immediate pursuit of power, since acquiring, maintaining, and demonstrating power allow us to acquire political and economic objectives. Hence, international relations are characterized by rivalry and conflict, where all states pursue and defend their national interests and all states pursue the same broad national interests to a greater or lesser extent. States first pursue their own self-preservation since the international system is anarchical and security is in short supply.

The second broad national interest is the economic well being of the population followed by the pursuit of a favourable world order and the pursuit of specific state values, such as democracy or socialism. National interests are achieved through the application of power, which, at times, depends on military capability, since the ultimate resolution of conflicts is war. Very powerful states, such as the United States, may not have to wage war to be influential as they can influence the behaviour of others simply because they possess significant power and have shown the will to use that power. But power is relative because some states possess more power than others and not all power can be used in all international contexts. Just because the United States possesses nuclear weapons does not mean that it can use them, or threaten to use them, for example, in a fishing dispute with Canada.

States are the most significant actors because they are more powerful than other international actors, such as **intergovernmental organizations** (IGOs). States have the capacity to tax their subjects and use those resources to pursue foreign policy objectives. Further, they can mobilize their populations to create militaries that serve to protect or expand the state and its sovereignty. States are sovereign in the sense that they are not obliged to do what other states tell them to do. There are no higher authorities even in today's international system than the national state. And, since there is no world government, the international system is anarchical characterized by turmoil, discord, and conflict.

Since human nature is immutable, international politics is immutable. International politics is, thus, perpetually characterized by self-reliance and the struggle for power. The international system is inherently conflictual, where peace is only a temporary condition and is always in jeopardy. Realism is an analytical model that holds for all times because the basic nature of state relations never changes. There is no progressive evolution as is the case in domestic political systems with their evolution toward democratic and free institutions.

A major variant of realism is neo-realism, also known as structural realism. The major difference from realism is the neo-realist emphasis on the international system itself instead of the state and its leaders. The structure of the international system is still characterized by a lack of overarching authority but equally important is the distribution of capabilities within the system. It is the nature of the system and the distribution of capabilities, or relative distribution of power, that defines the nature of international events. All states are basically alike in their functions—they all perform the same basic tasks despite different constitutions, ideologies, or cultures. They differ significantly only in regard to their power. Hence, change in the international system occurs when great powers rise and fall along with a shift in the balance of power. The only way to minimize conflict among actors is the maintenance of a balance of power. It is a highly deterministic analytical model with no room for the will of individual decision makers and minimal options for states.

The hegemonic model is defined by a preponderance of power by one state in relation to all others in the international system. The hegemon provides the values and the rules—in other words, the leadership—that maintain effectively functioning political and economic systems defined by peace, stability, and prosperity. It is a system that serves the interests of both the hegemon and all other actors in the system. The hegemon must maintain its unique position because instability arises when a hegemon weakens and a challenger moves to erode the influence of the hegemon. Instability is dangerous because it disturbs both the international and regional balances of power, thus creating conditions for war.

A critical obligation of the hegemon's leadership is the maintenance of a prosperous international economic system. Since the global economy today is defined by capitalism, this means the maintenance and expansion of the benefits of free trade. Hegemony is not merely pragmatic, for the benefit of the hegemon; a benevolent hegemon provides economic benefits to all other actors. To sum up, the realist model assumes power-seeking and antagonistic individuals who organize themselves into political actors that we call states. The resulting international system is one of anarchy that finds stability either through a balance of power or the domination of one state, the hegemon, over all others. Either the state or the international system determines whether or not the system will be peaceful or prone to conflict.

Liberal Models

Major challengers to the realist models are **liberalism** and liberal institutionalism with their focus on the individual and co-operation. In contrast to realist models, liberal models are optimistic about human nature. Liberals assume that human nature is ultimately based on reason, that individuals share many interests and thereby engage in co-operative activities and that international society is progressive in its movement toward a more peaceful world.

Liberals, like realists, recognize that human beings are self-interested but, because they are also rational, humankind is perfectible or at least capable of improvement. Human reason can triumph over human fear and the drive for power. This human nature has a powerful influence over international behaviour. In the long term, international co-operation will dominate the propensity for self-interested conflict. The international system, from a liberal perspective, is characterized by relative peace, the promotion of global interdependence and the spread of human rights. Increasingly, common problems, such as SARS (severe acute respiratory syndrome) and AIDS (acquired immune deficiency syndrome) epidemics, are solved by state collaboration. States work together first out of self-interest, and increasingly, by the very success of that co-operation, working together becomes habitual and overrides narrow national self-interest. Since liberalism is ultimately committed to both political and economic freedoms for the individual, liberals also promote democracy, since it provides the greatest freedoms and rights for individuals. But democracy provides a great deal more than individual liberty. Democracy also promotes economic development by increasing political stability and decreasing government influence and possible corruption in the economy.

For students of international relations, however, the most important aspect of liberalism is that democracies foster international peace. Ordinary people, as opposed to princes, generally oppose war because they pay for war with higher taxes and with their lives. Furthermore, democratic peace theory posits that democracies do not fight wars against other democracies, since they are more likely to act co-operatively to settle mutual disagreements. Implicit in this model is the idea that increasing the number of democracies in the world increases the possibility for a more peaceful world.

The liberal institutionalist model is grounded in the idea that co-operation takes place increasingly within the context of transnational actors. The result is an international system characterized not just by interdependence but interdependence through specialized institutions. Institutions are essential, since the increased speed and spread of transportation and telecommunications have changed world politics dramatically by changing the global agenda from a narrow military security perspective to the need to emphasize shared problems that must have shared solutions. Common problems are no longer just the most immediate threats, such as security and epidemics, but are now increasingly longer-term and less spectacular problems, such as population growth, depletion of fish stocks, and environmental issues (e.g., global warming). The consequences of these threats are a "global commons" problem because they impact all states whether they contribute to the problem or not. Evidence of the importance of institutions is their growth. Currently, there are several hundred IGOs, such as the United Nations and the Organization of American States (OAS), but non-governmental organizations (NGOs), such as Red Cross and Greenpeace, are even more numerous, their numbers now exceeding 26 000 worldwide.

Despite the growth of transnational actors, solutions to global problems are exacerbated by economic inequality because economic globalization has increased the gap between the rich states of the North and the poor states of the South. The growing gap is not only morally unacceptable, it also accentuates other global problems. Growing poverty contributes to growing immigration and refugee problems, and environmental issues, such as access to food and energy supplies. Increasingly, as well, poverty contributes to local violence among peoples who have nothing to loose, with the danger of violence spilling over into neighbouring states or a whole region.

Liberal institutionalists argue that realists ignore the growth and strength of international civil society because of their pessimistic view of human nature. While there is no world government, the functioning of transnational institutions and the acceptance of norms of international law is leading to common habits of co-operative behaviour of both state and non-state actors, including individuals. Compliance with norms and rules is the result of a complex interaction between self-interest and morality. States and other international actors adhere to rules, since it is in their long-term interest to do so, not only because of tangible benefits but also because other actors' adherence to rules makes the international system more orderly, predictable, and peaceful. In contrast to realism, liberal models view international organizations and non-governmental groups being as important as states. In the international system, these models project the replacement of international anarchy with interdependence and a growing international civil society.

Radical Models

The third analytical model in common application is radicalism. Radicalism does not begin with an assumption about human nature. In contrast to realism and liberalism, radicalism assumes that politics is the result of forces of economic production, that economic systems result in human exploitation and inequality, that capitalism—the economic driving force today—is expansionist, and that capitalism must be replaced by more egalitarian economic and political systems.

Radical, here, does not have the usual connotation of extremism. Instead, radicalism proposes solutions to underlying or root causes. It is normative because of its commitment to change. The change comes in the form of the elimination of global capitalism in order to establish a new international economic system based on a different distribution of power that ends exploitation of the weak by the strong and what is termed the "new imperialism." Imperialism in the contemporary context does not mean the existence of an empire because there is no direct and formal political control over other peoples as was the case historically. Formal control has been replaced by less formal control, but control no less for the benefit of the imperial power. Imperialism today is self-sustaining. The imperial power establishes the economic and political rules of the game, and weaker states have to make choices on the basis of those rules. The mechanism of control is the global capitalist economy, which is dominated by the United States, other developed Northern states, and the international institutions that they have formed, such as the World Bank and the International Monetary Fund (IMF). These international financial institutions have inordinate influence over the daily lives of the poor of Africa, the Middle East, and Latin America, as well as their governments.

While the specific methods of control vary, the imperialist objective is to keep the poor states of the South in their unique place on the lowest rung in the global division of labour. Although called free trade, the global exchange of goods and services is unequal. The South sells natural resources, agricultural products, and labour-intensive manufactured goods, often using outdated production methods. In turn, the North exports high-profit, high-technology manufactured goods (such as computers and medical equipment) and essential services (such as banking). Neither do the states of the North practise free trade when it harms their own economic interests. The governments of the North interfere in the marketplace, when it is to their advantage, by subsidizing research and development or protecting important economic sectors from external competition because they are important to security of supply or because they have a competitive edge in the export market (such as agricultural products for the United States).

Direct political control of the South is not necessary because economic imperialism is essentially self-sustaining. In order to earn hard currency to repay debt or acquire essential imports, including military equipment, the South must sell their goods. They cannot withdraw from the international economic system without serious economic or political consequences. But because the exchange with the North is unequal, the South keeps falling further and further behind economically. When hard export earnings are insufficient for current needs, the states in the South must either borrow or depend on international aid. Default is a difficult option because that would cut off the debtor nations from further international borrowing.

There are times when economic conditions are so serious that they must borrow from the International Monetary Fund (IMF) to maintain liquidity. As a condition for the loan, the IMF extracts concessions called structural adjustment programs. These programs are designed to attract private investment and raise export earnings by changing domestic economic policies. This can range from the adjustment of exchange rates, more often than not currency devaluation, to cutting expenditures by cutting social programs in order to balance the budget, and to cutting domestic subsidies for struggling industries. The result is a political control exerted through the influence of international institutions, in this case the IMF. Further control comes with ties among the elites of the North and the South states. Elites in the South are personally enriched by their status in their economic system and resulting political status. Sometimes, they are further enriched by bribery or, for example, more subtly through having themselves or their children educated in the most prestigious schools and universities in the North. Imperialism uses culture (or soft power) to inculcate the idea that capitalism is not only a way to get rich but also the best and most efficient way to structure economies. When capitalism is internalized, the imperialist system is not challenged.

At the 2004 World Social Forum, Indian political economist, Arundhati Roy, condemned the new imperialism, arguing that the contemporary complex system of multilateral trade laws and financial agreements effectively institutionalize global inequality. "Why else," Roy asked, "would it be that the US taxes a garment made by a Bangladeshi manufacturer twenty times more than a garment made in Britain?" "Why else would it be that countries that grow cocoa beans, like the Ivory Coast or Ghana, are taxed out of the market if they try to turn it into chocolate? . . . Why else would it be that after having been plundered by colonizing regimes for more than half a century, former colonies are steeped in debt to those same regimes and repay them some $382 *billion* a year?" Roy concludes that "no individual nation can stand up to the project of corporate globalization on its own" (2004, 13).

There are moments in world affairs when imperialist power is exerted more overtly. This can be accomplished through foreign aid programs, including the training and equipping of militaries and police forces. In some cases, direct intervention is deemed necessary. Anti-imperialists often point to such examples as the American intervention in Iran (1953), Guatemala (1954), the Dominican Republic (1965), Granada (1982), and Panama (1989). These interventions range from the prevention of revolution, especially socialist or communist, to suppressing revolutions, and to overthrowing governments that threaten vital economic interests.

It is capitalism that drives imperialism. Capitalism needs empire for the supply of raw materials, such as oil, which are often available only in the South. Multinational corporations need the opportunity to invest in the South in order to cut costs and increase profits. Minimal governmental intervention in the poor states, lack of environmental regulations, low taxes, and low wages all contribute to the corporate bottom line, hence the export of jobs from the North to the poor South. Finally, capitalism needs expanding markets because their productive capacity is greater than their domestic market can absorb. Without international expansion, the imperialist economy can go into recession.

Radicalism differs from realism and liberalism in a number of important ways. First, the source of international behaviour is the domestic and international capitalist systems. Human behaviour is structured through these larger systems of production and exchange. While the state is an important international actor, it is an agent of economic interests defined by dominant socio-economic classes, transnational elites, and multinational corporations. According to a radical perspective, the international system is not characterized by anarchy (realism) or interdependence (liberalism) but, instead, by a rigid stratification of power and wealth among the states of the North and the South. Most importantly, the radical perspective is normative in the sense that it opposes the global capitalist system, imperial domination, and the resulting exploitation and impoverishment of the vast majority of the world's population.

Back to the War

WE SHOULD NOW RETURN TO THE REASONS WHY THE UNITED STATES WENT to war against Iraq, with the subsequent loss of American lives and the huge bill for American taxpayers. A realist would focus on such explanations as the presence of WMD, alleged Iraqi support for Al Qaeda, American support for Israel, the pursuit of stability in the Middle East, and ensuring a secure supply of energy necessary for long-term American economic security. The essentially unilateral act by the United States reinforces the realist explanation for the war. We may want to argue that the lack of proof regarding WMD or ties to Al Qaeda negates both reasons for the war as well as a realist interpretation of the occupation.

Not so. A study of decision making shows us that the issue is not reality as much as it is the perception of reality. In this instance, it does not make any difference whether the WMD were there, as long as the Bush administration believed them to be there. There is now evidence to suggest that the Bush team may have been misled by the American intelligence community in its assumptions. But even without the WMD, Middle East security is essential to the United States because of the presence of energy that fuels the American economy. Further, from an American perspective, Israel is the only democratic and reliable ally in the Middle East, not to mention the influence of the powerful pro-Israel lobby in the United States. Since the potential for positive change in the Middle East is minimal, or even potentially threatening to American interests, the United States decided to act. Ultimately, of course, the United States has the power to act unilaterally and pursue its national interests, however defined.

Liberal analysts can pursue one of two strategies in evaluating American policy. They can point to the upholding of Security Council resolutions argument and the objective of Middle East stability as significant liberal goals. In addition, there is a long-term benefit to a liberal international system through the elimination of the non-democratic and repressive regime of Saddam Hussein. A second strategy from a liberal perspective is to condemn the American-led War on Iraq as a pursuit of realist objectives at a time when state security concerns should be secondary to other global threats. The fact that the United States acted almost unilaterally and did not give UN inspectors sufficient time to finish their work supports this interpretation. By implication, the American claim of support for UN resolutions and the moral argument regarding the toppling of a murderous regime are so much rhetoric for a basically self-interested pursuit of national interest. American unilateralism also suggests that the United States was acting as a hegemon, especially in view of its unbending attitudes toward the views of its potential allies.

The radical perspective is clear. The War on Iraq was an attempt by the United States to secure a long-term oil supply by establishing a friendly regime. In addition, American companies benefited directly and immediately through the economic rebuilding process in Iraq. Regional economic stability is enhanced by the elimination of an undependable regime, possibly resulting in a new regime that is not a threat to Saudi Arabia and the energy-driven economic system of the region. The dilemma for the radical analyst is that there is no direct (clearly stated by the administration) evidence for their position. The radical argument rests on the capitalist nature of the international economic system and by the influence on American foreign policy by economic elites, such as Vice-President Cheney. The differences between the United States and its allies are nothing more than evidence of different capitalist economic interests that translate into differences over the Iraqi policy.

Summary

It is generally agreed that the administration of President George W. Bush returned to realism after the Clinton administration's attempts to turn American foreign policy in a more liberal direction. The Bush administration is committed to strengthening the American military as is evidenced by its emphasis on a ballistic missile defence system. It also has refused to join the International Criminal Court due to the possibility that its military personnel could be charged while serving American interests abroad. Other realist evidence is the disdain that the administration has shown for international institutions and norms. It has refused to join the Kyoto Protocol, has withdrawn from the Anti-Ballistic Missile Treaty, and continues to be critical of the Landmines Treaty because of its need to maintain land mines in South Korea to protect itself against a land attack by a very large North Korean army.

After September 11, 2001, the War on Terrorism has increased America's belief that military power is the major deterrent against terrorist attacks. In fact, it is possible to argue that there is a significant hegemonic strain in American policy, especially after 9/11. The Project for a New American Century, an organization that included Vice-President Cheney, Secretary of Defense Rumsfeld, and Deputy Secretary of Defense Wolfowitz emphasizes a global challenge and role for the United States as the leader in maintaining peace and security in Europe, Asia, and the Middle East. This new thinking

continued

takes as its point of departure the assertion that the terrorist threat is not just to the United States but also to the rest of the world and that the United States has a moral duty to fight freedom's fight wherever it may be. It is, thus, up to the United States, because of its unique abilities and its commitment to democracy and freedom, to maintain stability and peace in the international system.

While it is possible to explain American policy in radical terms, it is a more difficult task because the evidence is more circumstantial. The other difficulty for the radical perspective is that while it is opposed to American foreign policy, it does not prescribe what the United States should do, except in some very general ways. The argument that the United States must stop intervening in the internal affairs of other states becomes an argument for American isolationism. The United States had isolationist tendencies prior to World War II and was, therefore, criticized for its late entry into that war. The anti-imperialist argument translates into debt forgiveness and protectionism for the South's economic interests at the same time as the world's economies are increasingly tied together. The questions for students of international relations are: which perspective to choose, and on what grounds? Our review of models of international relations suggests that multiple levels of analysis, as well as moral and empirical factors, are embedded in the way we choose to interpret contemporary world politics.

Discussion Questions

1. Research the backgrounds to the "reasons" for the invasion of Iraq in order to more fully understand the actions of the Bush administration, and categorize the "reasons" according to the levels of analysis.
2. Do you think that the United States is a hegemon? Why, or why not?
3. Has terrorism become the new Cold War for the United States?
4. Do you agree that International Organizations (IOs) are "better" able to deal with global problems than states? Why?
5. Which model (realist, liberal, or radical) do you choose to use in critically evaluating state behaviour? Why?

References

Roy, Arundhati. 2004. "The New American Century." *The Nation.* 9 February, 11–14.

Further Readings

Beitz, Charles R. 1999. *Political Theory and International Relations.* Princeton: Princeton University Press.

Cox, Robert W., ed. 1997. *The New Realism: Perspectives on Multilateralism and World Order.* New York: St. Martin's.

Legro, Jeffry W. and Andrew Moravcsik. 2001. "Faux Realism: Spin versus Substance in the Bush Foreign Policy Doctrine." *Foreign Policy*, 125, 80–82.

Mearsheimer, J. 1993. "The False Promise of International Institutions" in M.E. Brown *et al. The Perils of Anarchy: Contemporary Realism and International Society.* Cambridge, Mass.: MIT Press, 332–377.

Spegele, Roger D. 1996. *Political Realism in International Theory.* Cambridge, U.K.: Cambridge University Press.

Wight, Martin. 1991. *International Theory: The Three Traditions.* Leicester, U.K.: Leicester University Press.

Zacher, Mark W. and R.A. Matthew. 1995. "Liberal International Theory: Common Threads, Divergent Strands" in *Controversies in International Relations: Realism and the Neoliberal Challange.* New York: St Martin's. 107–150.

Weblinks

The Project for a New American Century
www.newamericancentury.org

International Theory
www.irtheory.com

The English School
www.leeds.ac.uk/polis/englishschool

BBC: Was the War in Iraq Justified?
http://news.bbc.co.uk/1/hi/world/middle_east/3033959.stm

CHAPTER 23

INTERNATIONAL ORGANIZATIONS

Objectives

In this chapter, we shift our focus to the arena of world politics. International organizations are a central part of politics at the global level. To gain a fuller understanding of international organizations in all of their variety and complexity, this chapter will provide an introduction to international organizations and an overview of their place in the wider arena of world politics. Every country in the world belongs to international organizations. Many individuals also belong to international organizations. These organizations are partially defined by the major organizing principles of world politics, among them, state sovereignty, anarchy, and global governance. This chapter discusses these principles as well as the origins and evolution of international organizations. It describes the critical distinction between intergovernmental and non-governmental organizations. Finally, it identifies some of the central preoccupations influencing the current and future role of these organizations in world politics.

TOM KEATING

Introduction

International organizations are a prominent feature of world politics. As we enter the twenty-first century, there are thousands of organizations active on the world stage. Every country in the world is a member of at least one international organization, and most countries participate in many. Canada has been one of the more active participants in these organizations, having joined dozens of them through the years, ranging from the universal, multi-purpose United Nations to the regionally focused Arctic Council. For many countries, including Canada, these organizations are a very important forum for conducting foreign policy. International organizations are not, however, just for states. Many individuals belong to organizations whose membership and activities cross national borders. These non-state or non-governmental organizations have increased in number and influence, and many of them play a significant role in such areas as international trade and regional and global environmental politics. International organizations have a long history but have proliferated most dramatically in the second half of the twentieth century. They have become a permanent, influential, and often controversial feature in the daily lives of governments and billions of people throughout the planet. It is possible to learn a great deal about international organizations by studying particular organizations, such as the United Nations or the European Union, or non-governmental organizations, such as the International Committee of the Red Cross or Amnesty International. The immense variety of organizations, however, suggests a slightly different approach, one that examines features common to many different organizations.

As an integral part of world politics, international organizations have been influenced by many of the principles and practices of world politics, particularly as they differ from those in domestic politics. It is particularly beneficial to understand the meaning and significance of **state sovereignty**, **anarchy**, and **global governance**. An understanding of these concepts provides a good starting point from which to examine the origins, evolution, current practices, and possible futures of international organizations.

The International Context

INTERNATIONAL ORGANIZATIONS HAVE BEEN TRACED BACK TO 1397. SINCE the time of Dante, in the early fourteenth century, international organizations have been advocated as an alternative or complement to the system of independent sovereign states. Since that time, they have been invented and reinvented repeatedly in attempts to find effective means for facilitating and regulating political, economic, and social interactions that cross national borders. Proposals for institutions that closely resemble the United Nations and the European Union date back to the seventeenth century (Hinsley, 1963). Many of these proposals were concerned primarily with eliminating or reducing international conflict, primarily among

European states. While the authors of these proposals, such as Sir Thomas More, William Penn, and Immanuel Kant, might be impressed with the extensive network of international organizations that exists today, they would likely be disappointed that these organizations have not prevented warfare within and between states. By the latter half of the nineteenth century, international organizations were more likely to be devoted to matters of international commerce than to conflict. This trend has continued in the contemporary period.

As with most political institutions, international organizations do not operate in a vacuum. Instead, they exist in an array of political, economic, social, and cultural activity. This activity has had a significant influence on the origins and evolution of international organizations. Particularly noteworthy are two prominent features of the global political arena—state sovereignty and anarchy. The first distinguishes the participants in world politics, separating national governments (or states, as they are most commonly labelled) from the private individuals, groups, and corporations that also participate in world politics. *State sovereignty* refers to the legal (*de jure* sovereignty) and empirical (*de facto* sovereignty) condition whereby states recognize no higher authority either domestically or externally and are, thus, free to act as they wish. Sovereignty emerged as an influential governing principle of world politics after the Thirty Years War ended with the Peace of Westphalia in 1648. The war and the resulting peace settlement legitimated the autonomous power of states over and against that of the Church and the Emperor as well as potential domestic challengers.

Sovereignty is often presented as an absolute term suggesting both autonomy and capability, but few states have ever possessed absolute sovereignty. Most states are constrained by limited capabilities and restrictions imposed on them through international agreements, including those overseen by international organizations. The widespread acceptance of the principle of state sovereignty, however, has meant that states must give their consent to be bound by international law and other commitments that might arise from being members of international organizations. International organizations, in turn, are restricted in their capacity to interfere in the internal affairs of sovereign states. This is best reflected in Article 2 of the UN Charter that reads in part: "Nothing contained in the present Charter shall authorize the United Nations to intervene in matters which are essentially within the jurisdiction of any state or shall require the Members to submit such matters to settlement under the present Charter."

State sovereignty has reinforced a second feature of world politics—the absence of a single central authority or government to regulate political interaction at the global level and enforce international law. *Anarchy* refers to the absence of government at any level. The significance of anarchy in world politics has meant that sovereign states operate in a world with no permanent authority to make and enforce laws. Authoritative institutions at the global or regional level would restrict the sovereignty and autonomy of states, something that states have traditionally resisted. As a result, states (increasingly working with private individuals, groups, and corporations) make their own rules, and determine how and by whom they are to be administered and enforced. The process by which rules are made and enforced in world politics has been called global governance and defined as "governing, without sovereign authority, relationships that transcend national frontiers" (Finkelstein, 1995, 369) The process is both complex and fascinating because of the absence of authoritative procedures and institutions. When private citizens and groups are involved, the process becomes even more complicated. As an aspect of this process, the establishment of international organizations and their ongoing participation in global politics involves a delicate balance between the preservation of state sovereignty and the development of authority structures at the international level.

Classifying Intergovernmental Organizations

AN INTERNATIONAL ORGANIZATION MAY BE DEFINED AS A FORMAL INSTITUTION that facilitates regular interaction between members of two or more countries across national boundaries. Such a definition would yield thousands of entities. There are, however, several criteria by which one can sort out the vast array of international organizations that populate this planet. One important initial distinction is to identify two separate categories of international organizations. The first, **intergovernmental organizations**, or IGOs, are composed of sovereign states. There are between three and four hundred IGOs actively involved in world politics. The United Nations (UN), is the pre-eminent example of an IGO. The European Union (EU), the International Monetray Fund (IMF), the North Atlantic Treaty Organization (NATO), and the World Trade Organization (WTO) are other well-known examples. A second category of international organization is **non-governmental organizations**, or NGOs, whose members are private citizens or national affiliates of groups composed of private citizens. In the mid-1990s, there were over 10 000 NGOs. Most NGOs are of little interest for students of world politics, while others emerge as important political actors for selected issues. Some, however, such as the Red Cross (formally known as the International Committee of the Red Cross), Greenpeace, and Amnesty International, have an active and ongoing involvement in world politics.

Intergovernmental Organizations

Intergovernmental organizations (IGOs) are a permanent feature of world politics in the twenty-first century. As suggested, one of primary motivating factors in establishing these organizations has been a desire to limit or prevent wars between states. French novelist Victor Hugo captured a common sentiment: "A day will come when bullets and bombshells will be replaced by votes, by the universal suffrage of nations, by the venerable arbitration of a great sovereign senate, which will be to

Europe what the Parliament is to England" (cited in Goodspeed, 1959, 3). For many people, some form of world government through international organizations offered the best solution to continued bloodshed. Consequently, scholars and practitioners devised elaborate plans for international organizations as the core of a world government (Hinsley, 1963). It is also evident that the most significant efforts to establish IGOs have taken place during or immediately after major wars. For example, the two major institutional experiments of the twentieth century were set up after the World Wars. The League of Nations was established as part of the Treaty of Versailles ending World War I in 1919 and the United Nations in 1945, at the end of World War II. In the latter case, the commitment of states to establishing an international organization was so strong that discussions on the UN began as early as 1942, long before the outcome of the war was known.

While peace may have been the primary motive in most proposals for international organizations—the preamble to the UN Charter, for example, reads: "We the peoples of the United Nations are determined to save succeeding generations from the scourge of war, which twice in our lifetime has brought untold sorrow to mankind,"—the vast majority of organizations have been created to serve economic and social needs. In an analysis of international organizations, Murphy identified their two principal tasks as fostering industry and managing social conflicts (Murphy, 1994, 32–37). He also argued that in addition to warfare, an equally important influence on the creation of international organizations has been the different phases of expansion and reform of the international political economy, commencing with the second industrial revolution in the late eighteenth-century. "They have helped create international markets in industrial goods by linking communications and transportation infrastructure, protecting intellectual property, and reducing legal and economic barriers to trade" (Murphy, 1994, 2).

The range of activities undertaken by international organizations is exemplified by the UN and its network of specialized agencies. While the primary objective is to maintain peace and security, as a multi-purpose organization, the UN has also been involved in many areas, such as economic development (UN Development Program), health (World Health Organization), communications (International Telecommunication Union), human rights (Office of the UN High Commissioner for Human Rights), and social concerns, such as refugees (Office of the UN High Commissioner for Refugees), women (UN Development Fund for Women), and children (UN Children's Fund). Other intergovernmental organizations have been established to serve more limited and specialized mandates. The World Trade Organization (WTO), established in 1995, focuses on matters related to international trade; NATO is primarily concerned with security issues; and some institutions, such as the Arctic Council, are concerned with regional issues.

Intergovernmental organizations can also be distinguished on the basis of their membership. A few organizations that are open to all states, such as the UN, are described as universal. More commonly, organizations restrict membership to states with similar historical roots, regional connections, or strategic concerns—for example, the Organization of American States (OAS), the Commonwealth, and NATO. Regional organizations have, in certain instances, emerged as important alternatives to the more universal institutions, particularly in matters of trade and finance. The European Union (EU) and the North American Free Trade Agreement (NAFTA) stand as the important regional organizations in the international political economy.

The World Trade Organization (WTO), established in 1995, has emerged as the most prominent IGO in the global political economy. Led by the developed economies of the North, the WTO focuses primarily on international trade, promoting policies of trade liberalization. It developed out of the General Agreement on Tariffs and Trade (GATT) first signed in 1947. The GATT's original objective was to reduce and eventually eliminate tariff barriers to international trade. Reincarnated as the WTO, it has since become involved in a wider range of trade-related issues. The restricted activities of the WTO have been challenged by some critics who argue that it is not possible to separate trade from other issues, such as the environment and labour practices. To date, attempts to have the organization deal with these adverse effects of trade have been strongly resisted by many members of the organization. The trade liberalization agenda of the WTO has also been challenged from within the organization by coalitions of developing nations led by Brazil and India from outside and by various civil society organizations that have been disadvantaged by WTO-sanctioned practices, most recently and effectively at the institution's 2003 meeting in Cancun.

Intergovernmental organizations vary extensively in their structures, procedures, capabilities, and budgets, but there are some common elements worth mentioning. Most organizations have a permanent secretariat that oversees the day-to-day operations of the organization and are led by a secretary general, president, or director, who is selected by the member governments of the organization. They do not have any independent sources of revenue and, thus, remain dependent on member-government contributions. The representation of states in the IGOs is generally based on the principle of political equality. At the same time, the decision-making structures and procedures actually employed in these organizations commonly accept a certain inequality in status and power, allowing more powerful states a greater opportunity to control the decisions of the organization.

The decision-making process in most IGOs is based on some combination of negotiation, consensus building, and formal votes. The sources of influence within this decentralized and diffused policy-making environment are extremely varied. Obviously, one's power in the world has some effect on one's ability to wield influence. Beyond this—and the more formal power structures found in such places as the UN's Security Council—states can employ a variety of techniques, such as diplomatic skills or technical expertise, to shape the outcome of the decision-making process within international organizations (Young, 1994). Unlike a national legislature, there are no organized political parties, but there are often coalitions of states that share common views and that co-operate to achieve specific objectives. These coalitions have become an active part of the process of global governance in international organizations and are very prominent in such institutions as the WTO and the UN.

Non-governmental Organizations

Non-governmental organizations have been defined in various ways. One of the more encompassing definitions can be found in two UN resolutions that refer to "any international organization which is not established by intergovernmental agreement . . . including organizations which accept members designated by government authorities, provided that such membership does not interfere with the free expression of views of the organizations" (UN General Assembly Resolutions 288 [X] and 1296 [XLIV]).

This definition encompasses an incredible amount of diversity. As Scholte writes, the membership of such groups include "academic institutes, business associations, community-based organizations, consumer protection bodies, criminal syndicates, development cooperation groups, environmental campaigns, ethnic lobbies, foundations, farmers' groups, human rights advocates, labor unions, relief organizations, peace activists, professional bodies, religious institutions, women's networks, youth campaigns and more." Scholte also divides their membership into three categories: conformists (those who seek and uphold existing norms), reformists (those who aim to correct the regime's flaws), and radicals (those whose purpose it is to transform the social order). Business or professional associations, think-tanks, and foundations belong to the conformist category. Social-democratic groups and associations of academics, consumers, and human rights, relief, or trade unions compose the reformist category. Finally, the radical category consists of anarchists, environmentalists, fascists, feminists, and religious revivalists—those with "respective implacable oppositions to the state, industrialism, liberal values, patriarchy, militarism and secularism" (Scholte, 1999, 2).

The term *non-governmental organizations* is also generally restricted to nonprofit organizations and, thus, excludes multinational corporations and other nefarious commercial activities, such as drug cartels, that operate across national boundaries. Many groups have taken to calling themselves **civil society organizations** (CSOs) to distinguish themselves more explicitly from the government and to reinforce their connections with civil society. First, it should be noted that most of these NGOs have absolutely nothing to do with world politics as it is most commonly understood. As an individual, you might take some interest in the World Ninepins Bowling Association or the World Rock 'n' Roll Confederation, but these groups are likely to contribute little to ending the conflict in the Middle East or alleviating poverty in Haiti. On the other hand, the World Jewish Congress or Oxfam might have a significant role in these issues. NGOs have been around for a very long time and have been actively involved in the politics of global governance for centuries. In contrast to IGOs, where there is a considerable amount of similarity in organizational structure and decision-making processes, there is an amazing degree of variety among the more than 10 000 NGOs in terms of such things as organizational structure, decision-making procedures, and budgets.

In contrast to IGOs, most NGOs have developed out of concerns for specific issues on the part of individuals and groups. Amnesty International, for example, emerged as a result of the work of British lawyer Peter Beneson, who, in the early 1960s, began to advocate for the humane treatment of prisoners in foreign countries. It has since developed into the world's most active and effective defender of individual rights. In 1977, Amnesty International was awarded the Nobel Peace Prize. The International Committee of the Red Cross, which originated in the mid-nineteenth century, also as a result of an individual's (Jean Henri Dunant) concern for the welfare of injured combatants, was awarded the first Nobel Prize for peace in recognition of its work in providing humane treatment for victims of conflict. The Red Cross remains one of the world's most active humanitarian assistance organizations. In 1997, another NGO, the International Campaign to Ban Land Mines (ICBL), was awarded the Nobel Peace Prize in recognition of its work to pressure governments to sign the Ottawa Treaty, which bans the deployment of anti-personnel land mines. The ICBL developed as a result of a number of individual efforts, in many countries, to press governments to eliminate their reliance on anti-personnel land mines. It subsequently developed a close working relationship with the Canadian government to push for the adoption of an international treaty. The landmines treaty–making process (often referred to as the Ottawa Process) illustrates the dynamics of NGO involvement in global governance. It is, for example, interesting to note that the ICBL was led by an American, Jody Williams, but found that it was able to work more effectively with Canadian government officials in Ottawa than it was with its own government in Washington. The American government did not even consent to sign the Ottawa Treaty that had been so strongly promoted by this American-based NGO. It is also worth noting the extensive and direct involvement of NGOs alongside state representatives in the diplomatic process leading to the Ottawa Treaty (Cameron, Lawson, and Tomlin, 1998).

Not all NGOs win peace prizes. Nor are they as effective as these three have been in influencing the course of world politics. Most NGOs are rather modest operations; however, they are becoming an increasingly important participant in the politics of global governance (Matthews, 1997).

In recognition of this increased involvement, certain NGOs have pressed for and been granted more direct participation in institutions. The UN and the World Bank, among others, have begun to develop more extensive contacts with NGOs. NGOs have also become particularly active around various UN conferences that were held during the 1990s on such issues as population, women, human rights, and social development. NGOs have used these venues as an opportunity to voice their concerns about policies at both the national and international levels and have achieved some success in shaping the agenda of these conferences. Even the UN Security Council has consulted with representatives of selected NGOs in such areas as human rights and peacekeeping. All of this activity reflects an increasingly significant role for NGOs in the process of global governance. Many states, as well as certain IGOs, however, have been reluctant and slow to respond to NGO demands, and as a result, these groups have been less successful in influencing policy. Their efforts, however, point to a potentially significant development in the area of global governance. More extensive, direct, and effective involvement on the part of NGOs would see traditional nationally based political activity. Interstate negotiations would be replaced by policy making at the international level, involving representatives of national governments acting alongside representatives of non-governmental organizations representing the interests of the "public."

Competing Perspectives

THERE ARE A VARIETY OF THEORETICAL DEBATES SURROUNDING THE CURRENT status and future direction of international organizations and global governance. These reflect the major theoretical debates in the literature on international relations (Cox, 1992). We will briefly review three of the most prominent arguments about the sources and potential role of IGOs in world politics. The first, or realist view, holds that international organizations play at best marginal roles in world politics and are little more than a reflection of the interests of the governments that created them (Mearsheimer, 1994–95). Viewed from this perspective, international organizations have no independent influence of their own. States use IGOs to protect or enhance their relative power position in the system. Among realists, hegemonic stability theorists argue that a dominant power (hegemon) uses IGOs to organize support and compliance from other states. In their view, a hegemon is essential for the creation and maintenance of IGOs (Keohane, 1984).

An alternative view, usually labelled liberal institutionalist, holds that international organizations are both important and influential on the world stage (Young, 1994). This view holds that states co-operate out of a sense of common purpose that emphasizes absolute gains and mutual interests, rather than narrowly defined self-interest. As a result, states are not only concerned with maximizing their own gains relative to other states in the system but are also more generally concerned with the effects of co-operation on the system as a whole. While accepting the importance and influence of states, liberal institutionalists also argue that organizations, once created, acquire a degree of independence from their member governments and are effective in shaping the behaviour of these governments. Further, they argue that states tend to comply with many of the rulings of international organizations and abide by the principles embedded in them. International organizations are, in this view, considerably more than a mere reflection of states' interests and power. Some liberal institutionalists go further in arguing that there has been a transfer of authority from the states to international organizations such that these organizations have taken on responsibility for areas previously under the jurisdiction of national states.

A final collection of views takes a more critical perspective on international organizations. Proponents of these critical approaches argue that international organizations hold the potential for bringing about a radical transformation in the practice of world politics (Cox, 1992). For example, while they may accept the view that IGOs reflect the interests of their more powerful member states, they argue that these same institutions provide an opportunity for less powerful states to pursue their own interests and perhaps design policies in opposition to those being pursued by more powerful states. This view has also emphasized the potential influence of NGOs to alter the course of world politics and argues that international organizations are a critical area for global political and economic reform. More than the other two approaches, these approaches emphasize the historical and political context in which international organizations operate and argue that changes in such areas as technology and in the increased globalization of economic activity create a different environment in which these organizations must exist and respond (Murphy, 1994). Some of these analysts take an explicitly normative view of international organizations and identify them as a source of global governance which is more democratic, just, and humane than the existing international system (Falk, 1995).

Current Issues and Debates

GIVEN THEIR PROMINENCE, IT IS NOT SURPRISING THAT INTERNATIONAL organizations have been the source of considerable debate and controversy. Differences over the American-led invasion of Iraq in 2003 led to charges and countercharges about the role and effectiveness of the UN in monitoring compliance with its own resolutions as well its ability to control the behvaiour of its most powerful member governments. The World Trade Organization has also been subjected to much criticism for not adequately addressing such trade-related problems as environmental deterioration and economic and social inequalities. One of the ongoing dilemmas that confront international organizations is the balance between the sovereignty of member states and the power of the organization to take and enforce binding decisions that infringe on this sovereignty. This raises important and challenging questions about the acceptable degree of institutional interference in the domestic affairs of states. For example, many advocates would like to see international organizations interfere to protect the human rights of oppressed peoples in such countries as Myanmar, Rwanda, or China. At the same time, others worry about the possibility that international organizations might interfere to protect the interests of foreign investors or interfere with domestic environmental and labour standards. Additionally, there are profound differences among member states over the nature and scope of intervention by international organizations. Many governments in the developed capitalist countries support international organizations that act in support of free market principles, while governments of weaker countries are concerned that more powerful states will use international organizations to control their policy options.

The balance between effective international institutional intervention and respect for state sovereignty will be one of the major considerations shaping the future role of international organizations. Part of the difficulty arises from the fact that most IGOs are explicitly designed to protect and reinforce the sovereignty of their member governments, however, many proponents of global governace demand that the organizations take on a more interventionist role to defend human rights, protect the environment, or promote economic reform. Most IGOs recognize the independence, sovereignty, territorial integrity, and formal equality of member governments. This, in turn, makes it difficult for these organizations to take action against a member government unless that member government consents to such action. At the present time, however, there has been widespread acceptance of the position that the domestic practices of sovereign states are a matter of international concern. "The old notion that what goes on within the state is a matter of sovereign privacy . . . has been swept away. In its stead, we have installed the doctrine that world order entails political stability, democratic governments, respect for human rights, general economic well being, ethnic harmony, and peaceful resolution of conflicts within states, no less than co-operative and peaceful relationships among them" (Claude, 2000).

These developments have raised a number of new responsibilities for international organizations, yet often without any concomitant attempt to expand their capacity or authority to address such issues. A number of areas of international and domestic politics are now regulated by international organizations. This is especially evident in Europe, where the EU has assumed responsibility for vast areas of domestic politics. The result has been to transfer responsibilities and power for some policy areas to international organizations. For example, international trade and financial institutions increasingly intervene into domestic social affairs by imposing monetary and fiscal constraints on national governments. The net effect has been to increase the salience of international organizations and international agreements in national policy debates. This is particularly true of poorer countries but is, to varying degrees, significant for all countries that are extensively involved in international trade and other activities. The increased involvement of international organizations in areas previously within the domestic jurisdiction of national governments suggests that there has occurred a diminution of state sovereignty. These are but a sample of the many issues surrounding international organizations. Global governance has always been an important issue, but the increased number and variety of organizations on the world stage have made it one of the more important and complex issues for the twenty-first century.

Summary

International organizations have become a permanent and prominent feature of world politics. There has been a tremendous growth in the number and variety of international organizations, especially in the last half of the twentieth century. Intergovernmental organizations have originated out of a shared concern for the elimination of war and for managing trans-border problems. Many advocates of a more peaceful international system have argued for the need for international organizations to provide for global peace, order, and justice. Others argue that international organizations merely reinforce the position of the powerful states and interests in the international system. While interpretations on the role and influence of international organizations vary, it is evident that as a result of the salience of cross-border issues—such as environmental pollution, the AIDS epidemic, refugees, and economic globalization—international organizations will continue to be a central part of world politics in the years ahead.

Discussion Questions

1. Should sovereign states transfer some of their authority to international organizations?
2. Are non-governmental organizations influential participants in global politics?
3. How do international organizations contribute to international peace and justice?

References

Cameron, Maxwell A., Robert Lawson, and Brian Tomlin, eds. 1998. *To Walk without Fear.* Don Mills, Ontario: Oxford University Press.

Cox, Robert. 1992. "Multilateralism and World Order." *Review of International Studies.* 18, 61–80.

Falk, Richard. 1996. *Humane Governance.* University Park, Pennsylvania: Pennsylvania State University Press.

Finkelstein, Lawrence. 1995. "What Is Global Governance?" *Global Governance,* 1, 376–372.

Goodspeed, Stephen S. 1959. *The Nature and Function of International Organization.* New York: Oxford University Press.

Hinsley, F.H. 1963. *Power and the Pursuit of Peace.* Cambridge: Cambridge University Press.

Keohane, Robert. 1984. *After Hegemony.* Princeton: Princeton University Press.

Matthews, Jessica. 1997. "Power Shift" *Foreign Affairs.* January/February.

Mearsheimer, John. 1994–95. "The False Promise of International Institutions." *International Security.* 20, 82–104.

Murphy, Craig. 1994. *International Organization and Industrial Change.* Cambridge: Polity Press.

Scholte, Jan Arête. 1999. "Global Civil Society: Changing the World?" www.warwick.ac.uk/fac/soc/CSGR/wpapers/wp3199.PDF.

Young, Oran. 1994. *International Governance.* Ithaca, NY: Cornell University Press.

Further Readings

Claude, Inis L. 1971. *Swords into Plowshares: The Problems and Progress of International Organization.* 4th edition. New York: Random House.

Keck, Margaret, and Kathryn Sikkink. 1997. *Activists Beyond Borders: Advocacy Networks in International Politics.* Ithaca, NY: Cornell University Press.

Weiss, Thomas, David P. Forsythe, and Roger Coate, 1997. *The United Nations and Changing World Politics.* 2nd edition. Boulder, CO: Westview.

Weblinks

Most international organizations have their own websites, including, for example, the United Nations, at
www.un.org

Most non-governmental organizations also have their own sites, including, for example, Amnesty International, at
www.amnesty.org

For other non-governmental organizations, check
www.oneworld.org

There are also some comprehensive listings of international organizations and issues involving these organizations on the Internet, including
www.globalpolicy.org

CHAPTER 24

INTERNATIONAL FINANCIAL INSTITUTIONS

SUSANNE SOEDERBERG

Objectives

International financial institutions (IFIs), such as the World Bank and the International Monetary Fund (IMF or the Fund), continue to play an important role in managing monetary and development issues in the world. Yet, these institutions have undergone important changes since their inception in 1944. The key task of this chapter is to examine these changes in the role of the IFIs. Do these organizations function to effectively regulate the international economy in the interests of all states and societies? Or do they merely facilitate the continuance of the current *status quo* that works for the benefit of particular states? Because IFIs are intimately involved in the functioning of the current global economy, it is essential to explore their historical emergence in the post-war period in order to understand their current role. This chapter traces the regulation of international monetary and trade relations to World War II, when world leaders established a rule structure called the Bretton Woods system (BWS). Next, the chapter describes the key roles of the

IFIs within this larger regulatory structure. It then looks at three main factors leading to the collapse of the BWS. We then survey the volatile landscape of the post-BWS. Following this discussion, we turn our attention to the roles of IFIs in the current era of globalization. Finally, we consider the critical issue of who benefits from the post-BWS.

Introduction

Archaeologists tell us that humans have been engaged in trading activities for most of recorded history. The earliest market economies depended on **barter**, or the trading of goods directly for other goods. However, with the rise of capitalism in the seventeenth century, markets became the principal mechanism of organizing society. This led to the extension of monetary transactions. Money also facilitated trade between countries. Economists argue that money allowed nation states to adhere to the **principle of comparative advantage**. According to David Ricardo, this principle holds that the best way for countries to achieve prosperity is to trade those things they can produce most competitively and to buy those things that other countries produce most efficiently in terms of cost. The principle of comparative advantage, however, does not fully capture the nature of economic relations between countries. Because some states are more economically and militarily powerful than others, they enter into exploitative relationships with weaker states. This kind of unequal and exploitative relationship between states is termed imperialism. A historical example of imperialism is the exploitation of natural resources and labour power in the "new world," by the former imperial European powers of Spain, France, and Britain. Trade between states has also become complicated by periods of protectionism, when some states create national barriers to block the import of goods from competitor states. Tariffs, which are duties or taxes levied on certain imports, are the most common way that states protect the interest of their national industries. The consensus among economists, however, is that in the long term, protectionism inhibits the growth of competitive enterprise.

How have nation states sought to mitigate the occurrence of protectionism and to regulate the international economy? An early attempt was undertaken by Great Britain in the nineteenth century. Under the unchallenged rule of Great Britain, the world economy was temporarily stabilized from 1870 to 1914 through the application of the Gold Standard. Nevertheless, the institutionalization of trade and monetary regulation is relatively recent, occurring only at the end of World War II with the establishment of the BWS.

The Bretton Woods System (1944–71)

In July 1944, representatives of 45 countries met at Bretton Woods, New Hampshire, to design a multilateral post-war system, through which the trade and monetary relations of the non-communist world could be regulated in a stable manner. An overriding concern for the policy makers who were present at Bretton Woods was to avoid another Great Depression as experienced in the 1930s. The policy makers believed that the length and severity of the Depression was exacerbated by rampant protectionism in the 1930s and by a lack of commitment by individual states to the creation of a stable international monetary and trade regime to guide national policy.

To this end, the key policy makers present at the Bretton Woods conference attempted to construct an international agreement that would promote international political and economic co-operation. Specifically, the Bretton Woods system was a set of rules that would govern the economic relations between member countries through a fixed exchange rate system (also known as the "fixed-but-adjustable rate system"). Under this system, the United States defined the value of its dollar in terms of gold: one-ounce of gold was to be equal to (or at par with) US$35. The BWS established that world trade would be conducted in American dollars. The United States, however, was required to maintain gold reserves to back up its dollar. Traders, thus, could, at any time, exchange their American dollars for gold at the set price of US$35 per ounce. Other countries fixed the value of their currency in relation to the American dollar. The Canadian dollar, for example, was fixed at a rate of US$0.925 between 1962 and 1970 (1993). Under the fixed exchange rate system, member countries agreed to keep the value of their money within 1 percent of this par value. If they thought that change in the value of their currency would help their economy, they discussed this issue with other members in the forum of the IMF and obtained their consent before doing so. The underlying motivation behind this mechanism was to keep currencies stable and predictable. Thus, in contrast to today's economy, there was little motivation for currency speculation—buying and selling currencies for profit. This par value system lasted from 1944 to 1971.

Later in this chapter, we will explore some of the reasons why the economic stability created by the BWS began to erode in the 1970s. First, however, we will take a closer look at the so-called "sister institutions" of the BWS, namely, the World Bank and the IMF.

The IFIs of Bretton Woods

The World Bank

The initial role of the World Bank, or what is also referred to as the International Bank for Reconstruction and Development (IBRD), was that of a financial intermediary providing finance for post-war reconstruction in such sectors as agriculture, transportation, and energy. The World Bank provides creditworthy countries access to international capital markets on more favourable terms than they could obtain otherwise because it acts as a guarantor. For some developing countries now, and in the past, borrowing from the Bank has been the only way to obtain long-term finance, which usually runs anywhere from 15 to 20 years. When the many colonies of European imperialism gained independence in Africa and elsewhere in the 1960s, the World Bank arranged loans for large-scale development projects, such as dams, bridges, and power plants. In most instances, the contracts to build these large infrastructural projects in the developing countries were obtained by enterprises from the industrialized world.

By the late 1950s, it became clear that a growing number of developing countries were having problems meeting the requirements to borrow on the World Bank's terms. To address this problem, in 1957, the World Bank created the International Finance Corporation (IFC) to assist these states in obtaining finance from private lenders—that is, commercial banks. In 1960, the International Development Association (IDA) was established to finance projects in poorer countries on more favourable terms than the World Bank's (e.g., loans are arranged for a 40-year timeframe). These institutions are referred to as the World Bank Group. The main objective of all these institutions is the same: to promote economic and social progress in the developing countries by increasing economic productivity. This goal is achieved by providing credit and loans as well as economic and technical advice to both private and public sectors in the South (Bakker, 1996). By the 1970s, developing countries increasingly turned to the private banks for development capital, while the World Bank began to focus on the elimination of poverty. Aid given by the World Bank to fight against poverty was tightly linked to the recipient country's economic and social reforms.

Up to the time of the debt crisis, which occurred in the early 1980s, World Bank lending was increasing in importance as a source of development finance. The perceived success of the Bank in its early years led to regional satellites that included the Asian Development Bank, the Inter-American Development Bank, and the African Development Bank.

The International Monetary Fund

Unlike the World Bank, which is considered a development institution, the IMF is a monetary institution. The fundamental role of the IMF was to oversee exchange rate relationships in a fixed, but adjustable, exchange rate system. As mentioned earlier, the fixed exchange rate system was established to encourage worldwide economic growth and stability by enabling member countries to pursue domestic growth polices that would be reflected in positive balance-of-payments statements. Drawing on the experience of the 1930s, the IMF sought to alleviate trade deficits because of the fear that they might eventually threaten the entire world economic system. To avoid the possibility of disrupting economic stability, the IMF lent money to countries facing a balance-of-payments problem. Where did this money come from?

The IMF does not make loans in the conventional sense. Rather, it swaps one type of monetary asset for another. For example, "a member with a weak balance-of-payments position and in need of hard currencies (stable currencies that are in demand, such as the American dollar) will exchange some of its own currency for the currencies of members with strong balance of payments" (IMF, 1999c). To illustrate, after the 1994 peso crisis, Mexico could hypothetically purchase one million American dollars with an equivalent amount of Mexican pesos (one million pesos), even though a peso was only a fraction of the value of an American dollar. Within a certain period of time, however, Mexico would have to buy back its pesos with American dollars. This purchase–repurchase strategy explains why the Fund's resources do not change—"only the composition of its currency holdings" (IMF, 1999c).

The organizational structure of the IFIs is similar to that of corporations. A member government owns a number of shares that is determined by how much money it has paid into the IMF. Clearly, some shareholders are far more powerful than others. The United States and other affluent countries have had a much higher proportion of shares and, thus, higher representation in the IMF and the World Bank. For example, the Group of Seven (G-7) industrialized countries plus the rest of the European Union, representing a mere 14 percent of the world's population, account for 56 percent of the quotas and, thus, voting rights in the IMF executive board. The size of a country's shares or quotas clearly establishes an internal pecking order among Fund members since these quotas determine the voting power in the Fund. It should be noted that the original rationale behind the shareholder regulatory structure of the IMF was to avoid the gridlock that is common to many international organizations, such as the United Nations. Nevertheless, to get particularly significant changes or decisions through the IMF, such as a change in the Fund's articles, an 85-percent majority is required. Thus, any member or group of members capable of collecting 15 percent of IMF shares possesses the ability to block decisions. In order for the required majority to be obtained, the United States must agree to the changes being proposed because it holds 18 percent of the Fund's quotas (Krueger, 1997). This highly unequal shareholder-based power structure means that the IMF has a serious democratic deficit.

The General Agreements to Tariffs and Trade

While the IMF was created to prevent financial instability and the World Bank was devised to finance economic recovery, the General Agreement on Tariffs and Trade (GATT) was created to prevent discriminatory trade practices, such as those that flourished in the 1930s. The basic goal of the GATT was not to regulate trade, as its successor the World Trade Organization (WTO) currently is empowered to do. Rather, the GATT was intended to facilitate freer trade on a multilateral basis. Freer trade has been facilitated through a series of international negotiations (known as "rounds") over the past 50 years, each lasting several years. The number of states involved in these rounds has grown over this period as well. In 1947, for example, 23 states participated, whereas the last 7-year (Uruguay) round, which concluded in 1993, included 107 states.

The GATT attempted to centralize trade negotiations and also to make certain that trade liberalization would be, in turn, applied to all states. The core principle of the

GATT is non-discrimination, aimed at preventing the emergence of privileged trading blocs that act in a protectionist or discriminatory manner against third states. To deter this type of discriminatory practice, the GATT relied on the most-favoured-nation clause (MFN). The MFN is invoked when a concession established with one state would automatically be applied to other states. In effect, the MFN turned out to be a powerful policy tool in seeking greater trade liberalization in the world economy. For example, if Canada agreed to lower tariffs on American beer, it would be required to apply that same tariff to all other countries selling beer to Canada.

The Collapse of the Bretton Woods System

THREE INTERRELATED WORLD EVENTS LED TO THE BREAKDOWN OF THE Bretton Woods System in the early 1970s: (1) the rise in the Euromarkets, (2) two significant hikes in the price of oil by the Organization of Petroleum Exporting Countries (OPEC), and (3) the end of the fixed exchange rate arrangements. It is important to examine these events because they shed light on the demise of the Bretton Woods system. They also represent the roots of the 1980s debt crisis discussed below. First, the Euromarkets, or Eurodollar markets, began to emerge as a major force within the world economy. Simply stated, Euromarkets are an organized market for foreign currency deposits. A Eurodollar deposit, for example, is nothing more than American dollars deposited in a bank outside the United States. Banks were attracted to these foreign currency deposits due to the perceived profit opportunities arising from the comparative regulatory freedom accorded such activity. American banks, in particular, found the offshore market irresistible in that it allowed them to bypass domestic reserve requirements and interest-rate limitations as well as the widening array of capital controls imposed by Washington in the 1960s to cope with the American balance-of-payments problem (Cohen, 1986, 24).

Second, the growth and power of the Euromarkets was closely tied to further acceleration in the internationalization of banking activity, especially with the skyrocketing oil prices in 1973–74 and again in 1978–79. Two immediate consequences of the oil shocks were the rise in imbalances in the pattern of global payments and the phenomenon referred to as "petrodollars." Because most countries were experiencing a downturn in their economies during this period, many, particularly in the developing world, found it difficult to make payments on the rising cost of petroleum. Simultaneously, the cartel known as OPEC purchased American dollars with their huge profits and reinvested these dollars in the unregulated Euromarkets, where their investments would receive the highest return. Banks operating in the Euromarkets, and especially American banks, provided huge loans to cash-strapped governments in the developing world.

The third, and decisive, factor that led to the demise of the BWS was the recessionary climate of most countries, particularly the United States. The effects of economic "stagflation" (high unemployment mixed with high inflation rates) translated into growing balance-of-payments problems for the country. In response to mounting domestic pressures, the Nixon administration in the United States turned inwards, taking a protectionist stance. In 1971, the American government suspended the dollar's gold convertibility. This move was motivated by the fact that there were simply not enough American gold reserves to adequately meet international demand for gold. In 1973, the American government abandoned the fixed exchange rate system and effectively did away with the BWS. From this point onward, national currencies would be determined by the forces of supply and demand in the global marketplace. This is what is meant by floating exchange rates. Governments became responsible for maintaining the value of their currencies at market value.

Problems in the Post-Bretton Woods Era

AFTER 1973, GOVERNMENTS BECAME INCREASINGLY RELIANT ON GLOBAL financial markets to sustain their countries' balance of payments. During the 1970s, a good chunk of these capital flows went to the developing countries in desperate need of funding. Financial markets were interested in investing in these developing countries because the latter posted higher interest rates (which translates into a higher return on investment) than most advanced industrialized countries at the time. Banks loaned haphazardly to the developing countries, such as Brazil and Mexico. This precarious financial situation was not to last long, however. In August 1982, Mexico announced that it could no longer meet the interest payments on its loan, never mind the principal amount. After Mexico's proclamation, a plethora of developing countries around the world followed suit and threatened to default on their loans. This event was known as the debt crisis, and, as we will learn below, it had important ramifications for the role of the IMF.

Since the 1980s' debt crisis, the international community has not created an international mechanism to deal effectively with debt crisis, as witnessed by the bankruptcy of the Argentine government in 2001. It was the largest sovereign default in history. The lack of policy mechanisms is puzzling, considering that the fastest and largest component in the growth of global financial assets is debt, such as government debt (Greider, 1997). The immediate implication for the interstate system is that nation states compete with each other for capital flows. In fact, signalling creditworthiness and demonstrating the investment potential and benefits of a country have become overriding preoccupations of governments in order to lure and retain capital investments. This competition for capital from international lenders, in turn, has led to the reordering of policy agendas. For example, government support for education, pensions, and social welfare has been reduced (and sometimes eliminated), all in the name of remaining competitive and creditworthy in the global economy.

Unlike the Bretton Woods system, which was predicated on state intervention, the post-Bretton Woods era is marked by increased power of markets over states, or what is generally referred to as **neo-liberalism**. This term refers to the diehard and naive belief that the constant liberalization of financial markets and trade will lead to some sort of magical self-healing and self-adjustment of the economy in which all societies will benefit. This new policy orientation was reflected in the development model pursued by the IMF and World Bank in the 1980s—what has become known as the **Washington Consensus**. This model suggests that market liberalization of trade, privatization of government-owned industries, and deregulation of financial markets will lead to greater prosperity and sustainable economic development.

IFIs in a Globalizing Era

The World Bank

With the increasing intensity of the world economic crisis in the late 1970s, the World Bank gradually began to become more cognizant of the importance of a sound economic policy, such as balanced budgets, low interest rates, and decreased levels of government spending; they also realized that the transference of responsibilities from the public sector to the private sector were integral to development. From the perspective of the World Bank, loans to improve a country's infrastructure were ineffective without a healthy economy to sustain developmental progress. Of course, another important motivation behind the Bank's desire that the countries implement sound economic management was to ensure that they could also pay back their loans to the international financial institutions. Hence, in the 1980s, the World Bank shifted its focus from development or aid to structural adjustment loans (SALs), a type of conditional loan, which we will discuss below. This modification in the World Bank's policy orientation represented a significant departure from its earlier focus on infrastructure development. Taking a lead in the establishment of the new neo-liberal model of economic development, the World Bank now swiftly disbursed money to support policy reforms, such as market liberalization, privatization, economic stabilization, and deregulation. These latter reforms are know as Structural Adjustment Policies (SAPs), that are assumed to lead to prosperity and sustainable economic development. Thus, the SAPs, which are issued by the World Bank, may be seen as an attempt to lock in nations to the principles of the Washington Consensus.

Policy prescriptions based on the Washington Consensus have assisted in transferring wealth to the Northern hemisphere by ensuring that loans issued by large banks (mostly American-based) were repaid. But, they have done little to alleviate poverty levels in the Southern hemisphere. Indeed, the 2003 United Nations Development Program's *Human Development Report* indicates that poverty remains a serious problem for the majority of the Third World, particularly South Asia and Sub-Saharan Africa (UNDP, 2003). All in all, SALs and neo-liberal policies have gone hand-in-hand to erode the already low levels of social spending, and to encourage the privatization of health and education as well as the forced export of food products. Clearly, such policies have led to increases in malnutrition and illiteracy, and to deteriorating levels of basic health standards for the general population. In the early 1990s, the World Bank admitted that its predominant, top-down, economic focus has had a deleterious impact on the developing world and has once again turned its focus to poverty elimination, albeit within a neo-liberal framework. To rectify this, the World Bank has sought to reinvent itself in the mid-1990s, under the larger ambit of the Comprehensive Development Framework (CDF). The latter describes a holistic long-term strategy, in which the developing countries are encouraged to "own" and direct the development agenda by building stronger partnerships among governments, donors, civil society, the private sector, and other development stakeholders in implementing the country strategy (World Bank, 2002).

The IMF

Because of its ability to wield larger amounts of money and to interfere more deeply in a country's macroeconomic policy-making processes, the IMF has been far more controversial than the World Bank in recent years. The chief concern of the IMF's critics is the structural adjustment policies (SAPs) that it has consistently forced on the developing countries since the early 1980s. Individuals across the ideological spectrum have heavily criticized the SAPs for appropriating a large chunk of a developing country's economic sovereignty and for contributing to increasing poverty, economic dependence, and financial instability. These criticisms have particularly been levied at the IMF's response to the Asian crisis of 1997 (Soederberg, 2004). For the debtor countries, new money was available only to pay off old debts. These new loans were negotiated through new standby arrangements with the Fund. In this way, the IMF was able to ensure that the debtor governments would co-operate with its so-called conditionalities. Basically, this term refers to a commitment that debtor nations must make to the IMF before receiving any funds. In effect, the debtor country is pressured to adhere as closely as possible to the Fund's SAPs or risk being cut off from external markets and experiencing a lengthy loss of access to external sources of funding, such as development aid.

The SAPs involve two basic phases: (1) economic stabilization, and (2) economic restructuring along neo-liberal lines. The first phase, economic stabilization, aims to engender what the IMF considers sound economic fundamentals. To this end, the Fund encourages the debtor nation to undergo budget cuts, currency devaluation, interest rate increases, and outward-oriented trade and investment policies and credit squeezes. The second phase involves "necessary" neo-liberal structural reform, such as trade liberalization, privatization of state enterprises, deregulation of the country's banking system, liberalizing capital movements, and tax reform.

Since the collapse of the BWS, particularly after the debt crisis of the early 1980s, the Fund has increasingly changed its role from an institution that managed a stable international exchange rate system to one of managing international economic and financial crises by acting as the global lender-of-last-resort and offering economic advice to the developing countries. In the process, the IMF has helped ensure that the developing countries implement and adhere to neo-liberal policy practices and, more generally, to the narrow contours of the Washington Consensus. To this end, the Fund has become the main organizer of international debt agreements by lending to countries facing debt crises and serving as the axis around which negotiations occur. Private international lenders insist on linking their rescheduling agreements to the Fund's seal of approval for a debtor's economic policies.

Although the SAPs ensure that international lenders are reimbursed, they have been less than successful in promoting sustained economic development in the developing world. The SAPs have created harrowing social and economic experiences for the majority of residents of the debtor nations. Almost two decades of IMF-inspired economic restructuring has been marked by increased poverty rates in the developing world. In response, the Fund's former Managing Director, Michel Camdessus, has stated that poverty in the developing world is a key threat to the growth and stability of the world economy (IMF, 1999a). In fact, as in the case of the World Bank, the IMF has responded by making reduction of poverty one of its two key policy pillars, the other being, of course, macroeconomic reform. However, experience suggests that the two goals may be contradictory.

By 1987, primarily due to the SAPs, the banks had largely recovered from the debt crisis and were reluctant to reenter the game of debt financing in the developing world (Kapstein, 1994). This had two important implications regarding the changing role of the IMF. First, official lending (i.e., loans largely from the IMF and individual governments) supplanted commercial funds by the mid-1980s. Second, new, more mobile, and less vulnerable players, such as **mutual funds**, arrived on the scene as a source of financing in the debtor countries. A mutual fund is basically a collection of bonds or stocks that allows investors to avoid risking all their money on one single company. As we saw earlier, the amount of money wielded by these new financial actors dwarfs government economic resources in the more prosperous industrialized world, not to mention the Southern hemisphere. This translated into increased instability for debtor nations.

In this light, the new role of the IMF may be seen as either a financial intermediary or a crisis manager. Both these roles are geared toward stabilizing the world economy. After the Mexican Peso crash in December 1994, for instance, the Fund's role as crisis manager took on new dimensions in avoiding collapses of the international payment system. In April 1995, financial ministers and central bank governors of the leading members of the Fund committee called for "stronger and more effective IMF surveillance of its members," especially with respect to "unsustainable flows of private capital," overextended credit, and speculative activity in member countries (Pauly, 1997, 127). This move was designed to strengthen further the Fund's primary mandate of surveillance over the economic policy-making in the developing countries. To promote this new role, the G-7 countries agreed, in June 1995, to establish an emergency financing facility, which would provide quicker access to IMF arrangements with strong conditionality, as well as larger upfront disbursements in crisis situations. In addition, the Fund was to use its new leverage to encourage countries to become more transparent. Debtor countries were required to publish regularly economic data about their levels of short-term indebtedness, the amount of international reserves (i.e., American dollars) held by the countries' central banks, and so forth (Pauly 1997, 128; IMF, 1999b).

These transparency requirements were based on the assumption that the root causes of the recent financial crises in the South were largely due to policy error, if not outright corruption on the part of the governments involved. This assumption was clearly articulated during the Cologne Summit of the G-7 industrialized countries in June 1999 and the attempt to create a so-called "New International Financial Architecture" (Soederberg, 2004). The basic goal of this new financial architecture is to balance financial liberalization with stability by encouraging greater openness and accountability among debtor countries while allowing the South to integrate more fully into the global economy. Interestingly, the highly deregulated international financial markets, whose players are motivated by insatiable voracity and risk-seeking thrills, have not been admonished.

The World Trade Organization (WTO)

In 1995, the GATT was transformed into the WTO. The WTO, which is a multilateral institution designed to promote, monitor, and adjudicate international trade, builds on the GATT framework and covers all areas of trade, such as manufactured goods, services, and intellectual property. Almost all of the world's major trading countries are members of the WTO. As of 2003, the WTO has 146 member states. The WTO, like the World Bank and the IMF, possesses a democratic deficit in that its decision-making processes (an international bureaucracy of 500 people) take place largely out of the parameters of public scrutiny. An equally disturbing aspect of the WTO is its ability to override or change democratically passed laws concerning trade at the national level. Thus, the issue of state sovereignty seems to be in contradiction with the fundamental aim of the WTO, namely, to widen trade liberalization.

Summary

This chapter has examined the changing roles of the IFIs in the global political economy. Both the World Bank and the IMF were created at the Bretton Woods conference in 1944. They were formed in an attempt to avoid the economic ills of the Great Depression. These institutions functioned fairly well up to the early 1970s, when the United States abandoned the gold standard. The general crisis of the world economy created new tensions between national policy autonomy and international economic stability. The emerging landscape of the global political economy is marked most notably by powerful international financial markets. This phenomenon has had great implications for national governments and domestic economies, since both are highly dependent on private, unregulated capital flows. States have become increasingly competitive in attracting and retaining capital investment. Given the uneven nature of interstate relations, the wealthier nation states are able to secure a larger amount of capital flows than those in the South. Against this backdrop, IFIs have become preoccupied with stabilizing the volatile world economy and have, therefore, perpetuated economic inequality between rich and poor countries.

In light of such criticisms, the IMF and the World Bank have attempted to present a new and more socially just and transparent agenda. Nevertheless, as the critics rightly point out, both institutions still operate behind closed doors and are largely unaccountable to the vast majority of the global population. This distinct lack of democratic accountability has furthered the charge that today, as well as during the time of the BWS, the IFIs reflect the interests of the most powerful national economies in the world, especially the United States.

Discussion Questions

1. In what ways have the roles of the IMF and the World Bank differed in the Bretton Woods system (1944–71) and the post-Bretton Woods phase? Do you think the IMF and the World Bank have outlived their usefulness in the post-Bretton Woods era?
2. Lately, there has been much talk about tearing down the IMF and the World Bank and creating more democratic and accountable institutions to deal with financial and economic crises and development issues. Do you agree with this position? Why? Why not?
3. Many countries of the South are caught in the vicious cycle of the so-called "debt trap." Do you think that the recent campaign for debt forgiveness might mitigate the swelling levels of abject poverty associated with this "debt trap"? Or, should debtor countries swallow more of the same bitter medicine prescribed by the IMF, namely, "structural adjustment policies"?

References

Bakker, A.F.P. 1996. *International Financial Institutions.* Heerlen, The Netherlands: Open University of the Netherlands.

Cohen, Benjamin. 1986. *In Whose Interest? International Banking and American Foreign Policy.* New Haven: Yale University Press.

Greider, William. 1997. *One World, Ready or Not: The Manic Logic of Global Capitalism.* New York: Penguin Press.

Held, David, Anthony McGrew, David Goldblatt, and Johnathon Perraton. 1999. *Global Transformations: Politics, Economics and Culture.* Stanford: Stanford University Press.

IMF. 1999a "International Financial Policy in the Context of Globalisation." Remarks by Michel Camdessus Managing Director of the International Monetary Fund at the Konrad Adenauer Foundation Frankfurt, Germany, October 11, 1999. www.imf.org/external/np/speeches/1999/101199.HTM.

———. 1999b "IMF Surveillance." September 5, 1999. www.imf.org/external/np/exr/facts/surv/htm.

Krueger, Anne O. 1997. *Whither the World Bank and the IMF?* Stanford: Washington: National Bureau of Economic Research (NBER) Working Paper No. 6327.

Pauly, Louis W. 1997. *Who Elected the Bankers? Surveillance and Control in the World Economy.* Ithaca, NY: Cornell University Press.

Ruggie, John Gerard. 1982. "International Regimes, Transactions and Change: Embedded Liberalism in the Post-war Economic Order" *International Organization,* No. 36, 2 (Spring).

Soederberg, Susanne. 2004. *The Politics of the New International Financial Architecture: Reimposing Neoliberal Domination in the Global South.* London: Zed Books.

United Nations. 2003. *Human Development Report 2003.* New York: Human Development Report Office, United Nations Development Programme.

World Bank. 2000. *World Development Report 2000/2001: Attacking Poverty.* Washington, D.C.: World Bank.

———. 2002. *World Development Report 2002: Building Institutions for Markets.* Oxford: Oxford University Press.

Further Readings

Boas, Morten and Desmond McNeil. 2003. *Multilateral Institutions: A Critical Introduction.* London: Pluto Press.

Gowan, Peter. 1999. *The Global Gamble: Washington's Faustian Bid for World Dominance.* London: Verso Books.

Pettifor, Ann. 2003. *Real World Economic Outlook: The Legacy of Globalization—Debt and Deflation.* London: Palgrave.

Weblinks

International Monetary Fund
www.imf.org

The World Bank
www.worldbank.org

Inter-American Development Bank
www.iadb.org

African Development Bank
www.afdb.org

Asian Development Bank
www.adb.org

The World Trade Organization
www.wto.org

Webcasts

The Sum of Its Parts—How the IMF Lends
Keeping Track—IMF's Oversight of the Global Economy
www.imf.org/external/mmedia

NEWS ITEM: GAP GROWING BETWEEN RICH AND POOR.
artizans.com

CHAPTER 25

GLOBAL INEQUALITY AND POVERTY

Objectives

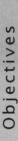

Inequality and poverty are enduring features of virtually all human societies. And, arguably, inequality is a constitutive feature of the global economy in an era of intensified globalization. Although global inequality and poverty often are discussed in tandem, they are conceptually distinct. Inequality is inclusive of both poverty and social welfare. Global poverty denotes the existence of people worldwide whose basic needs are not met and whose standard of living are below the norm, as determined by the societies or regions in which they live. Global poverty is a problem because people are living below subsistence, in conditions of immeasurable suffering, and this negatively impacts their life chances. Ultimately, global poverty is a profound waste of human potential. Global inequality, by contrast, refers to the skewed distribution worldwide of income, consumption, and other indicators of socio-economic well-being. Income and consumption are unequally distributed between the poor countries in the South and the rich countries in the North, and this concentration of wealth is deepening. Thus, inequality calls into question the fairness of the global economy and the legitimacy of institutions of global

MALINDA S. SMITH

governance. The two concepts are interconnected insofar as a major factor in the increase in global poverty is the unequal distribution of wealth and power between the North and South and the extent to which this reflects relations of domination and exploitation. Both global inequality and poverty pose ethical challenges for academics, policy makers, and non-governmental organizations committed to poverty reduction and a more just world order.

This chapter explores various dimensions of inequality and poverty in a globalizing era. It has several objectives. It maps contested conceptions of poverty, from low-income and consumption to notions of human development and social exclusion. Second, the chapter looks at measurements of poverty, including the World Bank's poverty line; the United Nations Development Program's Human Poverty Index (HPI), and the International Fund for Agricultural Development's Integrated Poverty Index (IPI). Finally, the chapter takes stock of poverty reduction and related international development targets (IDTs).

Introduction

Income inequality between rich countries and poor countries is increasing in a global era. Where the income gap between the world's rich and poor countries was 3:1 in 1820, by 1950, it was 35:1; by 1997, it was 74:1; and by 2002, it was 82:1. A mere 20 percent of the world's population in the rich countries owns 86 percent of the world's gross domestic product (GDP). The combined wealth of the world's three richest *individuals* is greater than the combined GDP of the world's 48 poorest *countries.* While, global *per capita* output has risen by 90 percent over the past 30 years, this is not true for Africa, where the real *per capita* income has declined; it is lower than in 1970. Africa is home to most of the countries in which at least 50 percent of the population are below the poverty line. Of the 65 countries the Bank has identified as low-income or poor, 40 are on the African continent, as are 16 of the 20 poorest countries (Aninat, 2000; UNDP, 1999; Prabhakar, 2003).

While the data for the Middle East and Latin America are less grim, they do show that *per capita* income in these regions is stagnant or growing significantly lower than in the North. In Asia, often advanced as the good news story for regional economic development, the picture is uneven. In South Asia, home to 515 million poor people—more than the populations of Canada, the United States, and Mexico combined—the outlook is bleak and worsening. A recent regional development report noted that "during the globalisation phase about half-a-billion people in South Asia have experienced a decline in their incomes" (*Times of India Online*, February 14, 2002). The report concluded that globalization has conferred benefits on "a small minority of educated urban population," but overall income inequality has increased.

International financial institutions (IFIs), such as the International Monetary Fund (IMF) and the World Bank, have reluctantly acknowledged that their development strategies, which prioritized economic growth—and underemphasized distribution and social well-being—have failed to limit the uneven impact of globalization.

Eduardo Aninat, the IMF's Managing Director, states: "Overall, the number of very poor—those living on less than $1 per day—has stayed roughly the same over the past decade; only limited progress has been made in reducing the share of the world population living in poverty" (Aninat, 2000). Data from the World Bank Development Group show that the incidence of global poverty fell by an insignificant 0.2 percent in the decade between 1988 and 1999 (World Bank, 2001).

Despite claims of the "death of distance" that accompany contemporary globalization, geography does matter in global mappings of the incidence and severity of poverty. The statistics cannot tell the whole story of the extreme conditions of destitution, ill-health, hunger, chronic underemployment and human in/security that many of the world's population live in. Some 1.3 billion of the world's population live in abject or extreme poverty, below the poverty line of US$1.08 dollars per day. Of these, 70 percent are located in rural areas. However, by 2005, the "urbanization of poverty" is expected to increase as one in two people are born into urban spaces. The highest percentage of rural poor is concentrated in Asia (633 million), followed by Sub-Saharan Africa (SSA) (204 million) and Latin America and the Caribbean (76 million). An additional 1.5 billion people live below the poverty line of $2 per day, and their numbers increase by 25 million per year. In total, some 2.8 billion people—almost half of the world's population—live on less than $2 per day (World Bank, 2004).

The fact that 70 percent of those living in extreme poverty are girls and women also reinforces the **feminization of poverty**. According to Nilüfer Cagatay (1998, 3), the feminization of poverty is a short-hand concept that captures at least three things: first, there is a higher *incidence* of poverty among women; second, there is greater *severity* in the experience of poverty by women; and, third, the incidence of women's poverty is *increasing* compared with the incidence among men. Women are disadvantaged in both urban and rural areas in their access to nutrition, education, health services, and employment and wages. As well, both the very old and very young are adversely impacted by poverty. Over 40 percent of all children in the South—one-half billion—live in hazardous conditions in overcrowded shantytowns and urban slums or eke out an existence hustling as street children (UNICEF, 2000, 1).

The stubborn persistence of poverty reinforces Henry George's observation made over a century ago: "The association of poverty with progress is the great enigma of our times" (George, 1880, 6). George's prophetic observation remains true today. Never before has the world created so much wealth, nor been more capable of a fairer and more equitable distribution. Nonetheless, the current era is characterized by the "paradox of plenty" (Brodie, 2004), in which increased wealth creation is accompanied by increased destitution. This paradox is not unique to contemporary globalization. In the nineteenth century, capital expansion under *Pax Britannica* saw an increase in world trade and an improvement in wages and working conditions in the North. These same global processes left stagnant and at subsistence level the wages and working and living conditions in the South (Bata and Bergesen, 2002, 2–6). By the late-twentieth century, the dominant trend was income concentration and a widening gap between rich and poor countries. Scholars differ in conceptualizing this polarity, as "uneven globalization," global "winners" and "losers,") and "global apartheid" (Kennedy, 1993). There is consensus, however, that inequality and poverty are unevenly distributed within and across geopolitical spaces.

A Genealogy of Poverty

LIKE SO MANY CRITICAL CONCEPTS IN THE SOCIAL SCIENCES AND HUMANITIES, explanations of poverty are robustly contested. Definitions of poverty are shaped by cultural norms and values. Differences arise over how poverty is defined and measured and over the policies designed to reduce and, ultimately, eradicate it. Understandings of poverty are shaped by the unit of analysis, space, time, and severity. The unit of analysis may be an individual, social group (e.g., gender, age, ethnicity), country, region, or the globe. The spatial dimensions of poverty include the incidence and severity of poverty within countries, such as between rural and urban areas, and across countries, such as between North and South. Poverty is shaped by time, with conditions of poverty being either temporary or chronic. Another dimension of poverty relates to its intensity or severity, such as between relative deprivation and absolute destitution. What any definition of poverty minimally entails is recognition "that significant numbers of people are living in intolerable circumstances where starvation is a constant threat, sickness is a familiar companion, and oppression is a fact of life" (Kanbur and Squire, 1999, 1).

Relative poverty concerns the unequal distribution of income within a given society. It suggests that a person may be able to acquire adequate food, clothing, and shelter but that this exhausts their resources, leaving nothing for other things, such as telephone, transportation, or even reading materials. Trying to capture the cross-cultural variations in the daily lived-experiences of the poor is difficult. Can we—and if so, how do we—compare deprivation in an affluent society, such as Canada, with, for example, the experience in an impoverished society, such as Haiti or North Korea? In Canada and the United States, some people are poor relative to others in these societies. However, the poor in the North American region may be considered wealthy in relation to the poor in South Asia. Absolute poverty is of another existential order. In 1978, then World Bank president Robert McNamara coined the concept to characterize a condition "so limited by malnutrition, illiteracy, disease, squalid surroundings, high infant mortality, and low life expectancy as to be beneath any reasonable definition of human decency" (quoted in Singer, 1979, 158). Absolute poverty denotes a condition of extreme destitution, in which a person's income and living standards are so inadequate that they lack the most basic necessities for survival, such as food, water, and shelter.

Throughout history, philosophers, economists, and novelists, among others, have tried to make sense of the empirical and experiential dimensions of poverty. In the *Leviathan* (1651), philosopher Thomas Hobbes suggests that an individual's consent to a social contract would enable her to escape a life that was "poor, nasty, brutish, and short." A supreme authority would guarantee civil order, industry, and the conditions for wealth creation. In *The Wealth of Nations* (1776), economist Adam Smith argued that national wealth was created through a market-based economy, free trade, and an "invisible hand" that somehow ensured balance within the economic order. By contrast, in *Capital* (1867), Marx saw neither an authoritarian regime nor an invisible hand as necessary or sufficient for understanding the contradictory tendencies in the accumulation of capital that led to the creation of wealth for a few and, simultaneously, the impoverishment of the majority.

There are theological and ethical conceptions of poverty. The examples of the late Mother Theresa, the "Saint of the Gutter," and various Roman Catholic Friars and Buddhist monks suggest that a spiritual understanding of poverty may require a vow of poverty. This vow is a voluntary, personal renunciation of private and communal material property and a means to achieving spiritual well-being. Ethical conceptions of poverty may entail judgments about "moral bankruptcy," in which an individual's laziness or personal choices lead to debilitating vices, such as gambling or crime. Conversely, absolute destitution and starvation can lead to crime, and ethicists have debated whether it is best to understand thievery in such cases as a personal choice or the outcome of structural inequities. The moral dilemmas posed by poverty are mapped in the novel *Les Miserables* (1935). Jean Valjean goes to jail for stealing bread for his daughter and sister and, ultimately, becomes a social outcast despite heroic efforts to change his life's circumstances and reintegrate him into society. The example of Mother Theresa focuses our attention on voluntary action and personal choice as causes of poverty, whereas the story of Jean Valjean points to structural and societal factors that impose social limits. Throughout history, there have been conflicting political and social responses to the poor, ranging from empathy and compassion to pity, moral distain, and even fear.

Understandings of "who" the poor are have shifted over time. During the Middle Ages, there was a social class that comprised **paupers** who met or supplemented their basic needs through the charity of churches or private philanthropy. There were moral overtones to the early nineteenth century **Poor Laws**. First introduced in the United Kingdom, these laws served as a disciplinary mechanism to get the poor off the streets and into poor houses, where they could be taught the value of work. The poor themselves were blamed for their own plight, not the economic or social structures. "The central tenet of popular versions of the 'underclass' argument," Byrne (1999, 1) argues, "is that miserable conditions are self-induced—the poor do it to themselves."

In the twentieth century, IFIs, such as the IMF and the World Bank adopted a narrow conception of poverty. Since the mid-1940s, poverty has been conceptualized in terms of gross national product (GNP), household income, consumption, and monetary access to the market. The World Bank defines poverty as "the inability to attain a minimum standard of living." This minimum standard of living benchmark was further subdivided into two other criteria: (1) the ability to purchase minimum daily nutritional requirements as determined by the society in which one lives, and (2) basic needs that are shaped by an assessment of "the cost of participating in the everyday life of society" (World Bank, 1990, 26). In both cases, the World Bank prioritized income and consumption, rather than a broader notion of social well-being.

The meaning of poverty began to broaden in the 1990s, with the UNDP's introduction of the idea of **human development**. It provided an understanding of development and poverty beyond economic indicators. This change in thinking was strongly influenced by Nobel prize winner, Amartya Sen, and his influential book, *Development as Freedom* (1999). In it, he argued: "Development requires the removal of major sources of unfreedom: poverty as well as tyranny, poor economics as well as systemic social deprivation, neglect of public facilities as well as intolerance or overactivity of repressive states" (1999, 3). Similarly, the UNDP's conception of human development prioritized non-monetary and social-well-being indicators, such as access to health care and knowledge, political and cultural freedoms, and participation in the everyday life of the community. Given the shared aim of expanding capabilities, both the World Bank and the UNDP came to conceive of development as freedom. However, where the Bank focuses almost exclusively on economic freedom and financial and material well-being, the UNDP tries to capture a broader conception of freedom, one that is inclusive of social, political, and cultural freedom.

By the mid-1990s, conceptions of poverty had broadened to encompass an understanding of **risk** as a determinant of transient or chronic poverty. One form of vulnerability arises from variable employment, income, and living standards. Vulnerability arises from the lack of social and political rights that impacts human in/security. Risks can arise from complex factors, including environmental and health hazards, such as crop failure and famine; personal insecurity, such as rape or land eviction; and macroeconomic shocks. "Many of today's non-poor may turn out to be *tomorrow's poor* if they are subjected to routine risks and if the costs of coping with such risk have to be met only through harder options" that make it difficult to avoid the poverty trap (B. Sen, n.d., 2–3). Those with more resources are better able to deal with risk-exposure and have greater access to risk-coping mechanisms.

Thinking on poverty further broadened to encompass the concept of **social capital**, which, proponents argue, is the "missing link" in development discourse and policy. In a nutshell, social capital suggests that "relationships matter" and that "who" we know, including our social networks, constitutes a kind of capital. The concept of social capital is broader than the understanding of **human capital** that emerged in economic discourse in the 1960s, to connote "the economic value to firms, individuals and the wider public of such attributes as skill, knowledge and good health" (Field, 2003, 9).

The French sociologist Pierre Bourdieu first developed the idea of social capital in the late 1970s. He distinguished between social, cultural, symbolic, and economic forms of capital. Bourdieu was cognisant of the fact that the "accumulation of social capital" could reinforce class cleavages and social relations of domination (1980; 1986). The rich would use their better-developed networks to maintain their status. This more critical conception of social capital is not the one now extant in development and anti-poverty discourses. The dominant conception owes its genealogy to American social theorist Robert Putnam. In the early-1990s, Putnam described social capital as "features of social organisations such as networks, norms and social trust that facilitate coordination and cooperation for mutual benefit" (Putnam, 1993, 67).

Putnam emphasized the importance of moral obligations, especially social values, such as trust, and social networks, such as "civic" or voluntary associations. Social trust became linked to notions of empowerment through social networking and participation.

While the debate about the relevance of social capital for development began in academic circles in France and the United States, a variety of actors soon picked up the concept. The World Bank and other official bodies, such as the Organization for Economic Co-operation and Development (OECD), first embraced the concept of social capital as a way of integrating social theory with economic theory, claiming that human well-being depended on economic development (Field, 2003, 9). Promoted by the World Bank, social capital soon became associated with faith in civil society organizations as important stakeholders in a host of good governance and anti-poverty initiatives. Some critics see social capital is a "chaotic concept" (Bankston and Zhou, 2002), one that lacks coherence and is too frequently used in inconsistent ways by social theorists, development specialists, and policy makers. Others argue that Putnam's conception, as well as that of the World Bank, occludes unequal distribution of wealth and also social relations of domination and exploitation in the accumulation of financial and social capital. A similar critique is levelled at Bourdieu's use of "capital" as a metaphor for social relations. Capital has a specific historical association with conventional economic discourse, and thus, Bourdieu's language also "helps blur crucial issues of power and control" (Field, 2003, 137).

The mid- to late-1990s witnessed the emergence in Europe of the idea of **social exclusion** in theorizing on poverty. Social exclusion widened the conceptual gap in how poverty is understood in the North and the South. The earlier conception of poverty within the European Commission (EC) referred to limited material—social and cultural resources that excluded a person's participation in a "minimum acceptable way of life,"—as determined by the states in which in they live (Schultz, 2002, 120). Like human development, social exclusion was much broader than income-poverty. The concept soon became pan-European and replaced poverty in European Commission social policy. The concept first emerged in French policy discourse as a way of addressing "new poverty" and the problems that arise from inadequate social insurance and social safety nets for the chronically un- and underemployed. Walker and Walker (1998, 8) differentiate the concept as follows: "poverty as a lack of material resources, especially income, necessary to participate in . . . society and social exclusion as a more comprehensive formulation which refers to the dynamic process of being shut out, fully or partially, from any of the social, economic, political or cultural systems." Walker and Walker go on to emphasize that social exclusion is also lodged in rights discourse and, thus, can be seen either as the denial or non-realization of rights of social citizenship.

There are competing conceptions of social exclusion. Ruth Levitas distinguishes between redistribution, moral underclass and social integration approaches (Levitas 1998). Another typology is offered by Hilary Silver (1994), who distinguishes between conceptions of social exclusion that corresponds to different political philosophies. Republicanism focused on solidarity and social disintegration; liberal philosophy focused on specialization in individual action and social exchanges; and social democrats prioritized monopoly, by which they sought to show that "the excluded are simultaneously outside and dominated." Despite the diversity of paradigms, what each offers is a broader understanding of the "multiple forms of social disadvantage—income, social, political, and cultural—and thus encompasses theories of citizenship and racial-ethnic inequality as well as poverty and long-term unemployment." However, one of the problems with social exclusion, critics argue, is that it has become "the predominant form of social injustice" (Bessis 1995, 13). Some usages of the concept have either replaced or sanitized conditions of exploitation. Exclusion is one form of contemporary exploitation (Byrne 1999, 57) insofar as the rich increasingly do not need the labour power of the poor, further deepening the latter's social dislocation.

Today, the narrower definition of income and subsistence is used primarily in explanations of poverty in the South, and the more multi-causal conception of poverty as social exclusion is used in the EU. An important cautionary note is whether, over time, the spatially specific definitions of poverty will distort our understanding of "who" the poor are as well as lead to a kind of geopolitical–conceptual gap in understanding "why" some people are poor.

Measuring Poverty

By any measure, the growing gap between the North and the South, as well as the incidence and severity of poverty for half of humanity, is among the most significant global challenges in the twenty-first century. The next objective of this chapter is to explain how poverty is measured. Given the disparate definitions of poverty, it is not surprising that there are divergent conceptions of how best to measure it. Such differences also have implications for policy coherence and assessments of the effectiveness of pro-poor policies and global poverty reduction strategies. There are several well-known measurements used to distinguish the poor from the non-poor.

The orthodox measurement of global poverty is a monetary conception that has been used by the World Bank since 1945. In a nutshell, people are poor if their incomes fall below a specified benchmark that the World Bank has called the **poverty line**. The World Bank argued that "a universal poverty line is needed to permit cross-country comparison and aggregation" (World Bank, 1990, 27). It operationalized its minimum standard of living, or basic needs threshold, in terms of **purchasing power parity** (PPP). For the world's poorest countries, the poverty line is based on a daily-income figure of $1 dollar per day per person in 1985 dollars. Those who fall below $275 *per annum* are considered extremely poor. In its third global poverty report in 2000, the World Bank adjusted its poverty line to $1.08 in the 1993 PPP. Using this measurement, some 1.3 billion people are income-poor. Using a poverty line of $2 per day, the number increases to 2.8 billion people.

While the poverty line does allow cross-national comparisons based on a head count, it is a blunt measure for assessing precisely how far below the poverty line individuals are living and what is meant by improvement. Further, and despite the World Bank's claim of an objective and universal standard, the income-poverty line varies across regions, with Latin America using a US$2 per day measure and Russia and Eastern Europe using US$4 a day as the poverty threshold. As well, there is no straightforward way of determining the incidence of poverty or the standard of living in Sub-Saharan Africa, where the poverty line is based on US$1, compared with Eastern Europe, where a threshold of $4 is used. Nor do the poverty-line thresholds tell us much about the intensity of poverty for those either on the line or well below the line (Gordon and Spicker, 1999). The limits of the poverty line measurement have given rise to efforts to determine the **poverty gap** and a **Poverty Severity Index**. The poverty gap measures the percentage of the population living below the poverty line and allows a composite of the incidence and severity of poverty within countries. The Poverty Severity Index measures the intensity of poverty insofar as it focuses on individuals living well below the poverty line and, hence, in conditions of extreme deprivation.

The **Human Development Index** (HDI) is one of four composite indices that have been produced by the UNDP since the publication of its first *Human Development Report* in 1990, under the direction of then Finance Minister of Pakistan Mahbub ul Haq and Indian Nobel laureate for Economics Amartya Sen (see, Sen, 1999). The HDI is the best known of the international development indices designed with the aim of measuring achievements in human and social well-being (see Table 25–1). Each index attempts to measure inequality and human well-being beyond economic growth and the rise and fall of income and consumption. The HDI replaced the previous development measure, the Physical Quality of Life Index (PQLI), which prioritized physical and material well-being. It expands notions of quality of life beyond physical subsistence by trying to assess qualitative factors, such as the freedom to make choices in employment and lifestyles, access to public education, and freedom from political repression.

TABLE 25.1 *Measuring Human Poverty*

Human Development Index (HDI) (UNDP)	Human Poverty Index (HPI) (UNDP)	Integrated Poverty Index (IPI) (IFAD)
• Life expectancy at birth	• % of people expected to die before age 40	• Poverty line (head count) and income gap ratio
• Educational attainment (education and literacy)	• % of illiterate adults	• Income distribution below poverty line (life expectancy)
• Standard of living (GDP *per capita*)	• Access to health services	• Annual rate of growth of *per capita* GNP
	• Access to safe water	
	• % of children under 5 who are malnourished	

The **Human Poverty Index** (HPI) is a composite index designed to better understand uneven development and a conception of poverty that is not exclusively monetary. Sudhir Anand and Amartya Sen first proposed the index (1996). Subsequently, it appeared in the 1997 *Human Development Report* launched during the United Nations International Year for the Eradication of Poverty. The HPI-1 for poor countries in the South measures deprivation understood in terms of vulnerability and risk in areas of health, knowledge, and overall economic well-being. In the first instance, health deprivation is measured in terms of early death or life expectancy before age 40. Knowledge deprivation is measured in terms of adult literacy. Overall economic deprivation is measured in terms of three variables; access to clean water, health services, and the percentage of children under five years who are malnourished (UNDP, 1999). The HPI-2 for rich countries measures life expectancy before age 60; adult functional literacy rates; the percentage of people living below the poverty line; and employability assessed in terms of long-term unemployment rates (the "new poverty"). There are at least two notable differences between HPI-1 and HPI-2. The HPI-2 assumes a longer life expectancy than HPI-1 (20 years) and assumes that employment is central to human development.

The **Gender-related Development Index** (GDI), like HPI, measures the experience of human deprivation and adjusts for health and knowledge deprivation and overall economic well-being as experienced by girls and women. It also looks at the differential share of income for women and men. Overall, the HPI and the GDI are closely related to the HDI in measuring life expectancy, knowledge, and standard of living. However, there are at least two important distinctions that relate to units of analysis. First, the HDI calculates aggregate social and economic data on a country-wide basis. In contrast, the HPI and the GDI focus on a cross-section of the national population defined by their conditions of deprivation. Second, where the HPI focuses on health and education deprivation, the GDI includes a focus on comparative income shares.

The **Integrated Poverty Index** (IPI) is an economic measure that can be traced to the composite poverty index first developed in the mid-1970s (Sen, 1976). The IPI is one of four poverty indices developed by the IFAD to assess the incidence of human deprivation in rural areas. The IPI calculates four cross-cutting measures that include a headcount measure of the incidence of rural poverty, income gaps, gross national product (GNP) *per capita*, and life expectancy. The Food Security Index (FSI) measures countries for food in/security and people that face risk and vulnerability due to food shortage, hunger, and starvation. The Basic Needs Index (BNI) examines rural poverty, using health and knowledge deprivation. Finally, the Relative Welfare Index (RWI) is an average of the IPI, the BNI, and the RWI and can take values between one and zero, with one indicative of the worst conditions of poverty. The IFAD also disaggregates its data to produce a Women's Status Index (WSI) that examines the incidence of deprivation for girls and women in rural areas. It uses these data as a basis for designing concrete policies to reduce and ultimately eradicate poverty. The WSI, like GDI, is important to the ongoing battle against the feminization of poverty both within and across geopolitical spaces (Gordon and Townsend, 2002).

Taking Stock of the Poverty Reduction

IN THE MID-1960S, ROBERT MCNAMARA MADE GLOBAL POVERTY ERADICATION the priority of his World Bank presidency. Over 30 years later and despite a number of professed commitments to poverty reduction, the international development targets (IDTs), and the Millennium Development Goals (MDGs), little progress has been made. The primary objective of this section is to briefly review these "missed targets" and "broken promises" (Oxfam International, 2000).

At the 1995 World Summit for Social Development (WSSD) in Copenhagen, some 117 governments reached consensus on a global agenda for poverty reduction. They committed to reducing global poverty by half by the year 2015. The Summit's Declaration and Program of Action characterized poverty reduction as "an ethical, social, political and economic imperative of human kind." The Summit also endorsed the 20/20 Initiative, which called for South governments to spend 20 percent of their domestic budgets and Northern governments 20 percent of their foreign aid budgets on funding anti-poverty and social programs in education and health. A year later, the "donor's club," comprised primarily of the Development Assistance Committee (DAC) of the Organization of Economic Cooperation and Development (OECD), affirmed the Copenhagen consensus on poverty reduction. The DAC also committed to related IDTs in areas of social well-being, including literacy, education, and health services. In September 2000, the UN Millennium Summit opened in New York with a call by world governments to eradicate poverty, and some 149 countries committed to do so as well as to achieve the related MDGs. All the major international organizations released substantial reports on poverty.[1] The consensus since Copenhagen was that "the social" mattered and that greater investments were needed to reduce poverty, illiteracy, and health deprivation (see Table 25.2).

If current trends continue, the global community will fail to achieve the goal of reducing extreme poverty in half by 2015, with perhaps the exception of East Asia. Imminent failure is also true for related MDGs. Poverty will not be reduced in Sub-Saharan Africa, North Africa, the Middle East, Latin America, the Caribbean, or Eastern and Central Europe. Population growth, combined with a static incidence of poverty, means that there are as many people living in poverty today as in 1990. Current World Bank projections suggest that the ranks of the poor will grow by 235 million more poor people over the next decade, and half of these will be born in Sub-Saharan Africa. Given the growth in population and the increasing incidence of extreme poverty, this region is unlikely to achieve the goal of poverty reduction until 2147—over 132 years after the original target date.

In 2005, the global community will have the first opportunity for stock taking, as this is the target date for the elimination of gender disparity between boys and girls in primary and secondary education. At least 60 percent of poor countries will not

TABLE 25.2 *Global Development Targets/Millennium Development Goals (MDGs)*

International Development Goal	International /Millennium Development Target	International Establishment of, and Recommitment to, Targets
• Eradicate extreme poverty and hunger	• Reduce extreme poverty by half by 2015	• 1995 UN World Summit for Social Development (Copenhagen), March • 1996 DAC of the OECD • 2000 Millennium Summit (New York), September • 2002 World Summit on Sustainable Development (Johannesburg)
• Achieve universal primary education	• Achieve universal primary education by 2015	• 1995 UN World Summit for Social Development (Copenhagen), March • 1995 Fourth World Conference on Women (Beijing), September • 2000 Millennium Summit
• Promote gender equality and empower women	• Eliminate gender disparity in primary and secondary education by 2005	• 1994 UN International Conference on Population and Development (Cairo), 5–13 September 1995
	• Achieve universal education by 2015	• Fourth World Conference on Women • 1995 UN World Summit for Social Development • 2000 Millennium Summit • 2002 World Summit on Sustainable Development
• Reduce child mortality	• Reduce the child mortality rates by two-thirds by 2015	• 1995 UN International Conference on Population and Development • 2000 Millennium Summit
• Improve maternal mortality and health	• Reduce the maternal mortality rates by three-fourths by 2015	• 1994 UN International Conference on Population and Development • 1995 Fourth World Conference on Women • 2000 Millennium Summit

continued

• Improve access to primary health care and reproductive health services	• Improve overall access for all by 2015	• 1994 UN International Conference on Population and Development
• Combat HIV/AIDS, malaria, and other communicable diseases	• Halt and reverse the incidence of HIV/AIDS infection, malaria, and other major diseases by 2015	• 2000 Millennium Summit • 2001 UN Special Session on HIV/AIDS (New York), June
• Ensure environmental sustainability	• Reduce by half the percentage of people without access to clean water	• 1992 UN Conference on Environment and Development, 3–14 June
	• Significantly improve conditions of 100 million slum dwellers by 2020	• 2000 Millennium Summit
	• Integrate principle of sustainable development into national policies	• 2002 World Summit on Sustainable Development

SOURCE: "Millennium Development Goals," from *Human Development Report 2003* by United Nations Development Programme, © 2003 by the UNDP. Used by permission of Oxford University Press.

achieve this goal, and if current trends continue, it is unlikely that the goal of universal education will be achieved by 2015. Current estimates by the World Bank suggest that it will be at least another 15 years before this goal is achieved in Sub-Saharan Africa (Brown, 2004, 4). Over 125 million children in the South were not enrolled in school in 2000. This figure is projected to increase by an additional 75 million by 2015. The African region accounts for one-third of all children out of school, and this figure is projected to increase to two-thirds by 2015. This trend will pose serious challenges for Africa's ability to reduce extreme income-poverty, particularly in rural households and among girls and women. At present, the continent is spending more on debt repayment than on either education or health care.

An equally important social development target was established in the area of health services, including reducing child mortality, improving maternal health, improving access to primary health care and reproductive services, and combating HIV/AIDS, malaria, and other communicable diseases. On the basis of the current trends, the global community will fail to achieve any of these goals by 2015. Only in Latin America and the Middle East is child mortality reduction on track. By 2015, an additional 3.8 million children will die before age five, and some 60 percent of these will be in Sub-Saharan Africa. On the basis of the current projections, it will be another 150 years before Sub-Saharan Africais able to achieve the MDG to reduce child mortality. Deaths due to preventable diseases will continue to increase. Some two million people die from tuberculosis annually. Another million die from malaria.

There are over 40 million people living with HIV/AIDS, and in some countries in Sub-Saharan Africa, as many as half of the population is infected. These diseases are preventable and treatable through existing knowledge, drugs, and technology. Yet, in almost all cases, the death toll continues unabated because of a lack of financial and human resources and affordable generic drugs.

The United Kingdom's Chancellor of the Exchequer, Gordon Brown, published an editorial in February 2004 in which he stressed the challenges posed by poverty and HIV/AIDS and why it was important for rich countries to act. "Four people a minute die of AIDS. Eleven-million children are orphaned in Africa alone. Another 20-million are expected to lose one or both parents in the next six years." Brown issued an urgent call to the North "to act on the scourge of poverty and disease" (Brown, February 16, 2004). "Madness" is how World Bank president James Wolfensohn characterized global spending priorities in the new millennium (Fickling, 2004). Wolfensohn challenged the rich countries to take seriously the global commitments to poverty reduction and the skewed global spending priorities. For example, over a trillion dollars a year is spent on defence, 20 times more than is spent "on trying to give hope to people" (Fickling, 2004). Less is being spent on development aid and poverty reduction in 2004 than was being spent 40 years ago. Further, despite "free trade talk," rich countries spend some 350 billion dollars on domestic agricultural subsidies and tariffs, while the same countries spend a paltry 50 billion dollars on foreign aid to poor countries. Foreign aid levels have been in free fall for over a decade. "We have got it tremendously wrong," Wolfensohn insisted, "in the way in which we are addressing the questions of poverty, development and its importance." Belatedly, the 2001 Financing for Development Conference in Monterrey and the 2002 Social Development Conference in Johannesburg began to think about how to finance development. As defence spending suggests, the issue is not a lack of financial resources, rather one of political will. There is much reason for pessimism as the lack of progress on IDT and MDGs suggests. Whether Brazil's President Luiz Inacio Lula da Silva's call for "a New World Social Contract" is possible remains to be seen (da Silva, February 16, 2004).

Summary

This chapter examined inequality, the contested concept of poverty, and diverse indices and measurements of this global social issue. It suggests that the uneven impact of capital accumulation on a global scale laid waste to many of the assumptions of the post-colonial developmental state, particularly the optimistic view that poverty alleviation and social well-being would accompany economic growth. A deepening of global polarization has resulted from successive waves of economic globalization, failed development policies, and the many unfulfilled international promises to eradicate world poverty. While the goal of poverty eradication—and interim goal of reduction—remains worthwhile, the history of global initiatives to end poverty has been littered with broken promises and dashed hopes. If there is a shortage or "lack," it is in the area of global leadership and political will to tackle global inequality and the scourge of poverty.

Endnote

[1] The World Bank subtitled its report *Attacking Poverty* (2000/2001), and in 2003 and 2004, its reports all prioritized poverty reduction. In March 2000, UNICEF released *Poverty Reduction Begins with Children.* A month later, the UNDP followed with *Overcoming Poverty* (2000) and again in 2003 with *Millennium Development Goals: A Compact among Nations to End Human Poverty.*

Discussion Questions

1. What do you think is the most compelling explanation for the incidence of poverty?
2. Is "social capital" the missing link in development theory, strategies, and policies?
3. Do you think the divergent approach to explaining poverty—subsistence income in the South and social exclusion in the North—will lead to a geopolitical–conceptual gap that impacts (a) how we understand poverty; (b) who we consider poor; and (c) why some people are poor?
4. Which measurement of poverty best captures the complex issue of poverty?
5. Do you think it is likely that poverty will be eradicated in your lifetime?

References

Aninat, Eduardo. 2000. "Making Globalisation Work for the Poor." Remarks by Mr. Eduardo Aninat, Deputy Managing Director of the International Monetary Fund at the German Foundation for International Development, Berlin, March 14, 2000.

Bankston, C.L. and M. Zhou. 2002. "Social Capital Process: The Meanings and Problems of a Theoretical Metaphor." *Sociological Inquiry,* 72, 2, 285–317.

Bata, Michelle and Albert J. Bergesen. "Global Inequality: An Introduction," *Journal of World-Systems Research,* 7, 1 (Winter 2002), 2–6.

Bessis, Sophie. 1995. "From Social Exclusion to Social Cohesion: A Policy Agenda." Management of Social Transformations (MOST), Policy Paper No. 2 (2–4 March), www.unesco.org/most/besseng.htm (accessed 18 February 2004).

Bordieu, Pierre. 1980. "Le capital social: notes provisoires." *Actes de la récherche en sciences sociales,* 2–3.

———. 1986. "The Forms of Capital" in J.G. Richardson, ed., *Handbook of Theory and Research for the Sociology of Education.* New York: Greenwood Press, 241–258.

Brodie, Janine. 2004. "Globalism and the Paradoxes of Social Citizenship." *Citizenship Studies,* 8, 4 (November).

Brown, Gordon. 2004. Speech by the Chancellor of the Exchequer Gordon Brown at the "Making Globalisation Work for All—The Challenge of Delivering the Monterrey Consensus," United Kingdom Treasury, London, February 16, 2004.

Byrne, David. 1999. *Social Exclusion.* Buckingham: Open University Press.

Çağatay, Nilüfer. 1998. "Gender and Poverty." UNDP Social Development and Poverty Elimination Division, Working Paper Series No. 5 (May).

Da Silva, Luiz Inacio Lula. 2004. Speech delivered at the "Making Globalisation Work for All—The Challenge of Delivering the Monterrey Consensus." United Kingdom Treasury, London, February 16, 2004.

Fickling, David. 2004. "World Bank Condemns Defense Spending." *Guardian Weekly*, Saturday, February 14, 2004. www.guardian.co.uk/print/0,3858,4858685-103681,00.html (accessed February 14, 2004).

Field, John. 2003. *Social Capital.* London and New York: Routledge.

George, Henry. 1881. *Progress and Poverty*, 4th edition. New York: Blackwell.

Gordon, D. and P. Spicker, eds. 1999. *The International Glossary on Poverty.* London: Zed Books.

Gordon, D. and P. Townsend, eds. 2002. *Breadline Europe: The Measurement of Poverty.* Bristol: The Policy Press.

Kanbur, Ravi and Lyn Squire. 1999. "The Evolution of Thinking about Poverty: Exploring the Interactions." September 1999.

Kennedy, Paul. 1993. "Preparing for the 21st Century: Winners and Losers." *The New York Review of Books*, 40, 4 (February 11).

Levitas, Ruth. 1998. *The Inclusive Society? Social Exclusion and New Labour.* London: Macmillan.

Oxfam International. 1995. *Poverty Report.* Oxford: Oxfam UK.

———. 2000. "Missing the Target: The Price of Empty Promises." Report to the Special Session of the General Assembly to Review and Access Implementation of the Declaration and Programme of Action adopted by the World Summit for Social Development, Geneva, June 26–30, 2000.

Prabhakar, A.C. 2003. "A Critical Reflection on Globalisation and Inequality: A New Approach to the Development of the South." *African and Asian Studies*, 2, 3 (September 1, 2003), 307–345.

Putnam, Robert D. 1993. *Making Democracy Work: Civic Traditions in Modern Italy.* Princeton: Princeton University Press.

Schultz, Bernd. 2002. "A European Definition of Poverty: The Fight against Poverty and Social Exclusion in the Member States of the European Union." in *World Poverty: New Policies to Defeat an Old Enemy*, eds. Peter Townsend and David Gordon. Bristol: The Policy Press, 119–145.

Sen, Amartya. 1976. "Poverty: An Ordinal Approach to Measurement." *Econometrica*, 44, 2, 291–331.

———. 1981. *Poverty and Famines: An Essay on Entitlement and Deprivation.* Oxford: Clarendon Press.

———. 1999. *Development as Freedom.* Oxford: Oxford University Press.

Sen, Binayak, n.d. "Poverty in Bangladesh: A Review." Bangladesh Institute of Development Studies. www.bids-bd.org/za (accessed February 13, 2004).

Silver, H. 1994. "Social Exclusion and Social Solidarity: Three Paradigms." *International Labour Review* 133, 5–6: 531–578.

Singer, P. 1979. *Practical Ethics.* Cambridge: Cambridge University Press.

United Nations. 1995. *The Copenhagen Declaration and Programme of Action: World Summit for Social Development.* New York: United Nations.

———. 1999. "Further Initiatives for the Implementation of the Outcome of the World Social Summit for Social Development." Report of the Secretary General, Preparatory Committee for the Special Session of the General Assembly, New York: United Nations, May 17–28, 1999.

UNDP. 1995. *Poverty Eradication: A Policy Framework for Country Strategies.* New York: UNDP.

———. 1997. *Human Development Report: Human Development to Eradicate Poverty.* New York: UNDP.

———. 1999. *Human Development Report 1999: Globalisation with a Human Face.* New York: Oxford University Press.

———. 2003. *Millennium Development Goals: A Compact among Nations to End Human Poverty.* New York: UNDP and Oxford University Press.

UNICEF. 2000. *Poverty Reduction Begins with Children.* New York: UNICEF.

Walker, A. and C. Walker, eds. 1997. *Britain Divided: The Growth of Social Exclusion in the 1980s and 1990s.* London: Child Poverty Action Group.

World Bank. 1990. Assistance Strategies to Reduce Poverty. Washington, D.C.

———. 2001. *World Development Report 2000/2001: Attacking Poverty.* Oxford University Press.

———. 2004. *World Development Report 2004: Making Services Work for Poor People.* New York: Oxford University Press.

———. 2005. *World Development Report 2005: Imporving Investment Climate for Growth and Poverty Reduction.* New York: Oxford University Press.

Further Readings

George, V. and P. Wilding. 2002. *Globalisation and Human Welfare.* Basingstoke: Palgrave.

HM Treasury. 2002. *Tackling Poverty: A Global New Deal: A Modern Marshall Plan for the Developing World.* London: HM Treasury.

Townsend, P. and D. Gordon. 2002. *World Poverty: New Policies to Defeat an Old Enemy.* Bristol, UK: The Policy Press.

Watkins, K. 2002. *Rigged Rules and Double Standards: Trade, Globalisation and the Fight against Poverty.* Oxford: Oxfam.

Weblinks

World Bank Poverty Net
www.worldbank.org/poverty/index.htm

Third World Network
www.twnside.org.sg/index.htm

Focus on Global South
www.focusweb.org

The Development Gap
www.developmentgap.org

Poverty Mapping
www.povertymap.net

Southern African Regional Poverty Network (SAPRN)
www.sarpn.org.za

CHAPTER 26

GOOD GOVERNANCE IN A GLOBALIZING ERA

Objectives

The concept of **good governance** has emerged at the forefront of contemporary thinking about how to achieve development in the countries of the **global South**. Development theorists and policy makers use the term "good governance" to convey the idea that development requires more than implementing the right economic policies. Rather, development also involves political and social institutions and values. Indeed, in the mid-1990s, many authors and policy makers began to argue that an overemphasis on the economic dimensions of development had led to widespread failures in development strategies since the 1980s. Consequently, at the turn of the millennium, development theory has had to become more attuned to the insights of political science and sociology. In this manner, the World Bank has suggested that good governance represents a *missing link* in the conditions necessary to promote sustained development in the countries of the South. In the World Bank's presentation, good governance is about public administrations becoming more efficient, transparent, and accountable to their populations. These factors include curtailing corruption and enforcing the rule of

MARCUS TAYLOR

law equally and fairly. Given that the good governance strategy emphasizes the importance of political systems in the achievement of development, it represents an important step for political science in its relationship to development theory. This chapter highlights how different strands of post-World War II development thinking have conceived of the appropriate relationship between the state and the economy and, thus, the ideal relationship between politics and economics.

Introduction

We begin this exploration by asking ourselves what we understand by the notion of development. Drawing upon the classical political economy tradition of such authors as Adam Smith—whose 1776 book *The Wealth of Nations* is regarded as a milestone in economic thought—development has commonly been understood in terms of the ability of a society to produce the goods required to satisfy the needs of the population. Improving the capacity of societies to produce necessary goods offers a potential solution to scarcity and poverty. Furthermore, the process of removing humankind from an unending toil to achieve subsistence offers the basis for personal and social development by increasing the amount of time available to improve human potentials. This can, therefore, be seen as paving the way for social, cultural, and political progress.

This modern notion of development emerged with the birth of industrial capitalism in eighteenth century Europe, a time when processes of industrialisation and the mass production of goods were becoming more widespread. Development has subsequently been portrayed as a transformation of traditional agrarian societies to industrialized, mass consumption societies in the model of the capitalist countries of the West. In the period following World War II, the leading currents in development theory suggested that this transformation would be a natural occurrence in all regions of the globe. This belief that all countries would follow the same trajectory from traditional to modern industrial societies was known as **modernization theory**. The theory proposed that traditional societies would move in a series of stages from undeveloped agrarian societies through to fully industrialized ones. Societies were envisaged to adopt increasingly Western social and cultural attitudes and more advanced forms of economic organization at each step of the way. Put simply, in the modernization paradigm, development is a natural process of the rest becoming like the West. Since the post-War period, this conceptualisation of development as a transition from traditional society to modern society has been dominant in both the academic theory and also in guiding policy makers. Proponents in the West suggested that the transition from traditional to modern could be speeded up by the diffusion of Western values in underdeveloped societies. In the 1950s, therefore, a common form of development aid was the provision of clocks and condoms, which were intended to impart Western ideas of time and family management (Corbridge, 1995).

Competing ideas about development, however, have been extremely critical of modernization theory. First, authors who can loosely be drawn together under the paradigm of **dependency theory** suggest that modernization theory is flawed because it does not take into account global and historical dynamics. As such, dependency theorists argue that the underdeveloped countries of the South are part of a world economic and political system that frustrates their ability to achieve modernization. They emphasize the existence of an unfair trading system that began in the colonial period of Western domination and that continues to undervalue the products of the developing world. They also highlight the penetration of Southern economies by Western **multinational corporations** that control global research and technology and that repatriate profits and goods from the South back to the West. Finally, the extraction of wealth through the interest on debt has also been highlighted as an important factor that has held back countries in the South. Under these conditions, dependency theorists argue, the global South will not achieve the goal of modernization. Underdevelopment is not a question of societies being at a backward stage between traditional and modern but is the result of specific global historical relations. To avoid being trapped in a subordinate relationship to the North, therefore, dependency theorists recommend that the countries of the South refashion fundamentally their linkages with the advanced capitalist countries in a manner that allows them to pursue more independent paths toward development.

A more recent strand of thought, sometimes labelled **post-development**, offers a different critique of modernization theory. Post-development authors tend to question the concept of development as modernization. Given that the overall number of people living in poverty in the world has increased greatly over the last 50 years, that inequalities between the North and South have continued to grow, and that continued industrialization poses serious environmental questions, these authors suggest that we need to reconsider and move beyond the very idea of development as currently understood. This notion of development, they argue, is a profoundly Western idea that has been imposed on the South to the exclusion of alternative and locally specific conceptions of society and well-being. As such, post-development theorists often use complex strands of cultural theory to show how the language and practices of development serve to marginalize local forms of knowledge and community development schemes (Rahnema, 1997).

Post-War Development Strategies

National-Developmentalism

In the period following World War II, the colonial empires of the Western countries broke down into a host of newly independent countries. In the colonial period, these countries had been assimilated within a **colonial division of labour**. They exported raw materials to the Western colonial centres, where the latter were processed into industrial goods. Subsequently, Southern countries would then import back the industrial goods they required. With independence, however, there were both political and economic reasons for governments in these new states to try to break this colonial economic relationship and promote industrialization at home. Economists, such as Raúl Prebisch, at the United Nations Economic Commission for Latin America, argued that the value of raw materials would always tend to decrease compared with industrial products. Therefore, countries that concentrated on raw material production would be trapped into producing more just to be able to import the same amount of industrial goods. This provided an extremely influential rationale for attempting to break the colonial division of labour through industrialization in the South.

Promoting national industrialization became known as national-developmentalism, where industrialization was seen as the route toward modernization and development. It was widely recognized, however, that industrial development was unlikely to occur in many developing countries without significant stimulus. With markets in the South being relatively small and unstable, potential investors were unwilling to establish firms owing to the risks involved. Additionally, firms in the advanced industrialized countries were already mass-producing industrial goods, and therefore, it was often very difficult for local firms to start up owing to this competition. As a potential solution to some of these problems, states in the South began to play a considerable role by intervening in markets to establish the conditions for industrialization. Political intervention by states was deemed necessary to create the economic conditions in which the global South could industrialize and develop. Moreover, the example of the Soviet Union, which had experienced dramatic industrial expansion through state control of the economy, also gave weight to the importance of the role of the state in economic development.

It was envisaged that state-promoted industrialization would allow countries to replace industrial imports with locally produced goods. This development strategy is commonly referred to as **import-substitution industrialization** (ISI). Within the strategy of ISI, states attempted to shield domestic markets from foreign competition through tariffs. By implementing tariffs, foreign goods would have to pay a surcharge to the government on entering a country, and this made them more expensive in local markets. In turn, this meant that local firms were better able to succeed because they did not have to compete with cheaper foreign products. The ISI strategy did not mean that Southern countries were closed off from the global economy. On the contrary, under ISI strategies, Southern countries remained very much involved in the global economy. They continued to export raw materials and used the money earned from these to aid their industrial sectors. Also, countries often encouraged multinational corporations to set up local branch plants in order to boost domestic industries.

To complement these protectionist policies, states tended to make a series of direct interventions in the domestic economy to promote industrialization. These interventions included providing infrastructure (e.g., roads and electricity), loans, and technical advice for industrial development. More often than not, the money for these initiatives was taken from the earnings of raw material exports, which were reinvested by the state in order to create industry. In addition, states also tended to keep the price of food low in order to help create and sustain an urban working class that would work in the new industrial sectors. Provision of health and education services also aided this latter goal.

In the early years of its implementation, between the 1940s and the 1960s, the ISI strategy proved to be very successful. At this time, countries in the South benefited from a period of sustained economic expansion at a global level. High prices for primary exports on world markets allowed many countries in the South to redeploy these export earnings into industrialization projects. Also, the Cold War geopolitical environment led to political and financial support from major Western powers so long as the developing countries pursued capitalist, rather than socialist, modernization strategies. As such, the years between the end of World War II and the 1960s were ones of rapid economic growth in the South, with many countries experiencing considerable expansion of basic industrial sectors. These years also witnessed wider changes in society associated with industrialization, such as escalating urbanization as people left rural areas to come to the cities. However, these results were often extremely uneven and did not replicate the ideas of modernization theory of a smooth transition from traditional to modern societies.

It is possible to highlight two specific key weaknesses in the ISI development strategy. First, ISI tended to be successful only in building basic industrial goods industries (e.g., simple consumer goods, such as soap, shoes, and so on) but was far less successful in developing more sophisticated industries (such as steel, cars, and so on). Overall, many ISI industries did not reach the productivity levels of Western industries, making them inefficient in global terms. This meant that they could not export to the West and remained dependent on small domestic markets. As the productivity of firms within the ISI fell behind that of international firms, their products became less competitive, and this necessitated further help from governments, such as stricter tariffs, more loans, and so on. Second, at a social level, the ISI strategies focused heavily on the urban-industrial realm. This meant that new industries provided some good jobs for a relatively privileged urban industrial working class but left many others in both urban and rural areas in conditions of underemployment. These inequalities exacerbated social tensions in rural areas and, in Latin America, for example, led to the growth of massive urban shantytowns.

Such problems were greatly intensified by a global economic slowdown that took hold in the 1970s and which led to falling prices for raw material exports from Southern countries. Less money from exports meant less money with which to support industrialization. Moreover, escalating economic problems translated into growing social pressures as various social groups put pressure on governments to help them in times of economic upheaval. In response, states often attempted to overcome what were seen as short-term problems by borrowing money from international banks. However, many countries became very rapidly indebted at unsustainable levels. When, in the early 1980s, the United States of America raised interest rates, many countries in the global South faced insurmountable debts and bankruptcy. This crisis, which erupted in 1982, was known as the **Debt Crisis**, and marked a turning point for development strategies in the South.

Neo-Liberal Structural Adjustment

The Debt Crisis brought a dramatic culmination to the escalating social and economic problems that had been growing in the 1970s. In response to the crisis, there was a growing consensus that current development strategies needed to be changed. However, there was much less agreement about how the change should proceed. The strategy that became predominant across most of Latin America, Africa, and the Caribbean was one that promised a solution by creating a dramatically new relationship between the state and the economy (politics and economics). This strategy—commonly known as **neo-liberal structural adjustment** or the **Washington Consensus**—was strongly advocated by the IMF and the World Bank, which made access to their loans conditional on adopting this policy approach.

Neo-liberal structural adjustment is based on a theory drawn from neo-classical economics. It argues that all economic actions conducted between freely interacting individuals are beneficial for all parties concerned. By generalizing this theory to the level of the market as a whole, it suggests that markets present the perfect manner of harmonizing individual economic decisions to the benefit of society in general. As such, resting on the belief that markets promote rationality, efficiency and the optimal distribution of resources within an economy, neo-liberal theory proposes that development is best left to market forces.

In practice, this meant that the state should not intervene in the economy. In other words, economics should be free from political interventions. All of the forms of state intervention common to national-developmentalism were accused of being profoundly counter-productive. This was because, according to neo-liberal theory, state intervention did, at best, what the market would do if left to itself. At worst, state intervention created distortions in the economy that would eventually lead to economic stagnation and crisis. From this perspective, states are not in a position to assume an economic role as they are subject to human failures, including corruption and the promotion of the particular interests of powerful groups. In contrast, the market is understood as a rational institution representing the common good. To avoid economic stagnation and achieve development, therefore, the market should be freed from political intervention because, when allowed to proceed without interference, market forces will always bestow maximum benefits upon society (Fine, 2001).

The strategy of neo-liberal structural adjustment, therefore, sought to remove the state from as many of its economic and social functions as possible. Moreover, given the depth of the Debt Crisis in the global South in the early 1980s, it was suggested that this process of creating a minimalist state should occur as rapidly as possible. Many countries instigated what was termed **shock therapy**—a program of rapidly removing political regulation and interventions in markets. By following these basic premises, the idea was that the countries would resume strong and stable economic growth and that society in general would benefit. We can identify two key components of the neo-liberal strategy.

First, **economic liberalization** aimed at opening economies to global market forces by removing any barriers (such as tariffs) to the entry or exit of foreign products and investment. If local companies could not compete on a global level, then they were deemed to be inefficient and to be liquidated. With economic liberalization, investment was intended to move into areas that promised global competitiveness as indicated by market forces. Specifically, the countries of the South were encouraged to allow investment to concentrate in export sectors, including raw materials and agricultural goods. For example, if a country produces bananas at a price that is competitive on world markets, then this should be its area of specialization. As such, neo-liberal structural adjustment decreed that all countries should specialize in whatever economic areas that global market forces dictate and that the political intervention of the state should not be used to change those outcomes. Second, as the state was designated as the source of problems in the South, neo-liberal structural adjustment suggested that the state should be cut back as much as possible. This included drastically reducing government spending, tight control on budgets, large privatization programs to end state ownership of industries, and the promotion of the privatized delivery of social services, such as pensions and health care (Taylor, 2003).

When highlighting the strengths and weaknesses of this approach, it is worth distinguishing between short-term and medium-term effects. In the short term, neo-liberal structural adjustment successfully countered the immediate features of the Debt Crisis. As such, through the implementation of shock therapy, many countries with severe economic imbalances in the 1980s managed to significantly reduce these problems. Moreover, by cutting back on state expenditures, the strategy also managed to free up resources for states to pay back their debts to Western banks. This latter feature, however, has led some critics to suggest that neo-liberal structural adjustment had more to do with the interests of Western banks than the promotion of development in the South.

However, significant problems within neo-liberal structural adjustment became immediately evident. First and foremost, shock therapy caused intense social upheaval. The rapid removal of state protection for domestic industries led many companies into bankruptcy. This, in turn, created mass unemployment, falling wages, and growing poverty (Green, 2003). Moreover, the downscaling of social expenditures in such areas as education, health, and housing exacerbated this trend. Indeed, growing social polarization has been a common trend across Latin America and Africa in the era of neo-liberal structural adjustment (see Chapter 25). As starkly manifested in Russia's post-1990 experiences with neo-liberal reforms, rapid liberalization provided the conditions upon which individuals with significant resources were able to benefit greatly, whereas a substantial proportion of the population have been unable to find any satisfactory employment (Clarke, 2002). This raises questions about the soundness of neo-liberal theory, which sees the economy as the harmonious sum of freely acting individuals, rather than as a social institution characterized by asymmetrical power relations.

In the medium term, several features are worth noting. First, by asserting that countries should focus on exports to global markets, many countries (particularly Sub-Saharan Africa) have gone back to producing predominantly agricultural and mineral goods for export. Ironically, this has returned some countries to a situation that resembles the colonial division of labour—the very condition that national-developmentalism originally set out to change. Primary exports are vulnerable to turbulent market prices, and the overall trend has been for these prices to fall with respect to industrial goods. Furthermore, falling export prices has occurred, in part, because with many countries implementing structural adjustment programs at the same time, international markets for raw material exports tended to get flooded (Milanovic, 2003).

Second, international investment, which was intended by neo-liberal policy makers to be the driving force of the developing economies, has not gone to those countries that have been most faithful to neo-liberal policies. Rather, it has tended to go most heavily to those countries where the state has retained a more sizeable role in providing the conditions for investment, specifically the countries of East Asia, such as China, Korea, and Taiwan and the South East Asian nations of Malaysia, Thailand, and Singapore (Lieten, 2001). At the same time, in Latin America, where neo-liberal structural adjustment has been implemented more faithfully, the majority of new jobs have been created in small informal-sector companies, where there is little regulation, poor working conditions, and lower pay (Munck, 2002).

This raises an important question that has proved to be something of an Achilles' heel for the advocates of neo-liberal ideas at a global level. With very few exceptions, the countries that demonstrated the highest levels of economic development during the 1980s and 1990s were those that were far more cautious about embracing the free-market policies advocated by neo-liberal structural adjustment. As indicated in the previous paragraph, the countries that we have come to know as the "Asian Tigers," owing to their fast rates of economic growth during the 1970s to 1990s, have employed development strategies that in many ways contradict the neo-liberal emphasis on a minimalist state (Kiely, 1998). This factor, alongside others, forced such actors as the World Bank into an ongoing rethink of neo-liberal development strategies. The advent of good governance as a solution to development problems is a result of this rethinking.

Good Governance

FACED WITH THE FAILURE OF NEO-LIBERAL STRUCTURAL ADJUSTMENT TO deliver strong and stable growth, and its attendant social dislocations, the World Bank and other advocates of this development strategy were forced to reconsider some of their policies. As early as 1989, a World Bank report on Africa identified the lack of good governance as feeding growing poverty and uneven development on that continent. In the past decade, however, the concept had been widely embraced, especially after social movements attacked the World Bank and the IMF for their doctrinaire adherence to neo-liberal structural adjustment. At present, whenever the IMF and the World Bank lend money to the poorest countries in the world, these countries are expected not only to adopt neo-liberal economic policies but also to make a commitment to promoting good governance. These agreements are known as **Poverty Reduction Strategy Papers**.

The idea behind good governance is that while the goals of neo-liberal structural adjustment are to be retained, it is also necessary to provide an adequate political environment in which markets can operate to their full capacity. In this view, the reason that neo-liberal structural adjustment did not live up to expectations can be found in the failure of surrounding institutions to allow markets to work properly. In response, the notion of good governance presents a number of necessary political and social conditions that have to be met for markets to work effectively and bring about development.

Good governance proponents argue that in order for market-orientated development strategies to be effective, the political systems that surround them must be accountable, transparent, responsive, efficient, and inclusive. More concretely, this means that political institutions and the processes of making decisions and delivering public services must be free from corruption, open to public scrutiny, operate according to clearly established rules, and reflect the voices of all social groups, including the poor. An example drawn from the World Bank helps elaborate the good governance perspective. In respect to the fundamental issue of poverty, the World Bank emphasizes that such factors as corruption and political voicelessness impede poor people from adequately participating in markets and inhibit them from using their resources in the most efficient manner possible. This exclusion, thus, perpetuates their poverty. By clamping down on corruption and enabling poor people to adequately express their opinions in the political system, good governance is intended to create a much fairer society that will allow markets to provide benefits to all members.

In this manner, good governance refers to states providing the correct political framework in which market interactions can proceed smoothly, whether at the level of big corporations or of poor individuals seeking jobs. It includes helping disseminate important information about economic conditions and ensuring that all involved parties adhere to the formal rules and do not try to gain special advantages. Where decisions have to be made, good governance emphasizes that this should be done in an inclusive manner.

The question of whether we consider the good governance paradigm adequate to the task of promoting development largely depends on our wider understanding of market relations and development. To start, good governance emphasizes that, where structural adjustment has not worked, the inadequacies of the country's political institutions are largely to blame, rather than the structural adjustment policies themselves. Clearly, there is some substance to this argument. Fighting corruption and promoting the political participation of all social groups are positive goals. However, the World Bank appears to overestimate the importance of these factors in providing the conditions for economic growth. For example, China has been the fastest growing economy in the world over the last decade and yet would rank very low on the World Bank's scale of good governance. Furthermore, proponents of good governance also assume that all development issues can be resolved by a consensus among all involved parties. The history of development practice over the last half-century, however, has provided ample evidence that there are fundamental conflicts of interest that cannot be easily settled through consensual deliberations.

The good governance paradigm ultimately continues to rest on the neo-liberal premises that markets are inherently rational and that market-based solutions to development issues are the only viable solutions to uneven development and poverty. By blaming the political environment for the failure of structural adjustment to succeed, good governance denies that there may be inherent problems in the project of market-driven development. In this respect, good governance represents an amendment to neo-liberal structural adjustment policies, but it leaves intact the underlying idea that free markets and a minimalist state is the only route though which to achieve development.

Several issues can be raised with this perspective. First, it is far from certain that outside of the models of World Bank economists, markets operate in an entirely rational manner. For example, the integration of many countries with global financial markets in the 1990s led to serious social and economic dislocation, when global financial panics created several large financial crises, including the Mexican Peso Crisis of 1994–95 and the East Asian Debacle of 1997–98. Second, in claiming that integration into global markets is the primary cure for poverty in the global South, the World Bank ignores how market integration can reproduce poverty. For example, the global textiles industry involves large networks of female workers in South East Asia who labour for poverty-level wages to create clothes that are sold in the West. Third, there is significant amount of evidence that direct state intervention can be pivotal to establishing viable industrial sectors. Many sources indicate that state investment can encourage private investors to follow suit. This has been the experience of the East Asian countries that have been most successful in promoting economic development (Kiely, 1998). In short, it is far from clear that the state cannot play an important role in promoting economic development. In fact, growing evidence suggests that building state capacity in manners that transcend the limited goals of good governance is an extremely important facet of successful development strategies.

As a final point, it is also worth noting that it is somewhat hypocritical of international organizations, such as the IMF and the World Bank, whose decisions are undertaken behind closed doors, to promote transparency and accountability as essential factors in client countries. While many observers suggest that the World Bank and the IMF should be leading by example, the dominant forces involved in these organizations (such as the United States executive) prefer to keep key decision-making processes away from public scrutiny and inclusion.

Summary

This chapter has introduced important debates in development theory, with a focus on how different perspectives understand the appropriate relationship between politics and economics. It has underscored how development has often been seen as a process of countries proceeding toward a modern industrial society. In the immediate post-World War II period, the strategy of import-substitution industrialization argued that in order to achieve modernization, the state would have to become a central player in the economic development of the country. The profound crisis of many of these countries in the 1970s and 1980s, however, created a space in which other ideas emerged. Neo-liberal structural adjustment was the strategy that became ascendant, not least owing to the political pressure exerted on governments by the World Bank and the IMF. This strategy reversed the earlier emphasis on state intervention and suggested that markets would work best if left with minimal political direction or regulation. In turn, the failure of neo-liberal structural adjustment to deliver on its promises of sustained economic development has led to a new emphasis on good governance as being a necessary pre-condition for markets to work effectively. Nevertheless, many questions can be asked as to whether good governance represents a significant enough change to the original neo-liberal paradigm to adequately address the latter's failings.

Discussion Questions

1. What is development? Should development be considered as a process of "the rest" becoming more like the West?
2. Was neo-liberal structural adjustment an adequate response to the crisis of development in the early 1980s?
3. Is the achievement of good governance sufficient to promote development in the global South?

References

Clarke, S. 2002. *Making Ends Meet in Contemporary Russia: Secondary Employment, Subsidiary Agriculture and Social Networks.* Cheltenham: Edward Elgar Press.

Fine, B. 2001. *Social Capital versus Social Theory.* London: Routledge Press.

Green, D. 2003. *Silent Revolution—The Rise and Crisis of Market Economics in Latin America.* 2nd Edition. New York: Monthly Review Press.

Kiely, R. 1998. *Industrialisation and Development: A Comparative Analysis.* London: Routledge.

Lieten, K. 2001. "Multinationals and Development: Revisiting the Debate" in Schuurman F., ed., *Globalization and Development Studies: Challenges for the 21st Century.* London: Sage.

Milanovic, B. 2003. "The Two Faces of Globalization: Against Globalization as We Know It" *World Development* 31, 4, 667–683.

Munck, Ronaldo. 2002. *Globalisation and Labour.* London: Zed Books.

Rahnema, M., ed. 1997. *The Post-Development Reader.* London: Zed Books.

Taylor, M. 2003. "The Reformulation of Social Policy in Chile, 1973-2001: Questioning a Neoliberal Model" *Global Social Policy* 3, 1, 21–44.

Further Readings

Corbridge, S., ed. 1995. *Development Studies: A Reader.* London: Arnold.

World Bank. 2001. *World Development Report 2000/1—Attacking Poverty.* Oxford: Oxford University Press.

Pincus, J. and J. Winters, eds. 2002. *Reinventing the World Bank.* Ithaca, NY: Cornell University Press.

Weblinks

The World Bank's site for governance issues
www.worldbank.org/wbi/governance

The Third World Network
www.focusweb.org

The Development Gateway
www.developmentgateway.org

Glossary

absolute monarchy A state form resting on the claim that absolute power is vested in the monarch by God.

accountability The answerability of government representatives for their actions and inactions. It is a multi-faceted concept that usually implies such questions as accountability to whom? for what? and by what means?

accumulation policies Governmental actions designed to ensure that businesses operate as profitably as possible. Examples include low rates of taxation, minimal regulations, and investment in infrastructure, such as roads and telecommunications.

act utilitarianism This moral theory is a common variant of **consequentialism**. It stresses the utility likely to result from one's action or choice. In its moral context, utility tends to be defined in terms of the increase of pleasure and the decrease of pain.

ad-hoc committee A legislative committee established to investigate particular issues or events that normally disbands at the conclusion of its review.

agency A force, an acting subject, capable of transforming society.

agents of political socialization Institutions that serve to socialize people about the political system and political action. Agents of socialization include the family, educational institutions, the media, and political parties.

ahistorical A theory or approach to politics that discounts the importance of history in explaining political outcomes.

alienated Marx used the term *alienated*, or alienation, to describe the separation of the worker from the goods produced and the decisions made by the bourgeoisie under the capitalist mode of production.

alternative service theory The transfer of responsibility for program and service delivery to private sector providers, nonprofit organizations, or new public sector organizational forms.

anarcho-syndicalism A form of anarchism that calls for workers to be organized into "management" groups (syndicates) to collectively make decisions and organize production.

anarchy The absence of government at any level. The significance of anarchy at the international level is that it means, in effect, that sovereign states operate in a system in which there is no permanent authority that makes and enforces laws to regulate the behaviour of these states or the behaviour of other actors in world politics.

auditor general An officer of Parliament whose role it is to annually examine the government's financial management and report the findings to Parliament.

austerity A condition facing local governments globally as demands for municipal services grow but own-source revenues remain static (at best) and transfers from senior government levels decline.

authoritarian A dictatorial regime based on force, or the threat of force, and obedience to authority among the ruled.

authority Socially approved power and legitimacy. Weber identified three types of authority—traditional, charismatic, and rational-bureaucratic.

autonomy Self-direction; the ability to think, choose, and act solely on one's own, without guidance from another person or group. Individuals are described as autonomous when they are able to give themselves their own moral and intellectual guidelines.

baby boomers The generation born in Western societies between 1944 and 1965.

backbenchers Assembly members in parliamentary systems who are not members of the cabinet. These members sit in the back of the assembly, since the front benches are reserved for cabinet members.

balance of payments A summary of a country's transactions with the rest of the world. It effectively reports receipts earned through export trade of a country's goods and services as well as payments made to other countries for the import of goods and services. The balance of payments also tracks financial flows entering (recorded as gains) and exiting (recorded as losses) the country.

barter A system of exchange that transpires without money.

beggar-thy-neighbour Any policy that aims to increase a country's own competitive edge at the expense of another country's economic performance.

behaviouralism An approach in political analysis, dominant in the United States in the 1960s, that emphasizes the study of observable and quantifiable political attitudes and actions of individuals and the scientific search for enduring laws of politics.

bicameral system A political system in which the legislative assembly consists of two independent chambers.

bilateral An action or agreement taken by two parties, generally states.

biological determinism An assumption that a person's nature and possibilities are determined by biological factors alone.

boosterism A view of city politics in which the role of local government is to support expansion of the community's entrepreneurs at the expense of any and all other objectives.

bourgeois ideology A term associated with Marx that refers to those belief systems that serve to mask the inegalitarian nature of power relations under capitalism and preserve the power of the bourgeoisie.

bourgeoisie A term most often used in Marxist analysis to refer to the social class that owns the means of production, often also referred to as the capitalist class.

brokerage party A party that takes a non-doctrinal approach to politics and focuses on maintaining unity by providing all groups it perceives as significant with a voice.

bureaucracy An organization defined by a hierarchy of offices, by written communications and rules, by a clear division of labour, and by employment based on technical qualifications. Bureaucratic organizations are the norm today.

cadre political party A type of political party, small in membership and focused on winning elections. It is financed by a small number of large donors, usually corporations.

capitalism An economic system organized on the basis of private ownership of the means of production and the employment of wage-labour.

cartel party A new form of party organization funded by the state.

caucus A group of sitting legislators from each party or a meeting in which the group discusses party policy and strategy.

charismatic authority Power and legitimacy accorded to individuals on the basis of their extraordinary personality or other personal qualities.

checks and balances A set of institutional measures adopted in presidential systems allowing the legislative and executive branches to effectively check the power of the other branch.

citizenship Membership in a nation-state defined by territory and sovereignty. Membership is typically accompanied by various rights and obligations. There are three important aspects of citizenship in liberal democracies—liberty (freedom), equality, and solidarity (feelings of belonging).

city-regions Used as a synonym for census metropolitan areas. In Canada, this refers to an urban core, and its working commutershed, with a population over 100 000. Although one city is usually the focus, the region may contain many other municipal governments containing the larger part of the population.

civic republicanism An approach to community that encourages commitment on the part of individual citizens to the public or community good.

civil rights Citizenship rights that are necessary for the protection of an individual's freedom. Examples include freedom of speech and the right to own property.

civil society The arena of political and associational activity located between the state and the family.

civil society organizations Nonprofit/voluntary associations of many diverse types—business associations, consumers, criminal syndicates, development groups, environmentalists, farmers, human rights advocates, labour unions, women's networks, among others—that participate in political activity and try to shape the policies of governments and intergovernmental organizations.

clash of civilizations A phrase coined by political scientist Samuel Huntington to describe emerging conflict between peoples and states of different civilizations. Civilizations are wide identities based on fundamentally different religious and cultural world views.

class analysis An approach to the study of politics and society that assumes that the most important explanatory factor is the division of populations by economic class and that politics is primarily about the necessary antagonisms between the owners of the means of production and non-owners or workers.

class politics A form of national politics, especially party politics, that is organized around citizen/voter identification on the basis of class position (working class, middle class, upper class) instead of on the basis of, for example, religion or ethnicity.

class struggle For Marx, this represents the antagonism between the bourgeoisie and the proletariat. This antagonism is one of the key defining features of the capitalist mode of production and one that will ultimately result in a social revolution lead by the proletariat.

Cold War The antagonistic relationship between the United States of America and the Soviet Union approximately between 1946 and 1991. Although these two superpower states (and their allies) frequently clashed, open fighting never occurred directly between them.

collective ministerial responsibility A principle found in parliamentary systems that requires cabinet members to be collectively accountable to the legislature for executive actions.

colonialism A practice of appropriating, dominating, and, in some cases, settling other territories and peoples, usually associated with European expansionism of the fifteenth to twentieth centuries.

colonial division of labour A system of economic and wealth production that divides labour, resources, and benefits unequally between the imperial power and the colony, the colonizer, and the colonized.

common law Judge-made law that is sometimes synonymous with unwritten law.

communitarianism Set of political ideas that emphasizes the importance of community ties, or of social relationships, to human happiness and the good life, in opposition to liberal-individualist interpretations of human needs or human nature.

community A group of individuals who identify themselves, or are viewed by others, as having something significant in common.

comparative advantage An economic principle that holds that a country will benefit the most if it specializes in trading the goods and services it can produce with the greatest relative efficiency and at the lowest cost (i.e., relative to other countries).

conditional grant A transfer of funds from one government to support the more local administration of its priorities and programs by another level of government on the condition that the recipient agrees to meet the donor government's terms and conditions.

confidence chamber A legislative chamber in parliamentary systems where the loss of a legislative vote normally requires the resignation of the executive.

consequentialism A set of political or moral beliefs that emphasize the moral importance of the consequences of one's actions and decisions. Consequentialist moral theory is contrasted to **deontology** and **virtue ethics**.

conservatism An ideology based on the belief that society is an organic (collective) whole. Moreover, conservatives believe that the best form of society is hierarchical—a society in which everyone knows their place, a society where some rule and the rest are ruled. Order and tradition, not freedom and reason, are key political values.

constituency A designated group of citizens who are entitled to elect a public official whose duties are to act for them as their representative. The term is also used in its plural form to refer to a set of electoral districts each containing its own set of constituents.

constitutional convention A non-legal constitutional rule that is not enforceable by the courts.

constitutional interpretation A method by which the judiciary undertake interpretation of written constitutions.

constitutionally entrenched rights Rights that are constitutionally guaranteed and, thus, may only be removed or added to by an amendment to the constitution, rather than by ordinary legislation.

constitutive representation The process of giving meaning to political interest by defining the political identity of those who are being represented.

core A term used in dependency theory to describe the developed capitalist countries (North) which exploit the underdeveloped periphery (South).

corporatism State control and mediation of relations among business, labour, and organized civil society sectors.

cosmopolitanism Rests on the idea that the contemporary world is becoming a single global community with shared values and interests that will require transnational democratic institutions for political action.

crisis From the Greek *kreinen*, which means decision, this word usually refers to a turning point after which things will be different.

Crown corporation A corporation owned by the government that engages in commercial activity often in competition with private firms. In most countries, such firms are called public corporations or government corporations.

cultural capital A term that stems from the work of sociologist Pierre Bourdieu, who argues that success in the educational system is determined by the extent to which individual students have internalized and conform with the dominant culture.

cultural identity A form of group identification resting on shared cultural characteristics, rather than, for example, shared class position. The term raises a central debate about whether equality in liberal democracies is best achieved by "difference blindness" or by recognizing and valuing "difference."

cultural studies An interdisciplinary (also called anti-disciplinary) approach to understanding power and culture. It draws from Marx and other writers to examine how groups with the least power use culture as a means to express resistance or identity.

culture A shared way of life that is transmitted socially, not biologically.

de facto In reality, despite what may be prescribed in a constitutional document.

de jure That which is prescribed in law.

Debt Crisis When Mexico defaulted on its foreign debt repayments in 1982, this raised the spectre of generalized debt default across the developing world and the collapse of many Western banks. The Debt Crisis was the culmination of growing economic crisis at a global level during the 1970s.

decision makers Individuals in government who make authoritative policy decisions on behalf of their states, such as presidents, prime ministers, foreign secretaries, secretaries of state, members of parliament or legislatures, and so on.

deductive method Analytical method that characterizes the normative field of political philosophy. Political philosophers start from an axiom (or principle) and then deduce from this principle.

delegate A representative who votes the way those he or she represents indicate. In practice, the term refers to anyone elected to a party convention regardless of how they approach their representative role.

delegate model of representation A perspective on representation that assumes that the actions of representatives should not be found to be at odds with the expressed wishes of the represented.

democracy Rule by many, characterized by leadership selection through elections, constitutionalism, and the rule of law. From the Greek *demos* (people) and *kratos* (rule).

democratic deficit A phrase used to describe the lack of trust in politicians and political institutions. Such cynicism is understood to reduce direct public participation in the process of politics because of a perceived inability to influence public policy.

deontology A liberal, individualist approach to ethics and politics that emphasizes the principles upon which one acts or judges. It is strictly a formal, rule-based moral theory because it ignores substantive questions concerning the consequences of one's actions, one's relationship to others, or one's commitment to particular traditions or communities. Deontology is contrasted to **virtue ethics** and **consequentialism**.

department A government administrative body over which a cabinet minister has direct management and control.

dependency theory A theory of development that attempts to explain the gap between living standards in the rich core-industrial countries and the poor peripheral countries of the South. It argues that underdevelopment in the periphery is the result of the exploitation of the countries in that area by core industrial countries, which perpetuates a situation of dependent relations that keeps the countries in the periphery "poor."

deputy minister A non-elected member of the bureaucracy who reports to a cabinet minister who assumes administrative responsibility for a government department.

deregulation The process of placing matters that had been subject to overseeing by state agencies outside the state's jurisdiction. Deregulation is a governmental practice associated with the neo-liberal state. It is justified on the basis that regulations needlessly impede the profitability of business.

descriptive representation The condition of descriptive representation is met only to the extent that our legislatures are a representative microcosm of the broader society.

devolution A transfer of political authority, usually by law or regulation, from one actor to another.

dialectical relationship A concept that proposes that history progresses through a process of thesis–antithesis that results in synthesis. A dialectical relationship argues that ideas and material circumstances interact to create historical change. Marx traces key outcomes of dialectical relations as the movement in history from slavery to feudalism to capitalism.

dictatorship An authoritarian or semi-authoritarian regime headed by one individual or a very small group.

dictatorship of the proletariat The stage immediately following socialist revolution, according to Marx. The dictatorship represents the empowerment of workers, the public ownership and management of production, and a transition phase to communism.

differentiated citizenship A conceptualization of citizenship that calls for an explicit recognition of group difference to ensure inclusion and full participation. This recognition would entail the public provision of resources and institutional mechanisms for the recognition and representation of disadvantaged groups.

direct democracy A system of government in which political decisions are made directly by citizens.

direct representation The idea or claim that a person can be represented only by someone whom they directly authorized to do so by voting for that candidate. Those who voted for a losing candidate in an election cannot be and are not represented by the winning candidate.

disciplinary power The ability to produce appropriate behaviours through social definitions of what is normal and expected. Conveys the idea of self-policing and the realization of social interests and goals without resort to force.

distributive justice A principle for guiding the fair distribution of things among people. For Aristotle, this principle entailed distributing more to those who are "good" than to those who are "not good."

discourse An internally coherent story or world view. Popularized in the work of Foucault, it advances the idea that the naming of things and their description through written or spoken language shapes both individuals and the material world around them. Different understandings of truth and reality are contained and find their meaning within discourses.

dividing practices Stigmatizing, controlling, and excluding different groups through the practice of naming as deviant—for example, homosexuals, or welfare dependents.

division of labour An economic system's determination of the specific roles and functions performed, and by whom, within production processes.

doctrinal party An avowedly ideological party that seeks to fit policies into rational value-oriented schemes. Ideological fidelity is more important than winning elections.

doctrine of utility The proposition that the standard by which all human action, public and private, should be judged is the greatest happiness of the greatest number.

domino theory or **domino effect** The idea that if one state falls to communist domination, other neighbouring states will also fall, either through direct aggression or subversion.

economic liberalization A process by which the politically imposed barriers to the movement of goods and money are dismantled.

egalitarianism A concept that encompasses a belief in the essential equal worth of all persons, and the view that social institutions should ensure equality of opportunity (economic, social, and political) for each individual to realize his or her needs and goals.

electoral formulae A rule system to determine the winner of an election.

electoral system A set of laws and regulations specifying the rules to be followed and the procedures to be used in organizing and conducting an election, especially as these pertain to indicating who may participate, the number of choices to be made, how voting is to take place, and by what rule offices are to be awarded to candidates based on their vote totals.

elite theory An approach to politics that assumes that all societies are divided into only two groups—the few who rule, usually in their own self-interest, and the many who are ruled.

empirical theory An approach to political analysis resting on the belief that knowledge is derived from what is observable, experienced, and/or validated by experimentation. It seeks to generate general explanations for seemingly distinct events through observation and comparison.

end of history A phrase used by political scientist Francis Fukuyama to describe the growing convergence of states and societies with a single, liberal democratic model of governance. The end of history refers to the end of the historic debate about superior systems.

epistemology A branch of philosophy concerned with issues of knowledge, its definition, what it is, how we acquire it, and the relationship between the knower and what is known.

equality A term conveying the idea of equal access to the political sphere, equal access to and benefit of the law, and equal access to social entitlements provided by the state.

essentialism The assumption that, by nature, all members of a group share the same core personal and social qualities. Essentialist thinking, for example, assumes that all women share the capacity to nurture.

ethics The philosophical study of standards of moral conduct and principles of moral judgment. Also called "moral philosophy." In general, a principle, belief, or value about what is morally good, or a system of such principles, beliefs, or values. From the Greek *ethos*, which means the general way of life of a culture or a people.

ethnic cleansing The systematic and forced removal or murder of members of an ethnic group from their geographic communities to change the ethnic composition of a region.

ethnocentric Prejudicial attitudes held by one group that feels its own values, customs, or behaviour are superior to any other. The term is also used in relation to political scientists who, often unconsciously, import assumptions or values from their own society into comparative research.

executive committee A part of council, chaired by the mayor and sometimes including the heads of standing committees, intended to co-ordinate municipal business and to give some limited political direction to council.

exploitation Marx argued that because workers must sell their labour power under the capitalist system, they are vulnerable to the whims and changes in economic fortune that beset the capitalist. This means that the workers' standard of living is constantly in jeopardy and that the worker is in a weaker social position as a result.

export-oriented industrialization An economic development strategy based on maximizing the export of national unprocessed and processed goods.

faction A division in society based on narrow group loyalty. Factions are seen as being at odds with the idea of the public good.

fairness A principle of distribution that is associated with equality in the modern era. For Marx, this principle involved redistribution, from each according to her ability, to each according to her need.

false consciousness A term, common in Marxist analyses, that conveys the idea that working-class consciousness is influenced by the dominant ideology of the bourgeoisie in ways that are not in the real interest of workers.

fascism A form of repressive authoritarian governance that eliminates democracy and maintains capitalism.

fatalism A belief that our fate is pre-determined by external forces, such as destiny or God.

federal constitution A constitution in which the sovereignty of the state is divided between national and sub-national governments.

federalism A political system in which constitutionally assigned powers are divided among two or more levels of government.

feminism A diverse set of ideas, grounded in the belief that patriarchal societies have oppressed women and united by the goal of claiming full citizenship for all women. Beyond this, feminists disagree about the roots of women's oppression, the appropriate strategies for contesting patriarchy, and about visions for a post-patriarchal society.

feminization of poverty A term describing the predominant gender of the poor.

feudalism An agrarian form of social and economic organization characterized by a strict hierarchy between the property-owning aristocracy and the landless peasants.

fiscal innovation New approaches that are developed to deal with fiscal austerity measures forced upon local governments; success appears to be correlated with growth in the high-tech and service economies, and with municipal co-option of local social movements; it may partly be measured by new participants in the policy process.

formalistic representation The condition of formalistic representation merely requires that legislative bodies are authorized and/or held accountable by regular elections.

franchise The legal right to vote in the election of some governmental official. Although the term *suffrage* is also used with this meaning, *franchise* specifies a right or privilege that is constitutional or statutory in its origin—that is, a formal legal right to vote in elections held in some jurisdiction.

freedom Traditionally meant the absence of interference and regulation in a person's life. It is coming to have a broader and more social meaning as the ability to live on one's own terms.

free vote A legislative vote that drops the requirement of party discipline normally adhered to in parliamentary assemblies.

fusion of power The integration of the executive and legislative branches in the parliamentary system.

gender A socially, politically, and economically constructed sex-code that prescribes what it means to be male or female in daily life.

gender parity Representation of men and women in proportion roughly equal to their distribution in the general population.

Gender-related Development Index Measures the experience of human deprivation and adjusts for the health and knowledge deprivation and overall economic well-being as experienced by girls and women.

genocide Acts committed with the intent to destroy, in whole or in part, a national, ethnical, racial, or religious group. Such acts include the killing of members of the group; causing serious bodily or mental harm to members of the group; deliberately inflicting on the group conditions of life calculated to bring about its physical destruction in whole or in part; imposing measures to prevent births within the group; and/or forcibly transferring children of the group to another group.

global city A modern-day city that has elaborate and independent economic, social, and political links with communities abroad that either subordinate, or bypass entirely, national and regional governments. Governing, social, and economic elites measure their community's success against other world cities outside their own national borders. Originally known as "world cities" as identified by urban planner Sir Peter Hall in 1966, and defined as post-industrial production sites encompassing those international firms who provide and innovate in corporate services and finance.

global economy Characterized by interconnected production sites all over the world that produce different component parts of a final product.

global governance The mechanisms and processes by which transnational actors—individuals, governments, non-governmental organizations, corporations—make decisions for and about the global community.

global insertion The economic and political location of a country within the global system of states and markets.

global South A term used to describe the heterogeneous countries that were once colonized by the West but have since won their independence. The term "global South" has increasingly replaced the terms "the Third World" and "developing countries."

globalism A world view advocating a single system of governance for the planet. Neo-liberalism is often described as neo-liberal globalism because it advocates the worldwide embrace of market-based principles of governance.

globality A term that describes the progressive shaping of the planet as a single political unit. Globality is associated with new communication technologies, the spread of consumerist culture, and population mobility and migration. Political issues and social problems are no longer isolated to one country but, instead, have global impacts and implications.

globalization The intensification of a world-scale reorientation of economic, technological, and cultural processes and activities that transcend state boundaries.

good governance The idea that in order for market-oriented development strategies to be effective, the political systems that surround them must be accountable, transparent, responsive, efficient, and inclusive.

governance The organized exercise of power; the manner in which we organize our common affairs.

government bill A legislative bill introduced by the cabinet in parliamentary systems.

harm principle The principle, classically attributed to John Stuart Mill, that a person's liberty can legitimately be restricted only to prevent direct harm to other persons.

head of government The position that assumes responsibility for the political and effective administration of government.

head of state The symbolic position that is assigned formal and ceremonial powers.

hegemony A term associated with the work of Antonio Gramsci to refer to the bourgeoisie's ideological domination of the working class, which results in the persistence of the capitalist system. Hegemony or *hegemon* is also used to describe the dominant country in the international system.

historical materialism A social-science approach based on the premise that a society's structure and political dynamics are driven by its mode of production.

human capital Emerged from economic ideas in the 1960s to connote the economic value of skills, knowledge, and good health to firms and corporations.

human development Promoted by the United Nations Development Program (UNDP) as a measurement of well-being that includes more than economic indicators. The UNDP annually publishes these results in a global **Human Development Index**.

Human Development Index See **human development**. A measure that combines life expectancy, adult literacy, Gross National Product, and education enrolments. It is used by the United Nations Development Program to compare countries with respect to human well-being. Country rankings are published each year in the UNDP Human Development Report.

Human Poverty Index A composite index designed to examine uneven development and poverty in terms that are not exclusively monetary.

human rights Rights that are asserted of all people on the basis that they are human beings.

humanism A philosophical belief system that puts an ideal person at the centre of philosophical reflection. This philosophy suggests that knowledge, happiness, and social and political fulfillment are entirely within human purview; religious or supernatural intervention in human affairs is not considered necessary. Rather than lament human imperfections, early humanists celebrated the human body, the ability to reason, and the capacity to produce beautiful art.

hybrid regimes Regimes that contain characteristics of two or more types.

ideal-type A mental model in the social sciences for categorizing and understanding social events.

identities The tendency of individuals and groups to develop a sense of who they are in relation to their shared cultural, sociological, and political attachments to each other.

identity-based community A group of people who share at least one identifiable characteristic, which members may carry into politics.

ideology A coherent set of ideas that explains and evaluates social conditions, helps people understand their place in society, and provides a program for social and political action. Ideology also consists of those beliefs and values that serve to legitimate a certain social order, the so-called dominant ideology, and those values and beliefs that may be said to oppose or challenge the dominant ideology.

imperialism An organization of the international political economy where the globe is divided among great powers into empires; associated with colonialism; for Marxists, the expansion of capital beyond single national markets.

import substitution industrialization A strategy for economic development in which state interventions are used in an attempt to build up a domestic industrial sector so as to reduce reliance on industrial imports.

indirect election A procedure for choosing office-holders in which the members of some group, organization, or governmental body, who are themselves directly elected by the citizens or by the members of their organization select the persons to hold an office from a set of candidates by voting among themselves.

individual ministerial responsibility Principle in parliamentary systems that requires ministers to assume responsibility before the legislature for the bureaucratic departments they direct.

inductive method An analytical method that aims to build empirically based theory or explanations from the observation of concrete events.

institutionalization A process whereby things that were once random or done with little conscious planning become deliberate, formalized, and expected.

instrumental representation The activity of acting or speaking for the represented.

Integrated Poverty Index Intended to assess poverty as experienced in rural areas.

interest-based community A group formed around concerns that bear directly, but not exclusively, on the members' political interests and that are usually represented in the political arena by organizations or interest groups.

interest party A political party that seeks to represent a particular interest in the electoral process, such as a region or a specific issue of concern. It does not make a full attempt to win power but raises sconsciousness about its concerns.

intergovernmental organizations International organizations that are composed of state governments, the United Nations being the pre-eminent example.

international community A group of governments, such as the United Nations, or the symbolic expression of the shared sentiments of people in different countries.

international division of labour A way of organizing the international economy wherein the factors of production (materials, labour, finance) are divided among countries.

international political economy A perspective on international relations that emphasizes the close relationship between economic factors, such as trade and investment, and political factors, such as policy settings and issues of distributive justice. IPE approaches generally analyze the interaction of states, markets, modes of production, class, politics, and culture in the international sphere.

internationalization of production The ability of companies to consider the productive resources of the globe as a whole and to decide to locate elements of complex globalized production systems at points that will produce the greatest cost advantage. It is reliant on an environment in which capital, technology, raw materials, and component parts are allowed to cross national jurisdictional boundaries with minimal or no regulation.

internationalization of the state The erosion of state authority in favour of external international forces that are able to exert tremendous influence on domestic agencies and on national policies.

international relations A field of political science concerned with relations among nation-states that engages philosophical, ethical, epistemological, and ontological questions in order to understand relations within the international sphere.

Jihad An Arabic word for "holy war" that is used by political scientist Benjamin Barber to describe the fanaticism of different cultural and national groups. These fanatics are allegedly at war with the growing influence of global consumer capitalism in their particular societies (see also **McWorld**).

judicial review The process whereby the courts judge the legality of political/administrative actions. Judicial review of the constitution refers to when the courts are asked to determine whether political/administrative actions conform to constitutional requirements.

Keynesianism An approach to the management of national economies that was developed by the British economist John Maynard Keynes. This approach was implemented by Western industrialized countries between 1945 and the mid-1970s. The central concern of Keynesianism was to counteract the boom-and-bust tendencies of capitalist economies. In periods of economic downturn, Keynesianism advocated increased public spending and lower levels of taxation to ensure that people would continue to purchase goods in the market. In periods of economic growth, public spending was to decrease and tax rates would rise, thereby curbing excessive growth and restoring balance to the public finances.

***laissez-faire* capitalism** A principle espoused by classical economists, such as Adam Smith, that government should minimize intervention in the capitalist market.

legal institutionalism An approach to politics that emphasizes the centrality of formal procedures, constitutions, and institutions.

legal-rational authority Power and legitimacy accorded on the basis of laws, formal rules, and impersonal procedures.

legal rights Rights that are recognized as law and therefore subject to authoritative adjudication and enforcement.

legal-rationalism A way of reasoning that follows the logic of the law.

legitimacy The quality of legal, moral, or social (among others) rightness. Since the beginning of the modern era, an act, decision, public policy, government, or law is most apt to be considered legitimate when it is based on reason. For instance, just as government is considered legitimate if it comes to power as a result of a fair and rational process, so a law shown to be irrational is considered illegitimate and struck down. In the medieval era, in contrast, legitimacy was conferred not by reason but by the authority vested in one of God's representatives, such as a king, priest, or another religious official.

legitimation Justification of the actions of the state to the population at large through policies that contribute to the authority of the state. Public health care, education, and transportation networks are examples of areas of public investment that are broadly supported by citizens and thus provide a rationale for the role of the state in their lives.

less developed countries A term of relative economic development that is normally used with reference to the poor Third World of Africa, Asia, and Latin America. Least developed countries were defined in 1971 by the United Nations Conference on Trade and Development (UNCTAD) as those with very low *per capita* incomes ($100 or less at 1968 prices), a share of manufacturing in GDP of under 10 percent, and a literacy rate under 20 percent.

liberal democracy The form of government prevalent in contemporary Western countries. Governments are selected through regular elections in which all citizens of voting age are eligible to participate. Liberal democracies are particularly concerned with protecting the freedom of individual citizens against the arbitrary use of power by the state. Hence, some formal expression of the rights of citizens can be found in the constitutional documents of liberal democracies.

liberal democratic theory A political theory arising out of the Western European liberal revolution of the sixteenth, seventeeth, and eighteenth centuries that emphasizes the importance of freedom, equality, rights, reason, and individualism.

liberal feminism A perspective that sees women's oppression as resulting from unequal treatment of women and men by laws, opinions, and social practices and that regards equal rights and empowerment through gender socialization as the solution.

liberal internationalism A belief that the natural global order has been subverted by non-democratic leaders and by such policies as the balance of power. Adherents believe that contact between people, who are essentially good, will lead to a more pacific world order.

liberalism A political theory and ideology that stresses the primacy of the individual and individual freedom. Freedom, in this instance, refers to the freedom of individuals to do as they wish without interference from others, whether these be governments or private persons. Liberals believe in a limited state where the power of government is restrained by such devices as constitutions. This ideology arose alongside capitalism.

libertarianism A "softer" variant of individualist anarchism that rejects government intervention in the market and social life. Libertarian thought is evident in today's political rhetoric, which promises to "downsize" government.

liberty Freedom from bodily harm, freedom of expression, economic independence.

lobbyist A person who contacts public officials on behalf of a client or an organization that they belong to or are employed by so as to influence public policy in a manner beneficial to their client or organization.

Magna Carta An important written element of Britain's constitution dating from 1215. It limited royal authority and strengthened the political position of the English aristocracy.

majoritarian electoral system An electoral system organized to reflect the principle of majority rule by requiring that candidates or parties obtain an absolute or a relative majority of the total valid vote cast to win control of an elective office.

majority government A situation in which the governing party controls more than half of the seats in the legislative assembly in a parliamentary system.

maquiladora Foreign-owned business enterprises that have been set up in Mexico in order to exploit cheap labour and low production costs and where local labour is afforded little legal protection. Maquiladora often entail a system in which components are made in the United States, shipped to Mexico for assembling, and reshipped across the American border duty-free.

market Taken broadly, this sphere includes economic transactions related to production, exchange, and distribution. Today, most societies can be characterized as *market societies* in which the social worth of individuals and groups is determined by *market principles*, such as ownership, price, income, costs, and supply and demand.

mass party An avowedly democratic political party organization possessing a large membership and active in recruitment. Joining the party involves agreement with principles, and members provide a good deal of financial support. Party conventions decide on policy.

mass politics Political activities citizens can engage in without having to invest large amounts of time, effort, or money. Examples include voting, signing petitions, protesting, writing elected officials, and joining political parties or interest groups. Mass politics must be distinguished from elite political participation, which requires special skills, intense levels of commitment, and particular resources. As well, entrance to elite political roles, such as candidate or officeholder, union leader, or president of an interest group, is partly determined by such factors as public opinion, voting behaviour, and/or by the gatekeeping functions of activists within the organization.

McWorld Derived from the name of the fast food restaurant chain, McDonald's. This term was coined by political scientist Benjamin Barber to describe the negative cultural and political influences of global corporations. These influences include cultural homogenization, the erosion of democratic values, and the provocation of the "intolerant fanatics" around the world (see also **Jihad**).

means of production The physical and human factors of economic production processes (land, technology, infrastructure, capital, labour).

means-tested social programs Social programs available only to those citizens who can demonstrate that they do not have adequate resources to purchase a service in the marketplace. People in this position are required to reveal their level of income and are often required to provide information regarding the conduct of their personal lives.

mercantilism A governing philosophy, common in Europe prior to the Industrial Revolution, that measured a country's wealth by the amount of precious metals it held. It is also associated with colonialism and the division of the world by the Great Powers for exclusive commerce.

military-industrial complex A concept that refers to an interest in high defence spending shared by military professionals and military weapons producers.

ministerial responsibility A principle found in parliamentary systems that requires the cabinet members to be collectively accountable to legislature for executive actions.

minority government A situation in which the governing party controls less than a majority of seats but more than any other party in the legislature in a parliamentary system.

mixed electoral system A system that combines both majoritarian and proportional representation mechanisms.

mixed-member proportional system A type of electoral system that combines a primary tier of seats in a representative assembly assigned to single-member districts with a pool of seats in the assembly assigned to a secondary tier composed either of a single national district or a set of regional districts. A majoritarian electoral system is used to elect the members representing single-member districts, whereas a proportional representation procedure is used to allocate seats in the secondary pool in a compensatory fashion to achieve overall proportionality between the vote shares of parties and the share of seats they won.

mode of production The way that a society organizes its means of production.

modernity A concept historically associated with the Enlightenment and its ideas of reason, progress, emancipation, and universality, as well as with the rise of commercial and industrial capitalism.

modernization A process and endpoint which all societies were assumed, by development theory, to evolve into. Modernization brought rational authority, industrialization, and societies with a complex division of labour.

modernization theory A theory that suggests that all countries progress through a similar series of stages, from traditional agrarian societies to advanced industrial societies.

moral rights Rights that are asserted (1) on the basis that they should be established at law, or (2) where there is a good justification for ascribing both duties and the power to demand that they be performed.

morality A principle, belief, or value; or the system of principles, beliefs, and values applied to conduct and judgment. Related to the Latin word *mores*, which means the general codes and guides for living that are accepted by a social group.

movement party A political party that arises out of a broad-based movement pursuing non-electoral goals, such as national self-governance.

multilateralism A form of co-operation among states marked by three distinct characteristics. First, that the costs and benefits of co-operation are shared by all participating states. Second, that co-operation is based on certain principles of state conduct that influence the relations among states. Finally, that states are committed to this co-operative behaviour for the long term and do not necessarily expect immediate results.

multinational corporation A company whose operations are located in two or more countries.

mutual fund A collection of bonds or shares that allow investors to spread and diversify their money, which, in turn, reduces levels of risk. Mutual funds are especially useful in international investments where information about foreign companies and markets is not accessible to the average individual investor.

nation A group of individuals who identify with each other (sense of community) based on common history, language, culture, and religion.

national interest A concept referring to the basic irreducible interests of a state (material and ideal) and criteria for action from a realist perspective.

nationalism A belief system that prioritizes or gives special significance to the nation as a focus of loyalty. The nation, in turn, is a particular form of community, with a history, tradition, and identity that it desires to promote and preserve.

nation-state An international legal entity defined by a specific territory, population, and government, possessing sovereignty. Because almost all states comprise diverse ethnic, national, and racial groups, some prefer the term *national state.*

natural rights Rights which people are said to possess "by nature" and not as members of particular societies.

negative rights An understanding of rights, entitlements, and liberty associated with classical liberalism. Negative rights entitle individuals to act without any interference from others. They are commonly associated with the freedoms of speech, assembly, religion, and press.

neo-liberalism A modification of nineteenth-century economic and political theory that advocates deregulation of the market, a non-interventionist state, minimal controls on international economic interaction, and individual freedom and responsibility.

neo-liberal structural adjustment A strategy for economic development.

new international division of labour The global economy created through colonialism, characterized by an industrialized "centre" (the early-industrializing, colonial countries) and a "periphery" (the former colonies) producing raw commodities, began to be reorganized in the 1970s. In particular, there was "deindustrialization" in the West as companies relocated labour-intensive manufacturing to cheaper wage zones in the South, and a process of industrialization (either "dependent" or state-led, as in the East Asian countries) in parts of Latin America and Asia.

new multilateralism Co-operation among states to protect the security of people, rather than the security of states.

new public management A combination of structures, practices, and processes of public management that were in vogue in liberal democracies in the 1990s. At the heart of new public management is a critical analysis of traditional Weberian bureaucracy and the view that government agencies must be driven by a desire to achieve clearly measurable results.

new social movement theory Seeks to explain the historical meaning of the progressive mass movements that arose in the 1960s, in the context of sociological theories of conflict and change.

non-aligned states A group of states, the majority in the South, that were not aligned with either the Soviet Union or the United States during the Cold War.

non-governmental organization An organization that has as its members private citizens or national affiliates of groups composed of private citizens.

non-partisanship The conduct of elections in the absence of political parties. In its pure form, individuals stand for election as independents.

normative Related to the establishing of moral norms or principles. Normative claims, statements, or questions tend to contain such prescriptive words as *should*, *ought*, or *must*.

normative theory A theory that inquires into ethical questions and considers what is moral, good, and true.

notwithstanding clause A clause in the Canadian constitution that shields an act of the legislature from a judicial declaration of constitutional invalidity.

oppression The systematic and systemic subordination of one group to another.

ordinal ballot A ballot form in which the voter is asked to rank the candidates or parties to indicate his or her relative preferences among them. Also known as a *preferential ballot*.

paradigm shift A shift in the intellectual framework that structures thinking about a set of phenomena.

parliamentary system A system of government in which the executive is chosen from and derives its authority from the legislature.

participation Direct action or involvement in processes of decision making.

partisan Having to do with political parties; to demonstrate a particular allegiance to a political party.

party discipline An established principle in parliamentary systems that requires members of a party's legislative caucus to vote collectively on legislation.

party list ballot A ballot form in which each party's candidates for seats in a multi-member constituency are presented as separate lists, and voters must choose among the lists, rather than choosing among the individual candidates appearing on them.

patriarchical family A family form in which the father is the head and primary bread winner and the mother stays at home and takes care of the family.

patriarchy In the anthropological sense, the rule of the father over his wife and offspring (family, kingroup, or clan). In the modern sociological sense, the structuring of social relationships and institutions in such a way as to preserve the dominance and privileges of men in relation to women.

pauper A social class in the Middle Ages who met or supplemented their basic needs through the charity of churches or private philanthropy.

peacebuilding Intervention by foreign actors into conflict zones to build governmental institutions, democratic practices, and civil society.

peacekeeping Intervention by foreign actors into conflict zones to maintain peace among warring factions.

periphery A term used in dependency theory to describe the lesser developed regions of the world, which are dependent on and exploited by the developed core.

place-based community A group of people who share geographical, usually local, space and who may also have common interests or feelings of closeness.

plebiscitarian democracy A form of democracy that attempts to replicate the virtues of direct democracy through democratic mechanisms, such as referenda and recall.

pluralist decision rule A form of decision making that favours the option with the most votes, even if it does not constititute a majority.

pluralist theory An approach to politics that assumes that society is composed of individuals who join groups to influence political outcomes. Politics is seen as the competition among groups for preferred policies. It assumes that all citizens can form groups and that no group has a permanent advantage in society.

plurality electoral system An electoral system in which the candidate who gains the most votes wins the office being contested, even though that total may constitute less than a majority of the total valid votes cast. A plurality outcome is also known as a relative majority.

policy community All actors or potential actors who share expertise and interest in a policy area or function and who in varying degrees influence policy.

political culture A term popularized by Gabriel Almond that refers to a particular patterned orientation toward political action. The political culture approach attempts to empirically describe and explain these patterns by measuring the attitudes characteristic of a national population.

political rights Citizenship rights that encompass the exercise of a citizen's democratic rights within the political community. Examples include the right to vote and the right to stand for elected office.

political socialization The process by which people acquire their knowledge of the political system and attitudes toward political action.

political sociology A social-science approach that emphasizes the social and cultural composition of society and its relationship to the state.

political violence The use of physical force to affect power relations.

politics–administration dichotomy A view of democratic politics whereby politicians make policy decisions which in turn are implemented by civil servants. Few observers see the dichotomy as a valid description of reality.

Poor Laws First introduced in sixteenth-century England, these laws were designed to get the poor off the streets. The underlying premise of these laws is that the poor are responsible for their own plight.

popular sovereignty Also known as *popular rule.* Popular sovereignty exists when the ability to rule or govern is distributed equally among the population of a specific state.

positive rights An understanding of rights, entitlements, and liberty associated with such ideologies as reform liberalism or democratic socialism. Positive rights entitle individuals to the conditions in which they can maximize their chances for full development. They are commonly associated with an interventionist state and specific initiatives, such as public education, social assistance, and affirmative action.

post-development A strand of thought that rejects the notion of development as a profoundly Western-centric concept that has proved inadequate in meeting the needs of the non-Western world.

post-Marxist Approaches that share Marxism's critique of capitalism and its emancipatory objectives, but which reject what they consider to be the economic reductionism of traditional Marxist theory, as well as the scientific and predictive claims of Marx.

post-structuralist Theoretical perspectives associated, in particular, with the French thinkers Jacques Lacan, Michel Foucault, and Jacques Derrida and which have called into question many of the epistemological assumptions underpinning modern political thought (especially regarding the Self [or subject], knowledge, and power).

postmodern feminism A stream in feminist thought that challenges any universalizing or essentializing explanations for women's oppression, arguing that there is no single, unifying women's reality; focuses on exposing the patriarchal ideas inherent in language and discourse.

postmodernism A perspective in the social sciences and humanities that holds that reality is not given; rather, it is constituted by ideas, texts, and discourses (writing, talking). It displays scepticism toward Enlightenment notions of truth, arguing instead that many "truths" can co-exist. Postmodernism holds that modern political ideologies, with their emphasis on reason and a single political identity, silence social differences and impose uniformity and homogeneity on society.

post-sovereign A depiction of the current era, in which the state has lost its capacity to exercise sovereignty within its territorial boundaries.

poverty gap Measures the percentage of the population living below the poverty line within a given state.

poverty line An arbitrary statistical instrument that categorizes a population as being poor or not poor. There are many formulations of the poverty line and ongoing debates about the most appropriate measure.

poverty reduction strategy papers (PRSPs) In the later 1990s, the IMF and the World Bank refashioned their structural adjustment programs into PRSPs, which are intended to cover a wider range of issues, including aspects of good governance.

Poverty Severity Index Measures the intensity of poverty insofar as it focuses on individuals living in conditions of extreme deprivation.

power The capacity of individuals, groups, and political institutions to realize key decisions.

power of the purse A power of review over the expenditure of public moneys.

power over The idea that individuals, groups, or states are unable to realize their interests and goals due to external influences, constraints, and inequalities in resources.

power to The idea that individuals, groups, or states can realize their goals.

pragmatic party A non-doctrinaire party that competes strategically for public office. It is concerned with practicality and with winning elections and gears its campaigns to programs it believes will most likely lead to victory.

precedent Past judicial decisions declaring legal principles that have a bearing on present controversies.

presidential system A system of government in which the executive and legislative branches are independent and assigned distinct powers.

principle of commodification Marxist notion that, under capitalism, items are prized because of their exchange value rather than their use value. This makes all items (including labour) commodities of exchange.

principle of comparative advantage Economic theory that economic growth is best achieved when countries focus production on those things they do best, or that are associated with abundant natural resources.

private The realm of society that has been deemed "natural" and, thus, beyond the possibility of debate or change (often this has included the "market" and the family).

private member bill Legislation introduced by non-cabinet members in parliamentary systems.

privatization A process of shifting public or governmental services and functions performed by the state into the realm of the market and the home.

Privy Council Office An agency of the Government of Canada that provides administrative support to and policy analysis for the cabinet.

productivism A characterization of industrial societies (both capitalist and state-socialist), referring to the priority given to the maximization of production of goods, even when this cannot be shown to enhance quality of life and may even result in its deterioration.

proletariat A term used by Marx for the social class that does not own the means of production but is instead forced to sell its labour-power in exchange for wages.

proportional representation A system of vote-counting wherein the share of seats in a representative body that a party wins in an election is proportional, if not equal, to the share of the total valid votes cast for it in the election.

protectionism A government policy that protects a national industry or sector from foreign competition through subsidies or tariffs.

public bureaucracy The set of institutions and people who form the administrative machinery of government.

public–private dichotomy The gender-based division of personality characteristics, roles, and values. Women are associated with the private sphere of home and family and its accompanying traits, such as passivity, subjugation, and emotion. Men are linked to the public sphere of business and government and its virtues of individualism, rationality, intelligence, and freedom.

purchasing power parity A practice of adjusting currency rates so that the same proportion of income is spent to buy the same item.

quasi-divine A term suggesting that the source of authority is understood to be godly or divine.

radical feminism A view of women's oppression as resulting from systematic subordination of women to men, especially male control of women's bodies; advocates the eradication of sexual violence and the promotion of bodily autonomy for women.

rational decision making A process whereby important policies are undertaken only after careful delineation of the problem at hand, a thorough analysis of policy options, and a detailed comparison of the costs and benefits of different options. Most public policy making is thought, for many reasons, to fall short of such standards.

rationality A claim to a systematic way of thinking.

realism The dominant international relations theory in Anglo-American academies. It purports to explain the world by holding that the international sphere is dominated by sovereign states, that states act in their own interests, and that international politics is a struggle for power between states.

reason The ability to think, understand, analyze, form judgments, and draw conclusions logically. Reason or rationality is variously considered as (1) a general *capacity* particular to human beings (and perhaps some other animals), (2) an *activity* in which one engages, and (3) a *faculty* of the mind (as one of its components, or hardware).

rectificatory justice The principle of justice that emphasizes the idea of making things right and correcting for past injustice.

regime A mode of governance over the organized activity of a social formation within and across four spheres—the state, society, market, and global insertion.

regulatory agency A government body, enjoying independence from the government of the day, that makes and enforces rules for sectors of the economy.

representation by population A principle applied in the apportionment of seats in a representative assembly among regions, provinces or states, or electoral districts. It holds that the number of seats assigned to a given region, province, or district should be directly proportional to the share of the population of the nation (or higher regional unit) that resides in that region, province, or district.

representative bureaucracy A view that argues that the civil service should reflect in its composition the major social groups of the society.

representative democracy or **indirect democracy** A democratic system in which citizens elect representatives, who, in turn, make political decisions on behalf of all citizens.

representative sample A term used in survey research to refer to a sample that is a reflection of the larger population; that is, it has the same profile in terms of gender, age, income levels and so on of the larger population. It is crucial that a sample is representative if it is to give valid information about the larger population.

republicanism A political belief that holds that we are political animals. Republicans extol the virtues of positive freedom—the freedom of individuals to participate in the affairs of government.

responsible government A convention in parliamentary systems whereby the executive remains in power for so long as it maintains the confidence of the legislative branch.

revolution The overthrow of a given socio-economic and political order and implementation of a radical transformation.

revolutionary regime A regime where certain elites, groups, and/or the majority have overthrown the given socio-economic and political order and undertaken a radical transformation, usually in the name of a dominated or exploited majority.

rights A legal or moral entitlement.

risk A term used by social scientists to describe personal or social factors that contribute to poverty or personal injury.

rule of law A fundamental principle in liberal democratic political systems. All citizens of a country are governed by a single set of legal rules. These rules are applied equally and impartially to all. No political official is above the law. The rule of law empowers and constrains political behaviour.

sentiment-based community A community based on a sentiment that endorses shared values, common interests and goals, participation in public affairs, and ongoing relationships that bind groups of people together.

separation of powers An institutional arrangement reflecting the idea that the liberty of citizens is best secured in those regimes where the executive, legislative, and judicial powers are separated and not fused into one single authority.

sexual division of labour The division of jobs and duties along gender lines.

shock therapy A dramatic response to economic imbalances based on rapid economic liberalization and cut-backs in state expenditure.

simple candidate ballot A ballot on which only the names of the candidates, often with optional identifying information, appear, and voters are simply asked to indicate which one or more of these candidates they prefer.

single transferable vote A voting procedure employing a preferential (ordinal) ballot in which a person's vote can be transferred from one candidate to another in successive rounds of the counting procedure.

single-member plurality An electoral system that grants elected office to the candidate winning the most votes, rather than the majority of votes.

social capital Communal sentiments and actions stemming from these sentiments that add value to society and the political system. Individuals have social capital when they have the education and skills to integrate successfully into society.

social contract The argument by Hobbes and Locke that individuals in a state of nature by mutual consent and agreement form societies and establish governments.

social democracy A democratic regime that uses the state to implement egalitarian redistribution of the wealth produced by a largely capitalist economy.

social exclusion A term used to define those in society that are economically and socially marginalized.

social formation A term applied to a "country" encompassing its given societal, economic, and political systems.

socialism An ideology founded on the recognition of a fundamental division and conflict in capitalist society between social classes. Class divisions are based upon those who own the means of production (the capitalist) and those who do not (the working class or proletariat). The solution to class conflict lies in the public or common ownership of the means of production, a solution to be achieved either through revolution or by working democratically within the existing capitalist system.

socialist feminism A stream of feminist thought that sees women's oppression as fostered and maintained by capitalism and the patriarchal state; the solution lies in challenging the sexual division of labour in the home and the workplace.

socialization of debt A governmental action wherein it takes over the debt incurred by the private sector. In doing so, the burden of responsibility to pay back this converted public debt shifts from private businesses to the average taxpayer. One important consequence of this is the channeling of taxpayers' money toward bringing down the public debt and away from spending in such areas as health, education, and welfare.

social rights Citizenship rights that are necessary for well-being and, thus, for full membership and participation in the political community as defined by the standards and norms prevailing in that community.

social stratification A social hierarchy often based on income or status; division of society.

social welfare liberalism A philosophy of governing resting on the idea that the basic necessities of life should be provided by government for those who are truly in need, for those who are unable to provide for themselves through no fault of their own.

society Refers to the character and composition of one of the four spheres of regimes. Weber argued that the composition of a society would determine the type of state that would evolve, for example, primarily traditional societies would be ruled by monarchies. Marx also studied societies, particularly the way in which class divisions resulted under a capitalist system.

socio-economic growth (development) An ability to produce an adequate and growing supply of goods and services productively and efficiently, to accumulate capital, and to distribute the fruits of production in a relatively equitable manner.

solidarity Membership in the political community, and feelings of belonging associated with acceptance by that community.

sovereignty A legal (*de jure*) and actual (*de facto*) condition whereby states recognize no higher authority either domestically or externally and are thus free to act as they wish. A state's right to manage its affairs internally, without external interference, based on the legal concept of the equality of states.

Speaker of the House A legislative official responsible for overseeing and controlling activity in the legislative assembly.

stakeholders A group of individuals who have identified a common interest in a portion of the more general public interest. They may consider themselves as having a common, sometimes a proprietary, interest in a specific policy area.

Stalinism Refers to the regime of Joseph Stalin, who ruled the Communist Party of the Union of Soviet Socialist Republics (CP-USSR) and the government of the USSR from 1924 to 1953. The regime oversaw the rapid industrialization and increasing military power of the USSR but exercised extreme coercion over citizens, imprisoned, exiled, or "liquidated" suspected dissidents and is widely viewed as having betrayed the democratic, proletarian principles of the international communist movement. Communist parties in the West, which emulated the top-down bureaucratic structure of the CP-USSR and which continued to defend the legacy of Stalinism, were also labelled "Stalinist" by their new left opponents.

standing committee A relatively permanent legislative committee with set responsibilities.

standing orders A set of rules governing activity in the Canadian House of Commons.

state See **nation-state**.

state of nature An imaginary existence without government where all people are equal and free to act as they please.

statute A written law enacted by the legislature.

state sovereignty See **sovereignty**.

subculture A different shared way of life within the national cultural setting, characterizing a smaller grouping of people within a country.

subjective Situation in which the observer is part of what is observed or is affected by values and preferences.

surplus value A key relationship of exploitation between capitalists and workers. Surplus value represents the profit that the capitalist gains as a result of selling a product for more than is paid to the worker in wages.

symbolic representation To "symbolize" or be the concrete embodiment of that which was represented.

terrorism An act or repeated acts of violence against arbitrary and/or selectively chosen victims intended to serve political ends by instilling fear in a larger audience.

theory A coherent interpretation or story that orders and makes sense of the world.

Third World A term used to describe the majority of countries in the world or the vast majority of the world's population who live in conditions of poverty, underdevelopment and, often, political instability.

totalitarian An ultra-authoritarian regime that controls virtually all aspects of politics, society, and economy.

traditional authority Power and legitimacy accorded to individuals on the basis of custom or heredity.

traditional society A society characterized by inherited authority and low levels of industrialization, consumption, technology, and diversification.

transnationalized regime A form of governance carried out by international actors.

Treasury Board Secretariat A central agency of the Government of Canada that has responsibility for overall administrative and management policy.

trustee model of representation A perspective on representation that assumes that the first obligation of representatives is to employ their reason and judgment in deliberations regarding governing in the broad national interest.

tyranny of the majority A potentially omnipotent power of the majority. Constitutional guarantees are required so as to curb the majority's potential excesses.

unicameral A regime in which the legislature consists of only one chamber.

unilateral Actions taken by one actor or government.

unipolar moment A condition of global order in which there is a single centre of power.

unitary constitution A constitution in which the sovereignty of the state rests in one government.

universalism A view that laws and policies should treat all citizens the same, irrespective of membership in distinct cultural or identity groups. Universalism collides with demands for recognition and valuing of difference whereby cultural groups are granted distinct rights or treatment in laws and policies.

universal social programs Programs available to all citizens regardless of their income level or their need.

unwritten constitution A constitution where most of a country's key governing principles are not contained in a single document. These principles exist in a combination of written laws and conventions.

vanguard A cadre of dedicated revolutionaries. The concept of the vanguard was put forward by Lenin as a means to lead the working class to revolution.

virtue ethics An approach to moral philosophy that emphasizes human flourishing and the uniquely human virtues. Virtue ethicists draw attention to both the consequences of one's decision or act (as in **consequentialism**) and also to the principles guiding the decision or act (as in **deontology**), but they do so more with a view to judging the individual's moral character than with a view to judging the actions themselves.

vote of no confidence A vote of parliament that determines whether the executive maintains the support of the legislature.

wage–capital relationship The capital mode of production is defined by the relationship between the proletariat and the bourgeoisie. In this system, workers are forced to sell their labour-power to gain an income to purchase the goods and services they require to live.

war A violent political instrument which continues political intercourse through other means.

Washington Consensus Refers to tacit agreement between the International Monetary Fund (IMF), the World Bank, and the United States executive branch over the development policies that the developing countries should follow. The Consensus formed around the key issues of macroeconomic prudence, export-oriented growth, and economic liberalization.

welfare state A form of governance wherein government programs and policies are designed to protect citizens from illness, unemployment, and long-term disability. In modern political debate, a welfare state is said to have a "social safety net."

world system The idea that the international state system and capitalism have constituted an evolving single global system since the sixteenth century, with a core, periphery, and semi-periphery.

world view A collection of integrated images of the world that serve as a lens through which one interprets the world. It helps the individual to orient to the environment and to organize perceptions as a guide to behaviour, and it acts as a filter for selecting relevant information.

Index

Note: Entries for tables are followed by "*t*." Entries that refer to the "References" section are followed by "*n*."

D

N

O

P

Q

R

Y

Z